THE END OF CHIDYERANO

THE END OF CHIDYERANO

A HISTORY OF FOOD AND EVERYDAY LIFE IN MALAWI, 1860–2004

Elias C. Mandala

Social History of Africa
Allen Isaacman and Jean Allman, Series Editors

HEINEMANN
Portsmouth, NH

Heinemann
A division of Reed Elsevier Inc.
361 Hanover Street
Portsmouth, NH 03801-3912
www.heinemann.com

Offices and agents throughout the world

ISBN: 0–325–07021–0 (cloth)
       0–325–07020–2 (paper)
ISSN: 1099–8098

Library of Congress Cataloging-in-Publication Data

Mandala, Elias Coutinho.
   The end of Chidyerano : a history of food and everyday life in Malawi, 1860–2004 /
Elias C. Mandala.
       p. cm. — (Social history of Africa, ISSN 1099–8098)
   Includes bibliographical references and index.
       ISBN 0–325–07021–0 (cloth : alk. paper) — ISBN 0–325–07020–2 (pbk. : alk. paper)
       1. Malawi—Social life and customs. I. Title. II. Series.
DT3187.M36   2005
968.97'02—dc22   2005018237

British Library Cataloguing in Publication Data is available.

Printed in the United States of America on acid-free paper.

08   07   06   05   SB   1   2   3   4   5   6   7   8   9

Copyright Acknowledgments

The author and publisher gratefully acknowledge permission for use of the following
material:

Excerpts from Elias Mandala, "Beyond the 'Crisis' in African Food Studies," *The Journal
of the Historical Society* 3, 3/4 (Summer/Fall 2003): 281–301.

For Nyatwa and Wangani

CONTENTS

ILLUSTRATIONS

FIGURES

TABLES

ACKNOWLEDGMENTS

Long in the making, this book has benefited from the generosity and assistance of many people and institutions. Fellowships from the Woodrow Wilson Center for International Scholars and the National Endowment for the Humanities made it possible for me to concentrate on the project during 1993–94 and 1998. The Dean's Office at the University of Rochester has been as equally supportive, granting me leaves of absence and paying for my research trips to southern Africa. My thanks also go to Rebecca Hurysz and Helen Hull, Administrative Assistant and Secretary of the History Department, respectively, for giving a human face to the university bureaucracy.

My gratitude also goes to the following: Jim Duncan, the copyeditor; Seth C. Triggs, the cartographer; and the dedicated personnel of the University of Witwatersrand Library (Johannesburg) and National Archives of Malawi (Zomba). I am particularly grateful to Mr. Joel Thaulo of the Malawi National Archives, without whose knowledge and diligence I would not have accessed the unclassified but critical documents of the Shire Valley Agricultural Development Project. He has joined a long list of people whose assistance made a big difference in the course of this project.

The list of my Malawian supporters includes the late Edward Pereira Tembo, who, for three years before his sudden death in 1994, worked as my only research assistant. I will live to cherish his memory and to remember his wife and children. Among those who succeeded him in data collecting for this project are Symforiano Mwendo, Joseph Mizedya, and my brother's sons (Elias, Joseph, and John). And during my tours to Malawi, the following friends opened their doors to me: Sam Safuli, Kings Phiri, Wapu Mulwafu, Steven Mutuwawira, Enoch Mvula, and their respective partners. Besides giving me shelter and food, Kings Phiri and Wapu Mulwafu also supervised students who did research for me in the National Archives of Malawi. This manuscript is the work of many hands and minds.

I also feel indebted to those who read earlier drafts of this manuscript, especially Doug Dorland, Bill Hauser, Allen Isaacman, Dean Miller, Jesse Moore, Kai Pederson, Matthew Schoffeleers, and Jan Vansina. I have learned a lot from their comments and suggestions. Karen Fields read the manuscript several times, raised critical questions, and suggested literature, often beyond African studies. Her prodding—which I sometimes found annoying—proved as invaluable in shaping the argument of this work as the invited and unsolicited responses of the peasant women and men of the Tchiri Valley. Always generous with their time, the villagers opened my eyes to the complexity of the food system they have created and keep going. This study would have taken a more sensible shape had I not initially approached them with wrongheaded questions about "crises." They definitely taught me the difference between constructing a food system and writing books about food, which can take place even during Rochester's blistering winters.

A circle of friends in and around Rochester has helped make this tundra a warm place. I would especially like to mention Lowesha Kapijimpanga, Cromwell and Mary Msuku, Veli Nolutshungu, Zwelonke Simela, Francois Utazirubanda, Antoine and Francoise Uwimana, and Vicki Walters. Finally, I wish to register my deep gratitude to my sons, Nyatwa and Wangani, for their patience and understanding. I dedicate this book to them.

Elias Mandala
Rochester, New York, February 2005

ABBREVIATIONS

ADMARC	Agricultural Development and Marketing Corporation
ALC	African Lakes Company
APMB	Agricultural Produce and Marketing Board
BCGA	British Cotton Growers Association
CAT	*Central African Times*
CCDP	Chikwawa Cotton Development Project
CS	chief secretary
CSC	Christian Services Committee
CTO	chief transportation officer
DA	director of agriculture or Department of Agriculture
DANO	District Administration Native Ordinance
DC	district commissioner
FMB	Farmers Marketing Board
MCP	Malawi Congress Party
MFS	Master Farmers' Scheme
MNA	Malawi National Archives
MYP	Malawi Young Pioneers
NADD	Ngabu Agricultural Development Division
NGO	nongovernmental organization

NT	*Nyasaland Times*
OPC	Office of the President and Cabinet
PAO	provincial agricultural officer
PC	provincial commissioner
PRO	Public Record Office
SAGM	South African General Mission
SAP	*South African Pioneer*
SDO	special duties officer
SP	Southern Province
SUCOMA	Sugar Corporation of Malawi
SVADP	Shire Valley Agricultural Development Project
UMCA	Universities Mission to Central Africa

INTRODUCTION: PEASANTS DEBATE ACADEMICS ON FOOD, HUNGER, AND TIME

[T]ime's arrow and time's cycle is, if you will, a great dichotomy because each of its poles captures, by its essence, a theme so central to intellectual (and practical) life that Western people who hope to understand history must wrestle intimately with *both*—for time's arrow is the intelligibility of distinct and irreversible events, while time's cycle is the intelligibility of timeless order and lawlike structure. We must have *both*.[1]

What sort of science is it whose principal discovery is to make the very object it treats disappear?[2]

INTRODUCTION

This book about food in Africa is a migrant worker's story, and, like most such stories, it has two tails. The longer tail points to Africa, my homeland, and the shorter one to America, where I have spent much of my productive life. I begin with two accounts about food in America that, at different times, sharpened my appreciation of the art of provisioning back home in Malawi.[3] They say something about the social basis from which Americans produce knowledge about Africa.

The first is an episode that took place almost two decades ago, when I was a graduate student at the University of Minnesota. One day I was invited out to dinner, together with my wife and an American friend (whom I shall call "D") who had once worked in Malawi as a Peace Corps volunteer. We were to dine at the home of an American couple, and were greeted with two pieces of bad news upon our arrival. The wife was not feeling well, and their maid, who usually cleaned the house and helped prepare meals, had not shown up. But do not worry, we were told. We would go out to eat at a restaurant not many blocks from the house. We went off to the restaurant cheerfully, after drinking the wine D had brought, and the food at the restaurant was good.

Nothing unusual happened until the check came. The host looked at it and passed it around. D calculated, produced the amount of money he thought was his fair share of the meal, and passed the bill to me. I knew the price of my wife's and my own meal, but did not have the money to cover either. A naive African, I thought I was a guest and had not even brought a wallet to the restaurant! But taking courage, I discreetly asked D to lend me some money, and was relieved when I felt the cash in my hand. I do not remember many such embarrassing moments in my life, but, like other things, it faded from memory and lost meaning, until I joined the faculty of the History Department at the University of Rochester.

What reminded me of the Minneapolis incident was not experience in a restaurant or at the home of a colleague, but the monthly departmental meetings held at noon. At every meeting, I watched, with peasant curiosity, as one or two of my colleagues happily consumed food from their lunch boxes. They enjoyed their food while everyone was discussing grave matters about the department's future and when some people were hungry—an unthinkable display of selfishness in the village I came from. That brought me back to the Twin Cities, where, even as a guest in a restaurant, one had to eat from one's own lunch box. Here, even as colleagues discussed problems of collective import, one was expected, in a fundamental way, to ignore everyone else. Unlike my Minneapolis friends, though, my academic colleagues have the chance to propagate, through study, research, and teaching, attitudes that are specifically American, or perhaps Western. I see in the Minneapolis episode and in the Rochester ritual one reason some scholars have produced a literature that cannot recognize sharing—unless it is reinterpreted as a form of investment banking. Academics would clash with peasants, who define food mostly as an object of sharing.

ARGUMENT OF THE BOOK

As a migrant worker's story, this book relies on both rural and academic interpretations of history. From the two intellectual traditions, the project has learned to appreciate the value of the cyclical and linear dimensions of the past, arguing that linear time needs cyclical time to become time and vice versa. The two time frames have made it possible for this book to understand the food regime of the valley as a dynamic system that does not easily lend itself to such generalizations as "transition," "crisis," or "decline."

Thus, although a land of frequent *chilala* droughts and *madzi* floods that exacerbate *njala* seasonal hunger, the Tchiri Valley is not at the same time a region of recurrent *chaola* famine. (The book can document with certainty only two chaola between 1860 and 2004.) In the absence of political turmoil, drought and floods do not lead to chaola famine, largely because the valley contains both deserts of hunger and oases of plenty. Dearth exists as part of abundance. Moreover, these deserts of hunger and oases of plenty are more than spatial categories. Every day, villagers create deserts of hunger and oases of plenty as they both assume and avoid risk in their fields and experience the daily meal as both "feast" and "famine." The food economy of the valley has been a terrain of struggle, replete with possibilities for change.

The book argues, however, that the mere existence of structural tensions does not by itself create new orders. Human beings turn yesterday's disorders into the orders of today. And since they do this as social actors, questions oblige us to insert the food system into its larger context: the broad economic, political, and ecological shifts—of local and foreign origin—that make it easy for potential rebels to adopt new production techniques, new foods, new eating patterns, and new ways of teaching those habits. The food economy of the valley has indeed undergone enormous changes since the 1860s. But these transformations were not uniform in their depth or direction.

Cumulative developments of the linear order represented only one kind of change. Many other shifts were noncumulative, transient, reversible, and without depth. The agents of disorder could not always project the food economy in one particular direction, partly because some of them were too weak and partly because some friends of the old order were too strong, defending their positions behind the orderly routines of the day and season. The food system has had as many "pasts" as it has had many "spaces." Time and space become inseparable.

SPATIAL DIMENSIONS

In the Tchiri Valley, villagers created their food system in a physical setting that was simultaneously diverse and unitary. As the southernmost extension of the Great Rift Valley running from the Jordan River in Palestine to the Indian Ocean in Mozambique, the Tchiri Valley forms a single unit in space, distinct from other regions like the Tchiri Highlands and the Lower Zembezi (figure 0.1). Rising to only 100 feet above sea level, the mosquito-infested valley floor is hot, humid, and receives only 32 inches of rain per annum on the average. During my extended research trip to the area in 1979–80, the region suffered a serious drought, as it would do again in the 1990s.[4] The droughts compound the problem of soil depletion in some places, where years of cotton farming and cattle grazing have transformed the gray and brown soils of the rain-dependent drylands, *mphala*. That people continue to live in this area, and do so in large numbers, testifies to a reality that peasants alone can understand: this desert of hunger exists only as part of oases of plenty (see figure 3.1).

One such group of oases of plenty consists of fertile hill or mountain (*phiri*) areas like the 4,000-foot-high Thyolo Escarpment. Its western slopes, which drop in the region's two administrative districts of Chikwawa and Nsanje, receive more rain than the valley floor. In the decade between 1964–65 and 1974–75, this zone got an annual average 36.76 inches of rain.[5] Cultivators here usually grow enough food, especially *chimanga* maize (*Zea mays*), to feed themselves and sell to others, just as the people of the Gaga Hills, some 50 miles to the west of Chikwawa district headquarters (Boma), do. These hills form part of the Kirk Range that runs in a north-south direction from central Malawi down to the northern banks of the Zembezi River (figure 0.1). In the decade from 1964–65 to 1973–74, the region received an average of 45 inches of rainfall per year.[6] This area represents another oasis of plenty like the Chididi Hills—approximately 90 miles to the south on the same Kirk Range—where annual rainfalls averaged 38.49 inches from 1964–65 to 1973–74.[7] Other beneficiaries of this oasis of plenty, besides their own

Figure 0.1 The Tchiri Valley: Topography (created by Seth C. Triggs for the author)

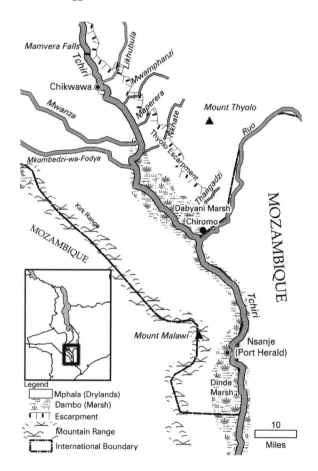

inhabitants, are peasants near Nsanje Boma and the nearby Khulubvi shrine of Mbona, the rain-giver and spirit guardian of the region. It should not come as a surprise, therefore, that villagers used to regard the Chididi Hills with the same kind of reverence and awe as they did the Thyolo summit. These were sacred places, attracting victims of hunger or war on the valley floor, and Mbona was supposed to feed them.[8] Parts of the Kirk Range and Thyolo Mountain mean more to the people of the valley than just a set of rocks and trees. They are oases of plenty and integral components of the reality we call the Tchiri Valley.

It is not only the fertile mountain regions that have encouraged villagers to think of the valley as a land with its own oases of plenty. The valley floor is itself a variegated ecosystem. The more extensive mphala drylands sandwich *dambo* marshes on both banks of the Tchiri River and its tributaries. Instead of relying solely on erratic rainfalls, peasants also work the rich and stratified alluvial soils of the dambo, trusting in the predictability of the annual floods of the Tchiri River—their Nile.

To appreciate the multiple ways the Tchiri River has enriched the social and economic life of the valley, let us take an imaginary canoe journey with chief Kasisi of Chikwawa District at the height of the dry season in October.

Photo 1 The Tchiri River at Chikwawa Boma (showing ferry cables, 1950s) (Matthew Schoffeleers's collection)

His village, known as Chirala, is near Mathiti Falls, the last of a series of rapids truncating the Tchiri River on its way from its source in Lake Malawi (figures 0.1 and 0.2). The year is 1953. The valley had experienced a devastating flood in February 1952. But as generally happens after a serious flood or drought, the following growing season (1952–53) was near perfect throughout the valley, especially in Chikwawa District. The rains came as expected and in the right amount and right distribution, giving the people of Chikwawa an unusually large bumper crop. Eager to secure money for the so-called hut tax, most villagers had dumped the maize from their *munda* gardens on the mphala drylands on the depressed Nyasaland market immediately after harvest in May. But big growers like Kasisi waited for prices to rise during the hungry season (October–March), and when they did not, the chief loaded a big canoe with his surplus maize of 10 200-pound bags. His destination was Mum'budi, a small Portuguese outpost on the east bank of the Tchiri River, where food prices were already shooting up. One district commissioner for Port Herald had people like Kasisi in mind when he bemoaned that "there is a great temptation to the natives of this area to sell their maize at well above market price, over the Portuguese border."[9] Kasisi did not know or care about what this officer told his superiors in Zomba. We will see in a moment how he regarded the international border.

From their Chirala Village, Kasisi and his canoe rowers would pass the following places on their way to Mum'budi (the figure after each name represents the place's approximate distance in miles from Chirala): Chikwawa Boma (5), Chiromo (55), Port Herald or Nsanje Boma (85), Nyachikadza's court (100), Marka-a-Gombe on the southern Nyasaland-Mozambique boundary (115), Megaza (125), and Mum'budi (170). By the time they reach Mum'budi, Kasisi and his men will have traversed the two main marshes of the valley: the Dabanyi (or what Europeans called the "Elephant") in the north and the Dinde (or the Europeans' "Ndindi") Marsh in the south (figure 0.1). Mum'budi is approximately 20 miles to the north of the Tchiri's confluence with the Zembezi at Mphanda-ya-Nyaganzi in Mozambique.

As they leave their village, Kasisi's rowers do not need much energy to move the heavy canoe. The current from Mathiti Falls is still strong and cuts steep cliffs on the western bank (figure 0.1). But after leaving Chikwawa Boma, the current becomes sluggish until it virtually dies out in the vicinity of the Mwanza River, which is the Tchiri's principal tributary from the Gaga Hills far to the west. Kasisi and his men are now entering the 40-mile-long Dabanyi, and had they made this journey in the nineteenth century, they would have met women from all over the valley distilling salt and men extracting wine from palm trees. But now they find mostly food cultivators.[10] As they move further down the river, they say good-bye to the Thyolo Escarpment on their left, which descends and finally disappears in the plain at about 10 miles to the north of Chiromo. At Chiromo, our travelers leave the Dabanyi behind,

Figure 0.2 Kasisi's trip on the Tchiri River, 1953 (created by Seth C. Triggs for the author)

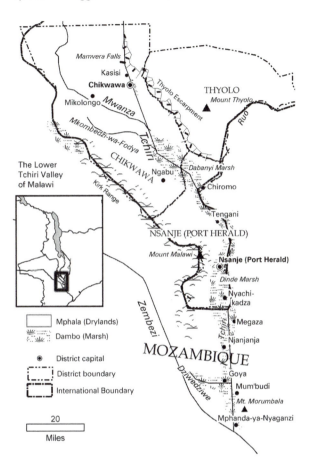

and the Tchiri River meets the Ruo, which starts in Mulanje Mountain and is the Tchiri River's largest and longest tributary from the east.

Kasisi remembers many stories about Chiromo, particularly those in connection with the Anglo-Portuguese conflict over the valley in the 1880s, in which his ancestors played a vital role. But he does not allow these memories to distract him. He does not want to spend the night on the Nyasaland side of the river and pass the Portuguese outpost of Megaza during the day. Megaza's colonists have earned notoriety for harassing travelers from Nyasaland. Thus, after buying some fish for dinner, Kasisi orders his men to proceed immediately. They reach Port Herald Township on the northern end of the Dinde Marsh. There is little activity on the Dinde, however, as the sun and its free light for agricultural workers had sunk behind the Chididi and Lulwe Mountains of the Kirk Range in the west. Pushing hard, the party passes Marka-a-Gombe, and around eight o'clock, they keep to the right bank to avoid detection by the Portuguese at Megaza on the left. They decide to spend the night at Njanjanja Village on the right bank of the Tchiri River, inside Mozambique.

The following morning is another day of visual contrasts. The east bank features very narrow marshes against the backdrop of the massive Morumbala Mountain, which they had started seeing from Chiromo and which drops sharply into the Tchiri River beyond Mum'budi. In contrast, everything is flat on the west bank, where the Dinde merges into the valley of the Dziwedziwe River from the west. Before disgorging its muddy waters into the Tchiri at Goya, the Dziwedziwe forms extensive marshes on both sides. Peasants from as far north as Nyachikadza's chiefdom in Nyasaland come to these marshes to collect *nyika* water lily in times of severe hunger. But no one comes to the marshes this year, as food is no problem throughout the valley. Years of hunger alternate with those of plenty, although peasants in other parts of the region are not that lucky even this year. Villagers living far away from the Tchiri River in the east, in a region generically known as Malolo, are already facing acute shortages; for these peasants the Tchiri Valley is an oasis of plenty this year. Their hunger is driving up food prices at markets like Mum'budi, where Kasisi quickly sells his maize to Indian traders at 150 escudos per bag, which is three times the rate they could get in Nyasaland. Satisfied, the chief buys cloth for his wives and children and sugar for making *kachasu* liquor back at home. The return journey begins at approximately three o'clock in the afternoon. The canoe is much lighter now, but the going is still hard because they are fighting against the current. They pass Megaza late at night and pitch camp at Mzimu Village, which is still inside Mozambique.

Once on the other side of the international boundary the following day, Kasisi and his men take a closer look at the Dinde (figure 0.1) in Nyachikadza's chiefdom. Most of the chiefdom's villages stand on a ridge, running parallel to and at about a mile from the Tchiri River. Far to the west, they can see nothing but maize gardens, which, as they are told, stretch up to the Dinde channel, separating the dambo from the mphala drylands (figure 3.2). Then, after about 15 miles from Nyachikadza's court, they leave the Dinde at Port Herald Boma. In the next 30 miles, the party travels through the Tengani chiefdom on the west bank. But there are no significant marshes on this side of the river, and Tengani's people survive mostly on munda farming on the mphala. It is hot and the land is very dry. Women and men are busy preparing the land for planting in November and hoping that Mbona will give them adequate rains as he did the previous season. Some families have already started the annual hunger season, and the travelers cannot procure fresh provisions from Tengani's munda-dependent growers. They therefore rush toward

Chiromo, where they can get green maize from cultivators of *dimba* gardens in the Dabanyi marshes.

After spending the night at Chiromo, Kasisi and his entourage enter Dabanyi, and, moving slowly, they are able to identify the various dimba-farming activities at the height of the dry season. As in the Dinde, in the Dabanyi the evergreen *bande* grass lining the river gives way to gardens in varying phases of cultivation.[11] People are busy securing their livelihood. Some are burning reeds, bande, and elephant grass to open new dimba gardens. There is smoke everywhere, rising from the lower portions of the dambo that have just emerged from the floodwaters. On these drifts, peasants are sowing fast-ripening crops, while plants on the higher sections of the dambo are more advanced. Some villagers are already eating the maize seeded earlier in the season. Others are weeding their beans and sweet potatoes (*mbatata*), the harvesting of which effectively closes the dimba season in December. While the mphala drylands are virtually "dead" now, the dambo features crops in different stages of development. To be sure, these crops do not eliminate all forms of food insufficiency, but they do protect the population against the kinds of hunger that attracted the attention of scholars and international aid agencies to other parts of Africa during the last quarter of the twentieth century.

TIME MATTERS

This book was originally inspired by the debates over the problem of hunger in Africa. I call these debates the "crisis literature," for they were preoccupied with sudden, dramatic scarcity, and, for the most part, they responded to the Ethiopian and Sahelian famines of the 1970s and 1980s. The publicity surrounding these disasters renewed Africanist interest in food matters. The disasters attracted the attention of young people looking for dissertation topics and encouraged older specialists in rural and development studies to reexamine their research findings and assumptions in light of the problem.[12] Africa's agricultural and agrarian history thus witnessed a rush to relevance.

In the event, however, the rush to relevance bogged down, because the very terms of the debates—"the food crisis in Africa"—made it virtually impossible to think about Africa historically. For that, an adequate conception of time is fundamental, and my abiding purpose throughout this book is to sketch its contours. The crisis literature provides little in this regard.

The Crisis Literature

We know a good deal about micro-environments, systems of cultivation, and forms of domestic organization in specific localities; in some cases we also know how particular patterns of production, strategies of livelihood,

and social relations have changed in the course of commoditization, population growth, or changes in policy and political structures. How to combine
these pieces of evidence and analysis into an explanation of *growing* food
deficits across the continent remains something of a puzzle.[13]

I distinguish between two main streams of thought in the crisis literature.[14]
The first gives priority to environmental factors in the etiology of famine,
directing attention to natural conditions such as soil structures, rainfall patterns, and climatic variability.[15] According to some scholars, these same
forces shaped the very character of African societies and history.[16] Nature
itself determined African history. The highly respected economic historian
E. L. Jones spoke for many when he wrote,

> In Africa man adapted himself to nature ... Without a sizeable agricultural
> surplus there was neither much incentive to develop private property ... At
> the root of all this seems to have been the infertility of the soil; pervasive
> insecurity as a result of conflict and slave-raiding, even before the advent
> of the Portuguese; and a hot environment of such ferocious human and
> animal diseases that population and market size, and draught power, were
> held down ... *The defects of the environment did indeed strike so close to
> the heart of economic life that it is not clear what indigenous developments
> were possible.*[17]

Neo-Malthusians round off Jones's story by suggesting how a combination of
"primitive" grazing and farming techniques and an "explosion" in animal and
human populations aggravated the continent's food deficits.[18] This ecological
deterioration and the food crises it causes have stood in the way of "development" everywhere on the continent, with the exception of South Africa and
pre-independence Zimbabwe, where settlers' agriculture, philanthropy, and
foresight harnessed the natural evils of the region.[19] Some people have called
this interpretation "Whiggish"—together with other formulations of environmental determinism, it competes with what I shall call the "liberal" (or
second) narrative of the crisis literature.[20]

Liberals reject environmental determinism and propose to understand
Africa's food deficits in political, social, and economic terms. Accordingly,
those liberals who joined the debate as rational-choice theorists have inter-
preted the crisis as an outcome of the failure of African governments to
provide incentives to peasant producers. These scholars argue that to placate
the more politically articulate urban consumers, including their own employees, states in Africa have depressed food prices, leading villagers to reduce
production. Africans' miseries arise from the fact that "rational" peasants
operate in "imperfect" markets.[21] Another such explanation, the "food versus
cash crop" theory, locates the crisis in the diversion of limited labor and land

resources from food to cash crop agriculture.[22] Still other liberal scholars think that the deficits stem from the uneven development between the relations and forces of agricultural production. They argue that because of the limited privatization of productive resources, African farmers have used their incomes to defend precapitalist social relations that determine access to land and labor. As a result, there has been a "proliferation of patronage relations" but no "investment … in labor-saving innovations."[23] Africans' failure to revolutionize the forces of production becomes a major theme also among those who believe that the food crisis is part of a broader economic malaise facing the continent as part of the world economy.

The international economy plays two different roles in diagnoses that portray the food deficits as a symptom of economic maladjustment. For one group of analysts, including the World Bank, the continent's failure to feed itself follows directly from the fact that it is not sufficiently integrated into world markets.[24] For these commentators, the solution to the problem lies in greater integration, which Africans can do by exploiting their "comparative advantage" in primary-commodity production. Such participation may not guarantee self-sufficiency in food—indeed, self-sufficiency need not be a goal—but full participation will generate enough income for Africans to purchase food on the international market. For another group, however, precisely this greater integration figures as the principal cause of Africa's food deficits.

At the hands of sophisticated analysts like Michael Watts, the political-economic explanation tends to be very complex, addressing most of the issues raised in the foregoing discussion. It also becomes centrally concerned with the problems of long-term changes in the structure of entitlements and social inequality. As Watts aptly summarized the position:

> Short term changes in entitlements [famines] occur in the context of larger transformations in agriculture, in particular sorts of states, in terms of specific patterns of peasant differentiation and market development, and as part of wider processes of ecological change and deterioration.[25]

In Watts's model, food deficits represent one outcome of the dissolution and reconstitution of precapitalist societies in the age of imperialism. New economic and political pressures have created producers of exchange values out of a population that had been preoccupied mostly with use values. This transformation of Africans into wage laborers or cash-crop producers represents a monumental event that shifted people's relations with one another and with nature.

Liberal scholars admit that, over the years, Africans have indeed abused their natural environment, but they convincingly show that the reasons for this are not to be found in some natural or biological givens, but rather in economic and social-political processes. In colonial Zimbabwe and eastern Zambia, for example, villagers were forced to destroy their environment when the state herded them into crowded areas of poor soils.[26] Elsewhere, peasants undermined the ecological base of all production as they tried to accommodate cash crops without the benefit of new agricultural technologies.[27] Environmental perturbations like drought assumed a new meaning in the face of these challenges, which also affected people's relations with one another.

As wage laborers or cash crop producers, Africans have been dominated by other social classes. Their incomes became subject to the exactions of the state and fell prey to the power of merchants and unpredictable markets, which promoted new forms of inequality and eroded old survival strategies. Colonial and postcolonial food deficits in Africa are thus radically different from their precapitalist antecedents.[28] In today's world, peasants starve not because there is no food, but primarily because they have no command over food. These are "capitalist" shortages that, according to most predictions of the 1970s and 1980s, were bound to get worse as the continent became more entangled in the capitalist world economy. Aggregate figures on food imports pointed to a hopeless future: "a year in the death of Africa"[29] was approaching.

Needless to say, producers of the crisis literature were not the only students of food in Africa. There were many others who researched and wrote about food outside the crisis mode, before, during, and after the 1970s and 1980s.[30] Several factors drew my attention to the crisis literature besides its dominance in the period I started this project. Scholars writing about the "crises" have tended to be historical and multidisciplinary in their approach, softening the boundaries that separate the different fields of African studies. Moreover, the more liberal versions deserve praise for rescuing the problem of hunger from the ethnocentrism—if not outright racism—built into environmental, demographic, and other forms of determinism. Thanks to their writings, it is now possible to teach American students about Africa's food problems without reinforcing the Western images of Africa. The crisis literature has made a valuable contribution, and the following critique is only meant to highlight the enormity of the intellectual challenges it had to deal with. These challenges go beyond the issue of food and touch upon the very heart of history as a science. Let the reader also understand this: I am not making a statement about the *quality* of this vast literature. Some of it is of the highest standards. I am only making a statement about its general *orientation.*

When I began this project in the 1990s, my principal objective was to chronicle and explain the so-called food crises of the Tchiri Valley, which seemed an ideal place to locate such a study. One of Malawi's poorest regions, the valley is notorious for its food deficits. I was to follow the liberal agenda with only one major difference—right from the beginning I wanted to expand the debate about the causes of famine with indigenous notions of want, which seemed to me a good starting point if I was to understand how rational peasants reason and plan in their farming activities. But by the mid-1990s, two problems came up. I had combed every archival and oral source at my disposal, but had found only two food crises that approximated the kind of shortages scholars have identified for the Sahel and Ethiopia in the 1970s and 1980s—the shortages of 1862–63 and 1922–23. (Peasants popularly call the 1922–23 scarcity Mwamthota.)[31] I was beginning to accept the idea that capitalism may not have fomented as many so-called famines in the valley as in other places, when I faced another and even more serious problem. If Mwamthota was indeed the last famine, how can one characterize the food situation in the area after 1923? I could neither discount nor explain why the region had earned its notoriety as a place of hunger, despite the absence of Mwamthota-like food shortages. I seriously considered the possibility of abandoning the project.

I was in the middle of this intellectual crisis about food crises when a political crisis in Malawi was resolved. The Banda regime, which had terrorized Malawians since independence from the British in 1964 and which had kept me out of the country since 1980, was forced out of office. I seized the opportunity and traveled to Malawi without a clear research agenda. All I wanted was to see the country and enjoy the new political freedoms, including the freedom to talk to elders without fear of the secret police. But nothing striking came out of this group of conversations, for my own focus on "famine" prevented me from hearing everything the elders said.

The real turning point came about a year later (1995), when I returned to Malawi and held an extensive conversation with Mrs. Sigresi and her husband, Lingstonya Zachepa, of Njereza Village, Chief Kasisi in Chikwawa District. Listen to her: "One doesn't see *nkute* [leftovers] in this area these days … in the past people never finished their *nsima* [they always left some nkute] … but today our children do not know nkute … because we don't have enough food."[32] The good lady is clearly describing a food deficit—which I was looking for—that differed markedly from the news-making Ethiopian disasters, with their gruesome pictures of emaciated children. No one organized televised concerts for Mrs. Zachepa's children, who went to school without eating breakfast on a regular basis. Nor were they the primary concern of academics, who abandoned the subject as soon as the Ethiopian-like crises disappeared from their televisions. Mrs. Zachepa is talking about a deficit of a different order—recurrent hunger (njala) that kills its victims without attracting national or international attention. Mothers in particular know and lament this kind of hunger. Mothers like her are also producers of food.

The discovery of njala[33] as something different from chaola famine represented a turning point for me. It sharpened my appreciation of the differences between rural and academic understandings of the food problem. Mrs. Zachepa's food system is grounded in space and time and rests on the indivisibility between linear and repetitive events. As an idiom and as a reality, nkute evokes two different but related time frames: the day, *tsiku,* and season, *nyengo.* Nkute is food left from yesterday, which is more easily available in some but not in all seasons. The season and day hold a key to an understanding of the material as well as ideological conditions of the peasant food system.

Peasant Intellectuals Respond

Instead of engaging the crisis literature by invoking the authority of Marx, Malthus, and other big guns in the pantheon of postindustrial philosophies,[34] this book turns to peasants whose knowledge about the problem rests on their direct experiences as food producers, consumers, and victims of hunger. They have developed not only sophisticated agricultural systems, but also ideas that seek to make sense of this important aspect of their lives. Above all, they make and implement the decisions that determine the indigenous food supply on a daily and seasonal basis. These orders of the day and season are so important that they have underwritten at least two major theories about the more routine aspects of social life.

The first is the golden-age theory that gravitates around the ideal that every member of the community deserves access to food and holds that the history of food falls in two radically different epochs: the indefinite past of plenty and the present era of hunger. The *chidyerano* communal meal, which grouped together members of different independent households on the basis of neighborhood as well as kinship, was the most distinctive feature of the food regime in the indefinite past of unlimited abundance. But the persistent hunger of the present rules out the possibility of chidyerano. Hunger and chidyerano cannot coexist.

Although powerful, the golden-age theory thrives alongside other world-views, particularly the "alternative vision." Central to this theory is the division of the meal between nsima, stiff porridge, and *ndiwo* (the American "stew," British "relish," or academics' "side dish"). In contrast to the golden-age theory, the alternative vision assumes a community of unequal members and graded foods. Not nsima—the central but unspoken issue in the golden-age theory—but the sharing of ndiwo emerges as the dominant theme in the alternative vision. The theory stresses conflict and does not divide history into a past of unlimited plenty and a present of inexorable njala. It acknowledges that feast can coexist with famine. Thus, according to female intellectuals, who are the most ardent proponents of this view, every meal is a feast for the elders and men of the community, with their established rights to ndiwo in general and, specifically, the more delicious portions of fish and meat, while every meal is famine for women and the young without those same privileges. A Chewa proverb condenses the women's theory: "The joys of being a community come to an end when you have to share ndiwo."[35] In this view, therefore, daily conflicts over ndiwo rather than long-term deteriorations in the system of food production brought an end to chidyerano. Daily routines can arrest history.

Both the alternative vision and the golden-age theory are about the repetitive. The ideal present and future of the golden-age theorists is the past, while social rather than temporal distinctions act as the organizing principle of the alternative vision. The two time signatures form part of what the geologist, paleontologist, and zoologist Stephen J. Gould called "time's cycle" or "the intelligibility of timeless order and lawlike structure" in contrast to "time's arrow," or the view of history as "an irreversible sequence of events."[36] As aspects of Gould's time's cycle, the golden-age theory and the alternative vision address the problem of order and represent peasants' collective protest against what Mircea Eliade appropriately called the "terror" of history[37]— unpredictable events that barely reach the surface in peasants' debates about life in general and food in particular.

I have yet to find among peasant intellectuals articulated ideas corresponding to Gould's time's arrow. But even if such a theory does not take a center stage in their debates, peasants know from their experiences that one cannot cross certain streams of life twice. Today's elders cannot revisit their youth, and no one can reconstitute the colonial state the way it existed. But, even more immediate, villagers clearly recognize the irreversibility of chaola famine. Chaola is an irrevocable event not only because it signifies the absence of food, but also because it subverts the rules of sharing the daily meal. Chaola abolishes history precisely because it is about both the absence *and* presence of food, and peasants appropriately give it (but not drought or njala) proper names. These names are not the kind people confer on their children in remembrance, or in an attempt to re-create the social identities, of their ancestors. Famine names embody the conditions under which those terrors of history occurred. They are historical markers, against which villagers date other events like the birth of someone.

These are all matters relative to time's arrow, although not necessarily the Whiggish time stretched back beyond memory and forward to a goal. But it is the kind of scheme that allows most people, including those in the West, to lead meaningful lives.[38] The dominance of cyclical time in peasants' ideas does not preclude conceptions of linear time.[39] Cyclical time needs linear time to become time, and vice versa. Gould's metaphor thus provides a more powerful tool for understanding history than the familiar genuflection to "change and continuity," which typically allows historians to drop into the frozen box of "continuity" anything they cannot plot along time's arrow. Gould's metaphor is about *different* laws of historical motion. Time's cycle cannot be about the "changeless" because it does not lead its own life independent of linear time. The two time signatures are intrinsically connected, giving rise to a conception of the food system that can be fundamentally different from that of the students of the crisis literature, who can see Africa's transition from the precapitalist to the capitalist era—but not the days and seasons constituting the transition.

Because neither the day nor the season has analytical space in their analyses, students of the crisis literature cannot control time's arrow or see food. Although their titles usually bear the word *food,* these studies are more concerned with the absence than with the presence of food. They contain little or no discussion of what peasants eat or what they miss as a result of the shortages.[40] For example, the closest *Silent Violence*—the most sophisticated among, and standard-bearer of, the crisis literature—comes to an analysis of patterns of food use is in a brief discussion of gift exchanges between patrons and clients and among social equals, all of which are inherently occasional.[41] To become an expert on food in the world's most underdeveloped continent, one does not need to know much about food; one has to learn about such matters as the "political economy" of its disappearance. Africanists cannot control time's arrow.

Since students of the crisis literature cannot apply brakes on time's arrow, they collide with peasants at several critical points in their respective conceptions of the food system. First, students of the crisis literature treat famine as the universe, with some famines being classified as "capitalist" and others as "precapitalist."[42] Villagers, like Mrs. Zachepa, would politely disagree, arguing that such a definition confounds the elementary rules of logic. For them famine is one subset of the larger phenomenon of food deficits, and njala is another. Moreover, while famine is an irreversible event, njala is not. Njala belongs to cyclical time, and since it occupies only one part of the year, it automatically stands apart from what comes before or after it. It interrupts the season of plenty, which has no analytical space in the crisis literature.

Second, peasants would clash with their academic interpreters on the relation between the routine and the rare. Preoccupied with famine, students of the crisis literature can barely see the ordinary, and the few who get momentary glimpses of it do so through the lens of the extraordinary. They understand the routines only through the crisis.[43] Thus, regardless of how the different parties understood gift exchanges in pre-British Nigeria, for *Silent Violence,* the transactions served no other purpose than to avoid famine: "These gifts and exchanges provided the social context of famine occurrence and constituted the admittedly brittle strands of an indigenous relief program."[44] These were the strategies of the "moral economy" of the precolonial era, and the next strongest indication that peasants may have enjoyed food under the pressures of dependent capitalism are tantalizing references to "ceremonial expenditures,"[45] which are never explained.

Peasants might well agree that moments of extreme want illuminate daily structures. They know, for example, that seasonal hunger heightens the tensions between the poor and rich and between the able-bodied and past or future workers. Some issues that barely catch the eye in good times do indeed become visible in moments of hardship. Mrs. Zachepa would argue, however, that it is simplistic to assume that knowledge of the unique will always illuminate the routine. The extraordinary sheds light on some but not all aspects of the routine, and it does so from a particular angle. She would, in particular, remind the researcher of the stories she had heard from her parents about the famine of 1922–23. Like the one before it, this *chaola* broadened the struggle for survival in such a way as to make all sorts of food the focus of conflict, including plants from the bush. Because villagers do not ordinarily fight for such plants, exclusive reliance on famine as a window on the everyday would lead to an everyday that may not exist on the ground. Mrs. Zachepa would therefore insist on the need to understand these routines in their own right. This and the previous disagreement lead to a third and even more profound disagreement about what history is.

Peasants would say history moves in unpredictable ways, because it involves free actors who every day go through the chaos of irreversible time in the midst of the predictable. Mrs. Zachepa would therefore clash with both environmental determinists and liberals, for, notwithstanding their differences, both schools of thought rely on the same trajectory: the so-called transition from precapitalist to capitalist forms of organization. For modern Whigs, capitalism in South Africa and Zimbabwe dealt a deadly blow to precapitalist famines that had regularly capped population growth in those societies.[46] For the more liberal interpreters, capitalism did precisely the opposite. Their analysis starts with the so-called precapitalist famines, which were necessarily mild as there were always built-in cushions of the "moral economy." With one mighty hand, capitalism removed this layer of cushions and placed the continent on an inexorable trip toward Hades. Not only does every food "crisis" become a "famine," but each famine must also be more serious than its predecessor. Thus, even after raising legitimate concerns about the validity of food-import figures as an indicator of Africa's levels of food production,[47] the same academics could still confidently declare that the continent was facing "growing" food deficits.[48] If Hegel's arrow positioned the German nation toward the future of unlimited abundance, the arrow of the crisis literature moved the continent toward its destruction.

It would not, however, be correct or fair to suggest that the students of the crisis literature are alone in this single-minded focus on time's arrow, and they would not deserve much attention if they were. They represent a broader trend of thought both within and outside African history. Modern history was born in political history's sequences of kingly reigns, wars, treaties, revolutions, and so forth. Its natural terrain is linear time, taken over from the legends and chronicles that preceded the birth of modern and would-be scientific history in the nineteenth century. That is one lineage. The other and more immediate lineage arises from African history, which, like most histories of oppressed groups, had its roots in struggle. Over and beyond the routine tasks of going to the archives and piecing together evidence whose producers never imagined would serve these particular agendas, African historians have had to battle an entrenched set of myths that made and still make the plunder of the continent's human and natural resources tolerable even among churchgoing people and academics of the West: the core of those myths is the idea that Africans did not have a history before the advent of the European colonizer, and that idea served colonial power. In Hugh Trevor-Roper's notorious formulation, precolonial Africa was nothing but a land of "the unrewarding gyrations of barbarous tribes in picturesque but irrelevant corners of the globe." Naturally, therefore, demonstrating the falsity of these myths has been a major task of the Africanist historian. But, tragically, the weapons of the weak have been the weapons of the powerful turned upside down. To write history, it seemed, one had to show that Africa had its own kings and queens.[49]

Nationalist historians have thus been able to find Hegel's state in every part of precolonial Africa, including those where probably none existed. There were even states whose most distinctive feature was that no one heard about them at the height of their power. Then the students of slavery in Africa, not to be outdone, not only discovered slavery as an institution, but discovered as well that the institution was heading toward the system of servitude of the American South. Next were the students of peasants. With powerful microscopes and prophetic vision, they could see in Mrs. Zachepa's neighbors, who sometimes ate better than she, the capitalist prototype. Such villagers' march from the alpha to the omega of capitalist development becomes even more unstoppable should they get 10 ounces of seed of a cash crop. Finally, there are the students of African women. On the one hand, they have explored almost every subject they can plot along time's arrow, advancing this, increasing that—even with the flimsiest and most ambiguous kind of evidence. On the other, only a few of these scholars have seen African women as food processors—the most significant daily occupation of most women on the continent.[50] Writing about such repetitive processes, which have no clear direction, would only validate the racist assumption of an Africa without history. The grand narrative behind these messages is that the African past was in no way significantly different from that of the West, and hence not inferior to it.

Trained historians have responded to the ideologues of imperialism in ways that testify to the force of the engine. The vehicle cruised through several red lights without stopping. Several studies should have halted, or at least slowed, the linear movement of African historians. Most important among these is Jan Vansina's *Tio Kingdom*—a social history born long before it could be understood. In this profound book, Vansina counterposed "large-scale institutions" with "the institutions of local communities" as one method to apply brakes on time's arrow.[51] But these studies and others like them[52] have exerted little or no impact on the production of Africanist knowledge. Africanists have fought their enemies on the terms set by those enemies. It has been an eye for an eye, and no one has turned the other cheek far enough to bring Africa's real history into view.

CENTRAL THEMES REITERATED

A major argument of this book is that we need both cyclical *and* linear time signatures to understand the history of the food system in the valley. Villagers placed the food regime in an irrevocable mode when they, for example, adopted new or abandoned old crops and when they went through moments of chaola famine. However, even such terrors of history as famine make sense only with reference to the routines as represented, among other things, by the orders of the day, tsiku, and season, nyengo. No transition from point A to point B in linear time can occur without the repetitive tsiku and nyengo.

In Malawi there are three nyengo: the cold (*masika*), hot and dry (*chilimwe*), and rainy (*dzinja*) seasons. These are the naturally constituted divisions of the year, but from an economic, sociological, and political point of view, the year has only two significant nyengo: the dzinja and masika. Focus on the dzinja allows this book to retrieve such repetitive processes as the cultivation of the region's major food crops and seasonal hunger, while analysis of the masika brings to the surface the past of such activities as harvesting and the annual rites of passage. Although season-sensitive, these activities also formed part of the order of the day, together with such processes that, like eating, did not respect the season. That these daily and seasonal routines enjoyed no independent life apart from the linear movement of time underscores the need to see many pasts in the history of rural struggles for food security.

A multidimensional view of the historical process highlights the indivisibility between order and disorder, between deserts of hunger and oases of plenty, between assuming and avoiding risk, between feast and famine, between abundance and hunger, and between the past and present. The book has, in other words, split the past into its constituent elements in order to see the internal connections and dynamics of the food system. Thus, although every chaola represents a rare and irrevocable event of the past, its victims understood it also as an aspect of their routines. A food shortage becomes a chaola when the sufferers subvert the quotidian rules of sharing food. Rare moments of absolute hunger become meaningful only with reference to the abundance of everyday life. Moreover, an analysis of the history of famines from the viewpoint of the seasons reveals a fundamental tension in the region's food system. Though famine-free between 1923 and 2000, the valley was never hunger-free during the same period. Every year a substantial section of the peasantry experienced a food gap before the new harvest. The presence of njala and absence of chaola are not mutually exclusive.

This book identifies at least two sets of connections to explain the tension. First, the valley is a land of both deserts of hunger and oases of plenty—areas of structural deficits and surpluses. Second, these deserts of hunger and oases of plenty were no mere spatial categories; they formed integral parts of the historical process. Every day, villagers created deserts of hunger and oases of plenty in their fields as they both assumed and avoided risk, as the logic of the garden pulled them both toward and away from specialization, both toward and away from reproducing in the fields the biological diversity of the natural world. The conquest of famine and persistence of hunger are embedded in these seasonally determined daily routines. The season combines order and disorder in ways that slow down the linear movement of time at another level. For example, the dzinja becomes an ideal season only insofar as it heightens the level of agricultural work, promising a future of plenty against the back-drop of present njala. Every year the dzinja and masika replay the golden-age theory's "present" of hunger and "past" of abundance, respectively. One does not, therefore, need to divide real time between an irreversible past of plenty and the present of hunger in order to see one central dynamic of the golden-age theory. Hunger and plenty can occupy the same time and space, as analysis of the greatest of daily routines—the meal—shows.

The daily meal was an exceedingly orderly process, with everyone knowing in advance who would prepare it and with whom they would eat. But, as suggested earlier, the meal also acted as a center of contention, declaring the right of everyone to food and the limited nature of that right. Every meal was a "feast" for some and a "famine" for others. The chidyerano communal meal was no exception.

Villagers locate the origins of chidyerano in times of plenty as well as in times of hunger. Both moments encourage sharing, one because there is so much food to go around and the other because there is so little. But what makes chidyerano a powerful metaphor is also the story of its ending, which is the primary focus of oral historians, interested in the past more as a precursor to the present than for its own sake. While some historians emphasize long-term deteriorations in food supply to explain the end of chidyerano, others focus on everyday conflicts over food that is there—ndiwo. In its very organization, the daily meal encourages both order *and* disorder in the community. The food regime operated as a terrain of conflict, with its own internal pressures for change.

This book makes three statements about change. First, it contends that the mere existence of pressures does not by itself create new situations; human beings do. Second, because humans make their history under specific conditions, questions oblige one to insert the food system into its wider field, including ecological shifts, population growth, processes of state formation, and new markets. Finally, the book argues that because these vehicles of change were of uneven strength and intensity, their outcomes defy easy generalization. Some were long-lasting and clearly irreversible, but many others were not. It is in order to capture this wide range of historical trajectories that I have extensively employed the golden-age theory and alternative vision and Gould's metaphor of time's arrow and time's cycle.

Like Gould, I am keenly aware of the pitfalls of dichotomies.[53] I do not employ the two sets of metaphors to close debate around two opposing interpretations. I see many possible theories of sharing between the golden-age theory and the alternative vision, and an assortment of time signatures between time's arrow and time's cycle. As the foregoing discussion has shown, Gould's "time's cycle" encompasses at least two ideals of the predictable: the orders of the day and season. The purpose of the dichotomies is to broaden the range of questions in an intellectually controllable fashion.

I tell the details of the above story in seven substantive chapters that fall in three sections, each of which has its own chronology or chronologies. The organization of the three parts reflects my own journey as a researcher into food matters over the past decade. Part I (chapters 1 and 2) contains the main elements of the original project. It analyzes the events leading to, and the social and political impact of, the famines of 1862–63 and 1922–23—all matters of linear time. Part II (chapters 3 and 4) focuses on the nyengo and especially seasonal hunger. Part III examines the daily routines of cotton and food growing (chapters 5 and 6) and the meal (chapter 7). Food has more than one past, which obliges the researcher to rely on more than one kind of source. Some sources do a better job at illuminating cyclical time, while others present the food system as a sequence of cumulative change.

SOURCES

I have made extensive use of the records of Dr. David Livingstone's Zembezi Expedition (1859–64) and Bishop Mackenzie's Universities Mission to Central Africa (UMCA) (1861–64), whose members were prolific writers.[54] These sources touch on almost every aspect of life in the valley, providing crucial information on the nature of the food economy in this era of the slave trade. In fact, the years between 1859 and 1864 are better documented than the remaining three and a half decades of the nineteenth century (1864–1900). Good reports on 1864–1900 are few and far between, and even the most detailed among them—like the unpublished letters and diaries of Fred and John Moir[55]—are of limited value for the student of food. There are no copious accounts about food, giving the distinct impression that no major food deficit interrupted the activities of the traders and missionaries. A famine, like the one of 1862–63, could have not easily escaped the diarists, given their

reliance on peasant-grown food.[56] References to the food economy become
more common with the establishment of the colonial state in 1891.

The Public Record Office in London houses some official records on
Malawi, but the more useful ones for this book are those in the Malawi
National Archives in Zomba. Annual, quarterly, and monthly administrative reports on the Tchiri Valley's Chikwawa and Nsanje Districts[57] provide
a rich source of information on the region's political and economic history.
Conscientious district commissioners have left for prosperity some of the most
valuable eyewitness accounts.[58] Equally inspiring are some of the Department
of Agriculture's records. Many field officers sent to their superiors in the
capital a mine of information that can become the basis of highly textured
farming systems analyses. The best among these records compare favorably
with those generated by the Shire Valley Agricultural Development Project
(SVADP), which starting in 1968 reported on the local cultivation practices
in many different ways, including multiyear surveys.[59] The surveys not only
complement but also make up for deficiencies in some government reports.

Some deficiencies in Malawi's official records resulted from pure acci-
dents. A fire in 1918 destroyed the Secretariat and most of records kept there
since the beginning of the colonial era. There are, as a result, significant gaps
in our knowledge of the first three decades of British rule in the country.
The gaps only compound the problem of structural shortcomings, reflecting
the knowledge and interests of the reporters. Government officials were, for
example, so committed to cotton that they left an inordinate amount of data
on the subject and made cotton agriculture the unspoken background to most
of their thinking on the food economy of the valley. One reads more about
an area's systems of food cultivation when it produced cotton. Agricultural
systems that did not produce cotton easily disappeared from the official radar.
Other kinds of biases interfered with official reporting on famine.

As the students of China and Russia know too well, official accounts of
famine have to be treated with caution. There was, for example, a clear political agenda behind the detailed accounts of the famine of 1862–63. Members
of Livingstone's Zembezi Expedition and the UMCA wrote copiously about
the famine in order to explain the failure of their respective missions and to
bolster the anti-slave-trade movement. Taken uncritically, these accounts can
easily reinforce European travelers' view of late-nineteenth-century eastern
Africa as a land of chaos in need of a saving hand from the West.[60] Slightly
different motives appear to have influenced British colonial descriptions of
the hunger of 1922–23. The same officials, who were quick to advertise the
sufferings of peasants under Portuguese rule in Mozambique,[61] tried everything to downplay the impact of the shortage in their districts. Thus, the more
conscious British accounts of the shortfall give the distinct impression that
not many people suffered seriously because of the effectiveness of colonial
relief programs.[62] Without oral evidence and raw statistical information,[63] this

book could not have treated the shortage as an instance of *chaola* famine. British officials were as committed in their determination to present the bright side of their rule as the African elites of the postcolonial era.

In postcolonial Malawi, the discrepancy between official chronicles and social reality grew wider as the Banda regime became increasingly repressive. Everyone, including agricultural officers, had to echo the party song, announcing how, under Dr. Banda, nothing could go wrong in the country; every year was a year of unqualified success. No one went hungry because peasants faithfully followed Dr. Banda's call for people to work hard in the fields and to adopt modern methods of farming. That we can draw the line between fantasy and reality in some of these reports is largely the result of the availability of statistical data generated by the SVADP and oral testimonies my research assistants and I recorded at different points between 1991 and 2004.

Used in this book as both evidence and theory, oral accounts about the food system of the valley fall in two broad categories. One consists of recollections of specific events that occurred at particular moments in the past, incidents like the introduction of new crops, major floods, famine, and other notable occurrences. Narratives about some of these events can become formal with the passage of time, and villagers sometimes date them. The second group of oral evidence covers repetitive processes like the gathering of wild roots and plants, the planting and harvesting of domesticated crops, food preparation, eating, seasonal hunger, and annual celebrations.

The past food economy emerges as many different things from the memories of men and women. At the risk of oversimplification, one can say that men's narratives take their logic from the golden-age theory. The food system emerges from their accounts mostly as a neutral zone of equal opportunities, without winners or losers. The emphasis is not on social distinction but the hiatus between the past and the present. Their world is miles away from that of the women, whose memories tend to gravitate around the hierarchical principles of the alternative vision, fulfilling thereby the prediction of a key Chewa proverb: "Those who eat bran have clearer memories than those who enjoy white flour." Gender or social position was not, however, the only factor shaping people's view of the past.

Another major factor to consider when assessing oral accounts about the food system is the indivisibility between the repetitive and the irreversible. Traditions about the Mwamthota famine of 1922–23 are very instructive in this regard. Unlike British officials, village historians make it very clear that Mwamthota was not another *njala*; it was a unique event. Nearly every elder in the 1990s knew something about it. Oral historians also spelled out the qualities that made it different from an ordinary *njala*. It subverted the quotidian rules of sharing, forcing people to steal from their neighbors. It was the hunger that abolished history. Mwamthota has left an indelible mark on the region's collective consciousness.

Villagers do not, however, remember every aspect of Mwamthota with equal force. Peasants told lively stories about their long journeys to places like Mozambique to work for food or get it free from relatives (see chapters 2 and 4). What is not immediately obvious to the listener is that these recollections owe a good deal of their vividness to the fact that they were not about one-time events. Every year during the hungry season a segment of the rural population lived off the bush and drew upon the resources of other villagers within and beyond the valley. Villagers remember the extraordinary events of 1922–23 with peculiar sharpness precisely because those events were not extraordinary. Linear time gets some of its force from the cyclical. Traditions about Mwamthota suggest that the converse may also be true.

Villagers are apt to "forget" those elements of the irreversible that have no bearing on the repetitive. On the one hand, oral historians are loud and clear in their representation of 1922–23 as a "rotten" moment, when the young suffered many hunger-related disabilities and when mothers abandoned or sold their children. In this regard, Mwamthota does not differ from the famine of the early 1860s, as it emerges from European records—our principal source for that calamity. But the Mwamthota of the oral historian is very different from the famine of the early 1860s (and 1949 in the Tchiri Highlands) in one aspect. Elders portray the plight of adult women as no different from that of their male counterparts. In their view, Mwamthota was a gender-neutral, "national" tragedy.

There may be valid grounds for accepting this view of the famine. Mwamthota had a different social and political context than the famines that came before and after it. In contrast to the early 1860s, there were no armed bands of foreign men trying to take advantage of the starving female population in 1922–23. Moreover, Mwamthota occurred several decades before the women of the region lost their economic independence. It came too early in the region's economic history to have had the same implications as the famine of 1949 in the Tchiri Highlands.[64] Mwamthota may have indeed been as gender-neutral as elders portray it. However, it is very well possible that one is here facing the effects of collective or structural amnesia. (Moreover, nearly everyone who reminisced on Mwamthota in the 1990s had been a child in the 1920s.) Mwamthota has become a turning point in the region's "generic memories," which are as much concerned with the real as with the ideal world.[65] Unlike memories about abandoning and selling children, the sufferings of adult women as women do not have a fertile ideological terrain to feed on among the Mang'anja. There are no patterned ideas to distinguish the unpleasant experiences of adult women from those of their male counterparts during the famine. Thus, even if historically valid, stories that reiterate the gender neutrality of Mwamthota owe part of their force to the ability of the dominant gender ideologies to resist deviations from the norm.

Oral history does not simply fill in gaps left by documentary sources; it also forms part of a community's theories about life. It should play a central role in the very definition of one's project, putting to rest the familiar division of labor that sends us to archives and libraries for "theory" and to the African countryside for "informants." Peasants' voices do open new ways of understanding their world. But, as the foregoing discussion has shown, to enter this world one needs to understand its history and culture, as well as its language.

LANGUAGE

Reviewers of my *Work and Control* raised two interesting questions about language.[66] First, they object to my use of the African "Tchiri," arguing I should have kept the anglicized term "Shire," despite the fact that no villager can recognize the term.[67] One reviewer went so far as to liken my attempt to de-anglicize the term to what he calls "Dr. Banda's imperialist penchant for 'correcting' spellings."[68] What the reviewer conveniently ignored is that Banda loved everything British and respected Scottish nationalism to the point that he kept for his country's only commercial center the name of an obscure Scottish village, Blantyre. The second criticism claims—without showing the consequences—that *Work and Control* could not realistically interpret the past of the Malawi section of the valley because it does not show competence in Portuguese, which was the official language on the Mozambican side of the valley.[69]

This criticism has more merit than the first, as a general rule. Historians need to know the language of the people whose past they study.[70] The reviewer has, however, identified the wrong language. Portuguese is largely irrelevant for an understanding of the history of the region. Whatever their earlier interest on the western or today's Malawian side of the Tchiri River, Portuguese officials stopped reporting about that bank of the river after fixing the international border in 1891. The pertinent European-generated reports on the west bank of the Tchiri are in English. The border was real in this regard. It only loses its significance in terms of inter-African relationships. There was considerable interborder activity between the two countries. But, as the foregoing story of Kasisi shows, the goings-on were largely clandestine, falling outside the immediate purview of both Portuguese and British officials. One does not need to know Portuguese to understand these hidden struggles; one needs to know the languages of the colonized, which I do. I am fluent in both Chichewa (Chimang'anja) and Chisena. In contrast, some of my critics have been writing histories of the region deaf and dumb to the languages of the region—with serious and demonstrable consequences.[71]

Competence in Chichewa and Chisena has allowed me to penetrate the world of the peasantry in several important ways. I was able to converse with the elders directly, thereby reducing the element of artificiality surrounding interviews conducted with the help of translators. I could follow leads, pursue new questions, and chat about matters of importance for the peasantry. Fluency in the two languages also prepared me well for the challenges of translation. As everyone knows, making the meanings of one language intelligible in another is no easy task. One cannot always rely on one's research assistants for an effective translation of some phrases, including proverbs. To render a proverb intelligible in another language, one needs a good grasp of both languages.[72] But even single words can cause a headache. As indicated earlier, *ndiwo* is "stew" for the Americans, "relish" for the British, and "side dish" for some academics. Moreover, neither "stew," "relish," nor "side dish" carries the extra baggage that *ndiwo* does. For a Chewa speaker, *ndiwo* stands not only for the meat, fish, and vegetables one takes with the nsima, it also stands for a system of sharing. Ndiwo defines the peasant world in original ways that do not reduce to Western terms. It is for this reason that I will keep key Chichewa terms in the text, although for quick comprehensibility, I will confine their Chisena equivalents to the glossary. The voices of "peasant intellectuals" are there not only to lend authenticity to the account, but also to depict the real world in which people live—be it the world of "feast" or "famine."

1

CHAOLA ABOLISHES HISTORY

The famines of 1862–63 and 1922–23 are irreversible events because no one can revisit them. They are also about cumulative change one can trace through the stories of the slave raids and Magololo and later British attempts to restructure the political map of the valley. However, as chapter 2 shows, chaola freezes history because it subverts the orders of the season and day. Villagers understand chaola not merely as the absence of food, but also as the perversion of the rules that govern the sharing of food on a daily basis. Precisely because chaola sabotages the everyday social identities of food, there is need to understand these identities on their own terms.

> Yes, chidyerano came to an end because … there is little food to share nowadays.
>
> —Mr. Bernard Demba

> Chidyerano comes to an end when some people eat meat alone in the secrecy of their houses at the same time as they enjoy other people's meat at the communal meal.
>
> —Mrs. Malita Chimtedza

1

POLITICAL CRISES AND FAMINE, 1862–1923

All the trouble that came on the Manganja was owing to the Rundo not doing as Rundos did in days gone by. They went from village to village all over the land, every year, and at each place they prayed to Pambi to send rain, and to keep away enemies. Then they were a happy people; there was no war, no starvation, but now all things were against them, for the Rundo cared for nothing but his pombi [beer] and his wives, shut himself up with them, and got drunk every day, and would go nowhere.[1]

The sale of the grain reserves had showed that those entrusted by the public had no regard for the welfare of ordinary people.[2]

But the slave-trade must be deemed the chief agent of the ruin, because, as we were informed, in former droughts all the people flocked from the hills down to the marshes, which are capable of yielding crops of maize in less than three months, at any time of the year, and now they were afraid to do so.[3]

INTRODUCTION

Peasants do not treat chaola famine simply as a natural event. Drought (chilala) may precipitate, but cannot by itself cause famine, which is also a political crisis, representing the failure of what I call the "crisis-management" scheme, which in the nineteenth century had two main components: relief and preventive strategies.

Besides the more "invisible" techniques of food production (see chapter 6), the preventive regime consisted of an "early-warning" system, out-migration, and "emergency" farming. The drought of the early 1860s and early 1920s led to famine not simply because they were unusually serious or because food production had been on decline. The system of food production was relatively healthy on the eve of both droughts. Drought became chaola mainly because there were political crises that disabled key elements of the crisis-management scheme. Both famines were irreversible events, with their origins in a series of cumulative shifts that undermined the relief and preventive regimes and, in general, rural responses to the natural phenomenon we call drought.

THE FAMINE OF 1862–63

A large field would be to offer a temptation to marauders and thus by sowing extensively, the whole would be lost.[4]

The drought that triggered the famine of 1862–63 affected the whole of central and southern Africa in varying degrees of intensity and duration.[5] In the Tchiri Valley, there were no planting rains from January 1862 to March 1863.[6] In other words, the drought covered the second half and both halves of the 1861–62 and 1862–63 rainy seasons, respectively. However, although serious, the shortages cannot by themselves explain the horrific disaster of 1862–63. Villagers died in such large numbers because the slave raids undermined their ability to do emergency farming or move to oases of plenty within and beyond the valley. Political instability trapped people in their deserts of hunger and compromised the early-warning system.

The Early-Warning System

The early-warning system, which announced the need for extraordinary action to meet a public threat, was religious in character and featured the *mchape* (witchcraft-eradication) and *nsembe* (sacrifice) complexes. Both rested on the belief that behind every natural distress, such as drought, pests, or epidemic diseases, were angry spirits or evil human beings (*mfiti* witches), and that, together with their subjects, political leaders could do something about the crisis. At the heart of both the mchape and nsembe was the idea that a properly functioning political community could prevent perturbations in nature from becoming social disasters. Beyond these similarities, however, there were important differences between the mchape and nsembe systems.

As part of witchcraft (*ufiti*) beliefs, the mchape complex made members of every social class capable of causing private and public misfortune. At the hands of chiefs, mchape could become, to invert James Scott's famous phrase, the "weapon of the powerful." Chiefs in trouble often employed the cult to neutralize their enemies, although this did not necessarily mean that the "weak" were entirely helpless. They enjoyed some protection in the fact that mchape specialists, who administered the *mwabvi* poison ordeal to suspected witches, did not necessarily form part of the official religious or political establishment, as the priesthood of the nsembe complex did.

The nsembe system consisted of the Mbona and *mgwetsa* cults.[7] Central to the two religious organizations was the idea that the spirits of angry royals could cause public misfortune, and that their living descendants could take action to "heal" the land (as the Shambaa would say). Thus, according to golden-age theorists like Chimbeli, whose words introduced this chapter, no chaola had visited the land when political leaders acted responsibly in the past. They would organize nsembe to appease the angry spirits. Mbona and mgwetsa cults were similar in that respect; they differed mainly in the scale of their respective political domains. While the mgwetsa focused attention on the well-being of what we now call "chiefdoms," the Mbona system enjoyed a broader allegiance; it was the religion of the Mang'anja "nation" that had developed as an integral part of the *lundu* state.[8]

According to the main thrust of Mang'anja mythology, Mbona was born of a virgin mother, who was also a sister of the founding lundu paramount. He was a great rainmaker, who consequently incurred the anger and jealousy of the lundu, his uncle. The lundu ordered Mbona's murder, which took place at Khulubvi in Nsanje. But vanquished as a human being, Mbona emerged as a worker of wonders again after his death. The miracles he performed as a spirit finally converted his former enemies, including the lundu, into his worshippers. They built a shrine for him at Khulubvi and placed a woman, known as the *salima*—"she who does not hoe"—as his consort and intermediary. The installation of a new salima and the rebuilding of the shrine, under the leadership of lundu rulers and their successors, became part of the nsembe the Mang'anja offered to Mbona whenever threatened by drought and other natural perturbations. As long as they listened to Mbona, the Mang'anja were assured of peace and prosperity, as they told members of the UMCA in the early 1860s:

> Bona [*sic*] was supposed eminently benevolent: when his power predominated war did not desolate the land; drought was unknown; he blessed the seed, and the fruits of the earth abounded; he was, in fact, a dispenser of peace and plenty as well as wise counsel.[9]

Thus, after receiving no rains between January and May of 1862, the Mang'anja turned to Mbona.

The custodians of the cult traveled from Khulubvi to the village of Mankhokwe, who then claimed to be the lundu.[10] The emissaries wanted a new salima to be installed at the shrine as part of a nsembe to Mbona. When the missionary, Horace Waller, visited the chief on 6 August 1862,[11] he found that the "village was occupied by the embassage of the spirit 'Bona' who had sent his men all the way from the rice village, Kulubvi for a wife according to custom ... On this occasion Mankokwi [had] to supply a wife."[12] Mankhokwe handed over a wife of one of his counselors to the custodians,[13] but the missionaries are silent on what happened afterward. There are no accounts of a salima's installation at Khulubvi that year.[14] For a sense of what such a ceremony might have looked like, one has to turn to the mgwetsa ritual that many members of the UMCA attended at Magomero in late 1861.

Missionary records indicate that the drought of 1861–62 struck the Tchiri Highlands earlier than the valley. People in the Tchiri Highlands were already in the grip of drought during the first half (November–December) of the 1861–62 growing season. The chief of Magomero, Chigunda, responded to the threat by organizing a mgwetsa, led by his sister in her capacity as the *mbudzi* priestess:

> Chigunda assembled his people in the bush outside the village, then marched with them in procession to the appointed place for prayer, a plot of ground cleared and fenced in, in the middle of which was a hut, called the prayer hut. The women attended as well as the men, and in the procession the women preceded the men. All entered the enclosure, the women sitting on one side of the hut, the men on the other; Chigunda sat some distance apart by himself. Then a woman named Mbudzi, the sister of Chigunda it was said, stood forth, and she acted as priestess ... The supplications ceased, Mbudzi came out of the hut, fastened up the door, sat on the ground, threw herself on her back; all the people followed her example, and while in this position they clapped their hands and repeated their supplication for several minutes ... When the dance ceased, a large jar of water was brought and placed before the chief; first Mbudzi washed her hands, arms and face; then water was poured over her by another woman; then all the women rushed forward with calabashes in their hands, and dipping them into the jar threw the water into the air with loud cries and wild gesticulations. And so the ceremony ended.[15]

As they did in mchape, everyone left nsembe ceremonies with two things: belief in the imminent end of the public threat[16] and a plan of action.

Participants in these ceremonies always knew they had to do something beyond prayer. Those taking part in liturgies to end an outbreak of measles understood that in order for their prayers to become effective, they also had to abstain from sex and to quarantine the sick in *msasa* temporary houses outside the village. Nsembe and mchape acted as a public forum at which villagers shared information about the availability of food in distant places and about the need to retool their emergency farming techniques. People had to reconfigure their responses because no two droughts were exactly similar (see chapter 3). Whether peasants actually translated such knowledge into lifesaving activities is not a foregone conclusion; it depended on existing political conditions. Political insecurity in the early 1860s removed both local and distant oases of plenty. Slave raids transformed the entire valley into one desert of hunger.

The Slave Raids

Evidence on the period immediately before 1862–63 goes a long way to support Amartya Sen's argument that famine can break out under conditions of agricultural prosperity.[17] The region's agricultural system was not in a crisis in 1859–61.[18] Abundance, rather than hunger, greeted members of Livingstone's Zambezi Expedition in the Tchiri River region in 1859. Peasants here had more to eat than their counterparts in parts of the Lower Zembezi that had been ravaged by the slave trade for decades. As Dr. John Kirk noted upon entering the Tchiri Valley in 1859: "There is no lack of food in these regions and a fine crop for the next year in the fields."[19] Thus, when Livingstone and his men could not get anything to eat at Thete in June 1859, they traveled all the way to Khulubvi (Nsanje) to procure rice.[20] They were so abundantly supplied that Khulubvi earned the epithet of the "rice village."[21] Two years later, in May 1861, a "crowd of well-fed, good-looking" villagers welcomed Rowley and the other members of the UMCA at Mankhokwe's village.[22] The missionaries easily secured their provisions, and their impressions of the region's ability to feed itself became sharper as they settled down. At Mikolongo village, near the Gaga Hills, everyone "looked well fed, all were well clothed, all were profusedly ornamented with beads, ivory, and brass rings."[23] The people of Mikolongo also exploited the dambo marshes of the Mwanza River, which could produce food even at the height of drought in 1862. In a few places that had come under the protection of the Magololo, Horace Waller identified maize in five different stages of growth, because, as he put it, "so rich is the soil [that when] one crop is taken up another [is] put in the same day the moisture filtering through the roots of the corn."[24] The slave raiders undermined the ability of most villagers to exploit such pieces of fertile land; they effectively turned natural oases of plenty into deserts of hunger.

Beginning in the late 1850s, raiding replaced slave "trading" as a result of several developments. First, there was an increase in the demand for sugar and cloves produced by slave labor on the French Mascarene and Zanzibar Islands. Second, the British anti-slave-trade campaign reached eastern Africa. The two conflicting trends had the effect of stimulating the international traffic in the valley. On the one hand, adroit slave traders who succeeded in selling their cargo on the Indian Ocean obtained high prices. And on the other, the more cautious middlemen, who did not want to collide with British antislavers on the east coast, turned to the ivory trade. But most ivory dealers in the interior wanted nothing but slaves. Thus, to engage in the ivory trade, dealers had to procure captives and join the more skillful hunters who sold captives on the east coast. Together, the two groups turned the valley and the Tchiri Highlands into one slave-raiding zone by early 1860s. The region was on a war footing, as Portuguese officials dispatched their raiders, who clashed or collaborated with other marauders like the Chikunda and Yao. They burned villages, killed very young children and the elderly, and drove the healthy and able-bodied to the slave markets. Warfare had replaced "peaceful" exchange with serious consequences.

Raiding denied village elders the control they had exercised since the 1830s, and there was, as a result, a dramatic shift in the social composition of captives from the valley. Every able-bodied person began to join the "less desirable" dependents, who had dominated the traffic when village elders acted as local middlemen. In particular, grown-up women, who comprised the nucleus of every Mang'anja community, began to feature prominently among the captives from the area. Most of the 84 captives that Livingstone and his companions freed at the outskirts of what is today Blantyre were women, including mothers with babies at their backs (photo 2).[25] Unlike European plantation owners, ivory hunters in the interior were more interested in female than in male captives.

As women, men, and children marched toward their destination under the order of the gun and *goli* slave stick (photo 2), their equally traumatized husbands, wives, and children abandoned their burned-down villages chaotically. They fled to mountains like the Thyolo Escarpment. Waller and other members of the UMCA subsequently found them there in the second half of 1862: "People had fled from war in the valley, to the summit of the [Thyolo] mountain: they had but little food with them, only a few pumpkins."[26] But it appears that the largest stream of fugitives from the old villages sought the shelter of the islands of the Tchiri River. Barely populated in the late 1850s, every island on the Tchiri began to team with refugees in the early 1860s. As one observer put it in late 1862: "The marsh is most singularly altered since last year: then there was not a soul to be seen, now there are *msasas* throughout it."[27] Lovell Procter was more specific when he blamed the changed settlement pattern on the slaver Matekenya: "Lower down the Elephant marsh [we] passed a great number of fugitives from Matikinya."[28] Similarly occupied were the islands above Chikwawa.[29] The slave raids had altered the settlement pattern of the valley.

In times of peace, villages straddled the line joining the dambo marshes and the mphala drylands on the valley floor. This was a strategic location that gave peasants easy access to both the mphala drylands and dambo marshes for agricultural purposes. The new settlement pattern denied them both microenvironments. Unlike the population movements of the normal hungry season, flight from war was a disorderly process. The fugitives that the UMCA missionaries met on the summit of Thyolo Mountain were not looking for the most fertile parts of the escarpment; they were driven by the need

Photo 2 Livingstone met with and released a gang of captives like this one at Mbami, near the modern city of Blantyre, in 1861. (D. Livingstone and C. Livingstone, *Narrative of an Expedition to the Zambesi and Its Tributaries and of the Discoveries of the Lakes Shirwa and Nyassa* [London: Murray, 1865; New York: Johnson Reprint Corporation, 1971])

for safety. Many ended up in caves and other inhospitable terrains. Similarly disadvantaged were those who fled to the islands of the Tchiri River. Unlike the wider Zembezi, which has islands large enough to accommodate people and their gardens, the islands of the Tchiri River are very tiny. No one lived there in times of peace; villagers occasionally used them only as gardens, and when they did so, men had to guard the crops against thieves toward the end of the growing season. War and insecurity turned the ordinary upside down in a double sense. First, the islands became home to many fugitives. Second, insecurity did not permit the refugees to grow food on the banks of the river.[30] Trapped on these islands, villagers also lost the will to live:

> The slave-hunting panic seemed to have destroyed all presence of mind. The few wretched survivors ... were overpowered by an apathetic lethargy. They attempted scarcely any cultivation, which, for people so given to agriculture as they are, was very remarkable ... They could not be aroused from their lethargy.[31]

Famine destroys the spirit, which is one reason peasants call it *chaola*, or that which is rotten.

Chapter 2 will explore rural experiences of this famine. Now, it is only important to stress that the combination of slave raiding and drought led to unusually high mortality rates,[32] and that oral history is correct in presenting chaola as a rare event. No society can afford to go through chaola as frequently as some versions of the crisis literature assert. Chaola turns society inside out and leaves a deep impression on everything it touches. The famine of 1862–63 restructured the political and intellectual history of the valley in such a way as to make it a relevant background to the chaola of 1922–23, which is popularly known as Mwamthota.

MWAMTHOTA: THE CHAOLA OF 1922–23

Much grain was used for beer to pay hut taxes. Instead of working one month and getting a rebate of 4s., he wastes grain to make beer and pays his 8s. tax. How native-like![33]

Magala ... were maplazi [fields] belonging to the chief ... the food from there was stored at the chief's palace. His people fed on this. The Mang'anja used to come to the chief's village in times of famine and scarcity ... There, their wants would be satisfied to the full.[34]

Mwamthota was a transitional famine, resulting from a series of cumulative changes between the murder of the last lundu incumbent by the Magololo in the early 1860s and the consolidation of British rule. Some of these pressures were economic, related to the rise of a new food market. But the more significant ones were political and religious, traceable to the measures taken by the British, Magololo, and other conquerors to reorganize the region's political and religious structures. These challenges to the old order disrupted the early-warning system at a time when the new rulers could not provide effective relief. Mwamthota was in this generic sense similar to the famine of 1862–63. However, it also differed from the earlier famine. While the first broke out because peasants were unable to freely move around in search of food and to do emergency farming, the second represented long-term interruptions in other strategies of dealing with natural calamity.

Like its predecessor, Mwamthota was precipitated by drought. Considering the Tchiri Valley as a unit, rain shortage suspended food production for two and a half consecutive growing seasons: November 1920 to April 1921, November 1921 to April 1922, and November 1922 to January 1923. But, as usually happens, drought started and ended at different times in the valley's three administrative districts of Chikwawa (or West Shire) in the north, Ruo (or Chiromo) in the center, and the Lower Shire in the south. (Ruo was abolished in 1925, with some of its parts going to Chikwawa and others to the Lower Shire, now christened Port Herald.) The Lower Shire District was the first to suffer.[35] Much of this district did not get rains in 1920–21, so that instead of harvesting, hungry peasants left the area for Mozambique and other oases of plenty in May 1921.[36] Many did not return to the district the following season (1921–22), which proved to be even drier. But the records are not clear about the district's condition in 1922–23, when many other parts of the valley also entered the era of drought.

One part of Ruo District, lying between the marshes in the west and the hills in the east—a region that officials sometimes referred to as the "lowlands"— commenced the long series of droughts at the same time as the Lower Shire District in 1920–21. In 1920–21, villagers from these lowlands obtained food from other parts of the district that had not yet experienced drought.[37] These luckier sections included the Makhwira chiefdom, which started its odyssey at the same time as Chikwawa District in 1921–22.

Chikwawa offers an interesting case in the relationship between famine and food production. On the one hand, the famine of 1922–23 was more severe in Chikwawa than in the other districts of the valley (see chapter 2); on the other hand, drought did not seriously undermine food cultivation in this district until 1922–23. But equally significant is the fact that this drought came after many good seasons. Mwamthota did not represent long-term failures in food production.

Like much of the valley between the 1880s and the 1930s (see chapter 6), Chikwawa registered exceptionally good harvests in the period immediately before 1922–23. There was a bumper harvest in the district in 1918–19, allowing villagers to sell 91 short tons of maize to the military.[38] The following season (1919–20) was equally good, with a meeting of chiefs in May 1920 boasting of "plenty of food to go around."[39] People were reportedly still celebrating different rites of passage until August, and the food situation remained good up to November 1920.[40] A spell of drought in February 1921 (the 1920–21 season)[41] did not ruin the year's harvest, and the season ended with a large surplus of maize.[42] Neither was the drought of 1921–22 unusually severe.[43] Between November 1921 and March 1922, the district received 15.05 inches of rain, representing 50 percent of the normal growing season.[44] For all practical purposes, then, drought disrupted food production in this district only in the 1922–23 (November 1922–February 1923) growing season. That the district subsequently suffered as much as, if not more than, the other districts of the region underscores the need to separate famine events from environmental perturbations. Mwamthota was a preeminently political event, requiring an understanding of change in the early-warning system, among other processes.

Mchape

Golden-age theorists are broadly correct in contrasting the past with the present in terms of the history of the preventive regime. The system suffered many setbacks between the early 1860s and early 1920s, as developments within both the mchape and nsembe complexes show. The Mbona cult lost much of its influence in the northern part of the valley under the Magololo, while Christian missionaries and British colonial rule set the custodians of the cult against each other and against the population. Meanwhile, the mchape system underwent two major shifts, as the British anti-witchcraft campaign undermined its public functions while new African rulers in the Ruo (Chiromo) District in the central part of valley deployed it mainly as a weapon against their rivals.

The area that came to be known as Ruo District emerged from the devastations of the early 1860s as a land of economic (see next section) and political experimentation. Lying outside the Magololo sphere of influence, the area attracted a large group of political entrepreneurs from the Lower Zembezi, such as the Chikunda, Mwenye, Phodzo, and Zimba. Intense competition among the foreigners heightened their sense of insecurity against one another and vis-à-vis their Mang'anja subjects. They were determined from the beginning to stamp out the Mbona and mgwetsa versions of the nsembe, with their symbolic and real pointers to the Mang'anja "nation." They instead turned to the mchape, which was deployable under any kind of political order. Subsequent British legislation to ban the cult only reinforced the private role of mchape, against the backdrop of influenza and smallpox epidemics.

Influenza and smallpox ravaged the valley for several years after the end of World War I. From November 1918 to August 1919, smallpox alone killed several hundred people in Chikwawa, where the epidemic was reportedly milder than in the Ruo and Lower Shire administrative districts. Many more people died in the Lower Shire District, where the outbreak coincided with the Duladula floods of 1918. The disease decimated impoverished villagers, crowded in temporary msasa houses on the mphala drylands after fleeing from the flooded marshes.[45] But even more devastating was influenza, which broke out in 1918 and lingered in the area until the 1920s. In Chikwawa, the epidemic attacked members of every social class, as the following annual report suggests:

> Influenza has entered the District and most villages infected ... Several of the Boma Employees have been down with it including Police, Machilamen & Residents personal servants, all of whom have had coughs and the result of the disease leaves them very weak and depressed. The Resident himself had also a slight attack but only laid up one day.[46]

The situation was as bad, if not even worse, in the Ruo District.

Strategically located at the intersection of the Tchiri River transportation system and the new railway line from Blantyre to Mozambique, the people of the Ruo District found themselves at the crossroads of the communicable epidemics. Moreover, decades of successful campaign against the mgwetsa and Mbona complexes denied the rulers of Ruo two legally acceptable methods of organizing responses to the public health crises. Their people thus turned to mchape, which, under the British, they could only use as a private instrument. The district led both Chikwawa and the Lower Shire in the number of recorded witchcraft accusations; almost every monthly report for the district in 1918–23 referred to incidents of witchcraft.[47] In 1919 the chiefs of the area devoted entire district council sessions to the subject.[48]

Ruo District reports throw light on the intellectual crisis the epidemics posed in the context of African and British legal systems. Villagers found nothing new in the nature of the accusations themselves. Peasants who had lost their relatives to the epidemics accused both men and women as witches;[49] brothers turned against brothers[50] and husbands against their wives.[51] However, no one, besides the British themselves, could make sense of the way the new rulers handled those cases that reached their courts. Under the Witchcraft Ordinance, the only people who escaped punishment were those who drank mwabvi and died—the real witches and "criminals" of the village community. Everyone else was punished.[52] Village headpersons were sometimes fined and locked up in prison for failing to stop the accusations or the administration of the poison ordeal.[53] But the injustices of the ordinance did not stop here; it victimized people who were already casualties of "traditional" society. Think of this woman, who must go into history books without a name: Her husband forced her to take mwabvi with him; he died but she survived.[54] She had proven her "innocence" in the eyes of her fellow villagers, and according to custom, she deserved a big celebration. But under British law, she got the very opposite. Like many others, she received a five-month prison sentence.[55] The world had turned upside down. The ban not only ruled out the possibility of a communal response to the epidemics, it also heightened tensions that made it impossible for people to creatively respond to drought as united communities.

Mbona

Political and religious change also disabled the Mbona early-warning system in the Lower Shire District. Unlike the entrepreneurs of the Ruo District, the more secure Magololo chiefs reinvented the mgwetsa tradition, which sealed their alliances with the former ruling Mang'anja families, and they resorted to the mchape only in times of crisis, as during the Anglo-Portuguese conflict over the valley.[56] But, like their counterparts in Ruo, the Magololo did everything to suppress the Mbona cult, which they perceived as a potential focus of Mang'anja resistance. Mang'anja historians dramatize the new rulers' hostility toward Mbona in many ways, including the allegation that soon after taking power, the Magololo chief Kasisi climbed the Thyolo Mountain, destroyed the shrine, and killed the principal functionary, whose head rolled down the mountain to form a pool on the valley floor.[57] While one can dispute the details of this story, the truth remains that the Magololo waged war against the cult. The campaign formed an integral part of their crusade to destroy Mang'anja political institutions, particularly the remnants of the lundu state. The killing of the last lundu incumbent at Mbewe-ya-Mitengo and war against Mbona thus emerge as one theme in the golden-age theory of history:

> From the time Mbewe was destroyed, the Mang'anja did not offer sacrifices to Mbona ... and began to live as if they did not have a Guardian Spirit of their own ... [with the result that] droughts visited the land year after year ... The Mang'anja lost the freedom that they used to enjoy in the olden days.[58]

Khulubvi officials subsequently blamed the immigrant rulers for the locust invasions of the 1890s:

> The cry of the River, as elsewhere (e.g. Domasi), is one of the locusts and the coming hunger. An old native prophet, who dwells on a mountain named Khulubvi ... has given forth that of late not enough attention has been paid him in the matter of offerings, and that it is he who has consequently sent the locusts to remind the people of their neglect. If, however, the Makololo chiefs and others who may have an interest in the matter, make some amends for the past neglect, he will reconsider his action, and take steps for the removal of the plague.[59]

There is, however, no evidence that the Magololo repented. They continued to stifle the cult, which, with its elaborate traditions, was out of place in the new political culture of autonomous chiefdoms. The cult survived only in the southern portion of the valley, which the British called the Lower Shire District.

After receiving a heavy blow in the early 1860s from Matekenya, who headed the Matchinjiri state,[60] the Mbona cult did make a recovery in the south. A key factor in this development was the fact that the Mang'anja regained their independence from the Matchinjiri after the defeat of the latter by the Portuguese in 1884.[61] Whereas in the central and northern sections of the valley it was the Magololo and other immigrants who "signed" the "treaties" ceding their power to the British, in the south only Mang'anja chiefs did so. Thereafter, the chiefs worked hard to revive the Mang'anja "national" identity as they spearheaded the campaign for the reinstatement of the lundu paramountcy and the restoration of the Mbona cult.[62]

The chiefs revived the Mbona tradition as they reconstituted their own power. They rebuilt the shrine, maintained a salima spirit wife at Khulubvi, and found a substitute for the lundu paramount in the Tengani family.[63] The Mbona presence was always strong in the Lower Shire District. British administrators never banned the cult, as it never posed a challenge to their control. Indeed, some officials openly supported the cult, even providing the black cloth used in ceremonies at the Khulubvi shrine. This alliance between the British and Mbona officials also helps explain the weaknesses of the mchape complex in the area. Like the British, Mbona officials and their political allies saw the highly decentralized mchape as a socially disruptive force.[64] The Lower Shire District entered the twentieth century as the land of Mbona. Only British efforts to use local elites in the administration of the region and the influence of Christianity can help explain why the cult subsequently failed to organize a public response to the droughts of 1920–23.

With the arrival of the members of the South African General Mission (SAGM) in the area in 1901, the Mbona cult came under a new attack. The SAGM appears to have offered a militant form of Protestantism, deeply imbued in nineteenth-century European cultural imperialism. Before they even understood what the cult was all about, they had already launched a broad campaign against it, condemning Mbona as the "Prince of Darkness." They required their converts to sever ties with Mbona, the "Devil," and after some time, came to believe in the effectiveness of their campaign against the cult. By 1916, articles about "The Defeat of Mbona, The Rain Chief" started to appear in the missionaries' newspaper, the *South African Pioneer.*[65]

The missionaries did not win many converts in the valley, but did weaken the cult. They drew a wedge between the cult and some of its key functionaries. Unlike the Catholics, who came to the valley in the 1920s, the SAGM adopted a top-down conversion strategy, concentrating on Mang'anja ruling families. With their headquarters at Lulwe in the hills, they built their schools and prayer houses in the villages of Mang'anja chiefs on the valley floor. And like everyone else, members of the ruling families who wanted to become Christian had to renounce Mbona, among other heathen practices. The list of such converts was not long, but it included Tengani chiefs, who were by tradition responsible for leading the population in nsembe ceremonies at the Mbona shrine. Tradition required Tengani incumbents to play a key role in the installation of a new salima spirit wife and the rebuilding of the shrine, which typically took place in response to drought and other natural calamities. (During the rebuilding of the shrine, Tengani chiefs were supposed to act as the central pole on which other officials constructed the roof's skeleton before placing it on the walls.) Many Tengani incumbents of the colonial era reneged on this responsibility on the grounds that they were Christian.[66] That was one challenge facing those interested in the Mbona cult in the early 1920s. The other setback at this point in time was political. Even those officials who had not converted to Christianity could not come together to organize a public response to the drought. They were fighting among themselves for political power in the wake of the District Administration Native Ordinance (DANO) of 1912.

Through DANO, the British sought to reorganize the political map of the region (and country) by drawing a sharp distinction between "village" and

"principal" village headmen. The exercise raised questions of long-term importance, although it was not these issues that bothered the "men on the spot." At
this point the British and their African underlings were primarily interested in
solving the more immediate question as to who would fill the positions of village and principal headman, a question whose seriousness varied by location.

It was relatively easy for colonial officials to implement DANO in
Chikwawa District, where they recognized as principal headman any
Magololo chief (or his descendant) who had signed treaties with the British
in the late 1880s.[67] But the situation was more complicated elsewhere. In Ruo
District, about 200 Magololo, Mang'anja, Chikunda, and other immigrants
vied for four positions of principal headman. As defenders of "tradition," the
British finally recognized as principal headmen a descendant of the Magololo
chief Chiputula (now known as Makhwira) and three Mang'anja claimants
(Mlolo, Ngabu, and Tengani).[68] The Lower Shire District—headquarters of
the Mbona cult—presented an even more intricate problem for the British.
Over 50 contestants vied for seven positions of principal headman, and, to
make matters even more difficult, they were all Mang'anja.

The Tengani incumbent of the time did not have to fight hard for recognition as principal headman and the most senior chief of the district. The
family exploited memories of their ancestors' encounters with Livingstone in
1859–64 and their position of seniority in the defunct lundu state. But other
contestants fought on less secure grounds. Some garnered the support of the
SAGM, but many others claimed recognition as leaders of the Mbona cult!
The cult was drawn into the politics of transition with serious short- and long-
term consequences. Descendants of the Chiphwembwe, Malemia, Mbango,
and Ngabu families—the principal ritual officials around Khulubvi—continue
to fight the battles over recognition to this day.[69] The more immediate conse-
quence was that, in spite of popular pressure, the feuding officials could not
come together and organize a public response to the droughts of 1920–23.[70]
The cult had entered one of its weakest moments, having lost Tengani and the
other officials to the SAGM and DANO, respectively. There was not another
serious rain shortage before World War II that did not lead to the rebuilding
of the shrine, installation of a new salima, or a public announcement of the
gravity of the situation and the need to retool the crisis-management kit. That
is one sense in which one can speak of Mwamthota as a political crisis. But
the chaola was a political crisis also in the sense that it represented the failure
of Magololo chiefs to provide relief; they used their surplus to supply a new
food market instead of feeding their people.

Magololo Bounty Collapses

Magololo relief programs grew out of the immigrants' knowledge of similar strategies in their original homeland in today's northwestern Zambia, and

their initial experiences in the Tchiri Valley. After their dismissal by David Livingstone at Chikwawa in November 1861, the 16 men lived on the generosity of the Mang'anja, who still had food to share with others:

> They [the Magololo] visited Mang'anja villages in order to get food from the Mang'anja. They visited first the Mang'anja who lived in Mlomba's village; and the latter were very generous. They killed goats and chickens for them, and gave them some food to take to their camp.[71]

They also stole from their hosts, as the immigrants themselves would later confess to the unsympathetic members of the UMCA:

> Well, it is true we have taken food when we wanted it, and what else could we do? We were left without food, without gardens, without sheep or goats, without anything but our guns. We can not go to the Portuguese. We can not go to Linyanti [capital of their country of origin]. We must stay here. What shall we do then? Die of hunger? No, not while we can take food. All men would take food rather than die.[72]

Then came the famine of 1862–63, which dramatically altered the balance of power between the immigrants and the local population. The chaola proved an unmitigated disaster for the Mang'anja, who were being hunted down by slave raiders. But the same chaola helped propel the immigrants to power. Armed with guns and knowledge of the region's political and general environment, they stepped up their elephant-hunting activities in the Dabanyi Marsh, ate the meat, and sent the ivory to the Lower Zembezi to fetch food, gunpowder, and more guns. Gunpowder meant more hunting expeditions that brought in more ivory, powder, food, and followers. The former beggars thus emerged from the famine as new rulers, with a large following of Mang'anja and non-Mang'anja clients who had submitted to the foreigners to survive hunger.[73] The Magololo were determined never to lose their subjects to the ravages of chaola.

The chiefs adopted an entirely new approach to eradicating famine, imposing over the existing preventive strategies a redistributive regime predicated on tributary relations. Even though the chiefs received fowls, goats, maize, and millet on special occasions, as when they supervised initiation rituals, the principal item of tribute under the Magololo was labor. Peasants undertook many projects at the chiefs' courts, like the building of new houses, but their primary obligation was work in the chiefs' large fields, known variously as *magala*. The chiefs' retainers at the court did the regular work in these fields, but during the rainy season, every village headperson would lead his or her subjects to weed the chief's fields. Then, at the close of the growing season, villagers would again help the chief's retainers to harvest, process, and store the grains in huge *nkhokwe* granaries that would become centers of food distribution in times of need.[74]

Magololo chiefs did not face huge logistical problems to feed their hungry subjects. Their chiefdoms were very small by modern standards; Mwita did not have more than 500 people in 1910–11.[75] He knew almost every family in his chiefdom. Rulers of larger chiefdoms, like Chiputula, instituted public granaries in the capitals of their senior village headpersons. The chiefdoms were so well run that European observers described the Magololo as having ushered in an era of "masculine" rule.[76] The chiefs gave grain and organized communal meals for their hungry subjects. The fact that these meals came with meat from the chiefs' hunting expeditions left a deep impression on their Mang'anja subjects. Oral historians remember the chiefs' generosity mostly through the idiom of the alternative vision with its emphasis on ndiwo stew:

> Meat? No, game was abundant in the country. One did not need to go far in order to kill game . . . and there was no scarcity of meat. [The] Magololo . . . employed their men to hunt wild animals . . . They would bring bundles of meat to the compound of the chief. That was fresh meat. People would eat as much as they wanted. They would sit there the whole day eating. Women from every village would be asked to come and collect the meat; they would get the meat free.[77]

It was programs like this that allowed the Magololo-controlled part of the valley to successfully keep chaola at bay until the chiefs withdrew their bounty at the turn of the twentieth century. The programs collapsed under the impact of a new food market.

Beginning in the 1890s, there emerged a new class of workers who needed food in the valley.[78] These included people who worked for the government or transport companies, and those on European cotton estates. For example, in July 1904 the Oceana Company employed 3,000 men at its Kaombe cotton estate (near Chiromo), about half of whom had been recruited from Central Angoniland (modern Central Region).[79] The debate about "feeding-the-natives" on European estates, which occupied so much space in the country's important weekly, the *Nyasaland Times,* was always a hot issue in the valley. Besides estate workers, there were men who serviced riverboats, laborers who constructed the railway line, and *mtenga-tenga* carriers, who transported European travelers in *machila* hammocks while carrying luggage on the head. The Shire Highlands Railways had 3,900 men on its payroll at the end of September 1904.[80] The presence of this large group of workers imposed a heavy burden on the region's food supplies.

According to one calculation, every week in 1912 the Shire Highlands Railways and Oceana Company needed approximately 1 ton of salt, 7 tons of beans, and 48 tons of flour to feed their combined labor force of 6,900 men.[81] No wonder, therefore, that the beginning of railway construction in 1904 was immediately followed by the erection of four grinding mills, the first three of which were owned and operated by the railway company at Chiromo.[82] While the three mills took care of the needs of railway employees, other employers looked to Mr. J. Sinderam's mill at Port Herald Township, which could grind 10 tons of maize flour per day.[83] "Feeding-the-natives" held the potential to become a big business, although different segments of the country's population responded to the demand differently.

European planters, seen by the government as the linchpin of the country's so-called agricultural development, rejected food (or maize) production right from the beginning. Only when under heavy pressure from the government did the settlers allocate any land to maize. High freight rates within the country and to outside markets made it unprofitable for them to grow this bulky and low-value commodity.[84] Instead, settlers wanted to monopolize the cultivation of the more valuable cash crops, such as coffee, cotton, and tobacco. They fought every government measure to encourage peasant production of cash crops. In their scheme of things, villagers were to stay away from cash cropping and specialize in maize production to feed the workers of European enterprise.

Africans in the valley responded positively to the demands of the new market, although for different reasons. Ordinary villagers needed money to buy new goods and to pay their taxes. Resistance to wage labor before the rise of peasant cotton agriculture drove many households to part with their food.[85] Their rulers, particularly the Magololo, saw in maize a new source of wealth, filling the void left by the collapse of key branches of the old nonagricultural sector.

The Magololo economy initially retained important features of the preceding Mang'anja era, particularly the division between agriculture, as the sphere of "subsistence" production, and nonagricultural resources as the basis of wealth. At the beginning, the chiefs generated wealth (imported cloth, guns, gunpowder, and people) by exploiting nonagricultural resources such as home-made salt, iron tools, and ivory. When the salt and iron industries crashed, as a result of competition from imported goods, the chiefs added sesame (*chitowe*) to the ivory trade. This was the pattern of accumulation that supported Magololo generosity with their surplus food. The chiefs subsequently faced a crisis of accumulation when the ivory and sesame trades collapsed in the late 1890s, just as the end of the slave trade threatened the economic power of West African rulers.[86] And, like their West African counterparts, the Magololo turned to agriculture, which in the period before the rise of cotton meant maize cultivation.

The chiefs became the region's big maize growers, taking advantage of the labor of their dependents, changes in the Tchiri water levels (see chapter 6), and their strategic location at the northern end of the navigable portion of the Tchiri River. (From here mtenga-tenga carriers started their arduous journeys to the Tchiri Highlands.) Having started selling maize to the Europeans in the 1870s already, Chikwawa under the Magololo entered the twentieth century with a well-established tradition in food transactions. (When, in the introduction, our imaginary chief Kasisi traveled to Mozambique to sell his surplus maize in 1953, he was following an old practice.) It was the only district in the valley that was sometimes allowed to export maize under the Native Food Ordinance of 1912 (see chapter 4). On the eve of Mwamthota in 1921, the district's farmers sold maize to the military, when poor peasants in the Lower Shire and parts of Ruo Districts were going hungry.

Chikwawa's maize revolution (see chapter 6) did not necessarily enhance the food security of the poor. To earn money for their taxes and other needs, parents sold the food that their children needed. By the beginning of the twentieth century already, the market had begun to generate a new type of hunger, stalking such diverse districts as Blantyre, Ruo, and Zomba.[87] Different in many other respects, including their respective ecologies, these districts shared one thing in common: they all hosted and fed large numbers of the new working class.[88] The new demands forced small cultivators to create a "surplus" out of "necessary" subsistence and enticed large growers like the Magololo to divert real surplus from relief programs. (During the drought of 1949, one official had the Magololo and other large growers in Chikwawa in mind when he complained, "The markets of Cholo and Blantyre presented a glittering attraction to those with full grain stores, and an immense tonnage must have made its way up the hills during the year; all efforts to control this export and to hold the surplus within the district for purchase by the less lucky were of no avail.")[89] Always valued as workers, one's hungry subjects became an unnecessary burden in the new economic environment.

In 1994, Mrs. Karota Tsaibola portrayed this breach of the tributary contract through the idiom of the golden-age theory:[90]

> Sir, these Magololo used to be generous people; generous with their food. No one suffered in those days. The chiefs fed anyone who went to their courts hungry. But what do you see today? They have large gardens but let their subjects die of hunger. The world has really changed.[90]

As if in anticipation to this accusation, 18 years earlier the Magololo chief, Joseph Maseya, had explained his ancestors' change of heart with reference to the fact that, as the new tax collectors, the British bore the responsibility of feeding the hungry.[91] Whatever its moral force, this ideal never became a reality in colonial Nyasaland. The ability of the country's British rulers to collect taxes far surpassed their capacity to feed the hungry.

Relief in British Style

Famine in Zimbabwe would not be helpful in understanding the conquest of famine in Malawi.[92] Relief did not play a significant part in the prevention of chaola in the country. The British helped defeat famine by default; their contribution was limited to their role as keepers of social peace. Otherwise, the Nyasaland government was either unwilling or unable to mount relief operations that could have made a difference in people's experience of hunger; on the contrary, through its unrelenting tax policy, the government can be said to have aggravated hunger in the country.

Although they usually used the term *famine* indiscriminately, government officials have responded to different food deficits differently both before and after independence. They did not treat victims of every food shortage equally. In general, they were more willing to assist the victims of the more dramatic and news-making floods than those suffering from shortages caused by the more invisible droughts. In 1918, for example, the British sold 40 tons of maize to the people who had suffered the Duladula (also known as Mmbalu) flood,[93] but did nothing to relieve the sufferings of victims of the 1920–23 droughts in the same Lower Shire District.

On the basis of government responses, one can identify three forms of relief (see chapter 4). The first consisted of the sale of food by different levels of the state, especially district councils, at what they called "cost price." This type of relief, which presupposed the availability of money in the villages, was the most common official response to a severe drought. The second was "food-for-work" projects that both colonial and postcolonial officials used to accomplish projects like road construction. The third was free or subsidized food. Such relief was rare because it required "famine" conditions or the existence of "the truly indigent." Government officials in Nyasaland defined the conditions for free or subsidized food so narrowly that aid was denied to entire regions and population groups even in times of severe shortage. Peasants learned very early in the history of British occupation that they could not put their fate in the hands of the government.

Colonial officials cited two considerations to explain their policy. Some argued that aid would create a dependency complex among the peasantry, and others refused to give assistance on the grounds that peasants impoverished themselves by overselling their produce at harvest time.[94] Behind both explanations, however, lay a more fundamental reality that explains the similarities between colonial and postcolonial aid programs. The rulers lacked the resources to mount an effective food program, as the stories of seasonal hunger (see chapter 4) and Mwamthota show.

After receiving dismal reports from many parts of the country, and after resisting the European planters' call for action, the government began to prepare itself for the possibility of relief operations in January 1922. It had become clear that if rains did not come within a couple of days, the administration would "be met with the most serious famine this country has ever seen and the purchase of some 50,000 to 100,000 tons of food" would "be necessary to stop countless deaths from starvation."[95] The government then adopted a multipronged strategy to ensure that drought did not lead to famine.

To begin with, the state deployed its authority under the Native Food Ordinance (1912), the Customs Ordinance (1906), and the Intoxicating Liquor Regulations (1911) to ban (a) the purchase of foodstuffs for resale or for export from any district in the country, and (b) the brewing and sale of beer. These rules were adopted on 31 January 1922 and communicated by telegram to all provincial commissioners and District Residents.[96]

Another component of the strategy aimed at mobilizing the support of European planters and their tenants. Planters had to give free seed to their tenants, and to encourage them to grow "catch" crops. They were asked to devote part of their own estates to the cultivation of food crops, which resulted in food production of about 35 acres in the Lower Shire and 400 acres in Ruo. They were to take stock of their reserves, which amounted to 8 tons of maize in the Lower Shire and 1.5 tons in the Ruo district. Finally, planters were to ensure that these stocks were well protected against pests.[97]

Still another strategy focused on District Residents, who were to explain the government's emergency measures (under the regulations of 31 January) and to encourage peasants to grow "catch" crops. Residents were authorized to purchase locally produced grain for seed and to distribute the seeds either free of charge or at a nominal price. Finally, the administration also requested that Residents compile and send, every fortnight, reports on the conditions and prospects of the food situation in their respective districts.[98]

One set of such reports, sent in the middle of February 1922, revealed the following situation. Of the colony's three administrative regions, only the Northern Province was expected to feed itself. The situation in the Central Province was mixed, with some districts faring better than others. Overall, no relief was anticipated for this region. It was in the Southern Province that the drought was severest, although the level of scarcity varied between and within districts. Chiradzulu was the only district that officials hoped would end with a modest surplus. Thyolo was declared to be in fair condition, although no one anticipated a surplus. Parts of Zomba and Blantyre were considered to be in dire condition, but no one thought relief would be necessary there. Sections of Fort Johnston, Mulanje, Neno, and Ruo emerged as candidates for relief, while the whole of Liwonde qualified for help. Finally, the report concludes that the Lower Shire was nearly hopeless. The "outlook," so the report goes, "is decidedly gloomy," and people were "leaving the district."[99] It was this set of reports and pressure from European planters that led the government into the final strategy, which was to look for food beyond the country's boundaries— a measure of last resort.

Budgetary constraints and high freight rates caused the government to proceed very reluctantly in its search for food from neighboring countries. It allowed every flicker of hope about improvements of the food situation within Nyasaland to halt the search for imported food and to revise downward the original estimate of the food needed in the country.

Between January and July 1922, Nyasaland officials called off their discussions with the government of Tanganyika twice. After receiving many frantic telegrams from Nyasaland beginning in January 1922,[100] Tanganyikan authorities acquired 950 tons of food for export by early March.[101] But, to their surprise, they were told Nyasaland did not need the consignment because the situation inside the country had improved.[102] The real reason was that food from Tanganyika was twice as expensive as that available in Nyasaland, according to the director of agriculture.[103] However, when it became clear that Nyasaland could not feed itself, a frantic search started again in April.[104] And so many officials were involved in this second round of negotiations that the governor of Tanganyika was thoroughly confused as to the amount of food that was being ordered.[105] In the end, Nyasaland's rulers were only too happy to take advantage of the confusion they had created to reject a consignment of 100 tons of rice that was ready for delivery in July.[106] The governor reneged on the contract under the pretext that he did not know of anyone in his administration who had made this particular order.[107] And after receiving the director of agriculture's revised estimate, the governor calculated the country needed only 1,000 instead of the original 2,560 tons. He ordered his men to purchase 1,070 tons, which would give the government a surplus of 70 tons.[108]

To reduce expenses, the government abandoned the plan to purchase the 1,070 tons from Tanganyika. Of the 1,070 tons, 500 would come from Beira in Mozambique, and the rest would be bought within Nyasaland: 200 tons from Mulanje, 120 from the Planters' Association in Thyolo, 100 from Chiradzulu, 25 from Neno, and 125 from Nkhota-Kota.[109] The aim was to hold down the cost of transportation, although if the Agricultural Department's estimates were correct,[110] maize from both Mozambique and Nyasaland proved to be more costly than Tanganyika's. Selling this maize at two pounds to the penny, the government charged villagers more than double what European buyers and the state had ever paid peasant producers.[111]

As in 1949, some District Residents protested at the price and tried in vain to soften the impact of the famine on the peasantry. In a letter to the provincial commissioner, the Resident for Chikwawa, Mr. R. H. Murray, pointed to the obvious fact that peasants had exhausted their purchasing power. Most had insufficient money to both buy maize at the government prices and pay their taxes. He therefore proposed that only the able-bodied be asked to pay taxes in 1922 and that anyone who bought one bag of maize be given another on credit. Peasants would repay the cost of the bag advanced to them in cash or labor the following year.[112] Few other suggestions created as much heated debate as Murray's mild proposal.

Although the provincial commissioner had some reservations about giving maize on credit,[113] he allowed the proposal to reach the governor's desk. In a series of interdepartmental exchanges, the governor reiterated the government's stingy relief policy in no uncertain terms. He was opposed to the idea of giving credit to peasants because, he argued, there was no legal basis on which the government could collect the debts. Like most other officials before and after him, the governor feared that giving food on credit would, like wholesale tax exemptions, "have the further mischievous effect of provoking idleness, when the circumstances of the time require the fullest employment and earning of money."[114] His only solution to the problem was to organize people for work. Let the able-bodied work on the Thyolo Road, where they would be fed and earn money to buy food for those who could not work.

In the above response, the governor was merely reiterating the country's relief policy, according to which "all those who can work and earn money to feed themselves and others dependent on them be made to work."[115] When it came to giving aid, even those officials who did not respect or understand African "tradition" were ready to appeal to peasant generosity; no African who had food could allow his or her relatives and neighbors to starve to death. Only a tiny minority, elderly women who had been abandoned and peasants without able-bodied relatives, needed government support. To extend government help beyond this small group of the "truly indigent" would only undermine peasants' "natural" generosity, according to these officials. So it took the Nyasaland government a long time before it started to organize relief operations.

The government began to distribute food in the valley in August 1922 and stopped on 6 March 1923. There were two stations serving the region: Mpemba in the north and Chiromo in the south. The author has no figures for the maize distributed from Mpemba, which took care of the needs of northern Chikwawa District[116] under the direction of the District Resident, Mr. R. H. Murray.[117] The Chiromo center, which came under the assistant agriculturalist, N. D. Clegg, served southern Chikwawa and the Ruo District.[118] The Lower Shire District did not receive any aid from the government in 1920–23: "The old Lower Shire district managed to carry on without any assistance from the Government in the form of famine relief."[119] The central government rejected many pleas for help, including the District Resident's request to distribute 60 tons of maize that was being destroyed by weevils and that had been "purchased with part of the profit made by the Agricultural Department on the sale of cotton grown by the natives of this district themselves."[120] The request was ignored in the country's capital in Zomba. All in all, the Chiromo depot distributed 344.19 tons of maize: 197.42 tons to the people of Makhwira and Ngabu, and 146.33 tons to those in Mlolo and Tengani. Of these, only 84.46 tons, or less than a quarter, were issued free.[121] Peasants bought or worked for the remaining consignment, which proved to be grossly inadequate as 1922 slowly gave way to 1923.

The demand for maize rose so high toward the end of 1922 that officials thought of importing 200 more tons in November, and anticipated the possibility of another 300 tons by December.[122] Whether they imported the maize is not clear from the record. What is beyond dispute is that Mr. Clegg found himself in a difficult situation between December 1922 and January 1923. His stocks ran so low in December that he contemplated the possibility of reducing what each family could buy per week from 50 to 40 pounds.[123] The situation was saved not by the government relief effort, but by the arrival of the rains.

Like the peasants in his jurisdiction, Clegg was more than thankful to the heavens when rain fell toward the end of the first week in January. He informed his superiors that given the rains, people could feed themselves in two or three weeks, which would allow him to reduce rations to 10 pounds per household a week by 19 February.[124] As it turned out, however, this prediction proved premature. The rains stopped for about a week and crops began to wither, which led to the gloomy report of 22 January 1923.[125] But by 26 January, he was able to paint a more optimistic picture. Rains had returned to the land, and he looked forward to reducing the rations to 10 pounds per family per week in three days.[126] There was a drop in the demand for food for purchase by 7 February. Some people had started eating wild grains and tubers as others climbed the hills to purchase green maize from other villagers. Peasants tried to avoid the government's relief program, which required them to participate in communal work.[127] Orders for purchased rations petered out again toward the end of February, and the station was closed on 6 March.[128] If they could have eaten the ink and paper that went into this relief program, no peasant could have died of hunger in 1922–23. The drought has left a long trail of paperwork. But they needed food, which their British conquerors could or would not provide; the British in Nyasaland provide a classic example of imperialism on the cheap.

CONCLUSION

Students of the crisis literature have classified some famines as capitalist and others as precapitalist. Capitalist chaola were food deficits in the midst of plenty, while their precapitalist predecessors were crises of "*absolute* shortage of the foodstuffs."[129] The unstated assumption here is that while capitalist

famines carried the imprint of their political contexts, their precapitalist counterparts did not. They were merely the result of the unchanging "technical
limitations of the productive system"[130] and the "peculiar relation between
persons and commodities."[131] They did not reflect disruptions in people's
relationships with one another in relation to food. But even more incompre-
hensible is John Iliffe's identification as precapitalist those early colonial famines in Zimbabwe that occurred under the brutal "pacification" of the country
by John Cecil Rhodes's "pioneers."[132] In his model, there is no possibility
that capitalism itself may have been responsible for some of the crises. All
one sees is the triumphant hand of colonial capitalism defeating "famine" in
Southern Rhodesia and brightening the "dark" continent. Nyasaland's coat of
arms declared the advent of light (*Lux in Tenebris*), even when those whose
eyes were supposed to be opened became permanently blind and starved to
death.

This book sees every famine as a social and political crisis. It is impossible
to predict the outcome of a drought, because the effect of any climatic distress
depends on how society handles it. The droughts of the early 1860s and 1920s
inflicted so much suffering because neither the old nor new kinds of responses
worked. On this basis, all famines are of the same order.

To argue that all famines are of the same order is not to deny their differences. The famine of 1862–63 was indeed different from that of 1922–23. The
two chaola arose out of different political struggles that disabled different elements of the crisis-management scheme. In the early 1860s, drought became
famine because political instability, resulting from the slave raids, confined
peasants in their deserts of hunger and ruled out the possibility of emergency
farming. The victims of Mwamthota faced different setbacks. The region's
invaders destabilized the early-warning system without providing effective
relief. To understand the two famines, one needs to bring into the picture their
changing contexts, which were thoroughly human and political.

To map out a historical context—which is the way social scientists typically explain events—is to prioritize time's arrow over time's cycle. No one
can revisit those backgrounds or the famines they gave birth to. Moreover,
analysis of what leads to a chaola implies an examination of cumulative
change—although not necessarily the straight path from one social order to
its opposite. This is the familiar terrain of the trained historian. Irreversible
time is the subject. But, like any other social outcome, famine is also about
the repetitive and time's cycle, drawing our attention to established survival
strategies and everyday practice.

2

In Times of Renewal and in Times of Disaster

The famine had done its work; the land was without inhabitants ... The villages were left standing, but not a single human being was found alive in them; skeletons were everywhere—in the path and in the villages. It was horrible.[1]
We hail from Machenjewa [in the Dabanyi]
A land without poor, sandy soils
Where no child could die of hunger
Where birds crapped flour
Where beer was always in great supply.[2]

INTRODUCTION

The stories that the late Mrs. Leni Pereira and other women told in 1991 about their experiences of Mwamthota[3] make it clear that to understand chaola famine, a one-time event, one needs to appreciate the more common and routine uses of food. The absence and presence of food are intimately connected, as are the rare and the routine.

In ordinary times, different rules guide access to different kinds of food or different phases of the same kind of food. To simplify a complex reality, villagers in the valley treat crops in the garden before harvesting, and food in the granary as the exclusive property of the people who grew or acquired it.[4] Thus, the village headman who, during the hungry season of 2002 in Malawi, forced his female subject to give other villagers part of the maize she had received from an international relief organization flouted the normal rules of sharing.[5] The community had no right to such food. By contrast, peasants regard as a communal asset cooked food that reaches the table as well as crops left in the garden after harvesting. Domesticated food in those two phases of their social biography assumes the same status as wild plants, which are by definition available to every member of the community. But food attains its highest social status when it satisfies the needs of dead ancestors and therefore loses all those physical characteristics that make it precious among the hungry.

Hunger becomes chaola when it upsets the above pattern of rights and obligations and obliterates the fine distinctions between the different phases of domesticated food. Chaola turns the ordinary on its head. On the one hand, it reduces all provisions to the status of wild food—good only for biological reproduction—and on the other, it converts those same wild foods into the "private" property of those who can defend their "rights" against others. Under chaola, food retains its social character only to the extent that it heightens its victims' appreciation of the ordinary and, in particular, the orderly sharing of the masika season of plenty.

THE MASIKA SEASON OF PLENTY

When the harvest begins to ripen ... there begin the *batukes;* this is a name given to drumming, dancing and singing in general, but each entertainment has its own style and special name such as *kateko, gondo, pembera,* etc. which can be told by practice. These *batukes,* which last until October, the month in which cultivation starts afresh, keep the Maravi entertained all this time, and meanwhile they lead no other life than drinking *badwa* [beer], dancing, and singing, and remaining in a state of continual intoxication.[6]

The above quotation comes from the diaries of the Portuguese traveler A.C.P. Gamitto, who passed through what is today's central Malawi between 1831 and 1832. His description corroborates peasants' accounts of what used to happen in the past and continues to occur, in some form, even today. (The following analysis will stick to the past tense of oral history, because some practices it refers to have ceased to exist or changed; see chapter 7.) However, being a foreigner, Gamitto did not understand the meaning of what he saw. Villagers were not simply drinking as alcoholics. The dancing, drumming, and drinking formed part of the great festivals of the masika season of plenty, which drew attention to the social functions of food. Some peasants shared food with their social equals and superiors expecting help from the recipients in times of need. But this was only one motive behind the food transfers. Peasants also used food to enjoy the good life, to appease the spirits, to renew social relationships, and to teach their children about the community's morals and values. Every year, the masika season brought to life the lost Eden of the golden-age theory and provided a forum for women to collectively retool their expertise as food processors and cooks.

Beer Brewing

Unlike the preparation of the daily meal, cooking food and brewing beer for the great feasts of the masika season was a collective enterprise, depending on the cooperation of neighbors, friends, and relatives. Extra-household labor was especially vital to the success of the second funerary rituals or nsembe—one of the most solemn occasions marking an individual's transformation from being a human to a spirit—which will act as our principal, though not only, example in the following discussion. The nsembe featured several kinds of communal meals and *mowa* beer, whose preparation almost invariably made the organizers of the last funerary rites turn to the food and labor resources of the wider community, including *shamwali* friends.[7] This was a friendship peasants established and nurtured on the basis of food transactions.

One step above the ordinary *bwenzi* friend, the shamwali were strategic friends, spread over different parts of one's region. True, they were friends to visit in times of distress, but they were also people with whom one enjoyed the pleasures of life. Heads of poor households could afford bwenzi but not shamwali friends, for it was expensive to maintain such a relationship. To visit a shamwali, one needed many gifts, including the proverbial "basket-of-flour-and-chicken." The host reciprocated in kind, serving the visitor with nothing less than a whole chicken. The more affluent would kill a goat and brew beer to celebrate the visit with their neighbors and bwenzi. The visitors would return home with food and beer leftovers and a deep sense of indebtedness. They would be among the first to come to the nsembe organized by their shamwali, bringing not only their mouths and their food, but also their labor and technical expertise.[8] They would join other women in cooking food and preparing beer.

Mowa was the most important alcoholic beverage in the valley.[9] Villagers sometimes brewed it for sale, although this appears to have been the least important function of mowa. The rich brewed mowa to entertain friends and relatives they had not seen in a long time and to celebrate a new harvest, which was, as one commentator put it, "to get rid of the surplus of the preceding season."[10] Peasants also held beer parties to thank friends and neighbors who had assisted them in weeding, harvesting, building a new house, or hauling a canoe from the forest to the village and from the village to the river. Individuals who took and vomited the mwabvi poison ordeal after being accused of being witches also celebrated their innocence with mowa.[11] Finally, mowa formed an essential element of the more elaborate forms of wedding (*chikwati*), puberty ritual (*dzoma*), and especially nsembe.[12] People almost always brewed mowa as part of the nsembe for dead married adults.

Beer brewing was a complicated process, directed by a woman the Sena called *nyatchenka*. People did not normally have to go beyond their friendship and kinship circles to secure a nyatchenka; they typically found one among the wives of *tsabwila* funeral friends and the dead person's sisters (*nkhoswe*). It was also not uncommon to find the wife of the funeral friend and the nkhoswe acting as two nyatchenka at the same nsembe—each supervising her own pots of beer. The nkhoswe would ideally assume responsibility over the beer that went to the *kachisi* shrine; the tsabwila's wife would take charge of the beer that served the public. This was largely a risk-avoidance strategy because the outcome of the process was always uncertain. Two nyatchenka were employed to make sure that if the brew of one specialist went sour, people could turn to the other set of pots. The fear of ending with a bad brew also explains the taboos against sexual intercourse by anyone involved in the brewing, and the prayers that accompanied the initial soaking of grains for making *chimera* malt.[13]

The soaking of chimera grain formally declared the beginning of the nsembe and the departure from the private domain of all foods to be used for

Photo 3 Women brewed mowa beer in these specially made earthen pots (1950s). (Matthew Schoffeleers's collection)

the ritual. Food started its long journey toward becoming an asset of the entire community and the spirits. In Mang'anja areas, people solemnized the occasion with a performance of the *nyau* masked dancers.[14] Sena villagers held a similar ceremony, during which the nyatchenka led a small congregation of close relatives in a prayer that emphasized one's immortality as a grandparent.[15] Several days after this ritual, women removed the grain from the water, spread it on mats, and covered it with banana leaves for several days. This allowed the grains to germinate and become ready for pounding, an activity that set in motion the second phase of beer brewing.

The second phase, whose details varied by location, was a protracted business that lasted at least seven days.[16] Led by nyatchenka, women spent the first day making malt by pounding, in a wooden *mtondo* mortar, the grain they had soaked on the first day of the first phase. They then mixed regular flour with water to create *phala* porridge in large pots, and closed the day by adding chimera malt to the phala. (On this day women sometimes soaked more grain to be turned into chimera on the last day.)[17] There was little activity the following day, when the brew was left for its initial fermentation. The second most important operation came on the third day when women reboiled the chimera-containing phala of the first day to make *mulusu*. Generating mulusu was a daylong process that drastically reduced the initial brew to a few pots of mulusu.[18]

Women did not disturb the mulusu on the fourth and fifth days, waiting for the first signs of vigorous fermentation, which usually came on the sixth day. That was when the nyatchenka and her assistants initiated and completed three critical operations within 12 to 24 hours.[19] First, women pounded the grain soaked on the first day of the second phase to produce chimera malt, adding the new chimera to the fermenting mulusu. They call the result of this process *matanthi*. When the matanthi started to ferment, they dropped more chimera into it to make *chale*.[20]

While the nyatchenka was busy manufacturing chale, other women started the second major operation. They cooked more phala, dropped chimera into it, and started boiling the mixture.[21] After this gruel had cooled down, the nyatchenka began the final operation, which was to mix chale with the new phala, containing chimera. The result was *phumbi*, which became ready for drinking after heavy frothing.[22] Men, who had taken no special role in the brewing process, would emerge to take charge of the drinking and eating that characterized the final days of the nsembe.

Drinking and Eating

Participants in a nsembe ate three kinds of meals, roughly corresponding with the three social uses of food outlined in the introduction to this chapter.

The greatest was the nsembe offering itself, in which food lost all its earthly value to feed the spirits. Next was the communal eating and drinking—the great chidyerano that brought together people from within and beyond the community. Finally, there were the all-female meals that lasted throughout the second phase of beer brewing.

In one sense, the all-female meals of the beer-brewing phase reflected the daily meal better than the other two meals. Women took these meals to regain the energy spent in brewing. But the meals differed from their regular counterparts in several other ways. They separated women from men in a radical way, as women comprised the only eating group. Men, who provided the firewood and ndiwo stew, did not participate in the meals prepared specifically for those engaged in beer brewing. Nsembe meals were at this stage like those in all-female *maseseto* initiation for girls.[23] The eating provided women, some of whom had permanently moved to the beer-brewing site from far away, an opportunity to exchange ideas, including new strategies of dealing with seasonal hunger in the months to come. For the time being, however, they enjoyed their all-female universe, where the lines of inequality only followed social age and technical competence. Led by the nyatchenka specialist(s), elderly women enjoyed the best ndiwo and those parts of fish and meat normally reserved for male elders.[24] Female elders became "men" in relation to the younger women. But the absence of men and other stakeholders limited the ability of nsembe at this point to reproduce the entire power structure. Nsembe would reaffirm the status quo only in the closing days, when everyone joined the eating, drinking, and dancing that attracted Gamitto's attention in the early 1830s.

Coming immediately after the offering of beer and food to the spirits, the communal meal featured many kinds of food and mowa. Villagers looked to such parties as occasions of enjoyment, when they could escape, even if momentarily, the hard realities of daily life. They also loved beer parties because they were rare. Beer brewing was a complicated process, and the end product was perishable. Only chiefs and the rich could afford to have mowa on regular basis.[25] Otherwise, most villagers had to wait for the big feasts to have a taste of beer. They drank a lot of mowa whenever they could get it. But such consumption of mowa, like the eating and dancing that characterized these feasts, was an orderly process that upheld the legitimacy of the existing social hierarchy.

Guests drank and ate as members of a kinship group, a profession, or as companions of a strategic friend (shamwali). For example, the deceased's maternal relations would get their pot of beer and food as a separate group from the paternal relatives. Similarly, a strategic friend, nyatchenka, head drummer, village headperson, and funeral friend would each receive food and beer as a leader of his or her own group.[26]

Photo 4 Drummers take a rest after entertaining participants in a major rite of passage (1950s). (Matthew Schoffeleers's collection)

The amount of food ordinary participants ate at these ceremonies depended on what their respective leaders received and on their willingness to share it. Some leaders allowed very little food and drink to trickle down; they would either consume much of it themselves or save it for their families back home. Others tried to impress their followers by giving them as much food and mowa as possible, and to that end they sometimes openly demanded more from their hosts.[27] Unlike the daily meal, which operated as a terrain of undeclared rights, privileges, and tensions, the communal meal exaggerated power. This was, however, social power and not the kind of physical force that otherwise determined access to food in a chaola famine (see pp. 62). This is power that flowed from one's position as an elder and earthly representative of the ancestors. Beer and food offerings to the spirits of the departed constituted the third meal, which gave nsembe its distinctive meaning. This meal is synonymous with the term *nsembe*.

Nsembe featured a broader range of food items than the first or second meal. Besides mowa, which was a necessary ingredient, organizers furnished a long list of foods, including nsima, rice, fish, meat, different kinds of bread and pastries, and every other delicacy of the area.[28] This was a meal of thanksgiving to the ancestors and ultimate source of abundance. Among the Sena, the task of consecrating these foods typically fell on the deceased's sister and the wife of the funeral friend. They transported the victuals to the kachisi shrine, which stood some distance away from the deceased's house. The wife of the funeral friend carried her pot of beer up to and left it at an arch gate made of twigs or reeds, constructed halfway between the house and the shrine. The sister of the deceased would later take this and her own pot of beer into the shrine, where she did the offering. She dished out each food item from the *lichero* winnowing basket and placed it on banana leaves covering the kachisi floor. This done, she would pour the brew into smaller pots that were half-buried in the ground.[29] Finally, she would recite the panegyric song of the deceased's clan to mark the dead person's formal entry into the powerful world of ancestral spirits, leaving his or her *mdzukulu* grandchildren to occupy his or her position on earth.

Only grandchildren and spirits ate and drank the consecrated food and beer. To allow the spirits to drink their mowa, the funeral friend pierced the bottoms of the pots to let the liquid seep into the ground. Next came the grandchildren. In a complete reversal of the ordinary, the grandchildren feasted on the delicacies left inside the shrine.[30] The only reminder of the routine was the fact that, as in everyday life, they were the beneficiaries of leftovers. But these were leftovers of an entirely different order—delicious food left by the spirits. And in an ironic reminder of what villagers say was a frequent practice among the hungry during a chaola famine, children fought for the leftovers. Whether it nourishes the body or soul, the story of food is always about human social relations. Several years later, these same children would formally be taught about food in initiation and wedding (chikwati) ceremonies. Parents then would then use food to make sure that their way of life did not die with them.

In a wedding ceremony, food did not only entertain the bride, bridegroom, and their guests. It also stood at the center of the formal instructions given to the newlyweds. Most articles that the bride received as gifts reminded her concretely of her role in food production and processing. The list included such items as carrying and winnowing baskets, small and large pots, plates, hoes, and knives.[31] These presents came as part of the instructions on how to take care of the community's food needs. Such lessons on provisioning took up much of the pedagogical time spent in dzoma, maseseto, and other puberty rites.

The lectures capped a lifetime learning experience. Girls started to learn about farming, cooking, and food processing at a very early stage. They played the roles of mothers and wives around the age of five, when, for example, they built miniature houses, pots, and so on in a "game" known as *makumbi* (or "little houses"). Around 10, they joined the boys of their age in hoeing gardens, and their contributions to agriculture increased as they began to scare birds and predatory animals from the fields. Besides guarding the crops, girls also drew water from the river or wells, cooked real meals, and helped their mothers in every aspect of food preparation. Puberty rites came after they had gained almost all the technical expertise involved in cooking meals—after they had become the technical equivalents of their mothers. The instructions they received at puberty and wedding ceremonies merely reinforced and gave coherence to the disparate technical knowledge they had already acquired.

Thus, while instructors spent time on the technical skills needed in food production and preparation, the substance of much of their teaching aimed at creating women who appreciated provisioning as a social value. As providers, women had to balance the needs of their husbands and those of the community, which was not always an easy task (see chapter 7). Some of the initiation rituals that looked bizarre to foreigners were meant to prepare girls for this kind conflict. For instance, one common practice in maseseto required girls to "steal" chicken from their parents' pen. They had to demonstrate their ability to catch and kill the chicken without allowing it to make noise—in anticipation of their role as participants in a communal meal, when they would "secretly" feed their husbands with food that never reached the public meal.[32] The great feasts of the masika season celebrated abundance by heightening the specifically social and spiritual functions of food, which get lost in the "rotten" world of chaola.

IN THE "ROTTEN" WORLD OF CHAOLA

As the people perished the wild-beasts increased upon us … they wandered about more, because there were no inhabitants in the villages to check them.[33]

The slavedealers of Tette now bring food and with it buy the starving and dispirited inhabitants.[34]

The poor wretches are shot in their attempts to steal the corn which is grown here & there on the banks.[35]

Peasants in the valley call famine *chaola,* which denotes the "rotten" state of affairs, partly because it disrupts the normal interactions between human beings and nature and partly because it subverts people's relationships with one another in relation to food. In sharp contrast to its multiple functions during the masika season, under chaola food plays no other role besides the physical survival of the individual. But, though now functionally equivalent to wild plants and roots, all foods become ndiwo, the daily symbol of social power, with this one major difference. The struggles can become internal, fought on the basis of physical rather than social strength. That its victims still go through chaola as human beings, as the stories of courageous mothers show, testifies to the force of their prior experiences and promise of bounty. No society can permit chaola to become a routine; it is an episode, which nonetheless leaves its mark on people's relationships with one another and with nature.

Shifts in Human Relations with Nature

Famine is about death, but to number the dead is not merely a matter of census collecting. To begin with, the issues are complex. In a chaola, hunger kills its victims in many different ways. There are diseases related to malnutrition, which exact a heavy toll especially on the old and children.[36] Then able-bodied adults die of exhaustion as they scavenge the forests or travel in search of food.[37] Others lose their lives when caught stealing food. Death greets people everywhere in a famine. All this makes it extremely difficult to calculate who dies in a chaola. Moreover, as students of Chinese and Soviet history know too well, political agendas determine official mortality rates for different famines, and the two famines examined here are no exception. Thus, while colonial officials left only fragmentary accounts about Mwamthota, travelers like Livingstone minced no words about the devastations brought by the famine of the early 1860s.

British travelers have left graphic descriptions of death resulting from the famine, emphasizing the role of the slave raids in bringing about this disaster. It would, therefore, be quite tempting to dismiss these accounts as part of the British antislavery campaign. Moreover, there can be no doubt that David Livingstone and other visitors to the region, like the missionaries of the UMCA, used the events surrounding the famine to explain the failure of their respective missions.[38] The travelers had every reason to exaggerate the impact of the famine.

It is possible, however, to defend the general picture created by Livingstone and his companions about the famine on at least four grounds. There were, in the first place, at least half a dozen individuals who wrote about the devastation, ranging from people who, like David Livingstone, had a political agenda, to "marginal" men like Horace Waller, who do not appear to have entertained big ambitions. The early 1860s are one of the best-documented periods in the history of the valley. Second, while some of these records come to us as books, which are by definition highly structured, many others are not. There are at least five diaries that corroborate the central message of the structured accounts.[39] Third, while some travelers questioned Livingstone's representation of aspects of the region's economy prior to the 1860s, there is a broad agreement among all sources about the famine's catastrophic impact.[40] Finally, it would be virtually impossible to explain certain events without accepting the general thrust of the travelers' accounts. Only a catastrophic event can, in particular, make sense of the region's conquest by the 16 Magololo immigrants. The famine effected in the valley what epidemic diseases had done in the conquest of Latin America by the Spaniards. It reduced the Tchiri Valley to a mere ghost of what it had been in the 1850s.

Instead of the lively communities that had greeted them in the late 1850s, Livingstone and his companions found a somber and frightfully silent Tchiri River Valley in the first quarter of 1863:

> It made the heart ache to see the wide-spread desolation; the river-banks, once so populous, all silent; the villages burned down, and an oppressive stillness reigning where formerly crowds of eager sellers appeared with the various products of their industry.[41]

The eager sellers of cotton and food had also disappeared from Chikwawa, which now presented the travelers with a totally different picture:

> Wherever we took a walk, human skeletons were seen in every direction, and it was painfully interesting to observe the different postures in which the poor wretches had breathed their last. A whole heap had been thrown down a slope behind a village … Many had ended their misery under shady trees—others under projecting crags in the hills—while others lay in their huts, with closed doors, which when opened disclosed the mouldering corpse with the poor rags round the loins—the skull fallen off the pillow—the little skeleton of the child, that had perished first, rolled up in a mat between two large skeletons.[42]

Horror also welcomed the Europeans who ventured beyond Chikwawa; the 50-mile road from Chikwawa in the east to Mikolongo in the west was littered with dead bodies. And at Mikolongo itself, a village once famed for its prosperity, an average of 10 persons were dying of starvation each day in March 1863.[43] The famine had exacted its toll, and "the land was desolation."

Rowley may have exaggerated in his estimate that "ninety per cent. of the Manganja" had died of famine by February 1863.[44] But he and his companions were certainly right in their explanation of the high mortality rates. So many people perished not merely because there was drought; the catastrophe had its deepest roots in the ongoing slave raids. As Rowley summarized the situation: "war *and* famine had done *their* work."[45] Livingstone was even more emphatic on this point:

> But the slave-trade must be deemed the chief agent in the ruin, because, as we were informed, in former droughts all the people flocked from the hills down to the marshes, which are capable of yielding crops of maize in less than three months, at any time of the year, and now they were afraid to do so.[46]

The slave raids had trapped villagers in their deserts of hunger and tipped the delicate balance between society and nature in favor of the latter. Nature triumphed in a double sense. Famine not only killed people by the thousands, but it also undermined the ability of the few survivors to control their natural world after the rains of March 1863.

The rains revived the animal and plant kingdoms faster than the sickly remnants of the old human population. Everywhere, new vegetation engulfed the empty villages, and without human beings to look after them, gardens that would have carried crops became free range for wild animals. "Now," lamented the sober-minded Kirk, the "grass is high, [and] the people are gone."[47] Beasts roamed with such unprecedented freedom that the missionaries at Chikwawa spent sleepless nights guarding their diminished flock of goats and chicken against ferocious hyenas and leopards.[48] So aggressive were the predators that they attacked the emaciated human beings in broad daylight. The natural world had won the day—with assistance from society. Without such help, however, the famine of 1922–23 did not drastically alter the nature-society equilibrium. Mwamthota exacted a lighter toll on the peasantry despite the ineffectiveness of colonial relief programs.

British officials, who defined their mission as beneficial, downplayed the devastation that took place under their stewardship. Instead, they touted the efficacy of their paltry relief programs:

> The chief trouble in the district has been the shortage of food and in consequence famine insued [*sic*], but owing to the assistance of the Government in obtaining Maize and relieving the situation, by rationing Exempted people, old and infirm and selling to others at a normal price, the death rate amongst the population has been very low.[49]

In truth, British relief programs did not make a real difference in rural experiences of hunger in the early 1920s or in subsequent food shortages. Villagers survived hunger on their own (see chapter 4). The British and their postcolonial successors in Malawi played a positive role in the story of hunger mainly by default, as keepers of social peace, which allowed villagers to engage in different strategies of the crisis-management scheme. Unlike their ancestors, villagers in the early 1920s were able to do emergency farming and, in particular, to abandon their respective deserts of hunger for oases of plenty within and outside the valley. Migrations played a key role in softening the impact of the droughts of 1921–23.

The absence of open political violence allowed hungry peasants to move in many directions, as the story of Chikwawa District illustrates. The district acted as a magnet for many hungry villagers between 1920 and 1922. It received refugees from Ruo District's lowlands and the entire Lower Shire District. Chikwawa also fed fugitives from the Thete Province of Mozambique, whom the Mang'anja historian E. Chafulumira calls the "Nyungwe."

The Nyungwe and other peoples in Mozambique, to the south of Nyasaland, suffer hunger regularly to this day ... But because the Mang'anja practiced dimba farming, famine was rare. People from those hungry places used to come here in search for food and some of those, not willing to return to their deserts of hunger, decided to stay here permanently.[50]

In 1922, the Nyungwe or some other refugees from the Thete region became the subject of a colonial memo, stressing British benevolence:

[Twenty-five] Natives from Portuguese Territory were brought in to the Boma in starving condition and were treated to the best of the ability of the SAS the Police and every assistance of the Capitaos of the Boma to the Resident to save them, but I regret to report that a great many died and the remainder on getting stronger went away to their country.[51]

Their decision to leave the district proved to be a wise move. Chikwawa would be another hungry place within a few months, setting in motion another pattern of migrations.

Chikwawa began to export its hungry residents in 1922. First among those to leave were the newcomers who had come to the district at the beginning of the food shortage in 1921. "Of the large numbers of Portuguese natives who entered the district during the famine of last year," wrote the district commissioner, "a very large proportion returned to their own country early in the year."[52] Some natives of the district joined the former immigrants. They all went to Mozambique, just as many residents of the Lower Shire District had done in 1921: "As generally happens when there is a shortage in this district a large number of natives are moving to the Zambesi."[53] And statistical data tend to confirm these anecdotal references to population movements.

The existence of statistical information on who left the country shows that although ineffective as providers of relief, the British in Malawi were determined tax collectors. Thus, while officials in the capital—Zomba—were happy to get the sanitized reports about the food shortage, they also wanted know the reasons for the drastic decline in the taxpaying population. And the answer they got from the Tchiri Valley was that hunger had driven peasants out of the country. "According to the census figures as shown on report," wrote the district commissioner for the Lower Shire, "some 2000 people appear as not having paid tax, these have left the District and gone to the Portuguese territories adjoining mostly ... owing to the famine condition through which the District has passed."[54] His counterpart in Chikwawa faced a similar deficit. In 1921, Chikwawa's predecessor—known as the West Shire District—had 11,441 people. But this number had dropped to 10,640 by 1923.[55] And the decrease was more significant than it appears on paper. The

Chikwawa of 1923 was a much larger unit, incorporating not only the West Shire of 1921 but also the densely populated Makhwira chiefdom on the East Bank (formerly part of Ruo). Many people had left the district and others had died, as oral history often depicts the condition of the early 1920s.

A large corpus of oral evidence defines the term *Mwamthota* as a condition of high mortality *and* emigration:

> The word [Mwamthota] means death, people dying; many died while others looked for food. [Mwamthota also means] population movements; people moved into all directions because of hunger. People were just moving from one place to another. And that is why they call it Mwamthota.[56]

Some of the emigrants moved to the Tchiri Highlands and other parts of the valley, but many others ignored the international border and went to Mozambique.

That many people died in and left Chikwawa vindicates the profound insight of Amartya Sen.[57] There is no necessary relationship between chaola and long-term developments in food production. Drought struck Chikwawa later than the Lower Shire or Ruo District. And in Chikwawa the drought lasted for only one growing season. Moreover, the district entered the chilala drought from a stronger agricultural base than the other districts. Chikwawa had experienced successive seasons of bumper harvests (see chapter 1). Yet chaola killed more people in Chikwawa than in the other districts. Indeed, the term *Mwamthota,* which highlights the "rottenness" of chaola better than the other names people have given to the hunger of 1922–23, is a specifically Chikwawa name. Like its predecessor, Mwamthota was as much about the natural world as it was about distorted social and political relations.

The Social Relations of Chaola

Although relevant, demographic shifts do not by themselves constitute chaola. Peasants in the valley regard high mortality rates and population movements as part of chaola only when they coincide with the subversion of the normal rules that govern people's relationships with one another in relation to food. Chaola is about both the absence *and* presence of food. It upsets daily routines in contradictory ways, so that reliance on famine as a window on the routine may lead to a partial or distorted view of the ordinary. Chaola cannot act as a carbon copy of the routines. Under chaola, all kinds of food lose their respective social and religious identities and only retain their physiological functions; all foods become "wild" plants. But while in ordinary times wild plants are there for anyone who needs them, under chaola, they assume the social character of crops in the garden, food in the granary, and, particularly, ndiwo stew. Chaola nullifies the golden-age theory, while upholding the discriminatory conventions of the alternative vision. Every type of food becomes the property of those powerful enough to assert their rights against others. These are not, however, necessarily the socially powerful. Indeed, the privileged would not fight for some of the foods that become a source of conflict under chaola. The struggle is internal—among the hungry themselves—and is decided on the basis of physical rather than social strength. Famine turns the orderly world of the peasant into a Hobbesian terrain of all against all, promoting "stealing" over sharing and the integrity of the single household over the chidyerano communal meal. Chaola amplifies the spirit of seasonal hunger to the extreme.

Chaola exaggerates the njala season, strengthening people's ties to distant friends and relatives at the expense of their relations with neighbors and coparticipants in a chidyerano meal. The spirit of generosity gives way to its opposite: *umbombo* stinginess. A man returning from a food search would not enter the village in broad daylight but would wait until nightfall. He needs the cover of darkness. And contrary to custom, the wife would pound any grain brought by the husband inside the house, prepare the meal for her family, and tell her neighbors she has no flour.[58] The neighbors would respond in kind, placing chidyerano and good neighborliness at risk. Trapped in their poor households, the more vulnerable members of the community, like children and the elderly, lose a layer of their normal entitlements to food and become disposable. Many resorted to stealing to get the food they needed.

Chaola victims stole not only from strangers, but also from neighbors. Some forms of pilfering that punctuated the chaola of the early 1860s and early 1920s would have certainly qualified as stealing under any circumstance. Even in good times, villagers would have treated as a potential thief the child who in January 1863 tried to get grain from a neighbor's house in a village near Chikwawa; they would have considered hard-hearted, but not criminal, the man who shot the child.[59] Similarly, the marauders in 1921–23 who terrorized travelers and seized their food would have deserved punishment under any circumstances.[60] But these were not the only instances of theft during a chaola; there were many others that became crimes only in the context of the expanded notion of individual "ownership" of food.

Some of the fights that tore village communities apart near Chikwawa in the early 1860s originated in struggles over crops in abandoned gardens, and, in particular, over *maphupu* stems and roots that had sprung on their own after the rains of March 1863.[61] These grew from the residues of the previous season, and in normal times, no one would have paid attention to them. Children and ruminants regularly helped themselves to such food without interference. But under famine, even leftovers from the previous season became a terrain of social conflict. Armed men guarded maphupu as jealously as they did a new harvest, taking to court anyone they caught stealing their crops. Between October 1862 and February 1863, the missionary Procter recorded at least seven such cases.[62]

Some were brought to the missionaries' attention because their protégés stole the food: "This morning," wrote Procter, "we had another grief on account of our men. Kataruma, the chief of Chikwawa, came early to complain that some [of our people] went to his place yesterday & stole a lot of corn from the gardens around."[63] But in many other instances, the thieves were ordinary villagers, who were sometimes stabbed to death and thrown in the Tchiri River: "As we neared the village," bemoaned one missionary, "we passed the dead body of a woman with two arrows on it, the first only of eight that we saw floating by on different days, miserable spectacles of the effects of famine, some having been probably killed while robbing gardens."[64] Stories about Mwamthota take this theme one step further. Chaola victims also fought over wild plants.

Pax Britannica in the early 1920s made it possible for hungry peasants to turn to the roots, fruits, and cereals of the bush. Villagers scavenged the forests so thoroughly that both written and oral sources on the subject are unusually rich in detail.[65] These stories are so vivid also because food collecting is an annual ritual. Every hungry season a significant portion of the region's population survives by foraging (see chapter 4). Foraging under Mwamthota differed, however, from seasonal routines in one respect. During the njala season, the forest is open to anyone who needs it, but under Mwamthota the strong tried, sometimes successfully, to exclude the weak from the fruits of nature. Peasants tell many stories about this inversion of order, including accounts of armed men who held lamps of burning grass at night to simulate the glowing eyes of a lion. They would roar to frighten other gatherers away from fruit-bearing trees and to force others to abandon the roots and berries they had already collected.[66] Whether these dramatic events were common is beside the point. Peasants tell these stories to emphasize the uniqueness of chaola, which turns the social world to its natural opposite. This generalized disorder was not, however, limited to interhousehold or community relations; it also affected intradomestic relations, particularly social age and gender.[67]

Oral and documentary evidence portray the plight of women during the two chaola differently. European diarists—our only source for the period—paint women's experiences of the famine of 1862–63 as significantly different from those of their male counterparts. By contrast, oral sources—our main database—present the famine of 1922–23 as a "national" tragedy that did not dramatically upset women's ties to men. On gender, the Mwamthota of the oral historian emerges as a different disaster than the chaola of the early 1860s or the famine of 1949 in the Tchiri Highlands.[68] How valid are Mwamthota stories in this regard? Are they not merely a reflection of the dominant Mang'anja ideology of gender equality?

This book does not deny the power of the collective mind to suppress unpleasant experiences or departures from the norm. At the same time, it does not rule out in principle the possibility that Mwamthota was indeed gender-neutral. The women of the early 1920s may indeed have experienced chaola differently than their ancestors in the early 1860s. The two chaola had different social and political dynamics. In the early 1860s, the slave raids destroyed villages that constituted the spatial component of women's power and source of security in a matrilineal and matrilocal setting.[69] Those women who were forcefully taken from their burning villages ended up as food-dependent "slaves" in various male-dominated societies of the Lower Zembezi.[70] Their sisters, daughters, and mothers who managed to escape the clutches of the raiders faced a similar fate in the region itself. Traumatized, many fled to the hills and islands of the Tchiri River for safety (see chapter 1), where they lived on wild plants. But others sought protection and food in the new communities that were springing up in the region under well-armed foreign men, such as the Yao, the UMCA missionaries, and the Magololo. In those camps, the formerly independent food producers, some of whom had given food to the immigrants, became beggars.[71] Mwamthota took place under very different political environment.

There was no open political violence in the early 1920s. Under armed British peace, hunger did not create a large group of disposable women for men to exploit. But Mwamthota was also different from the chaola of 1949 in the Tchiri Highlands. Mwamthota occurred before the economy had significantly restructured the preexisting gender hierarchy. Wage labor, cotton agriculture, and other new economic pressures had not yet sharply divided the peasantry, as they would after World War II.[72] Mwamthota was a "class" famine only in the sense that it occurred in a colonial economy devised to benefit a fledgling European sector. Finally, the failure of the British to provide meaningful relief meant that most peasants deployed well-rehearsed survival strategies that did not necessarily give more power to men than women (see chapter 4). It appears that oral history is broadly correct in presenting Mwamthota as another njala season insofar as women's social and political relationships with men were concerned. The same cannot, however, be said about the experiences of the young.

The chaola of both the early 1860s and 1920s highlighted the vulnerability of the young, who were abandoned or traded for food by their parents. These experiences find support in ideologies that make social juniors the equivalent of things and in daily food practices. Every day, children come up at the short end of the conflicting ideals of the golden-age theory and the alternative vision. The extraordinary experiences of the young during a chaola are inseparable from the ordinary routines of everyday life.

As they do every hungry season today, children entered the chaola of the early 1860s and early 1920s from a position of disadvantage. The normal rules of sharing had denied them their full share of the limited protein-delivering ndiwo stew available to their community. Lack of stiff nsima porridge in times of famine only exacerbated their condition, making them victims of the worst forms of hunger-related diseases. A January 1863 eyewitness account depicted the children of Madugu's village near Chikwawa as "an awful sight their feet and eyes swollen terribly, their ribs nearly through the skin, and the stomach largely distended." The reporter continued, "A group was eating roots round a hut … another was almost blind with affection of the eyes very common now."[73] They were suffering from dysentery and had developed "sharp, distinct faces of thin men of 50 years of age."[74] That many perished resulted not merely from the immaturity of their immune system or inability to digest foods from the bush.[75] They died also because the rules of sharing ndiwo had been stuck against them in ordinary times. But the ideals of the golden-age theory also shaped the famine experiences of the young.

Attempts by parents, particularly mothers, to apply the principles of the golden-age theory could only have led to disorderly practices in the "rotten" world of chaola. Parents could only save their children by turning them into "things," which made sense given the prevailing definitions of social juniors as "animals." Thus, unwilling to helplessly watch their loved ones starve to death, some mothers abandoned their children with the hope, however faint, that someone would find and feed the children. Mothers transferred their responsibilities to people they did not even know—something unthinkable in ordinary times. Many children died, but some survived to tell the story, as Mrs. Patrishu of Mbande Village in Chikwawa District did about her own odyssey in 1922–23. After her mother had abandoned her on a road, some folks found, fed, and later returned her to her parents. She told this story in 1991, still grateful not only to the people who had rescued her, but also to her mother—"for her courage," as she put it.[76]

Other mothers "provided" for their children, particularly daughters, by selling them to wealthy individuals for food.[77] Peasants remember Mwamthota as a time when old men from Mozambique came to the valley to buy young women for wives.[78] Those who traded and abandoned their children tried to accomplish the same goal. They wanted to save life, as Mrs. Margaret Phiri from Kasungu District in central Malawi told reporters during the food shortage of 2002.[79] Asked why she had sold her children, she replied, "The children will starve to death if I keep them. They stand better chance of surviving with other people."[80] But selling children served another purpose. Parents also wanted to get food, which effectively turned children into providers of food—an inversion of normal practice.

It would, of course, be erroneous to suggest that the above stories constituted the totality of famine experiences. They were probably not the most common either. But, like accounts about generalized disorder affecting the entire community, these riveting stories about the real experiences of women and especially children serve a purpose. In the peasant world without statistics, they act as a medium to convey the extraordinary nature of chaola. An agent of social cohesion and renewal in times of plenty, under chaola food becomes a source of disorder, tearing families and communities apart. Chaola turns the ordinary on its head because it is as much about the absence as it is about the presence of food; it "abolishes" history. No society can afford to go through such chaos as frequently as students of the crisis literature imply through their indiscriminate use of the term *famine.* Over the centuries, peasants have developed a food system designed to prevent such "terrors" of history.

CONCLUSION

Peasants recognize the uniqueness of chaola in many ways, including the practice of giving each chaola a proper name, which they do not do for seasonal hunger.[81] The famine of 1922–23 is known by several names. Some call it *Kherekhe,* in remembrance of Mr. N. D. Clegg, the agricultural officer who supervised the sale of government maize at Chiromo. Some call the same famine *Bwana-Male,* after Mr. R. H. Murray, the district commissioner for Chikwawa, in charge of relief operations in the northern section of the district. But most call it Mwamthota. Moreover, Mwamthota is the only hunger that nearly every elder in the area can date with precision. Those who do not know how to read link it to administrative history, saying it occurred when Chiromo was a district separate from the Lower Shire and Chikwawa Districts. Those who had some schooling refer to it simply as the famine of 1922. Like its predecessor, Mwamthota was not another seasonal hunger or njala. It was, according to old Mang'anja informants, a chaola, or moment of rottenness.

Peasants treat every chaola as a landmark, separating one epoch from another. The famine of the early 1860s put an end to whatever had remained of the lundu era while Mwamthota closed the initial phase of British imperial control. But villagers also remember the two disasters as the famines that inaugurated a chaola-free era in the valley. Social peace and effective relief programs under the Magololo ended famine in the northern section of the valley between the mid-1860s and the establishment of British rule in the 1890s. The British record was more mixed. Initially, the British unleashed the forces of chaola. More effective as tax collectors than as providers of relief, the British also supported a new market that withdrew food from established consumption channels, including Magololo reserves, and compromised the early-warning system. The result was Mwamthota, which, however, proved to be the last chaola in the twentieth-century Tchiri Valley. The British contributed to the defeat of famine by default. Their mere presence as keepers of armed peace precluded open violence, making it possible for villagers to practice old survival strategies, which they augmented with food from the market (see chapter 4). This conquest of famine has affected many aspects of social life, including language.

The language of hunger has changed in two related ways. First, the term *chaola* has almost disappeared from the region's vocabulary. One hears it only from very old people, particularly those who experienced Mwamthota. People of the younger generation do not know or use it. The term has met the same fate as many other words that have vanished because the reality they used to refer to has ceased to exist.[82] Language does not have an independent existence from the lives of those who speak it. Second, the fact that seasonal hunger, rather than famine, has been the dominant form of food insecurity since the 1920s has expanded the meaning of the term *njala* to include those rare events people once called *chaola*.[83] Today, the term *njala* denotes both irreversible and reversible events. Parts I and II of this book are intimately connected.

II

Present Hunger
Against the Future
of Plenty

Certain aspects of the hungry season have clearly changed over the years. Ecological shifts, new markets, and government intervention have, among other things, restructured rural experiences of the annual food gap. Njala does not lie outside history. However, it is impossible to tell whether it has become more or less acute. Some pressures have exaggerated its impact, while others have softened its edges. But regardless of these shifts in its economic and social context, seasonal hunger remains for many households as predictable as it was a century ago. Some villagers trapped in these annual food deficits cannot hope to break the cycle, largely because the hunger season also happens to be the time they have to work hard in the fields raising the region's major cereals. And hungry peasants are not only ineffective workers, but some mechanisms they employ to survive njala take them away from their own fields. One hungry season ensures another. Drought and floods can compound the problem. But even a perfect growing season is only so in its contradictions, promising a future of plenty against the backdrop of present deficits. Abundance and scarcity do not occupy two separate terrains in the peasant world.

3

DROUGHT, FLOODS, AND SEASONAL HUNGER

Thus the existence of a pronounced hunger season can be established without making any elaborate quantitative investigation.[1]

Almost half of the 27 administrative districts in the country reported serious food shortfalls, in the wake of the worst floods to hit Malawi in recent years, according to World Vision. In the floods, which wreaked havoc earlier this year [2001], 15 people were killed and over 320,000 were left homeless. In addition, crops were destroyed just when the staple food, maize, was ripening.[2]

Then, our prospects as regards native food are sadly unpromising. The drought here still continues, one bright sunny day succeeding another in brilliant but disastrous splendour, beautiful for the present, but ominous for the future.[3]

There is a definite shortage of food in this district though the situation varies from village to village. The hill areas appear to have sufficient to last until next season. The shortage in low-lying areas ought to be alleviated by the produce of dry-season "dimba" gardens; in many cases however an unusually high level of water has prevented cultivation being started in these areas at the normal time, and they cannot be relied upon to contribute very much to the food supplies at least of the Southern half of the District.[4]

INTRODUCTION

As they celebrate the different rites of passage during the masika season of plenty, many villagers also expect, with the certainty of death, to alter their diets later in the year before the new harvest. Many anticipate surviving on one instead of the normal two meals per day. Some will replace the usual nsima stiff porridge made from cereals with sweet potatoes, nyika tubers, and other products of the bush. Villagers in the marshes will eat nothing but fish.

Mothers dread the prospects of hunger-related diseases that kill their children. Finally, many villagers fear that their neighbors will ignore their plight, as they cultivate ties with distant relatives and friends who can provide them with food for their immediate family members.

The above expectations are not about chaola famine, which no one can predict with confidence; peasants are thinking about recurrent hunger (njala), which weakens but does not subvert the rules of sharing and which confirms the golden-age view of the present as a structurally inferior time. Every season njala torments the inhabitants of the valley in ways that remind them of the region's place on the African continent. Seasonal hunger is a predictable event in the valley, as it is in many other parts of Africa that depend on only one main growing season per year. The experiences of the Tchiri Valley are typical in this regard. However, they are also unique. In the valley, the njala season is a period of great uncertainty. People fear floods and droughts that frequently exacerbate seasonal hunger. The expected and not-so-expected meet in seasonal hunger. The acute food deficits resulting from floods and droughts go a long way to explain the popular image of the Tchiri Valley as a hunger-prone region.[5] That these recurrent food gaps did not lead to chaola famine in the last seven decades of the twentieth century requires an explanation.

There are three kinds of answers to the above question. One directs our attention to the political context; famine occurs only under abnormal political conditions (see chapter 1). Chapter 4 will explore the second group of answers through its discussion of food exchanges and markets during the njala season. In anticipation of chapter 6, the present chapter focuses on the agricultural system itself. Villagers have over the centuries developed techniques of production that can mitigate the effects of climatic distress. Moreover, nature is not uncompromisingly evil. Floods and droughts rarely coincide in one season, and most droughts cover only one, instead of both, parts of the growing season. Finally, the Tchiri Valley does, as unit, contain both deserts of hunger and oases of plenty, making njala more acute in some than in other parts of the region. The indivisibility between space and time becomes sharply clear in a njala season.

The time that gives different meanings to njala is not, however, the same as chaola's. Each famine acquires its identity from the fact that it interrupts time's arrow. By contrast, njala belongs to cyclical time, which is one reason why it has easily escaped the attention of students of the crisis literature with their single-minded preoccupation with the so-called transition from precapitalist to capitalist forms of organization. Although it does obey the rules of irreversible time, as all social processes must (see chapter 4), seasonal hunger gets its logic from the repetitive. Thus, to understand njala, one needs to pay as much attention to historical time as to spatial differentiation. Floods and droughts tell the story of a particular place during the rainy season.

THE TWO PHASES OF THE HUNGRY SEASON

The need for food supplies from outside the district is likely to increase after September and reach its peak in the early months of next year.[6]

Every year, munda growers on the rain-dependent mphala drylands experience a food gap in two stages: the first starts in September and ends with the first planting rains in December, and the second is from December to March. (Njala occurs at different times for those who depend on dimba farming on the dambo marshes.) There is, of course, nothing fixed about these dates, because, like its ending, the beginning of njala depends on many factors, including the nature of the previous harvest. A poor harvest in one season almost invariably leads to an early hungry season.[7] September is a heuristic starting date for njala because hunger takes some of its features from the nature of rural work, and most villagers begin preparing their munda gardens in September (see chapter 6).

Another characteristic, besides the nature of work, that distinguishes this phase of the hungry season is that many more families live on homegrown food and other local resources. Hungry households turn to such food as the famous nyika water-lily bulbs and sweet potatoes from the marshes. Access to these roots allows people to contain the impact of njala within their communities. Planting rains in December mark the end of this phase of the hungry season. That the flooding of the marshes eliminates both sweet potatoes and nyika accounts, in part, for the severity of hunger in the second half of the wet season, from December to March. In fact, for many government officials njala starts only with the onset of the planting rains.[8]

The percentage of households that depend on food supplies from outside rises sharply between December and March. For example, in 1954 and 1957, the whole Nsanje District faced serious food deficits in December. "As to be expected," complained one agricultural officer, the situation in the district "worsened during the month [and hunger] became more severe."[9] It became necessary to import food from outside. The Agricultural Development and Marketing Corporation (ADMARC) sold only 1,524.152 metric tons of maize between April and December of 1976. This number nearly doubled to 2,791.463 metric tons in the next three months, between January and March of 1977.[10] But it was not only diminished food supplies that defined the hungry season in this phase; the second half also earned its distinctive character from the nature of rural work.

Hungry villagers have to work hard in their fields after the first planting rains, so there is a marked discrepancy between the amount of food they eat and the energy they expend. Sometimes peasants have to reseed their fields after the failure of the initial plantings. But the most common agricultural task confronting all growers is weeding, which people have to do repeatedly between December and February. Poor families always find themselves in a bind, having to choose between saving their crops from weeds and looking for food or money. Such a dilemma assumed special significance for tenant households on European estates during the first three decades of the twentieth century, when they were obliged to weed the cotton fields of their landlords in addition to their own—hence the unpopularity and eventual collapse of the estate sector in the valley. Some independent cotton growers subsequently faced a similar predicament, when the state forced them to cultivate cotton separately from their food crops. Rural resistance to this cultivation regime was, like the struggle against tenancy, as much about work as it was about njala. Finally, market forces also exacerbated njala in this period.

Market conditions make the second half of the njala season especially stressful in different ways. Villagers in places like the East Bank, the Chapananga chiefdom, the Dinde, and the Dabanyi Marshes cannot easily purchase food even when they have money.[11] There are no good roads connecting these places to major food depots like Bangula, and the rains only aggravate an already bad situation (see chapter 4). Peasants in these localities can therefore starve with money in their pockets. But even those villagers living next to the main lines of food supply can also suffer severe hunger because of soaring food prices. In 1957, for example, a 200-pound bag of maize in Nsanje District sold for 57.5 shillings during the first phase of the hungry season, but fetched over 70 shillings in the second half.[12] Similarly, peasants sold a 200-pound bag of maize for only 30–35 shillings at harvest time in 1962; but by February 1963 they had to pay well over 60 shillings for the same bag.[13] It was not, therefore, unusual to have large supplies of maize and a starving population in the same area toward the end of the wet season. Many families in Chikwawa went hungry in February 1981 despite the availability of food stocks at all ADMARC markets in the area; maize had become too expensive for the locals.[14] The market is a double-edged sword. It offers cash income at harvest time and exploits the hungry during the dzinja.

The increasing popularity of markets in rural survival strategies opens a window on the political and social dimensions of njala. Today, njala exists only for those without money, and it helps rich peasants maintain their power over their poor neighbors. Njala also illuminates the role of the state as a provider of relief and as an organizer of food markets (see chapter 4). The study of food markets allows one to see what is new in rural experiences of seasonal hunger, although these elements of time's arrow have not undermined the order and intelligibility of njala: every March, it fades away almost as silently as it came, giving way to the masika season of plenty.

Like its beginning, the end of njala does not have a fixed date; it varies according to many factors, including the economic position of its victims. Poor peasants begin eating their crops before they ripen, as Chief Tengani's subjects did in 1957. They started on their new crops while their rich neighbors still consumed their millet from the previous harvest.[15] The end of njala also depends on the crops people grow in a particular area. Unlike maize and the more popular millet (*mchewere*) varieties, the drought-resistant *gonkho* sorghum (*mapira*) is not a hunger breaker, since it does not get ready for picking until May (see chapter 6). The combination of slow- and fast-maturing crops makes the retreat of hunger in the valley a long, drawn-out process stretching from March to May. But one can treat March as the last month of the njala season because peasants start eating mchewere millet and maize in that month. As one official happily declared in March 1961: "At present there is a sufficient supply of all staples."[16] The demand for imported maize would fall precipitously, and food prices would also tumble.[17]

It is important, however, to remember that not everyone celebrates the end of hunger. Every year there are villagers who harvest nothing and who begin to get food from other peasants and traders as early as February.[18] For example, in March of 1973 and 1974 ADMARC and the state had to bring to the area 384 short tons maize for sale.[19] There is no season in which the valley as a unit achieves a 100 percent self-sufficiency rate. Njala is a highly variable reality.

DROUGHT AND DESERTS OF HUNGER

There was no appreciable surplus [of maize] in the Port Herald sector, but in Chikwawa, where the crop did extremely well, there was an estimated surplus of about 200 tons.[20]

Two questions immediately come to mind when one thinks about the variability of njala. The first is about the scale and intensity of hunger in historical perspective. Like the proponents of the golden-age theory, the crisis literature, which rarely sees njala as distinct from famine, proceeds on the assumption that food shortages (or "famine") have indeed become more acute and frequent.[21] This notion is especially consistent in that body of literature inspired by the underdevelopment theory; the message is that the more deeply Africa gets integrated into the world economy, the more acute its food deficits, and scholars have liberally used figures about the continent's food imports to substantiate the claim.[22] But I have found no evidence to bear out this assertion with respect to the valley as a unit.

There can be no doubt that some developments, like the rise of a new food market, the permanent inundation of the marshes, and land degradation, did undermine food production and intensify seasonal hunger in some segments of the population in certain historical periods.[23] But it is impossible to abstract from these cases a *general* trend or trajectory valid for the entire valley during the period covered by this book. Space, rather than irreversible time, remains a more reliable index in assessing the severity of njala. The Tchiri Valley combines both oases of plenty and deserts of hunger. The region owes much of its notoriety as a place of food deficits to its extensive deserts of hunger.

Deserts of Hunger between and within the Districts

A long-term historical perspective suggests the need to distinguish the Tchiri Valley's deserts of hunger in two related spatial dimensions. The first contrasts the southern—or roughly today's Nsanje—district with the northern or Chikwawa district (see figure 3.1). Nsanje has over the years earned the unfortunate reputation as the hunger capital of the valley.[24] Masked by the prosperity of cotton agriculture during the first four decades of the twentieth century, the district's inability to feed itself became especially apparent after

Figure 3.1 Deserts of hunger and oases of plenty (created by Seth C. Triggs for the author)

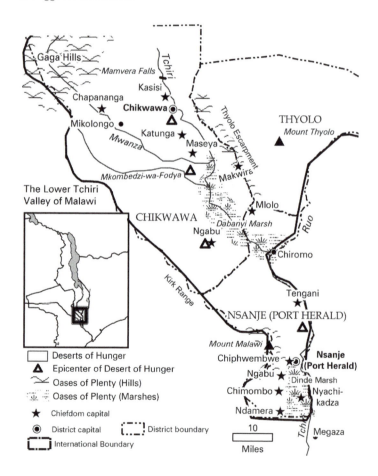

the Bomani floods of 1939. That was how the district's impoverishment came to contrast with Chikwawa's relative prosperity, based simultaneously on an enlarged cotton economy and a maize "revolution" (see chapters 5 and 6). Observers have described the two districts in different terms. When Chikwawa produced a surplus, Nsanje faced food shortages;[25] Chikwawa exported some of its maize, while Nsanje consumed all its sorghum and millet;[26] and when Chikwawa faced a mild shortage, Nsanje's would be "acute."[27] It was a tale of two "cities," as the 1950 report on the region made clear:

> The old Chikwawa District covered a total of 2,644 square miles, had a population density of 51 to the square mile and was comparatively prosperous from its heavy cotton crop, whereas Port Herald covered 747 square miles only, with a population density of 100 to the square mile and was possibly one of the poorest districts in the protectorate.[28]

But far more relevant than the Chikwawa-Nsanje distinction is the second contrast, which portrays each district as having its own oases of plenty and deserts of hunger. (Again, like most other aspects of njala, the differences between the two are not qualitative; they relate to matters of degree, as peasants in both areas experience the annual food gap in one way or another.)

The first desert of hunger in Nsanje District coincides with what agricultural-development experts classified as Nsanje South (figure 3.1). This area consists of the mphala drylands between the Dinde Marshes in the east and the slopes of the Kirk Range in the west, all the way from Nsanje Township in the north to Malawi's border with Mozambique to the south.[29] Once the center of cotton agriculture in the whole country, this area has emerged from the Bomani floods of 1939 as a perennial food-deficit region, caused, according to one interpretation, "by overcrowding on a poor soil."[30] As one antinationalist colonial administrator predicted in the late 1940s, political independence would mean nothing good for the people of this enclave:

> The District is notorious for its lack of agricultural progress and with the heavy density of population in the south living on land which has already lost much of its fertility, it is quite obvious that this is a subject which must take precedence over all others. Whatever progress might be made in other fields, whatever ideologies it may be possible to satisfy, all will be of no avail if the final result is an empty belly—and this emptiness is already too well known in the Southern part of the District.[31]

Unfortunately, he was right. Supplying the food needs of this area became the first order of business for the African leaders who assumed control over the state after the first general elections of 1961. They had to import food as a result a serious drought and the inundation of large tracts of the Dinde

Marshes. Food "supplies will be required in the Southern half of the District from some other source," wrote a somber district commissioner in August 1962.[32] And the problem has continued to frustrate all his successors, who also had to deal with the hunger problems of Nsanje North (figure 3.1).[33]

Nsanje North, which is almost synonymous with the large Tengani chiefdom, is the second major area that has made the district a net importer of food. Covering about three-fifths of the district's land area, the food deficits of this area have helped seal Nsanje's reputation as a hungry district.[34] One report in 1962 estimated "that by the end of December" approximately "90% of people in Tengani's area" would be "acutely short of food." (The corresponding figure for the hill areas was five percent.)[35] Unlike the peasants of Nsanje South, who sometimes looked to the dambo for relief in the form of sweet potatoes, their counterparts in Nsanje North did not have extensive marshes to cultivate even when the Tchiri water levels were low. As one knowledgeable official put it:

> As was to be expected, the food shortages became more severe as the month progressed. The people south of Port Herald were helped by the sweet potatoes from Dimba; the shortages were still most acute in the Tengani area.[36]

Without sweet potatoes, Tengani's subjects relied heavily on nyika water-lily bulbs from the Dabanyi and Dinde to their north and south, respectively.[37] They have also distinguished themselves for their ability to tap into maize grown in the oases of plenty, especially the Mlolo chiefdom on the East Bank.[38] Villagers living near the district's boundary with Chikwawa also procure provisions from markets in southern Chikwawa, although some of this food comes from the Tchiri Highlands and other parts of the district.[39] Southern Chikwawa is itself a net food importer.

Southern Chikwawa constitutes one of the district's two deserts of hunger. The other is a smaller unit, spread over the western sections of the Kasisi, Katunga, and Maseya chiefdoms (figure 3.1)—a region some reporters have referred to as the area "within a ten mile radius of the Boma [district headquarters] on the West Bank." Close to the Boma, the food deficits of this arc have regularly attracted the attention of government officials,[40] although they pale into insignificance when compared with those of the southern portion of the district. This is an extensive area on the west bank of the Tchiri River, running from the Mwanza River in the north down to the district's boundary with Nsanje in the south. Embraced in this region are southern Chapananga and the entire Lundu and Ngabu chiefdoms (figure 3.1).[41] Some officials have characterized this whole stratum as the area "far away from" the Dabanyi and the Tchiri River.[42] The epicenter of this desert of hunger, Makande or Ngabu Township, also happens to be the country's number-one producer of cotton since the 1940s.[43]

Little is known about this region's (figure 3.1) food problems before the 1940s, when officials treated it largely as the valley's "backwater" and "empty" space good enough only as an area to resettle villagers from the more "congested" Nsanje District. But this has changed since the 1940s, when the region emerged as the country's leading producer of cotton. In 1968, Ngabu became the headquarters of the Chikwawa Cotton Development Project (CCDP), which compelled officials to confront, in one way or another, the area's recurrent food problems.[44] A 1977 report estimated that 90 percent of the population in the area lived on food from the market.[45] The area's dependency rate on external sources skyrocketed to 98 percent in 1981.[46] ADMARC was sometimes unable to meet the region's food needs:

> The rest of the population [outside Chapananga and the East Bank] in the district are reliant on ADMARC Markets for their food requirements. This is very evident in the overcrowded ADMARC maize Markets and the numerous requests for the same in those areas where the ADMARC stores have sold out every bag. The demand for maize is so high that ADMARC constant efforts to maintain the grain's supply at her markets in the district appear to fall short of our requirements.[47]

Maize prices have always been high in this area. In 1966, for example, a 200-pound bag of maize sold for 40 shillings at Ngabu but for only half that amount in Makhwira's chiefdom on the east bank of the Tchiri River.[48] Southern Chikwawa may look traditional in many respects, but the region has definitely entered the era of modern hunger (see chapter 6). Drought only compounds the problem in this as it does in the other deserts of hunger.

Chilala Drought

Study of chilala incidents during the past 150 years suggests one reason why peasants rarely blame nature for their misfortunes. They view society as responsible for most of their miseries. The impact of every drought has been uneven. This is not only because of the strength of the agricultural system, but also because nature itself is not uncompromisingly evil. Droughts are highly variable in their intensity and duration; they rarely coincide with floods, and, most importantly, they take away with one hand and give back with another. The same rain shortage that undermines munda production on the mphala drylands also exposes large tracts of the fertile dambo for cultivation. The Tchiri Valley does not allow a single-tunnel vision, pursuing hunger without an idea of plenty or positioning nature as Africa's principal adversary.

Despite—or because of—their frequency, droughts are silent killers one cannot easily document. In contrast to the news-making floods, droughts are "nonevents," whose realness one can only define in negative terms. Peasants in the valley give names to floods but not to drought. To understand them, one needs to know a "perfect" growing season. But instead of drawing up an ideal type, consisting of different climatic variables, it may be more instructive to describe a real perfect season, as 1952–53 was in Chikwawa District. (The story was, as one can only expect from nature, different in Nsanje District.)

The season began with light showers on 1 October, as villagers prepared their gardens for planting. (The rains were heavier in the Gaga Hills, where they reportedly damaged planting ridges.) As usual, villagers did not plant with these rains, whose chief function was to get lazy cultivators back to work. Planting started in earnest the following month, when, as expected, rains fell throughout the district on 9, 10, and 11 November and, after a two-week interlude, on 26 November. A total of 3.96 inches had fallen at Chikwawa Boma by the end of November. Rainfall became more localized, however, in December, when during the first three weeks of the month, the district headquarters received only 2.88 inches. Villagers began to panic when the rains ceased altogether between 20 December and 7 January. However, rainfall resumed in the district on 18 January and became more regular and widespread, giving this critical month a total of 12.33 inches. Another total of 5.17 inches, spread over 10 days in February, took away the last fears of a drought in the second half of the growing season. March, which brought 5.21 inches of rain in 15 days, sealed the fate of this favorable season. Three days of rain in April, totaling 1.38 inches, closed this happy dzinja.[49] In all, 30.93 inches of rain fell between 1 October 1952 and 30 April 1953.

When judged on the basis of rainfall amount, 1952–53 was not an ideal season even in Chikwawa District. The 30.93 inches of rain fell short of the regional average by 1.07 inches. Moreover, this deficit, which resulted mostly from the December rainfall patterns—localized at the beginning and in complete cessation toward the end—threatened the failure of late-planted crops that began to wilt by the first week of January. What turned 1952–53 into a season of bumper harvest was the overall distribution, especially between December and March, when the district received 83 percent of the total rainfall against the statistical average of 85.[50] There are varieties of good seasons, just as there are many different kinds of droughts.

In Malawi, droughts come in two forms, depending on whether the shortfall occurs during the first (November–December) or second (January–March) half of the dzinja. The two kinds of drought are different in their impact, as the members of the UMCA recognized in the early 1860s, calling the November–December shortage an "early" and the January–March deficit a "latter" drought. Early droughts are less ominous because they only delay planting, while latter droughts kill crops that have already taken root. The missionaries closely monitored both types of drought, which, combined with the slave raids, led to a famine that adversely affected their enterprise.

The missionaries arrived in the country toward the end of the masika season of plenty in July 1861, and they faced no difficulty getting food at their Magomero settlement in the Tchiri Highlands. Then as the cold season gave way to the hot chilimwe in September, daily life began to change at Magomero. There was less drinking and drumming, and every able-bodied adult started preparing munda fields for the planting rains. Peasants worked their fields with such expertise that they impressed the missionaries, particularly their leader, Bishop Charles Mackenzie, who told his compatriots in Britain that Africans did not need European agricultural science. Like other Europeans, Mackenzie had come to Africa "to teach [these] people agriculture"; but, after seeing Africans at work, he admitted, "I now see that they know far more about it than I do."[51] The Bishop sent this message shortly before his untimely death near Chiromo during the missionaries' first growing season (1861–62) in the country.

Missionary records of the early 1860s emphasize the need to treat drought as an extremely variable phenomenon, not easily subject to generalization. It affected Magomero and those parts of the valley the Europeans knew (especially Chikwawa) in different ways. In the valley the shortage covered one and a half rainy seasons: January–April 1862 and nearly the whole of the next dzinja, from November 1862 to March 1863. The 1861–62 season started on a positive note in the valley. The area received heavy planting rains between 9 and 14 November 1861, and after a two-week break, the rains resumed and continued to fall throughout December, causing the Tchiri River to flood in some places.[52] The situation at Magomero appears to have been more mixed in this same period. If it ever rained there in November, then the rains must have stopped in early December, because the next thing one hears is the mgwetsa rain-calling ceremony organized by Chief Chigunda after receiving an order from his dead predecessor in a dream. The mgwetsa took place on 18 or 19 December with spectacular results:

> Singularly enough, before the ceremony was over a thundercloud passed over Magomero, and we had an abundant shower of rain; though the hills about us drew it away, and it was some time before it rained again.[53]

The rains did come back, so that on 7 February the missionaries boasted of having plenty of rain when Kankhomba from the Phalombe Plain complained "of the want of rain; they had so much sun that all the corn was being dried up & he asked us to pray for rain for him."[54] But it was only a matter of days or weeks before the drought also hit Magomero, prompting a disheartened Rowley to provide one of the best definitions of a latter (January–March) drought:

> The ground had been prepared, the seed sown: the rains came, the corn sprang up—all seemed as we desired it; and then the rains ceased: day by

day, week by week, and no rain; the fierce sun seemed withering the young corn, famine appeared imminent.[55]

Crops planted between November and December 1861 in the Tchiri Valley were also dying from this latter drought, as the missionaries would later learn when they abandoned Magomero and moved to Chikwawa in May 1862.[56]

At Chipindu, a village halfway between modern Blantyre and Chikwawa, the missionaries found everyone "sad at the prospect of failing crops."[57] But even more depressing news awaited them on the valley floor,[58] where nothing but "fields of withered corn" greeted them. The principal "crops of the valley had failed from want of the latter rain," wrote Rowley.[59] There were no celebrations in May 1862, and peasants anxiously looked forward to a better growing season beginning in November. Sadly, though, the first half of the 1862–63 season turned out worse than its predecessor. There was nothing at Chikwawa that mitigated the missionaries' experience of early drought.

The drought of November–December 1862 was typical of Malawi's weather pattern in several respects. The days were hot and humid, with temperatures rising to 100 degrees and above. Every afternoon there were tantalizing thunderstorms that declared the unfulfilled promise of a rainfall. Rowley's riveting description of that drought reminds this author of his encounters with the early drought of 1979–80.

> For many weeks we were anxious for the November moon; rain, said the weather-wise, must come then, it always did; but the November moon came, and the drought still continued in the valley. It did seem at first that it would be as predicted, for on S.S. Simon and Jude (October 28), the clouds, dense and black, gathered round about, the lightning flashed, the thunder reverberated among the hills; we momentarily expected a deluge of rain, but we had but the spray of the storm, which spent itself far away among the mountains. The earth about us was not moistened. Several times after this we had similar manifestations, which were followed by similar results. The clouds collected towards the afternoon, the wind became furious, a storm right overhead seemed imminent; but the seductions of the highlands proved irresistible, and away sailed the clouds, leaving us a clear sky from which descended an "unclouded blaze of living light." And so Nov passed away, and we had no rain.[60]

Had the rains come after November, people would have forgotten this drought the way they have done many others both before and after the 1860s. Early drought are less disastrous in their impact because all they do is to delay planting. Rains in December or January would have sent the villagers back to their gardens to partially reclaim the season. What turned 1862–63 into a catastrophe was the fact that this early drought was followed by a latter drought between January and March 1863.[61] Droughts occurring in these months leave villagers with hardly any opportunity to replant, although they do not necessarily become a precursor to chaola famine.

One reason that drought does not automatically lead to chaola is that munda cultivators have over the centuries developed strategies to deflect the effects of rain shortage. Chapter 6 will discuss these farming methods in detail; the purpose here is to stress the multiplicity of those strategies. One group consists of intercropping practices, which, once condemned as the epitome of peasant irrationality, are now accepted as the bedrock of rural science. Villagers grew in the same garden and at the same time many crops of differing drought-resistant capabilities. They combined maize, which is one of the least drought-resilient crops[62] with crops like gonkho sorghum that rarely die from drought. In the drought of 1979–80, 75 percent of the millets "died off completely," but the sorghums were reported to have "done much better."[63]

Drought will damage some but not all crops in a typical peasant field also because villagers stagger the sowing process, planting different crops and different varieties of the same crop earlier than others. A typical peasant garden mimics the biological diversity of the natural world, featuring crops in different stages of development during the same season. In 1964, for example, officials estimated that villagers planted about 50 percent of their maize crop early and the remainder late. In the same season, late-planted millet accounted for about 30 percent of the region's total millet output.[64] One and the same crop would weather drought differently. In 1980 early-sown cotton was reportedly "flowering and forming bolls" while its late-planted counterpart was "doing poorly."[65] While early-planted maize and millet did "fairly well," the late-planted versions were described as "very poor and in some cases a complete failure."[66] As one officer, who had waged a fruitless campaign against late planting, once congratulated himself: "This year has provided an excellent demonstration of the value of early planting of both food and economic [cotton] crops."[67] Whatever its merits in some years, the campaign was fundamentally flawed in that it did not try to understand the logic behind staggering and, in particular, how early- and late-planted crops fared during both normal *and* abnormal seasons. Staggering stabilized food supply by ensuring the loss of some but not all crops during both favorable and unfavorable seasons.

Finally, peasants extend the logic of this survival strategy when they raise crops in different ecosystems, like the dambo and mphala. Deserts of hunger are inseparable from oases of plenty.

FLOODS AND OASES OF PLENTY

One group of oases of plenty is comprised of segments of the Kirk Range and the Thyolo Escarpment, where rainfalls are higher and more reliable than on the valley floor. Another group consists of the dambo marshes in the Dabanyi,

Dinde, and banks of the Tchiri River's main tributaries. Every drought, these marshes attract growers from all over the valley, who, as in northern Nigeria, expand the acreage under food cultivation in the floodplains.[68]

The evidence on how drought boosts dimba farming is overwhelming. A severe drought in 1908 drove women from the Lulwe hills to the Dinde Marshes, where they grew and worked for sweet potatoes, carrying the tubers back home along what the members of the SAGM dubbed the "Sweet Potato Road."[69] About 40 years later, during the famous drought of 1949, people flocked to the marshes to do emergency farming. (Some of these villagers had left the marshes in the aftermath of the Bomani floods of 1939.)[70] According to district commissioner for Port Herald, Mr. P.M. Lewis:

> The great fall in the level of the river Shire has exposed large acreages of land on the east bank of the river above Chiromo, and on the west bank below Port Herald [Nsanje]. Advantage has been taken of both these areas to raise additional emergency crops during the year … planting of the more staple food crops and even cotton has taken place for the first time since the river flooded [in 1939] … , and will add greatly to the diet of these people.[71]

The bustling activity in the marshes led him to speculate on how the harnessing of the Tchiri River could release the region's agricultural potential: "It has been a vivid example," he wrote, "of what the effective control of the Shire means to the district as a whole, and the vast extent of highly productive land which is waiting to be used, if this control can only be achieved."[72] Nothing was done to harness the river, and three decades later, in 1979–80, villagers responded to another serious drought by increasing the acreage planted with maize and sweet potatoes.[73] And the impact of these efforts has been consistently positive.

When every munda crop around them withered for lack of rain in 1862, the members of the UMCA were impressed with something entirely different on the dambo still free from the slave raids:

> There had been no rain in the valley sufficient to moisten the surface of the earth for nearly eight months. On the line of river itself the consequent dearth was not apparent; for on the islands and along the banks, just those places which received moisture from the stream, you found *chimanga continually growing.*[74]

Dimba farming rarely failed in subsequent years. Officials often factored in dimba farming in their estimation of the effects of drought: "The Shire River is dropping most quickly and prospects of good and early dimba gardens are a certainty; the over-all food position in fact should give more than adequate supplies for the whole year."[75] The official, who made this observation in response to the drought of 1958, did not engage in daydreaming; he was speaking from experience. A decade earlier, in 1949, Chikwawa survived drought in a better shape than Port Herald or much of the country because of the success of emergency dimba farming.

The failure of dimba crops during the drought of 1949 brought Port Herald District to the brink of chaola famine. Two unexpected floods damaged dimba crops in the Dinde. Heavy rains in the Mulanje area in early April caused the Ruo and the Tchiri to flood, "ruining potato plantings and destroying a very promising maize crop."[76] Then, as people were trying to recover this brief flood, another came in mid-June, "causing severe damage to maize in" the Dinde.[77] Hunger became very acute in Port Herald. By contrast, for Chikwawa, which was not affected by the early floods, 1949 turned out to be almost a normal year despite the drought:

> In Chikwawa [District], with the exception of Ngabu and Ndakwera, a crop sufficient for immediate food needs was obtained from the dry land *and when the dimba crops, which were unaffected by flood, were added to this,* the year could be called practically normal, with small surpluses of maize in some areas.[78]

Livingstone and members of the UMCA were absolutely correct when they blamed the disaster of 1862–63 on the slave raids. Centuries of experience had taught the peasantry how to turn drought into an asset.[79] The valley became one undifferentiated desert of hunger only under political upheavals and, as the story of Port Herald District in 1949 illustrates, under certain forms of rare floods.

Madzi Floods

Like droughts, floods come in many different forms. Some floods affect the Tchiri River while others get confined to its tributaries; some are routine, coming and leaving the marshes as expected, while others are rare and disrupt food production. Flash floods are among the disruptive floods, which are, however, largely confined to the tributaries of the Tchiri River, such as the Ruo from Mulanje Mountain and the Luvunzu, Maperera, Mwamphanzi, and Thangadzi Rivers from the Thyolo Escarpment (figure 4.1).[80] They are common in the Makhwira and Mlolo chiefdoms, sandwiched between the western slopes of the Thyolo Escarpment and the Dabanyi Marshes. They can leave a trail of destruction during the rainy season, as events of 3 February 1953 in the Mlolo chiefdom illustrate. A wall of water overflowed Thangadzi River, moving trees, bananas, and bamboos, which in their turn flattened hundreds of acres of maize in the Chapinga and Mlolo villages. The floods killed a five-year-old girl in addition to chickens and goats.[81] The damage was so extensive partly because the floods came at night, unlike the Ruo madzi of 15 March 1967, which struck the Sankhulani and Chiromo triangle during the day. Although the Ruo torrent submerged many buildings and acres of maize and rendered 3,489 persons homeless, there were no reported deaths, and people were able to rescue most of their property as they ran away toward higher ground.[82] Many villagers returned to their homes in a matter of days, something that victims of some types of the Tchiri floods could not have done.

The Tchiri River system provides more examples of both rare and routine floods. I call the regular madzi "good" floods because they come when expected at the beginning of the rains in December–January and leave anytime between February and June, depending on the long-term trends in the flow of the Tchiri River. When the Tchiri ran consistently low between 1880 and 1940, good floods normally receded by February, exposing the marshes for food and cotton production for nearly nine months before the beginning of the next flood season. Before and after this period floodwaters withdrew from the marshes as late as July. But even when they receded in July, these floods were still good because they followed an established pattern. Predictability was an essential feature of good floods, which were to dimba agriculture what a normal rainfall was to munda farming. But every time they occurred, good floods reminded villagers of the possibility of what I term as "bad," "prolonged," and "early" floods.

Prolonged floods that linger on without retreating impinge on dimba farming the same way as early (November–December) droughts do to munda agriculture. They delay but do not kill plants, as early floods do. Early floods, which come anytime during the dimba growing season, are like latter (January–March) droughts that damage crops in different stages of growth. The Tchiri Valley is a very complex ecosystem.

Originally, early floods resulted almost exclusively from sudden and heavy rainfall in the sources of the Tchiri River's main tributaries, such as the Ruo from Mulanje Mountain. However, after the construction of the Liwonde Dam in 1957, early floods became common. The dam was initially designed as part of a multifaceted scheme that, if completed, would have supported many projects in the country, especially the irrigation of the mphala drylands and the draining of the marshes in the valley. The scheme would have—in the words of one governor—"revolutionized" life in the valley.[83] But financial constraints aborted this grand vision, so that the dam came to serve more limited objectives. Officials have opened and closed the dam to prevent flooding in the area above Liwonde and to facilitate the construction of bridges and hydroelectric power stations below Liwonde. That was how, as chapter 6 will detail, the dam turned out to be a curse instead of a blessing for those who depended on dimba farming in the valley. Officials have controlled the flow of the Tchiri River with little or no consideration of the needs of peasant growers in the Dabanyi and Dinde. While the closing of the dam made more dambo available for cultivation, the opening almost invariably led to early floods. Such floods destroyed dimba crops and forced villagers to dig up immature tubers of sweet potatoes in 1957, 1958, 1971, and 1974, among other years.[84] Peasants paid a heavy price for "development."

The combination of early with prolonged floods since the late 1970s has dramatically changed the face of the marshes. The inundation forced villagers, who had resisted such a move since the Bomani floods of 1939, to permanently evacuate the marshes.[85] One can find only a few isolated communities in the Dinde and Dabanyi today. Some of the displaced people now occupy the deserts of hunger and turn to the marshes only for fishing, collecting water-lily bulbs, and farming during the dry season. But because large tracts of the marshes are permanently underwater and uninhabited, the distinction between rare and routine floods has lost its relevance, and it is, therefore, proper to use the past tense when describing bad floods that used to force the inhabitants of the Dabanyi and Dinde Marshes to the mphala drylands on a temporary basis.

To understand how bad floods affected the lives of peasants in the dambo, we will use the roughly 150-square-mile Dinde before the 1980s as an example (figure 3.2). With a population that ranged from 5,000 to 10,000, the Dinde suffered at least nine bad floods, in 1918, 1925, 1927, 1939, 1952, 1957, 1963, 1967, and 1971.[86] Peasants went through each of these disasters in three stages, corresponding to the Dinde's three main topographies (figure 3.2). The first referred to the western or Malawian (as opposed to the Mozambican) banks of the Tchiri River. On the western fringes of the banks was a ridge (*mtunda*) where most villages were located. Finally, there was an extensive piece of land between the ridge in the east and the Dinde channel in the west; the channel separated the mphala drylands from the Dinde Marshes. Peasants called this third zone mphala in reference to the fact that they sometimes grew on it crops that, like cotton, were otherwise typical of the rain-dependent mphala drylands. A flood became bad when it inundated the three strata and forced people out of the ridge.

Like a good flood, a bad flood started by filling the banks of the Tchiri, engulfing the area within a few hours, a day, or a week, depending on the volume and speed of the Tchiri. The longer it took the river to submerge its banks, the greater the chances for people to save their crops, as was the case in the Chikwawa section of the Dabanyi in 1952.[87] Mature maize easily weathered this stage, and if the waters stopped or started to recede at this point, the result would have been a typical normal flood. The mighty Tchiri would have done a good job fertilizing the dambo. But more flooding after this stage would warn people about the possibility of a bad flood.

Figure 3.2 Ecology of the Malawi section of the Dinde Marsh (created by Seth C. Triggs for the author)

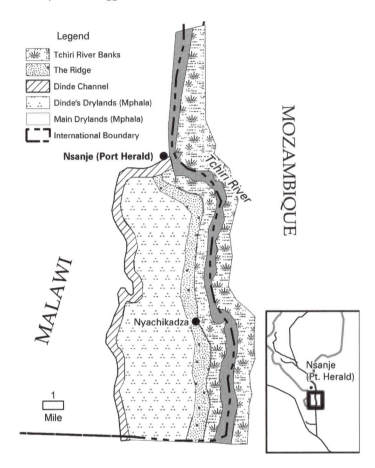

Two developments characterized the final saga of a bad flood. First, waters from the banks would break the ridge at its lowest points,[88] rushing to the west, and submerging every garden on the local mphala, in a clear warning about the impending disaster.[89] Some villagers would begin to prepare themselves for the possibility of a bad flood by erecting temporary msasa houses on the main drylands outside the Dinde.[90] But the stubborn ones would hang around even after their houses on the ridge had sunk many feet underwater in the second and final phase of a bad flood.[91] In some years, as in 1964, that kind of obstinacy paid off, but in other seasons, the resisters would be forced from the marshes after the entire Dinde had turned into one expansive lake. There was nothing but water in the Dinde in February 1952:

South of Port Herald, flooding was observed on both banks, gradually getting more extensive on the right bank than the left. Many villages were seen standing in water and south of the Border, floods spread out widely to east and west, though more pronounced on the west than the east, due to the higher ground in the Portuguese. It was almost impossible to trace the course of the river in this area except in isolated places.[92]

In the north, the Dabanyi was, according to the same report,

completely full, forming a huge lagoon, which reached down nearly to Chiromo. The lagoons on the right bank near Mbenge [*sic*] were also full ... Along the banks of the Ruo could be seen large areas of flattened reeds. The Ruo waters were heavily charged with silt, and it was very notice-able at the junction with the Shire how the river was flowing in two different coloured streams, moderately clear on the right bank, and thickly clouded on the left.[93]

The infamous Sinapolotali deluge of 1925 had proved to be even a bigger disaster:

Hundreds of people have been rendered homeless; in some places their huts have been completely submerged in water, whilst in others they are standing in three or four feet of water. Some of our out-station buildings have been under water, and many will have fallen. Huts and other build-ings have been seen moving down river. ... One heard many reports of loss of life ... One sad story was of a mother escaping in a canoe with her children, one of whom, the baby, most likely tied on her back, fell over into the water, and nothing could be done to save it. It will not be known how many have lost their lives until the waters assuage and the bodies are found.[94]

People lost their lives in these two floods because huge waves resulting from strong winds made it extremely dangerous for anyone to cross the swollen Tchiri River or Dinde channel toward the main mphala drylands. This cross-ing was known as *kuthawa madzi* ("running away from the floods").

Kuthawa madzi was a complex and carefully choreographed procedure. Well-to-do villagers who owned dugout canoes (*ngalawa*) had kuthawa madzi in mind. The need to cross the Tchiri River in times of a bad flood must have also been a consideration among the poor, when they helped their rich neighbors to haul canoes (in a rough form) from the forest to the village (where they received their final shape) and from the village to the Tchiri River. Such assistance was supposed to guarantee the availability of these lifesaving boats that supplemented those provided by chiefs.

Chief Nyachikadza, whose entire chiefdom was located in the Dinde, owned and deployed a fleet of several large canoes to ferry his subjects from the marshes to the main mphala drylands in Mozambique or Malawi.[95] (Nyachikadza and other chiefs referred to this responsibility when they asked colonial authorities to waive fees people had to pay for trees used in canoe making, but the British tax collector repeatedly rejected the request.)[96] The chief supervised the process for many days, as it sometimes involved virtually the whole population.[97] Only high winds reduced the effectiveness of this well-used procedure, as was the case during the floods of 1952, known as Madzi-a-Padri, when some of the chief's approximately 5,000 people lost their lives.[98] The Msasila flood of 1958 was a different story. The operation was almost 100 percent successful; there were no reports of death among the Dinde's 8,000 souls.[99]

Saving human life was only one objective of kuthawa madzi. Another was to rescue property and particularly foodstuffs. Again, there were many factors that determined the success of this aspect of kuthawa madzi. Cyclone storms always spelled disaster for those trying to salvage their foodstuffs. It also appears that people had more difficulty saving their sweet potatoes than other crops.[100] The success of the operation also hinged on the crop's stage of development; floods dealt a deadly blow to any crop in its formative days. The flood of 1958 destroyed almost all crops in the Dinde because they were planted late, while in 1952 peasants in both the Dabanyi and Dinde were able to salvage their relatively mature crops.[101] Many victims of the 1952 floods thus lived on their own food during the time they spent away from their villages. The few unfortunate ones depended on the hospitality of their hosts on the mphala drylands; bad floods turned upside down the normal relationship between the inhabitants of the dambo and mphala.

Some people who fled the marshes settled on the Mozambican mphala on the east bank of the Tchiri River.[102] When the Portuguese were still in control of the country, the fugitives lived on large estates owned by Portuguese settlers and had to obey the rules that governed African tenants on these estates.[103] Life was in that respect less complicated for the villagers who took temporary residence on the mphala within Nyasaland; they did not have to make any political adjustment. Indeed, Chief Nyachikadza moved his court to Nyathando Village in Ndamera's chiefdom,[104] where he adjudicated cases among the refugees, constituting a distinct jurisdiction from the chiefdom in which they were physically located. Regardless, however, of where they settled, the fugitives faced at least one common challenge.[105] They always went through a hungry season.[106]

Njala, in its formal sense as a period during which the refugees did not harvest any crop, started the moment they landed on the mphala. However, their actual experiences depended on many factors, such as the amount of food they had salvaged and the length of time they spent on the mphala. No one could predict the duration of life on the mphala because some floods receded faster than others. The marshes remained under water for four months in 1952, two in 1958, and only one month in 1971.[107] Finally, the state of the economy of the mphala also played a part in determining the severity of njala among the fugitives. Food was relatively more plentiful on the mphala after the harvest, which began in March. Peasants who evacuated the marshes in February, as happened in 1952, could not have expected much help from the mphala.[108] Like their hosts, they got some food from the bush and the market, and worked for money or food in places like the Kirk Range and Thyolo Escarpment—the second group of oases of plenty after the marshes. Frustrated government officials who advocated the forceful removal of peasants from the dambo did not understand what those peasants did. Bad floods nearly always started as good floods, which villagers needed to rejuvenate the dimba system; the two types of floods are inseparable, just as the valleys are inseparable from the mountains.

On the Mountains

Enjoying higher and more reliable rainfalls than their counterparts on the valley floor (see chapter 6), mountain farmers of parts of the Kirk Range and Thyolo Escarpment usually produced enough maize to feed themselves, export, and supply the needs of hungry peasants from other parts of the valley.[109] The Chididi and Gaga Hills on the Kirk Range and the western slopes of the Thyolo Escarpment do not normally become part of the region's deserts of hunger even in times of drought. In 1921–23 people from Tengani procured food from the Mlolo and Makhwira chiefdoms to the west of the Thyolo Escarpment. One reporter in 1941 summarized the observations of his predecessors and successors when he wrote that "famine does not occur" in Mlolo's chiefdom.[110] In 1955, hungry villagers from the Ngabu chiefdom deserted their well-stocked markets and traveled to Makhwira to purchase maize directly from other peasants.[111] Six years later, in 1961, when Chikwawa's perennial hungry areas subsisted on imports, the people of Makhwira ate homegrown food.[112] The following year, Mlolo's people in the northern part of Port District (Chiromo and Bangula) were reportedly less dependent on the market than their counterparts in the southern section of the same district:

> Maize is being brought into the district for sale at Chiromo and Bangula. Up to the present however there is *no great demand in the north of the district* and the rate of sale is less than ten bags per day at those two places. The price is about £2.5s per bag. In the south of the district very little maize is being offered for sale though *there is a strong demand.*[113]

And like much of Mlolo's chiefdom, the Makhwira area survived the serious drought of 1980 with little food from outside.[114] The government has fought a largely futile battle to keep off unlicensed maize buyers from the two chiefdoms.[115]

On the Kirk Range to the west of the Makhwira and Mlolo chiefdoms one finds two major oases of plenty with their epicenters around Chididi in the south and Gaga Hills in the north. The two areas nearly always produce a surplus, though little of this surplus reaches Malawi's official system of food supply. There are no reliable roads leading to the Chididi or Gaga Hills; the two regions are almost as inaccessible as the Makhwira and Mlolo chiefdoms on the east bank of the Tchiri (see chapter 4). Before the market's "liberalization" in the mid-1990s, the government had unsuccefully tried to keep off unlicensed traders who sometimes managed to reach these oases of plenty.[116] In the Tchiri Valley places of hunger exist only as integral parts of areas of plenty. Thus, while it is possible to predict—with the kind of certainty uncommon in social science—the coming and ending of the njala season, it is at the same time virtually impossible to measure, let alone forecast, the levels of want in any hungry season.

MEASURING AND PREDICTING THE INTENSITY OF HUNGER

Because njala threatened the tax base so frequently, colonial rulers and their African successors in Malawi tried by fits and starts to measure and predict the levels of the annual food gap in the country. These measures assumed an aura of emergency after a serious food shortage caused by drought or floods. The floods of 1952 set off a flurry of correspondence among the country's meteorologists, hydrologists, and water engineers on the flooding patterns of the Tchiri River system.[117] But this concern died almost as quickly as the floods did. Eight years later, the countrywide hunger of 1960 precipitated a lively debate on how to move food rapidly from areas of plenty to those of scarcity.[118] But nothing came from this talk either. The African leaders who took reins of the state in 1964 found a research station in the valley dedicated to an understanding of cotton but not the food system; they made their own forays into the virtually immeasurable world of seasonal hunger.

The new government's attempts to quantify seasonal hunger took officials and their experts along two well-trodden routes. First, they approached the problem from the perspective of the levels of food production. Basing their estimates on the amount of land available for agriculture, the "Garden Survey" of 1977–79 reached the stunning conclusion that a "vast majority of households in bad years and a substantial number even in good years" face hunger.[119] Another study confronted the issue by measuring what peasants produced and ate annually. Calculating that the 105,000 inhabitants in the CCDP (1968–73) could only grow 11,400 short tons of maize while every adult consumed 420 pounds of maize every year, the surveyors surmised that 50 percent of the food villagers ate was not homegrown.[120] Another variant of this method led officials to establish, through interviews with peasants in the same project area, the number of households that began the 1973 harvest season with the food they had harvested in May 1972. They discovered that only a third of the households reached May 1973 with food from the previous season, and the remaining two-thirds survived on supplies from other sources, including ADMARC.[121]

ADMARC points to the second method of measuring the region's food deficits. In this group of efforts, the postcolonial state made it the responsibility of every district commissioner, in collaboration with the district agricultural officer, to compile monthly estimates of the percentage of households dependent on the market (especially ADMARC) for their food supplies. For example, officials estimated that in January 1976, Chikwawa District's dependence rate on the market reached 98 percent.[122] (In December 1983 the corresponding figure was 90.)[123] The crop harvested in March 1976 brought some respite to the district, but the relief was always partial; between 10 and 50 percent of the district's households still looked to the market for their supplies in March.[124] Bureaucrats and politicians in the country's capital (Zomba and later Lilongwe) were especially interested in the March and October figures because of their assumed value in forecasting future needs.

Data collected in October were supposed to tell officials how serious hunger would be during the second half of the growing season, between December and March, while the March figures were to assess the new harvest's potential to feed the population in the next 12 months.[125] A 1960 March report from the valley prompted the central government to consider the possibility of forcing the Agricultural Produce and Marketing Board (the predecessor to ADMARC) to sell maize from its general reserve to African traders in Chikwawa District.[126] A year later, in 1961, one district commissioner for Port Herald included in his March report the following alarm:

> At present there is a sufficient supply of all staples, but the rate at which the new crop is being eaten means there will be a general shortage in a few months time, that is before people begin to harvest food from the Dimba gardens. Dimba garden planting has been generally delayed this year because the level of the water in the Dimbas has not fallen as rapidly as usual. It is also considered that there will be a quite severe shortage of food in November and December, because of the fact that the new crop is already being eaten and not stored away.[127]

Planning for njala left a long trail of paper in postcolonial Malawi, but with few if any tangible results in terms of relief or reliable data on the depth of seasonal hunger.

Two factors conspired against the good intentions of state officials who wanted to understand and predict the levels of the food gap. First, there was the human factor. While some government officials took their responsibilities seriously, others did not. They were either too lazy or incompetent to do the job well, especially after they were required to produce figures instead of detailed descriptions. Many sent their superiors in the capital nothing but mere guesses.[128]

More fundamentally, every official survey on the Tchiri Valley rested on one or more of the following false assumptions: that there was only one level of agricultural productivity, only one form of food production, and only one food crop. Every survey proceeded on the supposition that maize was the only food crop. While Malawians may eat more maize than any other nation in Africa on a per-capita basis,[129] not all regions of the country or the valley are equally dependent on maize. In some parts of the valley people grew and ate more millet and sorghum than maize. It was equally wrong to assume, as surveys generally did, that munda farming represented the totality of peasant production.[130] As the preceding discussion has shown, and as chapter 6 will detail, people in the valley engaged in other forms of agriculture besides dryland cultivation. Villagers combined munda with river-fed or dimba farming, which, as one district commissioner wisely admitted, made it extremely hazardous to predict the levels of want: "It is very difficult," he wrote, "to estimate what proportion of food people are able to supply from the remaining dimba crops, wild plants, etc."[131] The use of different microenvironments made the assumption about uniform levels of productivity untenable. One acre of the rich alluvial dambo produced much more than the same amount of land on the mphala drylands. The only predictable aspect of njala is that it will afflict the poor again next season. One does not need calculators or prophetic inspiration to understand this feature of seasonal hunger.

CONCLUSION

The Lower Tchiri Valley is not the place I would recommend to peasants who can make a living elsewhere. The villagers whose collective stories I tell in this book have faced challenges that are both unique and not so unique in Africa. Seasonal hunger afflicts peasants in many other parts of Africa that rely on only one main growing season. In those parts of Africa, njala is a cyclical event that arrives and leaves with the natural seasons. As Audrey Richards once remarked for the Bemba of northeastern Zambia, peasants of the Tchiri Valley live in "a society in which people regularly expect to be hungry annually, and in which traditions and proverbs accustom them to expect such a period of privation ... [annual hunger] is within the ordinary run of experience, and accepted as such."[132] Every growing season replays the

golden-age theory's view of the present as an inferior moment. Rural experiences of njala in the valley are in this sense not fundamentally different from
those of the Bemba or Tchiri Highlands. They are only different to the extent
that floods and frequent droughts increase the element of unpredictability and
exaggerate the severity of njala in the valley.

That these outbreaks of severe hunger have not always led to chaola famine
underscores the need to separate natural disturbances from social disasters.
Njala becomes chaola only when the social system fails. Nature becomes
uncompromisingly cruel only when the political environment traps the hungry
in their deserts of hunger. Otherwise, villagers have been able to contain the
effects of drought and floods and have thought imaginatively of the different
possibilities of their social and natural worlds, with the result that the Tchiri
Valley is one of the most densely populated regions of Malawi. That these
smart ways of "cheating" nature have not banished njala to the dustbin of history brings us back to the larger political field. In the absence of effective relief
programs and restructured state-peasant relations, every year poor villagers
succeed in preventing chaola by ensuring the return of njala.[133]

4

COPING WITH AND REPRODUCING HUNGER

In this connection I am to say that, although reports make it clear that there will be acute local food shortages in various places in the country before the next harvest, it is not expected that famine conditions as such will obtain, and you and the copy addressees of this letter are asked to note that this Ministry deprecates the use of the terms famine and "relief" in connection with the allocation of maize stocks to meet the currently expected shortages.[1]

A recent [2001] report in the "Malawi News" ... revealed that some villagers are now eating bitter roots and tubers from indigenous shrubs.[2]

Foraging for food has slowed up garden preparation.[3]

The old and the infirm were now definitely hard-pressed to find sufficient food and some people were reduced to a meal every other day.[4]

All activity is reduced to a minimum when food is short, and in a specially bad year garden work tends to be skimped.[5]

INTRODUCTION

On 17 October 1991, Mr. Anthony Chipakuza recounted his experiences of Mwamthota famine of 1922–23, providing vivid details of the hard work his parents did on a European-owned cotton estate to earn money for food. Two weeks later, on 3 November 1991, Mrs. Kolina Tambo corroborated Chipakuza's account of the famine, adding how men, after procuring food in distant places, would return to the village at night to avoid detection by their neighbors. Finally, on 5 November 1991, the late Mrs. Leni Pereira added her voice to the story of Mwamthota, with a focus on the long trips women made to the Dabanyi and Dinde Marshes to collect nyika water-lily bulbs, the processing of the bulbs, and the digestive problems the roots caused in some children.[6] All three interviewees recounted these aspects of Mwamthota with such detail and immediacy that one might think the famine had taken place only a few years before.

Villagers remembered these activities so vividly mainly because the processes are not simply about Mwamthota, which is a one-time episode. Working for the rich, eating roots, and taking meals in secrecy are not uncommon during the njala season. Every wet season thus reenacts some Mwamthota experiences. True, njala may not subvert the normal rules of sharing the way chaola does. At the same time, njala does weaken the ideals of the golden-age theory. Peasants tend to share less with their neighbors and more with friends and relatives in distant places who can give them food. Because it returns to the land every year, njala is about order, although, like everything else, it can only be orderly as part of the disorderly events of irreversible time. Time's cycle needs time's arrow to become time.

There is, therefore, a *historical* dimension to the food searches and foraging of the three narratives cited above. Had the interviewer closely questioned her, Mrs. Pereira would have told stories of how some parts of the marshes have become inaccessible as a result of the rise in Tchiri water levels. Mr. Chipakuza would have given an account of how rich African cotton growers replaced European cotton planters in the late 1920s. Finally and most importantly, the three historians would have emphasized the changing roles of markets and the government in shaping rural experiences of hunger. They would, in other words, reiterate the linear components of seasonal hunger. But, if pressed really hard, they would also explain why none of these shifts have ended njala as an annual event for a significant portion of the population. They would, in particular, refer to the failure of the state to ameliorate the sufferings of the hungry, a failure that has guaranteed the deployment of old survival strategies and the reproduction of njala and poverty in particular segments of the population. The force of time's arrow has not been strong enough to pierce time's cycle.

TINKERING WITH THE FORCES OF NJALA

The road from Port Herald southward to the PEA [Portuguese East Africa] border and the Zambesi has been in what I would describe as a disgraceful condition. It is in places a mere track and compares most unfavourably with the road to Dona Anna on the other side of the boundary.[7]

At the beginning of the month the food situation deteriorated rapidly, African Businessmen were charging up to £3:10/- for a bag of maize and by the measure maize was selling up to 6d per pound. At the district team meeting all locally stationed officers were of the opinion that "the trade" had forfeited any right to be allowed to handle the situation alone. The use of unfair measures was general, including cups with moveable bottoms. It was agreed that steps would have to be taken to force down the price of maize.[8]

The state in Malawi has intervened in the daily lives of hungry peasants indirectly by organizing the country's transport system and formal markets, and directly by selling food at "cost price," arranging food-for-work programs, and distributing free or subsidized food. But, as chapter 2 has already shown, budgetary constraints have always undermined the ability of the state to discharge its responsibilities on a regular basis and in times of emergency. Financial limitations provide a major line of continuity between the colonial and postcolonial relief policies in Malawi, although the country's postcolonial rulers have understood the politics of hunger better than the British, who had treated hunger largely as an administrative nuisance they could solve by legislating food markets.

Food Markets and the Transportation System

The state in Malawi passed important laws on the marketing of food in 1912, 1959–63, and the late 1990s. Written in response to the food shortage of that year, the Native Food Ordinance of 1912 is landmark piece of legislation in at least three ways.[9] First, it formally gave the government (the governor-in-council) the right to intervene in food markets on behalf of hungry peasants. Second, the law established, by what it said and did not say, the legal basis of the distinctions between estate and peasant production, and between African and non-African food traders. Like estate (but not peasant) production, African traders did not fall within the system of controls imposed on European or Asian dealers. African traders could ply the market without undue interference.[10] The third element of the ordinance addressed the problem of the export market.[11]

Although part of the ordinances of 1926, 1946, 1949, 1962, and 1963,[12] the export trade was largely uncontroversial except when the country could not feed itself and officials had to refuse applications for the export of essential commodities like rice, wheat, and especially maize.[13] The restrictions would target two population groups in the country. The first consisted of peasants living near Mozambique,[14] who, like the inhabitants of northern Chapananga in Chikwawa District, regularly sold their food across the border.[15] (Unlicensed traders from the Tchiri Highlands, operating in Makhwira and Mlolo chiefdoms, also attracted official attention in times of serious hunger.)[16] Indian and European dealers formed the second category of actors that became the focus of the antiexport legislation.[17] The interests of this group conflicted with European estate holders who did not regularly grow food but relied on peasant produce to feed their workers. The estate holders always fought hard against the export of food.[18] Largely unaffected by all colonial food export rules were African dealers, who had no legal existence.

Like many other colonial pieces of legislation, the Native Foodstuffs Ordinance of 1912 was based on racial distinctions. It placed African and non-African traders in two qualitatively different categories, recognizing the activities of non-African merchants but not those of African traders. The subsequent High Court decision that the law did not prohibit "natives exporting native foodstuffs" reaffirmed the racial division of the food trade.[19] European settlers and Asian (Indian) traders had to obtain licenses to move food from one part of the country to another. Obtaining such a permit was a long and complicated process, involving the trader, the district commissioner, and even the provincial commissioner if the food was to cross district boundaries.[20] Africans bought and sold food without much intervention from the colonial government. The ordinances of 1926, 1946, and 1949[21] did not upset the racial divisions of the 1912 ordinance, and the market's liberalization under the Produce Marketing Ordinance of 1959 actually gave African traders more clout.[22] Their fortunes began to change dramatically only with the passage of the Farmers Marketing Ordinance of 1962 and the Agricultural and Livestock Marketing Ordinance of 1963, which formed part of the postcolonial state's attempts to restructure the country's food and political economy.

Although the government and in particular the minister of agriculture, Kamuzu Banda (the future prime minister and life-president), preached the virtues of free enterprise, the bills of 1962 and 1963 stifled African entrepreneurship in the food trade. The creation of the Farmers Marketing Board (FMB) and its successor, ADMARC, consolidated under one statute the various laws on the produce market. It initiated a new era in the marketing of peasants' cash crops in three related ways. First, the new rules increased the powers of the minister of agriculture beyond what anyone could have imagined during the colonial era. Unlike the governor, who could only exercise his authority in these matters while "in-council," Banda, who held the Ministry of Agriculture throughout much of the 30-plus years of his reign, did not need such advice. No one could restrict his powers, and, as in other matters, he became a law unto himself. Second, the ordinances perpetuated the colonial dichotomy between peasant and capitalist production. The FMB was granted absolute monopsony over peasant produce but denied any power over estate produce and particularly tobacco, which became the favorite crop of the new political elite. The third and most significant feature of the two statutes relates to the transformation of the board into a business that had to sell produce at a profit and participate in profit-making ventures as a provider of loans. Dr. Banda and his cronies used these provisions to pump profits from the peasant into the capitalist sector,[23] and to turn independent traders into the agents and clients of the FMB and its successor, ADMARC. The era of independent African traders had passed.

Under the FMB and ADMARC, the maize trade became a highly centralized and politicized operation, which chipped away at the autonomy of African traders. Headquartered in Limbe, the board kept its Southern Region maize stocks at such markets as Balaka, Limbe, Luchenza and, within the valley, Bangula and Ngabu.[24] After receiving maize directly from the regional head-quarters in Limbe, officials at Bangula and Ngabu would send the food to "permanent sheds," which, in Chikwawa, overlapped with the district's major cotton markets, and in Nsanje were found at trading centers like the district's headquarters, Chiromo, Mankhokwe, Marka, Muona, Sorgin, and Tengani.[25] Only in times of emergency did officials permit food to move directly from Limbe to the permanent sheds.

In times of severe shortage, the board added another layer of markets below the permanent sheds. They called these "semi-permanent shelters," situated mostly in the villages of Native Authorities.[26] The board would sell at such local markets only in response to written requests by local politicians, made in accordance with a well-defined procedure. The politicians would first approach the board's local representatives at the sheds; then the representa-tives would forward the requests to the divisional supervisor at Bangula or Ngabu, who would forward the same to the Head Office in Limbe or to the Office of the President and Cabinet in Lilongwe.[27] Only after all these steps had been followed would the authorities sell food to hungry peasants at local markets and sheds.

When they did not purchase foodstuffs directly from the board's sheds, vil-lagers sometimes purchased maize from district councils acting as the board's agents. The councils were especially active in times of acute shortage, as in 1962, when the board concentrated its efforts on supplying bulk consumers in urban areas.[28] District councils bought the maize from the board at a standard price throughout the country and were required to charge a price that equaled the purchase price plus transport and handling.[29] But as time went on, poorly staffed councils found it increasingly difficult to operate under these regula-tions and were finally relieved of this responsibility by 1970, leaving private traders as the main dealers in places the board did not command a physical presence.[30]

Unlike in the pre-independence era, however, African traders now oper-ated as agents of the board. To become a trader, one needed the support of one's district commissioner, who initiated the procedure by drawing up a list of potential traders in his area and submitting it to the board's divisional supervisor at Bangula or Ngabu. Once approved, the nominee would sign a contract with the board, accepting his position as an agent under the direct supervision of the district commissioner.[31] After signing the contract, he would deposit cash with the divisional supervisor, who would place an order with the regional headquarters in Limbe for a food consignment to be shipped to Ngabu or Bangula.[32]

From Bangula or Ngabu, the trader would take the maize to a "Selling Point," which, having been authorized by the Regional Office in consultation with the district commissioner, would be clearly identified in the contract for two reasons.[33] First, traders were not allowed to sell maize within 10 miles of another ADMARC market.[34] The aim was to avoid duplication of effort, which, as officials argued, would prevent the trader "from getting a fair return for his work."[35] For the same reason, the board allowed only a few traders to operate in any given area. The other reason the contract specified the Selling Point was that the final price traders charged their customers depended on the distance between the Selling Point and the board's depot.[36]

The price any trader paid the board reflected the rate that the Ministry of Agriculture charged throughout the country and the amount of maize the trader ordered.[37] In 1968, for example, a trader who purchased 50 bags of 200 pounds each was charged 33 shillings per bag, representing a 10 percent discount on the prevailing national price.[38] The trader was allowed to sell this bag for 36s. 6d. anywhere in the country, plus the fee for transport and handling the maize from the board's depot to the Selling Point. In the late 1960s, this fee was fixed at seven pence for every ton-mile; the trader was not supposed to make a profit higher than the discount given by the board.[39]

To further curtail the agent's ability to make a profit, the board supplied an agent in a particular area with just enough maize to sell to direct consumers and to officially recognized subagents. Subagents would come under the supervision of the agent in the same way the latter was policed by the district commissioner.[40] And to ensure that no agent sold maize to unregulated middlemen, board officials reserved the right to inspect an agent's accounts without notice, in addition to the scheduled monthly reviews.[41] Board officials and/or district commissioners would cancel the contract of an agent with more maize than required in a particular area and issue him a contract that more accurately reflected the "existing demand in the area."[42] District commissioners were encouraged to question a consumer, a subagent, or an agent who seemed to be buying an "excessive amount" of produce.[43] Finally, district commissioners were also required to report agents who overcharged their customers and committed other malpractices. Such agents would lose their licenses and/or face penalties.[44] Under Dr. Banda's form of dependent capitalism, the maize trade was not supposed to operate on a profitable basis for African middlemen.[45] Only ADMARC had the right to make a profit and exploit the peasantry, buying a 200-pound bag of maize from producers at 25 shillings and selling the same to consumers at 45 shillings.[46] African traders must have welcomed the third important set of marketing regulations enacted in the second half of the 1990s.

Not much has yet been published about the marketing rules that took effect after the fall of the Banda regime in 1994. The regulations formed part of a structural-adjustment program that has led, among other things, to the privatization of the Malawi Railways and other parastatals. ADMARC has not yet been sold, but it has lost its former clout in the economy, competing with other players in the produce market. Peasants in the valley now sell their cotton to several companies besides ADMARC,[47] and they buy food from many independent dealers. The new rules have restored the kind of freedom that African traders used to enjoy before the draconian regulations of the early 1960s, although the impact of these changes on food security is not entirely clear.[48] It is one thing to promulgate new laws and entirely another to make them work on the ground.

Even at the height of the Banda regime in the 1970s and 1980s, the government of Malawi did not exercise as much control over the food trade as some of the legislation might suggest. As in other parts of Africa, formal markets in

Figure 4.1 Communications in the Lower Tchiri Valley (created by Seth C. Triggs for the author)

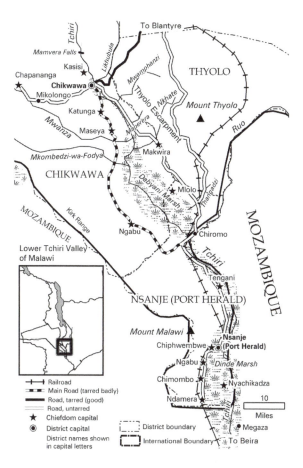

the valley constitute only one segment of the food trade; peasants engage in many more food transactions outside state-controlled markets. Moreover, the transportation system in Malawi is so "primitive" that the state has not always been able to deliver food in areas of need or to control the activities of independent traders. Every year, hunger exposes the limits of state power as an organizer of food aid, controller of merchants, and builder of a road system

Like Malawi itself, the Lower Tchiri Valley is a typical Third World enclave in terms of its communications (figure 4.1).[49] Since the completion of the Shire Highlands Railways in 1911, it has been relatively easy to move food into the valley from Thyolo, Mulanje, and other districts of the highlands, just as the completion of the bridge over the Zembezi River in 1936 increased the valley's links with the Indian Ocean. (The destruction of this bridge during Mozambique's brutal civil war made it more difficult to get food into Malawi during the serious deficits of 2000–2002.)[50] The Tchiri Valley is better situated in this respect than the central and northern regions of the country. What makes the valley a typical Third World region is the fact that this "developed" transport network, opening it to international markets, is supported by a backward or nonexistent internal communication system. The railway system bypasses and is poorly connected to many communities, including the entire Chikwawa District.

Chikwawa was for a long time linked to Blantyre by nothing but a dirt road along the treacherous Thyolo Escarpment.[51] Already a nightmare during the dry season, this 30-mile connection regularly failed during the rainy season, and villagers have horror stories to tell about the grueling trips they made to the highlands to get maize at Mbami during the famine of 1922. The situation has improved, however, since the construction of a tarmac road in 1965, but little has changed within the district itself.[52] The district's headquarters or Boma is poorly connected to all major population centers like Ngabu in the south, Makhwira in the east, and Chapananga in the west.[53] Peasants in the hungry parts of the district have no access to its oases of plenty.

There is, for example, no real road between the Boma at Chikwawa and the Gaga Hills of the Chapananga chiefdom. Each vehicle has to create its own path along the small, meandering track,[54] which is unfortunate because, as indicated earlier, Gaga is one of the most fertile areas of the valley. Farmers there consistently produce a surplus that they sell across the border in Mozambique because Malawian traders cannot get there. Gaga is in that respect similar to the Makhwira and Mlolo chiefdoms, which are also inaccessible oases of plenty. The only road that passes through the two chiefdoms from Thabwa in the north to Chiromo in the south does not need rains to become impassable; it is in a perpetual crisis (see figure 4.1).[55] The inhabitants of the region's deserts of hunger, like Ngabu, cannot reach this oasis of plenty, especially during the rainy season, and food prices are almost invariably lower on the East Bank chiefdoms of Makhwira and Mlolo than in West Bank deserts of hunger like Ngabu. In 1966, a 200-pound bag of maize sold for between 18 and 21 shillings in Makhwira, but the same bag fetched anything between 40 and 50 shillings in the Ngabu and Lundu chiefdoms.[56] Nsanje's regions of perennial hunger suffer a similar fate despite the presence of a railway line in the district.[57]

The railway in Nsanje has done little to connect the district's communities, as it follows the foothills of the north-south Kirk Range, whereas most people live close to the Tchiri River in the east and on the mountaintops in the west. (And heavy rains easily damage the poorly constructed, underfunded, and privately owned railway line, which ran over wooden bridges in its initial phase.) There is, for example, no reliable road between the railway line and places like Chididi and Lulwe in the mountains.[58] ADMARC often found it easier to ship maize by rail from Limbe to Bangula or Nsanje than to get it to places like Chimombo, Mbenje, or Tengani on the east side of the railway. Even more inaccessible than any of these places is Nyachikadza's chiefdom in the Dinde. This area remained isolated even during the dry season,[59] and bad floods only made the situation worse, creating a nightmare that local administrators anticipated with trepidation:

A more serious problem is expected to develop in the flooded area of Chief Nyachikadza when more rains come and when there will be no way of transporting the maize to the area. Most reliable transport is, usually, by canoe which is not safe when the water current is strong.[60]

What officials did not want to admit and what peasants knew was the fact that the chiefdom's isolation had as much to do with nature as with the way the state organized the economy. For the Portuguese the Tchiri River did not represent an obstacle; it acted as a highway they effectively utilized to transport their cotton from Megaza in the south to the railway line at Nsanje Township in the north. Motorized boats and barges passed through Nyachikadza's court and other places in the Dinde without a problem. Malawi's rulers failed to establish such a connection, so that even when they had money, as in 1963, the people of Nyachikadza could not purchase food because no trader could reach them.[61] There continues to be a wide discrepancy between the politics and mechanics of food supply.

There was, for example, no institution that could accurately assess the food needs of different communities in the country. The rule that a trader should get only that amount of food required by direct consumers in a given area presupposed a level of institutional knowledge that has never existed in Malawi.[62] Traders sometimes received more and at other times less than local demand.[63] What licensed dealers ultimately did with the food they could not sell to direct consumers was beyond the control of the state.[64] District commissioners and ADMARC were not in a position to monitor the daily activities of licensed traders after leaving the depot. Neither did the state have the power to enforce price controls in the countryside. When the demand for food was high, as in 1970, traders overcharged their clients, selling a 200-pound bag of maize for 55 shillings against the officially stipulated price of 40 shillings.[65] Peasants remember the activities of these traders with bitterness just as they also complain about the government and ADMARC.

Peasants recall with anger the rule that required ADMARC and its agents to sell maize in predetermined quantities. The stipulation made life easier for the sellers but not for poor villagers, who could not come up with enough money for the prescribed units.[66] But the official market during the Banda era frightened poor peasants on another ground. The ruling and only political organization in the country—the Malawi Congress Party (MCP)—used food markets to raise money, deploying the members of the notorious Malawi Young Pioneers (MYP) to extort money from poor villagers at food markets, in a process that reminds one of how the colonial state had used cotton markets to collect "hut" taxes. To buy (or sell) food (or anything) at the state-controlled markets, peasants had to show their current MCP membership card. The MYP were especially vigilant during the first half of the hungry season (September–December), when the party held its annual conventions. Expectant mothers had to buy cards for the unborn babies, and those without cards were physically abused and turned away from the market. Poor villagers do not forget this aspect of the Banda regime, although they may ignore its ineffectiveness as a provider of relief; on this score, Banda's government did no better or worse than its colonial predecessor or postcolonial successor.

Selling Food at Cost Price

Neither the colonial nor the postcolonial state in Malawi mounted meaningful relief programs in the valley, even though the country's African rulers have generally understood the politics of hunger better than their British predecessors. Unlike the British, Malawi's postcolonial rulers have not treated hunger as a mere administrative nuisance. Food shortages of all degrees have assumed political connotations for the new rulers. As president for life, Dr. Banda may not have been afraid of the country's hungry villagers; the heavens could not withdraw their mandate from him. But as a player in world politics, Banda did not want to represent himself as the "almighty" leader of a starving population. Even more concerned were his cronies, who needed to continually remind people of the benefits of independence. They recognized more clearly than the British the right of the people to expect assistance from the men and women they had voted into Parliament. Dr. Banda's letter, which provides the opening quotation of this chapter, implicitly accepts the notion that the state has a responsibility toward the hungry. The circular debates only the problem of division of responsibility between different layers of government and forms of hunger. Thus, in addition to engaging other levels of the state, postcolonial authorities have also worked closely with nongovernmental organizations (NGOs), whose influence has grown steadily after the election of a democratic government in 1994. NGOs most likely played a role in the creation of the Department of Relief and Disaster Preparedness. But, as recent events have shown, the mere creation of an agency has not strengthened the hand of the state as a provider of relief.

In Malawi, officials have tried to help hungry peasants by giving them free food, organizing food-for-work programs, and selling food at "cost price," or at purchase price plus transport and handling. Officials responded to most food crises in the country by selling food at cost price, under the assumption that villagers had money to buy food only if it was made available and rightly priced. By selling food at cost price, the state sought to correct such imperfections of the market as the absence of trading centers in some areas and, in general, the tendency for prices to skyrocket during the hungry season. The state was engaged in a contradictory drama, as it wanted peasants to survive on their own resources and to protect them against the free market. This contradiction showed itself in many ways, particularly the central government's attempts to shift responsibility over losses in the food trade to lower branches of the state.

After three decades during which they had acted as the only branch with responsibility to feed hungry peasants, officials in the capital (Zomba) began to engage other units of government more systematically in the early 1930s. Created in 1933 as part of indirect rule, Native Treasuries came to shoulder some of the cost of providing relief and were subsequently joined by the Native Development and Welfare Fund. But the greatest legal change came with the formation of statutory district councils under the Local Government (District Councils) Ordinance of 1953.[67] Thereafter, officials in Zomba tried to limit their responsibilities to the rare famine events, leaving the more recurrent njala in the hands of district councils and other levels of government.

Two things did, however, complicate this attempt at neat compartmentalization. First, no one knew the specific areas of responsibility between the central and local governments in Malawi,[68] and the problem has continued to this day. And even more complicated than the definitional ambiguity were the financial implications. Although always willing to assist their constituents, local officials lacked the human and financial resources for the kind of responsibilities Zomba imposed on them. Thus, each food crisis threw "the men on the spot"—district councils and district commissioners—in a "confrontation" with the men in the capital, the Ministry for Local Government, and the chief secretaries.

In 1952, for example, District Commissioner Lewis—a man who understood the local situation in Port Herald better than most of his contemporaries in the colonial administration—drew up a modest relief plan to help the victims of a bad flood in the Dinde Marshes. He wanted the Native Authority Treasury to purchase and sell at cost 60 tons of maize and 10 tons of rice and the central government to provide seeds (of sweet potatoes, beans, and maize) to the residents of the Dinde.[69] The provincial commissioner modified the request, proposing instead that the central government "bear half the loss, if any, on the seed account."[70] But the chief secretary's reply to the provincial commissioner's request was a blunt no: the government "is unable to agree to bear any part of such loss as may occur on the seed account." Not the central government, but the Native Authority Treasury and/or the Native Development and Welfare Fund should be prepared to bear any loss.[71]

The chief secretary reiterated the policy regarding the financial responsibilities of local governments in relief programs two years later in 1954. He announced that beginning 1 January 1955 the central government would formalize its long-standing practice of not subsidizing seasonal hunger. Money for relief in nonfamine operations would come as a component of the regular, local treasury funds:

> I am directed to inform you that as from 1st Jan, 1955 Famine Relief Funds will no longer be maintained as separate funds but will be embodied in the general reserves of N A or District Council treasuries ... local authorities should meet as far as possible the cost of any subsidization which may be necessary in cases of local food shortages which occur from time to time, but which are seldom true famines.[72]

But few local officials took note of the implications of this circular in 1954, when peasants had a bumper crop throughout the country. Administrators came to appreciate the significance of the directive four years later, in 1958, when a combination of drought throughout the country and bad floods in the valley led to severe shortages. District councils and Native Authorities found themselves unable to provide relief.

Thus, at a special meeting in April 1958, district commissioners called upon the central government to assume its responsibilities, arguing "it was neither right nor reasonable to expect local authorities to deal with" the severe, though nonfamine shortages.[73] The reply from the provincial commissioner was vague and open to all sorts of interpretations. It opened by reaffirming the "financial responsibility" of the Native Treasuries "as the agent of the central Government," and went on to absolve district councils of responsibility. But, the letter continued, the councils were free to provide financial assistance "should they wish to do so." The memo concluded by admitting that there was no real policy on the matter because no one could define the relationship between the central and local government in the country.[74] District councils came to assume a major role in relief operations after self-rule in 1961 mainly because the new rulers recognized better than their predecessors the political implications of rural hunger.

Thus, after making it clear that the crisis of 1962 was not a famine and did not therefore deserve free food from the central government, Dr. Banda, as secretary for natural resources and surveys, did make a concession. Financially strapped district councils could borrow money from the Ministry for Local Government, although such monies had to be returned immediately after the sales had been completed.[75] Councils would use the funds to purchase maize from the FMB and sell it to hungry villagers at cost.[76] That was how district councils without money could have engaged in the maize trade. In 1964 the Chikwawa District Council secured a loan of £1,250 to purchase maize for sale in the district's southern desert of hunger.[77] Records do not indicate whether the council repaid the loan.

Many district councils did not repay their loans, often for the same reasons that district commissioners had underlined in 1958. District councils were ill prepared for the kind of transactions the central government imposed on them. Their bookkeeping practices were unsatisfactory, and there were many cases of theft and embezzlement. Slowly, the councils lost much of their role in food distribution to the FMB and the almighty ADMARC, which effectively took over the government's functions as a seller of food at cost price. ADMARC also sold maize to villagers employed on the government's food-for-work programs.

Food-for-Work

Both colonial and postcolonial officials have treated hungry peasants as a pool of cheap labor for their pet projects. During the first two decades of the twentieth century, the British welcomed njala because it facilitated the recruitment of labor for European estates.[78] After the collapse of the plantation economy, hungry peasants provided labor for different projects that sought to transform the rural economy. In the food crises of 1941 and 1949, the government used its stocks of maize flour to entice peasants to excavate storm drains in Port Herald District.[79] Subsequently, officials employed hungry peasants in so-called development projects, ranging from road construction to the digging of latrines at schools and hospitals.

When it became clear that there would be a serious maize shortfall in many districts of the country, the government appointed Lt. Col. J. Holden as a special duties officer (in the Office of the President and Cabinet), with responsibility to assess the needs of the country and "advise on the kind of projects which may be introduced in the affected areas on which a fairly large number of the local people can be employed for them to earn money for food."[80] As a result of his consultation with government and MCP officials, Nsanje District (like many others in the country) qualified for a K4,000 (4,000 kwacha) relief fund, "whose sole purpose" was "to provide people with money to buy food."[81] Food was readily available at FMB markets.[82]

After securing the funds, officials spent several months trying to identify the project(s). The list ranged from such works as the digging of wells and latrines to the construction of kitchens at Nsanje Hospital to serve patients and their visiting relatives.[83] Then, after a subcommittee of the District Development Committee had decided on suitable projects, Col. J. Holden's committee deliberated for nearly a month before approving them and releasing the money—nothing more than K3,000.[84] Moreover, to give as many people as possible the opportunity to earn some money, no one was allowed to work more than one week.[85]

Information on how the program worked on the ground is sparse, but from the little circumstantial evidence there is, the operation does not appear to have made much of a difference. It lasted for only the month of February 1971, and with only K3,000 at their disposal, officials employed fewer people than is suggested by the amount of ink that went into its preparation. The first group of workers got their pay around February 15, when the FMB also reopened its maize markets.[86] Many villagers who wanted to work did not get the opportunity to do so. They confronted the administration in early March, although, in a typical ruling-class representation of the world, the official report simply condemned the poor as people who wanted to get money for nothing:

> The 3,000 Kwacha which the Government has provided to be used on Relief Projects (RP) created by the DDC [District Development Committee] appear to cause some confusion in the villages . . . Just for instance, yesterday, March the 5th, 1971, some 600 people, men and women all from Chief Malemia's area, gathered at my Office demanding free pay from the Government and through Chief Malemia and his village Headmen, I managed to convince them to go away from the Office. Quietly, they moved from the Office to their respective villages with their baskets in their hands.[87]

There was nothing in the experiences of this hungry "mob" that might have taught them about free money from the government; all they wanted was work, which the state of Malawi could not provide.

Njala also exposed the tensions among the ruling elite. The Ministry of Local Government did not trust the integrity of the district council, and the two bodies wrangled over a *potential* overdraft of K15 for three months![88] The impoverished central and local branches of government in Malawi appear to have worked well together only when administering a project funded by outsiders, as when they distributed free food in 1970.

Free Food

Free food distributions were rare because they required exceptionally disastrous and easily documentable circumstances. Victims of the more common but less visible droughts did not usually get free food from the government, as the preceding discussion of the January–April 1970 drought illustrates. The people who got the most out of the government's stingy relief projects were victims of bad floods, although the well-documented relief program of 1970 in Nsanje District was atypical, as it engaged international organizations.

The project, which ran from January to May 1970, was anything but the one-person—usually the district commissioner or agricultural officer—operation of the colonial era. The undertaking mobilized the resources of both the state and NGOs. There was a District Operations Committee, headed by the district commissioner and including such officials as the district's officer-in-charge (police), chairman of the MCP, and the district's representatives in Parliament. Then there was the Regional Operations Committee, chaired by the regional minister, G. C. Chakuamba, and consisting of the senior assistant commissioner of police for the Southern Region; officials from the FMB, MYP, Ministry of Works and Supplies, and Ministry of Health and Community Development; and most importantly, the personnel of the Christian Services Committee (CSC) and the Red Cross.[89] Not only Malawi's, but also the resources of the international community were involved in this politically charged undertaking.

The operations began on 5 January 1970 and covered two distinct areas. In the first, which lay between Bangula and Nsanje, the floods affected some 80 families (approximately 500 persons). They received food from the District Operations Committee between 5 and 9 January.[90] The second and larger area coincided with the Dinde Marsh from Nsanje in the north to the Malawi-Mozambique border in the south. Operating under the authority of the district commissioner and the officer-in-charge, a CSC team of four people (sometimes increased to eight) was responsible for transporting food from Nsanje Township and distributing it to the inhabitants of the marshes.[91] The first round of operations ran from 10 to 23 January, and the second from 28 February to early May. Villagers on or near the Tchiri River received their rations from Chief Nyachikadza's court, while those living away from the Tchiri River got theirs along the road between Nsanje and Marka. In all, the relief effort served about 9,000 people.[92]

It is impossible to establish the amount of food, clothing, and other goods that were distributed during the first round of operations between 10 and 23 January. There is, however, some information on the items peasants received during the second series of relief operations from 24 February to 2 May in the Dinde. About 138 tons of flour, rice, maize, oats, beans, and dried milk were distributed during this period.[93] The Red Cross and the CSC provided most of these supplies. The CSC had received some of the food from the Church World Service in the United States[94] and some of its money from Christian organizations in Malawi, the World Council of Churches, and Caritas (a Roman Catholic organization).[95]

This was without doubt the most generous and most comprehensive flood relief ever undertaken in the valley. Moreover, unlike the aid packages of the colonial era, which included only maize or maize flour, this relief program featured many other food items, such as salt, sugar, and dry milk. There was also a wide assortment of nonfood items, such as plates, blankets, quilts, trousers, shirts, dresses, and other clothing.[96] Finally, there was a liberal seed package that included 120 200-pound bags of seed maize.[97] Gone indeed were the days when men like District Commissioner Lewis sometimes fought a losing battle to convince their superiors of the need for seed subsidies.[98] The involvement of international organizations made the signal difference. Malawi's rulers could not run such an operation on their own.

Impact of State Intervention

British officials were both right and wrong to praise their relief programs.[99] Their relief projects helped peasants to the extent that they made food available on the market. Peasants could purchase food in remote places and, at times, at prices lower than the prevailing free-market rates. True, there were times when the central government overcharged hungry villagers, who would consequently boycott official markets.[100] But there were also times when the state sold its stocks at lower prices than those charged by independent traders. Moreover, government sales sometimes forced merchants to lower their prices, as was the case in 1958. At the beginning of January of that year, African businessmen at Nsanje market were charging up to £3 10s. for a 200-pound bag of maize. Then the district council and the Agricultural Produce and Marketing Board (APMB)—the predecessor to the FMB—saturated the market with large quantities of maize and forced prices to tumble.[101] Seven years later, in 1965, the Chikwawa District Council reacted to soaring prices by lowering the price of a 200 pound bag of maize to £1 18s. Private traders, who had been charging between two and three pounds, were forced to either drop their prices or withdraw from the area.[102] Officials were right to highlight this aspect of state intervention in the fight against hunger. But they were wrong in suggesting that state programs significantly improved the condition of those without money or too weak to work for money. Free food distributions were rare, and when they did come, they did so in amounts too small and too late to save people from starvation.

Strapped for cash, government officials in Malawi often used patently unreasonable measures to determine who deserved state aid.[103] In 1970, for example, the inhabitants of the southern Chikwawa and northern Nsanje districts received nothing simply because they lived in a cotton-growing zone.[104] It did not matter to government officials whether one actually grew cotton or not; all they wanted was to reduce the number of candidates for their bounty. Then, in contrast to the international operation of 1970, the government gave assistance to only 831 persons (not households) out of the 9,000 victims of another bad flood in the Dinde Marsh in 1971.[105] Moreover, such aid was often too little and came too late to make a real difference. The delays resulted from financial and organizational constraints. In particular, the government did not maintain a permanent organ to deal with emergency aid prior to the late 1990s. It responded to each calamity on an ad hoc basis. Thus, it took officials a whole year to organize relief for the victims of the drought of January and February 1970. Recipients of government aid in 1958 received food after they had already started harvesting their new crops.[106] Similarly, in 1971, the state came to the rescue of the "lucky" 831 inhabitants of the Dinde seven months after the floods had subsided and after some villagers had harvested at least one crop and forgotten about the disaster.[107] Officials in Malawi lacked the resources or the will to mount meaningful relief programs, as European planters complained again and again during the first three decades of colonial rule in the country.[108]

Assessing the significance of the "free" maize distributions of 1958, the administrator for Chikwawa asserted, "When it came down to the individual the actual amount of maize received was very small."[109] His counterpart in Nsanje agreed, saying that the maize distributions "by the village headmen [were] such that in many cases the old and the young, who were able to work, received similar quantities, *often only sufficient for one meal, so that not much true relief was felt.*"[110] Writing about the 1949 crisis, a distinguished district commissioner for Port Herald made the case for the irrelevance of state relief very sharply when he told his superiors in Zomba,

> Finally the ordinary villager, on whom alone the burden of hunger has fallen, is deserving of the utmost praise not only in the way *in which he has gone forth to fend for himself instead of falling back for help on what would have been an extremely embarrassed Government*, but also for the incredible amount of manual work of which he has shown himself capable, often in the most trying conditions.[111]

Even if they had merely wanted handouts, as some officials were fond of fantasizing, peasants in Malawi could not become dependent on the state for survival.[112] As in Nigeria,[113] the British in Malawi did not create a state upon which a hungry person could rely; Banda did not create such a state, and the post-Banda regime has not either, as the food deficits of 2001–2 showed. During much of the twentieth century, peasants in Malawi conquered famine with their own resources, including old survival strategies.

PEASANTS PREVENT NJALA FROM BECOMING CHAOLA

Many desperate people are reportedly eating maize husks and wild roots.[114]

Vast distances have been covered on foot or by canoe in the search for food and many and varied were the methods employed in obtaining it; direct purchase, barter for livestock, poultry, earthenware and even firewood, the hoeing of others [*sic*] gardens, living on luckier relatives and friends, and theft, have all played their part in the keeping of the population alive.[115]

Wild foods also played a very large part, and it is a pity that time did not allow for an exhausitive [*sic*] enquiry to be made into their wide variety, and a complete catalogue of them listed; although many are eaten every year, others such as the root of the "Nyezi" three [*sic*] which is made into a kind of mild beer, only the older people could remember being used before.[116]

Many of the people, old and young, were away working for their food.[117]

Fish has played a large part in this search; literally thousands would gather at Massenjere market on a Monday to exchange it for food brought down from the hills, and the unlucky ones would more often than not go up into the hills with it village to village in search for maize.[118]

Like any social phenomenon, seasonal hunger is part of time's arrow; it occurs in irreversible time. And there are many elements that buttress the historical character of njala in the valley. The environment that villagers exploit during the njala season has changed. Some plants have disappeared, and the Tchiri River today maintains very different water levels than it did in the 1920s. One can also cite several developments that have aggravated the problem of food availability in some areas. The emergence of a new food market has led some villagers to dispose of part of the food they and their families needed to survive.[119] The subsequent rise of cotton as a cash crop diverted attention of many labor-deficient households from their food crops. Finally, the cattle economy has posed a great challenge to certain forms of food production in the southern portion of the valley. These and other transformations have clearly affected people's experiences of njala. Njala *does* have a history.

Although significant, these shifts have not, however, altered the nature of njala in two ways. First, it is impossible to say whether njala has become more or less severe in the communities affected by the above transformations or in the Tchiri Valley as a unit. While some pressures have undoubtedly exaggerated the problem of food availability, others have ameliorated it. Poor peasants can engage in new income-generating activities, have access to many more markets where they can buy food, and, at certain moments, can get some food assistance. As a lived experience, njala has not moved in one particular direction, as the students of the crisis literature would have us believe. Second and more importantly, njala has not lost its fundamental character as a recurrent event. The failure of the state to provide meaningful relief has guaranteed the persistence of old survival strategies, including those that underwrite the annual return of njala among the village poor. None of the changes of the past 150 years have altered the fact that, like their ancestors, today's poor peasants can expect njala every year of their lives. Njala remains an orderly event of time's cycle.

Exploiting the Natural Environment

Broader economic and ecological shifts have reshaped the natural environment and some methods of exploiting it, but nothing has ended rural reliance on the rules of sharing the gifts of nature during the hungry season. As in the past, peasants today still look to the dambo during the first half of the hungry season, although some of these marshes are not in exactly the same condition as they were in the past. The western banks of the Tchiri River between the Mwanza River in the north and Mkombedzi-wa-fodya River in the south provide one example of a thoroughly new ecosystem. Once famous for its palm-wine trees and salt deposits,[120] this dambo has since the mid-1960s been drained and transformed into the huge Nchalo Sugar Estate. Villagers who still need the dambo to cope with njala have to go beyond the Sugar Estate, where, starting about August, they can still make salt, fish, and collect *mphambadza, ntchenjezi,* and nyika water-lily bulbs.

Nyika, ntchenjezi, and mphambadza belong to the same family of water roots, and villagers differentiate them according to several criteria. They say mphambadza is the smallest of the three and ranks lowest as a hunger reliever because it is the least available. Tastewise, mphambadza stands between the generally bitter nyika and the palatable ntchenjezi. It takes a lot of expertise to turn the prickly-skinned ntchenjezi into flour for making nsima, as Mrs. Tambo's account tries to capture:

> In times of hunger we used to go to Chisagadi River, when it was very low, in order to harvest ntchenjezi. We pounded ntchenjezi in a mortar, and after that we would grind it and used [the resulting flour] to make nsima. We also used it to make soft porridge for our children. The nsima would be really tasty. Ntchenjezi are similar to nyika except that they have a thorny skin. We scooped [from the ground] with *likombe* spoons and carried them to the village in large baskets. As we did this, the men would be busy killing fish with spears. There was an abundance of fish in those days. We would eat ntchenjezi with the fish killed by the men. We ate this with our children.[121]

But, as Mrs. Tambo also noted, people did not rely on ntchenjezi alone; they also looked to the more abundant nyika.[122]

Nyika collectors, who were usually women, started to forage in the marshes as early as August. The foraging would reach a peak at the height of the dry season in October, when women would spend their afternoons digging and transporting the tubers in a scenario brightly captured by District Commissioner P. M. Lewis in 1949:

> If a song of praise is to be raised for the way in which the people have got through this trying year, then it must be in favour of the water-lily bulb without which famine in its worst forms would undoubtedly have been seen; whole communities have lived on this root without any other form of food at all for weeks at a time, and the long string of men, women and children returning from the river, often from distant villages, with heavily laden baskets was reminiscent of the cotton markets at the height of the season.[123]

The more enterprising males organized nyika-collecting expeditions to Guwa in Mozambique, where they found almost limitless supplies of nyika. After several days of collecting, the men would return to Malawi with their canoes fully loaded with the tubers. Children would celebrate as their mothers prepared the roots into a meal. Some women boiled the roots, some roasted them, and others pounded them into flour for making nsima.[124] Many families lived on these roots until January, when the floods ended this form of food collecting in the marshes.[125] The second half of the njala season had started, and peasants would now look more to the resources of the mphala drylands.

The mphala drylands were not completely devoid of useful plants even during the dry season. There were important fruits like mangoes that the people of the valley floor began eating as early as October and finished off earlier than their counterparts in the local hills like Chididi or the Tchiri Highlands, where the fruits matured much later in the season. Villagers also supplemented their dwindling supplies of domesticated foods with wild fruits like *masau, bwemba* tamarinds, *matondo* African plums, and *ntheme* oranges.[126] Some fruits, like masau, never survived the dry season, but others took peasants well into the rainy season, which brings a wide range of early-maturing wild plants.

One group of these early-maturing plants of the bush consisted of millets and sorghums that officials sometimes referred to as "grass seeds."[127] Better known among these were *gugu, kapepe, mphunga,* and *khundi.*[128] Some of these grass seeds became available on the valley floor as early as January, and villagers from the hills would come down to collect them.[129] The seeds were popular because, in addition to their early-maturing qualities, they were so close to their domesticated cousins in structure and taste that villagers faced few difficulties preparing or digesting them. Older women are correct when they blame the changed vegetation for some of the misery they now bear during the hungry season. The valley has lost so much of its original vegetation that many villagers of the younger generation interviewed for this book did not know much about the grass seeds that embellish the written accounts of earlier food deficits.[130] They also know less about the roots from the mphala drylands that once sustained their ancestors during the wet season.

A number of roots on the mphala drylands helped to ease hunger during the wet season. Besides the roots of banana trees (*makhuli-a-nthochi* or *zibowa-za-nthochi*), hungry villagers dug up such tubers as *minyanya, mpama* wild yam, and *nyenzi* or *nyenza*.[131] These roots were generally more available on the hills than on the valley floor.[132] Villagers from the valley floor traveled to the hills to get the roots that women subsequently prepared in more or less the same way as the nyika and the ntchenjezi from the marshes. Women also made sweet beer or *thobwa* with some of the roots, particularly the nyenzi.[133] According to Mrs. Chasasa Fole:

> In the past we used nyenza roots to make sweet beer. We dug the roots, discarded bitter ones, and searched for sweet ones. When we found syrupy ones, we tried to get as many of them as possible. We would then peel off the skins, pound them in a mortar, and squeeze out any impurities ... Then we would take a large pot and put it on fire. When the water [in the pot] started boiling, we dropped the [pounded] nyenza into the pot. We stirred it when it began to boil. Those who had some flour [made from cereals] would at this point make a small amount of porridge to drop into the large pot. [Then] the beer would be ready for people to drink.[134]

Thobwa sometimes replaced regular meals in times of acute shortage. Well-to-do villagers also used thobwa to entertain their visitors, including those who had come to beg or work for food under the practice the Mang'anja call as *kusuma*.

The Social Impact

Whereas the market engages buyers and sellers as equals, kusuma implies a relationship of temporary dependency. People did kusuma when they got free food from relatives and friends or when they received provisions in return for work from nonrelatives. Parties engaged in this kind of relationship were typically located in different but often complementary ecological zones. Every year kusuma renewed the connections between the region's deserts of hunger and oases of plenty. Peasants from the deserts of hunger turn to friends and relatives in the Kirk Range and Thyolo Escarpment, and an unusually serious drought would send every munda cultivator, including those from the hills, to the Dabanyi and Dinde Marshes. There they would plant and work for sweet potatoes,[135] and, in so doing, announce the ability of the dambo to save the victims of drought:

Were it not for the large acreage of madimba which is available to the south
of Port Herald then it would have gone badly for those people who were so
unfortunate as to lose much of their mphala land crops.[136]

But this kind of movement would be reversed in the event of a bad flood,
when the inhabitants of the marshes would turn, for shelter and food, to
munda cultivators within and beyond the Tchiri Valley.

During a serious food shortage, kusuma took hungry villagers to regions
like the Tchiri Highlands as well as Mozambique. They would work in the
gardens of these strangers for weeks and even months before receiving their
compensation in food:

> You do kusuma when you embark on a long journey to procure food. You
> would visit a distant place and spend up to a month looking for food. You
> would not purchase the food with money, but you would work in someone
> else's garden, and you would not come back to your village until you have
> procured some provisions. That is the food you would take home.[137]

Some people never returned to their villages and became permanent immigrants in those far-flung places. Many individual and family migrations that
punctuate the history of all major food deficits started as kusuma trips.[138] At
the height of these crises, it was not easy to distinguish between those people
who left the region permanently and those who went away on temporary
basis.[139]

Villagers highlight yet another tension in kusuma. One could not always
tell whether the food one received was a gift or compensation for work. This
ambiguity comes clearly in the stories about women who tried to get sweet
potatoes from friends and relatives at harvest time. The women received
one bag or basket of potatoes after "assisting" their hosts in harvesting the
entire crop. Those who gave food in a kusuma relationship got free labor and
invested in a future return at the same time. Peasant generosity was as complicated as any other activity, including the sale of their labor and goods.

To get cereals for nsima, villagers sold such items as cotton, cattle, fish,
goats, pigs, chicken, mangoes, baskets, mats, spears, and *khasu* hoes.[140] But
the greatest asset of the poor was their labor power. Some parents and wives
procured food with remittances from their sons and husbands working outside
Malawi and within the country for such employers as the Nchalo Sugar Estate
and Factory. Some poor peasants worked for other villagers as musicians or
cattle herders. But the most common work was in the cotton fields.

Initially, hungry peasants worked on European-owned cotton estates, but
after the collapse of the settler enterprise in the late 1920s, many labored for
the region's rich peasants, known as *zunde* holders. Located mostly in the
Dinde and Dabanyi Marshes, large zunde cotton fields disappeared after the

Bomani floods of 1939. Thereafter, poor villagers looking for local employment opportunities turned to Chikwawa District, where cotton growers of every category needed more labor than their own households could provide. The demand for extra-household labor was especially high among growers who sprayed their cotton with pesticides and who raised the cash crop in separate fields from food crops. These growers became the main employers of the village poor.

The evidence linking cotton agriculture and seasonal hunger is both direct and indirect. Like other employers, cotton growers easily procured labor during the hungry months when work in the cotton fields consumed nearly 50 percent of a growing season's hired labor hours. Weeding in January took up about a third of these hired labor hours.[141] One farmer in 1996 had no difficulty getting twenty casual workers to weed his cotton,[142] as njala drove poor villagers to his farm. But the number of job seekers would drop dramatically toward the end of the hungry season in March, causing a severe labor shortage during the cotton-harvesting period around May.[143] Many cotton growers found themselves unable to harvest their crop.

In an attempt to solve the seasonal shortfall, European farmers during the first three decades of the twentieth century lobbied hard for legislation to bond their workers.[144] Rich African cotton growers did not get such support from the colonial government. But in the 1970s, the postcolonial regime encouraged the MYP to work for rich peasants in order to ensure the success of the Shire Valley Agricultural Development Project. It seems, however, that the impact of this strategy was limited. The MYP were too few to cover the needs of all growers in the area. Hunger was a more dependable ally of the rich.

Government officials were right when they denounced cotton for diverting labor from food production.[145] But not all understood the differential impact of the practice. It was not the cotton of poor people that benefited from the diversion of their labor; the labor that left poor people's food crops ended up in the cotton fields of the rich. But that is not the whole story. Njala also complicates the relations between the poor and rich.

Njala exposes the Janus face of the rural rich. Every year it makes them appreciate their wealth, as hungry villagers, including those who do not normally respect authority, bend on their knees for money or food. But, precisely because it drives the poor so low, njala creates a state of insecurity for the rich as well. In particular, hunger and humiliation make the poor appreciate that their poverty is caused by the wealth of their neighbors. The rich are what they are not only because they have access to good land and political favors, but also because they exploit the labor and other resources of the poor. Peasants express this understanding when they define the rich as, among other things, those who employ powerful *ntholera* magic to entice poor people's food into their granaries.[146] Villagers understand their misery—as well as their joys—as products of their society, so that with the cooperation of their headpersons, the hungry often harassed the rich. They would, for example, burn the houses and granaries of the rich, and drive them out of the village. Immigrants and the wealthy known for their meanness were especially vulnerable to such acts of violence.[147] Njala also imposes serious strains on the relations among the poor themselves.

Njala brings to a halt many rituals that unite the community and allow villagers to publicly enjoy good life. There is no food for such celebrations, and the community loses some of its energy, as Audrey Richards already found among the Bemba in the 1930s:

> There is little or no dancing in the hunger months, partly owing to the absence of beer. Few journeys are planned, and the children tend to play listlessly. Usually more good-tempered than the average English baby, they whimper at the slightest provocation.[148]

Richards understood the implications of seasonal hunger better than some British officials in Malawi, whose concern for law and order led them to overstate the "good" effects of njala:

> There being great scarcity of food in the District there was very little beer making and consequently less trouble than there would have been had there been much beer, practically no cases of adultery and assault were brought before the Courts.[149]

The absence of sex offenses, prosecutable under colonial marriage laws, did not mean there were no other offenses. Njala reduced some kinds of "sins" while raising the incidence of other types of violence, like those targeted against elders.

Hungry elders also became victims of internal violence and harassment. Njala weakens the position of the elders, who, although respected as custodians of agricultural expertise, do not contribute anything to the ongoing struggles against hunger. Elders become a burden, and a dangerous burden, especially when children die, as they frequently do at this time of year.[150] Instead of producing food, elders "eat" future producers; they are mfiti witches, who do not deserve to live. This dark and ugly side of the peasant world becomes especially obvious when economic and/or environmental distress exacerbate njala, as was the case during the Great Depression of the early 1930s. In a powerful reminder of the slave raids, elderly men and women of the Great Depression lost the protection of their children, wandering between Malawi and Mozambique in search for shelter and food.[151] Economic distress complicated the kusuma process for these elders.

Through kusuma and other practices, njala strengthens hungry villagers' ties to relatives, friends, and rich peasants in distant places, while imposing serious strains on relations within the community. Njala brings to the surface intracommunity tensions that rarely come to the surface in times of plenty, against the backdrop of a sharp discrepancy between heavy agricultural work and low caloric intake. Many families survive on one instead of two meals a day; a few do without eating for days on end.[152] Moreover, the meals one often gets these days are not normal. Peasants survive on sweet potatoes and the products of the bush like nyika as a substitute for the nsima stiff porridge—made from maize, millet, or sorghum. In places like the marshes, villagers would live on nothing but fish. Ideal meals become rare during the hungry season, which also challenges the principles and practices of good neighborliness.

As njala deepens during the second half of the growing season, many villagers find it difficult to share with their neighbors food procured from distant places or the market. Village historians remember the njala of the past as a time when many chidyerano-eating groups collapsed (see chapter 7). Hungry villagers took extraordinary measures to hide from their neighbors the little food they procured through kusuma or collecting in distant places. They ate such food at night as members of a single household. Gossip about these nocturnal meals would persuade other members of the eating group to respond in kind, so that the season of plenty found many chidyerano groups broken up or at the point of doing so.

Njala is thus similar to chaola in that it unifies the household against the wider group, weakening the spirit of the golden-age theory. But, unlike chaola, njala does not subvert the rules of sharing or generalize the application of the hierarchical rules of the alternative vision to every kind of food. Njala retains the struggle for survival within the social world, keeping in place the fundamentals of people's ties with one another in relation to food. Njala is a conservative force in other ways. It does not freeze history to become the basis of a new epoch. Peasants go through the agonies of njala believing good times are around the corner. Njala recycles history while giving substance and meaning to the golden-age theory's present as an era of persistent hunger and umbombo meanness. This year's njala season creates next year's.

The lack of calories limits the amount of work the poor can do in their own gardens, and many expend their labor away from their fields, scavenging the forests and working for the rich for food and money. Such villagers become the first to consume their crops long before the latter reach maturity. They dig out the young sweet potatoes and harvest unripe maize, millet, or sorghum to stave off starvation. They do not get the benefit of fully mature crops. Finally, they also tend to sell their foodstuffs at harvest time, when prices are low, and would be the first to turn to the same markets when prices are high. The upshot of all these practices is that they enter the hungry season early, which compromises their ability to open and take care of their fields;[153] every hungry season guarantees the return of another. Every year the poor prevent chaola through the same social processes that bring them into trouble in the first place. The Tchiri Valley successfully defeated chaola in the last seven decades of the twentieth century by perpetuating njala. Few other social processes are as predictable as njala.

CONCLUSION

To assert that njala belongs to the domain of time's cycle is not to remove it from history. Like everything else, njala does have a history, making one njala season different from another. Growers who reduced food to increase their cotton faced a different kind of njala than the one they had experienced before cotton (see chapter 6). Food markets have also changed rural experiences of njala. On the one hand, there are peasants who have increased their vulnerability to njala because they sell their foodstuffs cheaply at harvest, and on the other, there are villagers who survive njala more easily today because they can buy food on the market. As in other parts of contemporary Africa, in the valley njala is the scourge of the village poor; rich peasants do not know hunger—on the contrary, njala has become bonanza for the rich. Finally, state intervention has transformed rural experiences of njala in multiple ways, sometimes exacerbating and at other times moderating its impact. The njala of today cannot but be different from that of yesterday. Njala can provide a window on the evolving structures of governments, markets, and social inequality.

However, because none of the above forces has broken the cycle of the season, particularly the fact that villagers can only have one harvest per year, and because the poor survive njala only by reproducing it, this form of hunger remains a perfectly intelligible and expected event. It cannot rise to the status of an irreversible episode like chaola famine. Villagers do not give njala a proper name; it does not deserve one. Africanists can, for once, boast of their ability to predict social events. They can foretell the coming and going of njala with a degree of precision rarely enjoyed by some members of the scientific community. It is more difficult to end njala than to end chaola.

Breaking the njala cycle would require a radical transformation in existing technological and social relations. One way to consign njala to the dustbin of history is to empower the poor so that they can stop looking for food when they have to work their fields. Another is to restructure the technologies of food production and storage in such a way that villagers can have more than one harvest in a calendar year and can store their food for a longer period than they can presently (see chapter 7). Either method would entail a fundamental reorganization of peasant-state relations. In the absence of such a restructuring, njala will continue to sap the energies of poor peasants every year, with the state offering nothing more than temporary and inadequate fixes—the common thread weaving through the histories of the colonial, Banda, and Muluzi regimes in Malawi. After selling its maize reserves in a controversial move, the Muluzi government pleaded poverty when asked by donors to fund a survey on the extent of hunger in the country.[154] But a few weeks later, the same government found enough money to repair its television station.[155] Despite its loud rhetoric about poverty alleviation, the Muluzi government has had the same kind of priorities as its predecessors. There is always money for television stations and cotton projects (see chapter 5) but nothing for recurrent njala.

Seasonal hunger creates future disasters in the image of the present. As Richards and many others have observed, hungry people are, by definition, ineffective workers.[156] Moreover, they spend their diminished capacities for work away from their own fields at a crucial moment in the agricultural cycle,[157] when they should be weeding their gardens and replanting where crops have failed (see chapter 6). As one district commissioner bemoaned in 1958: "The food shortage has effected [*sic*] the strength of the people in weeding and a number of garden owners have been absent looking and working for food."[158] Full of weeds, the gardens of the poor can only yield poor crops, and this in turn ensures another bad harvest.

III

THE QUIET DAYS BEHIND THE NOISY TRANSITIONS

The great transitions that have preoccupied the attention of historians consist of nothing but a string of time units, including the day. Any transition requires daily processes to become time. And while some daily routines, like growing cotton and food, are season-specific, others are supraseasonal. Eating is one such habit. And historians have avoided these daily routines for good reason. Like eating, work in the field is a repetitive and predictable process. Peasants know in advance how they are going to dig the soil, who will prepare the meal, and with whom they will eat. The day of the food system is a highly structured domain. But, as the following chapters will show, the enemies of order are as many as its allies. One cannot, in particular, separate order from disorder. In their gardens, villagers create at one and the same time deserts of hunger and oases of plenty; they both assume and avoid risk. And every meal, including chidyerano, acts both as a feast and as famine, supporting those with and those without interest in the status quo. The question, therefore, is not whether the food system can or did change. One can take change for granted. In any age, tradition-respecting peasants are also potential rebels. The question is whether, or to what extent, rebels can transform the disorder of today into the order of tomorrow. And questions oblige one to insert the food system into its wider field. But one cannot limit this context to the so-called transition from the precapitalist to the capitalist epoch. The peasant world is too rich to be squeezed into only one straitjacket. The food system has changed along other trajectories.

5

IN THE LONG SHADOWS
OF COTTON, 1860–2002

The single most important economic factor in our lives was the price of cotton, which, during my boyhood, varied from a low of five cents a pound to a high of almost thirty cents. Unlike all the other crops we grew, however, there was always a cash market at the prevailing price.[1]

And after selling a bag its [*sic*] *never enough for buying a cloth or taxation but sweets* ... We want to be rich, therefore marketing system should be improved and price raised. Agricultural Department is doing excellent work to improve our methods of farming; we only hated it because of ridges. *It is now F.M.B. drawing back our progress, we want richness.*[2]

Up to now too much time has been spent trying to raise the productivity of the mass of the farmers. There is no telling whether this work has had any measurable effect. What I do know is that the larger farmers, and in particular the farms of my brother Ministers, have not been receiving the attention they require.[3]

INTRODUCTION

It may be premature at this point to pass judgment on the potential effect of the grow-more-cotton campaign the Malawi government launched in the valley in January 2002, but if history is any guide, this drive, too, will not alter long-term trends in output.[4] The state had embarked on similar campaigns in the past. During the entire decade from 1968 to 1978, it invested scarce financial resources into the SVADP (or "the Project"), whose principal mission was to raise productivity, increase the number of cotton (*thonje*) growers, and create specialists who did nothing but grow cotton.[5] The Project did not accomplish any of these objectives for many reasons, the most important of which was the gap between producer prices and the cost of production.

When villagers complain about high costs of production, they have in mind not only the money spent on wages, sprayers, and pesticides, but also the invisible and often incalculable cost of family labor. Cotton is an expensive enterprise in terms of the daily routines of the wet season, when the cash crop's labor demands collide with those of the food economy against the backdrop of recurrent njala. The discrepancy between its demands and rewards go a long way to explain, on the one hand, peasants' failure to acquire or effectively apply new technology, and on the other, their continued reliance on the labor of fellow villagers and their own involvement in multiple activities such as food production, cattle keeping, fishing, and wage employment. There are no cotton specialists in the valley today because nearly all growers need to grow food to survive, while others frequently need money from others sectors of the economy to subsidize cotton production. Among some producers, cotton has become parasitic on other industries. That villagers still grow cotton testifies to the cash crop's inherent strengths as well as the lack of alternatives. Thus, while for the state cotton is the only meaningful economic enterprise in the valley, for peasants the cash crop does not have a life of its own apart from other economic processes of the region. One cannot understand the history of cotton without an appreciation of the history of other activities within both the food and nonfood sectors of the economy.[6]

THE BROADER ECONOMIC CONTEXT

In the Lower Tchiri Valley, the nonfood sector entered the twentieth century as a much smaller segment of the rural economy than it had been in the 1860s. The iron, cloth, and salt industries—three key branches of the old nonagricultural sector—had collapsed. But this was not all. The region had also lost the ivory and sesame trades, which had inserted the region into the expanding international market during the last three decades of the nineteenth century.[7] In the larger scheme of things, therefore, the rise of cotton as a cash crop at the beginning of the twentieth century did not represent an expansion in terms of the region's list of economic activities; cotton merely replaced one of the lost branches, but with the particularity that it absorbed more human and natural resources than any of the old branches of production.[8] Cotton effectively plunged the valley into a monoculture—to the pleasure of British officials, who were always concerned with exports. But neither the British nor their subjects expected what came after the Bomani floods of 1939.

The floods initiated a new era in the region's economic and agricultural history. The Tchiri River remained so consistently high that peasants could no longer raise cotton in the fertile Dabanyi and Dinde Marshes, as some parts never rose above the floodwaters, while others emerged too late in the season to sustain the slow-maturing cotton. Peasants lost their best lands for cotton (and food) production, forcing British officials into a frantic search for a plan to raise productivity on the rain-dependent mphala drylands. But the high-handed nature of some of these attempts, particularly the use of force, contributed to the collapse of the cotton economy in Nsanje (Lower Shire or Port Herald) District outside the northwestern or Mbenje subchiefdom. Once the center of cotton agriculture in the whole country, Nsanje District entered the era of political independence in the mid-1960s without cotton producers. Subsequent official attempts to promote cotton in the region focused on the northern or Chikwawa district, which displaced Nsanje as the region's economic and demographic center of gravity. Moreover, the fact that Chikwawa was able to make this transition without significantly altering its economic structure amplified its differences with Nsanje. The end of cotton agriculture in Nsanje forced peasants to restructure the district's economy.

With little or no state support, peasants began in the 1940s to expand the nonfood sector, adding new branches of production and revitalizing old ones. The result was a dramatic increase in the region's cattle population, a resurgence of male labor migration, and an invigorated fishing industry. By the early 1980s, this segment generated about 84 percent (about K10 million) of the valley's annual income outside the food sector, while cotton's contribution had shrunk to a mere 16 percent (K2 million).[9]

It is not necessary or possible to give a detailed account of every branch of the nonfood sector; each branch is important enough to deserve its own study. The following outline of aspects of wage employment and the cattle industry seeks to serve three purposes. First, it highlights the fact that the story of cotton is only one among many important stories of economic activity in the valley. Second, it seeks to show that despite their differences, both cattle keeping and wage labor are similar to cotton in their ambiguous impact on food security. Like cotton, they have both undermined food production *and* increased villagers' ability to procure food from the market. The third and final purpose of the outline is to provide a background to the discussion of cotton's relationship with wage labor, its competitor and ally.

Table 5.1.
Malawi Kwacha to U.S. Dollar, 1975–2004 (approximate)

Year	1975	1980	1985	1990	1995	2000	2004
1US$	1.0	0.80	1.7	2.7	15	55	105

Notes: The kwacha was introduced in 1971 as half the British pound. Before this date, all measurements were in British sterling. Rates for all years are based on my recollections, except for those for 1985 and 1990, which are taken from http://www.photius.com/wfb1991/malawi/malawi_economy.html.

An important shift in the relative importance of cotton and wage labor occurred in the 1940s. After losing river-fed or dimba cotton in the aftermath of the Bomani floods of 1939, the valley joined other areas of Malawi as a labor reserve, so that by the late 1970s, 44 percent of the region's income outside the food sector came from wage laborers within the valley, in other regions of Malawi, and in foreign countries. The data suggest there was a significant change in the ratio between those who worked in foreign countries and in Malawi. Prior to the mid-1970s, most wage seekers from the valley headed for foreign destinations; in 1973–74, for example, 64.3 percent of the emigrants worked in foreign countries (44.5 percent in South Africa, 19.8 percent in Zimbabwe, and the remaining 1 percent in other foreign countries).[10] But this figure had dropped to a mere 12 percent by the early 1980s, when most wage earners worked within the country.[11]

Like most quantitative data in this book, the above figures should be treated with caution; they are only useful as indicators of broad trends for which there are other kinds of evidence. Qualitative evidence in this case does confirm the central message of the statistical data, though the swing in emigration patterns was probably not as sharp as the figures would make it. The Tchiri Valley's position as a labor market did alter in the 1970s, in response to both long- and short-term pressures in the region and the country. Most dramatic among the short-term factors was the 1974 decision by the Malawi government to ban all labor emigration to South Africa, following an airplane crash that killed 74 Malawians returning home from Johannesburg.[12] But even more important—and what one might suspect was the real motive behind the ban—were long-term transformations in the Malawi economy. The accident took place at a time when the African political elite, under Dr. Banda's leadership, was building the tobacco estate industry.[13] Tobacco farmers in the southern and central regions of the country also needed large numbers of low-paid workers while, within the valley itself, the SVADP and the Sugar Corporation of Malawi (SUCOMA) created new labor demands.[14]

SUCOMA started operating at Nchalo in 1965 and hired 2,000 workers a year by the late 1970s. The SVADP began in Ngabu in 1968 and engaged almost 1,500 workers every year by the late 1970s. Other employers, including the state, had 6,500 employees annually during the same period.[15] These 10,000 people employed in the nonpeasant sector earned an average of K221,600 a year—the equivalent of about US$250,000 in 1980.[16] But even a larger number worked for other villagers,[17] as we shall see later in this chapter. All wage laborers in the region received about 50 percent of the money from cotton sales. Cotton's relative contribution to rural incomes shrinks even further when one brings into the picture the burgeoning cattle industry.

The cattle industry grew rapidly between the late 1930s and early 1980s, when the number of African-owned cattle jumped from about 550 to well over 80,000.[18] (Between 1968 and 1975, the Tchiri Valley's herd increased at the rate of 12% per annum, compared to the national average of 4%.)[19] By the 1980s, about 37 percent of the Southern Region's cattle came from the valley, although it accounts for only 17 percent of the region's land area.[20]

According to one survey, the rapid increase in the region's cattle population was due to good grazing lands, low incidence of disease, and high fertility.[21] This may be true, but the explanation misses the political and economic dynamics of the industry, particularly the relations between those who own the cattle and those who depend on food cultivation. There are no fences marking off grazing grounds from cultivated fields, and no one stall-feeds cattle. Instead, cattle graze the same mphala drylands and dambo floodplains that farmers also use to grow their food and cash crops. Cattle owners and those who live by farming have conflicting interests, and the success of one group has often come at the expense of the other. The history of cattle provides an important window on the process of rural differentiation in the valley.

Having started in the mid-nineteenth century as the exclusive enterprise of the Magololo immigrants,[22] the cattle industry did not make headway in the pre-Bomani era. The few cattle-owing European settlers, Indian traders, and Africans were politically and economically too weak to challenge the interests of cotton-growing peasants and their powerful allies in Zomba, Liverpool, and Manchester. It was then unthinkable for cattle to graze on the dambo marshes, which grew cotton throughout the dry season from February to December. Cattle grazing was limited to the mphala drylands under certain restrictions. During the growing season on the mphala, which then lasted from November to September because of late-planted cotton, no cattle could range on the munda gardens of the mphala drylands. Instead, cattle herders drove their herd past munda fields toward the uncultivated slopes of the Kirk Range and Thyolo Mountains. Cattle were allowed to graze on the flat mphala only after the harvesting of cereals and cotton in September and before the planting rains in November. Cattle would then enjoy the traditional "rights" of children and small ruminants like goats, which scoured gardens of unpicked leftovers of maize and other crops, so long as they did not trample village plots of sweet potatoes and legumes. But events after the Bomani floods altered the balance of forces in favor of cattle owners.

The end of dimba cotton opened the marshes to cattle grazing for, although still important for many villagers, agricultural production on the dambo ceased to be part of the export-driven or "formal" economy, deserving official protection.[23] "Real" agriculture took place only on the mphala, where villagers grew cereals and cotton. But two agronomic changes after World War II lengthened the grazing period on the drylands from three (September to November) to nearly six months (May to November) a year. In 1951, the government required all villagers who grew cotton to raise it between November and May, and the subsequent collapse of all forms of cotton farming in Nsanje reestablished the "traditional" or precotton munda schedules. As they had done before the introduction of cotton as a cash crop at the beginning of the twentieth century, peasants in the new noncotton areas started and ended the production of major cereals between November and May. Cattle were more or less free to scavenge the mphala for nearly half a year, in addition to the dambo marshes, which were available throughout the dry season.

The post-Bomani era also brought about a new political and social context to the industry. The people who came to dominate cattle ownership in the post-Bomani era were anything but the politically marginal Indian or European traders; they were the local cadres of the all-powerful MCP, which helps explain the dramatic increase in the herd population and its uneven distribution. Only 20 percent of the households in the valley owned cattle in the 1970s. Over 80 percent of the region's cattle was owned by just 2 percent of these households, including Dr. Banda, who maintained a large herd in Chikwawa District. With Banda as an example, cattle owners have been able to convert, with impunity, the whole dambo and the mphala during the dry season into their private ranches.

There are no legal mechanisms for the small grower to fight against the large cattle owners, and, in a complete reversal to traditional customs, today the responsibility of protecting gardens against cattle falls not on cattle owners but on food cultivators.[24] Peasants who maintain small patches of maize and sweet potatoes on the dambo have to guard their crops against cattle throughout the growing season. In 1979–80, this researcher conducted many interviews with villagers in their dimba gardens, where protecting their crops against cattle was a full-time occupation.[25] Poor peasants were particularly bitter because the extra work imposed by cattle complicated their struggles to survive drought through dimba agriculture. Drought drew attention to a problem that, according to Mrs. Nsayi Kanting'u from Nsanje, munda cultivators face on a regular basis:

> There are so many cattle these days, so many herds that you cannot see even sweet potatoes in these gardens. Soon after you have planted the cuttings, and long before the vines have started spreading on the ground, cattle are there already to devour them. What is it that gives us famines? Is it not the beasts? There is no agriculture these days. If we eat sweet potatoes, it is only because we are stubborn enough to continually keep watch over the gardens.[26]

Cattle also undermined the experiment in guar production.

In an attempt to bring cash-earning opportunities to non-cotton-growing areas, the government introduced guar beans in Nsanje District in 1976–77.[27] The response was encouraging, with the percentage of households growing the crop nearly doubling from 46 in 1977–78 to 71 in 1979–80.[28] But the industry is in the doldrums today, with its original source of strength turned into its principal weakness. Peasants had responded with enthusiasm to the experiment not only because it provided a new income, but also because it neatly dovetailed with the calendar of food production on the mphala. People planted guar beans after harvesting maize and millet around April, and the beans grew during the dry or slack season. But cattle undermined this advantage. After avoiding the unknown plant for three seasons, the beasts discovered that guar beans could make palatable fodder.[29] They devoured the crop, forcing some cultivators to give it up and others to plant it at the same time as their major food crops.[30] The cattle industry has forced many villagers to turn to wage employment, including work on the dominant cotton economy.

IN THE WORLD OF COTTON

Cotton has dominated the economic landscape of the valley in three ways.[31] First, it has affected food security more profoundly than most other activities, creating jobs that allow the poor to cope with njala (see chapter 4) while diverting their labor from food production (see chapter 6). Second, cotton has overshadowed other economic activities in the bureaucracy's imagination and reports. The history of the region and its constituent parts filters through official sources mainly as a cotton producer. There are more archival sources on Nsanje than on Chikwawa in the pre-Bomani era because Nsanje was then the center of the cotton economy. But Chikwawa became the focus of official reporting after the district's emergence as the new epicenter of the cotton economy since the 1940s. Finally, no other crop or program of development has received as much private and public funding as cotton. As villagers spent their precious time and money to raise the cash crop during the hungry season, the state mobilized its own resources and those of the international community to promote scientific cotton agriculture.

The Campaigns

The individual progressive farmer, who will in future be called Chikumbe, will be the backbone of the agricultural advance of Malawi. I want all the efforts of all extension staff concentrated upon the production of Achikumbe.[32]

There have been five major campaigns to popularize cotton growing in the area over the past 150 years. Dr. David Livingstone mounted the first in the mid-nineteenth century, when he advertised the region's potential as a cotton-growing area that would help reduce Britain's dependence on the American South.[33] The campaign did not result in the immediate colonization of the region by British settlers apart from the fateful expedition of the UMCA, whose commitment to cotton was symbolized by their cotton gin. Although the gin became, in the words of Reverend Henry Rowley, the "most useless ... thing taken up to Magomero,"[34] Livingstone's dream did triumph in the long run. The first thing the British did upon taking control of the Malawi region in 1891 was to launch the second cotton campaign, premised on the idea that Africans would provide the labor under the direct supervision of European settlers. The project failed spectacularly, and the colonial government had to accept a cotton regime with Africans as independent producers. Besides organizing markets, the state did not intervene in peasant cotton agriculture before the collapse of the dimba subsystem in 1939. Attempts to revive the sagging cotton economy after World War II constituted the third campaign,[35] which subsequently merged with the fourth crusade known as the Master Farmers' Scheme (MFS).

Unlike its predecessors, the MFS was a national project, which, if successful in the valley, would have instituted a cotton-dominated economy revolving around a class of farmers who did nothing but grow cotton. Appreciating the difficulties of propagating "scientific" agriculture among thousands of "backward-looking" villagers, this project zeroed in on the master farmer, who would through example carry out the "civilizing" mission and act as the *Lux in Tenebris* in the dark African countryside.[36]

Recognizing the importance of their mission, the state did not make it easy for people to become master farmers. There was a period of waiting, preparation, and learning when potential converts were known as second-class master farmers. Like first-class master farmers, they had to follow at least five categories of agricultural rules, known collectively in the vernacular as *malimidwe.* The first required master farmers to consolidate their pieces of land into one block of at least 10 acres,[37] and the second dealt with soil conservation under the country's various natural resources ordinances. The drive for *mitumbira* ridges—planting mounds rising to about a foot high, and between one to two feet apart, which were supposed to act as a soil-conservation measure—fell under this category. Through the third set of regulations the government required master farmers to place at least a third of their holdings under grass, pigeon peas, or fallow for at least three years—they were to practice crop rotation.[38] The fourth and fifth groups of regulations set the standards for storing crops and growing trees. Finally, those aspiring to become first-class master farmers had to know something about animal husbandry and other rules that made them the linchpin of malimidwe. Master farmers of either grade were to become leaders in revolutionizing the countryside.

Master farmers were to spearhead capitalist development, based on private property in land. While no one had an idea about the specifics of this aspect of the project, colonial planners always proceeded on the assumption that a new system of land tenure was a necessary precondition to their ability to restructure peasant production. As one director of agriculture put it in the late 1940s: "No programme of rural development can be formulated without giving careful consideration to the subject of land tenure."[39] To accomplish their mission, therefore, master farmers were to take away land from the "conservative" peasantry, employ some of them as agricultural laborers, and drive the rest to the cities. The time had come for a social revolution.

To help the new class achieve its historic undertaking, the government dispatched real and prospective master farmers to Thuchila Farm Institute in Chiradzulu and the Tchiri Valley's "Lower Shire Farm Institute" at Makhanga, where they learned, through lectures and demonstrations, the benefits of "modern" farming. On a more regular basis, however, master farmers received technical assistance on a wide range of issues from *mlangizi* field officers. Finally, the government set up a bonus system to reward successful master farmers and, through the Native Authority Treasury, provided loans for the purchase of capital goods like cattle, carts, and ploughs and for tractor rentals.[40] It was not lack of commitment on the part of the government that, after a decade of effort, the scheme could boast of only 2 master farmers in Chikwawa and less than 10 in Port Herald District.[41] The scheme failed for other reasons, including those that came to plague the fifth and final campaign, launched by the independent government of Malawi.

The history of this campaign falls into three phases, each with its own name, although for reasons that will become clear later in this discussion, we will generally refer to it as the SVADP (or the Project)—the name of the second phase. During the first stage, from 1968 to 1973, the program was known as the Chikwawa Cotton Development Project (CCDP) and was administered through the Ministry of Finance's Department of Economic Planning. As its name indicates, the project dealt exclusively with cotton agriculture in Chikwawa and in the northwestern section (Mbenje subchiefdom) of Nsanje District. Nsanje's noncotton areas became part of the campaign only in the second phase, starting in 1973, when they renamed the program the Shire Valley Agricultural Development Project. Headed by a manager, the Project's activities covered the entire valley and went beyond cotton and beyond agriculture, promoting the fish industry, constructing feeder roads and markets, and symbolizing what experts once called "integrated" rural development. Not only natural scientists and economists, but also sociologists and anthropologists were involved in the project. Its agenda was "to revolutionize the entire life" of the region, to use the phrase made famous by Governor G.F.T. Colby two decades earlier.[42] The Project's third and final phase started after the expiration of World Bank funding in 1977–78. Now known as the Ngabu Agricultural Development Division (NADD), the project reverted to the Department of Economic Planning after inheriting the infrastructure, personnel, and general objectives of the SVADP; it proved to be as intrusive as the SVADP.

The Project tried to reshape the region's agricultural practices formally and informally. It provided formal education at four Rural Day Training Centers (Chikwawa District headquarters, Tomali, Sorgin, and Chiromo) and at a Residential Training Center at the Project's headquarters at Ngabu Township. Headed by a senior training officer, the Residential Training Center took care of the educational needs of the more affluent cotton growers, teachers of agricultural and domestic science in primary schools, and, above all, mlangizi extension workers.[43] Totaling about 250 at the beginning of the second phase in 1973–74, *alangizi* (the plural of mlangizi) were the foot soldiers of the Project's campaign for "scientific" agriculture.

Some alangizi met with villagers in small groups to listen to radio programs on cotton agriculture; 6,862 villagers participated in these sessions in May 1970.[44] Alangizi also distributed leaflets on a variety of agricultural topics,[45] ran puppet shows, and projected film shows to large audiences.[46] But most members of the extension team spent their time in informal contacts with peasants in their gardens. In August 1971, alangizi contacted 23,942 persons on an individual basis, and in January 1974, each of the 254 field workers averaged 12 contacts per day.[47]

The subjects covered during these meetings varied by the season and can be found in the Project's monthly publication—the *Monthly Advice.* Every issue of the magazine listed the topics alangizi had to focus on every month, starting with garden preparation, registration of cotton growers, distribution of cotton seeds, planting, weeding, thinning, cotton spraying, construction of cotton storage sheds, picking, grading, marketing, the uprooting and burning of cotton residues, and credit recovery. Field officers did not, of course, give equal weight to every topic. They did not, for example, spend much time teaching peasants how to plant or weed their cotton, but they spared no effort on cotton spraying, uprooting, picking, and mitumbira ridging.[48] Then, toward the end of the growing season, they promoted new techniques in cotton picking.[49] Finally, the Project tried to enforce old colonial rules that required growers to uproot all cotton plants by 31 July and burn them by 15 August.[50] The aim was to kill those pests that, like the dreaded pink bollworm, could not be destroyed by any of the existing pesticides.

The use of pesticides, more than anything else, gave the Project its distinctively postcolonial character. For although cotton pests had beleaguered the cash crop since its introduction at the beginning of the twentieth century, it was not until the 1960s that pesticides were used in Malawi to deal with the problem. The Project's management deployed all the media at its disposal to promote the sale of spraying machines and pesticides. An intensive but ineffective drive to sell sprayers in December 1970[51] did not discourage the management, who in the following year enlisted the support of local politicians to sell 1,800 knapsack spraying machines.[52] And as they were about to reach their target, officials added another 500 sprayers to the list.[53] Encouraged by this response, the chairman of the Project's Liaison Committee proposed that the FMB should give "spraying farmers preferential treatment as an inducement." The resolution was adopted, and the Project manager took up the matter with FMB officials, who subsequently treated "spraying" farmers as a special category of cotton growers deserving preferential treatment.[54] Every *Monthly Advice* touted the presumed advantages of spraying.

Initially, the Project sponsored two forms of spray technology: handheld spraying machines and air-spraying. The first ever air-spraying in Malawi's peasant sector was conducted in the valley in 1971, when 844 acres of cotton were treated with pesticides.[55] About the same number of acres were air-sprayed the following season, which also happened to be the last year of the experiment. They had to stop the trials for a variety of reasons. Most cotton fields were not contiguous and were interspersed with food crops, and cotton was in different stages of growth. Contributing to the high cost of the program (K20 per acre)[56] were frequent aircraft breakdowns, which only compounded the difficulties caused by the weather.[57] As a result, all applications for credit processed after 1971 were for loans to buy insecticides and handheld machines, including ultra-low-volume sprayers.[58]

A special unit of the Project's finance department, together with some local residents, formed a Loans Committee to review applications for loans for spraying equipment. These were short-term loans peasants had to repay each season after selling their cotton.[59] To qualify for the loans, a farmer had to be creditworthy, owing no money to the Project; must have earned a good reputation as a cotton grower through experience or by attending courses given by the Project; and had to cultivate at least two acres of cotton, ridge them, and use pesticides to raise productivity.[60]

According to the World Bank, which partially funded the SVADP, cotton production in Malawi increased by over two percent annually in the period from 1969 to 1985.[61] Malawi's cotton regime during this period relatively outperformed that of Nigeria and Tanzania, which also received so-called development loans from the bank. Malawi trailed behind only Cameroon and Senegal, where cotton was largely grown on virgin land.[62] Officials took these findings as evidence for the success of the handheld spray technology, which was the Project's most distinctive innovation.

The increases are less impressive when viewed in a longer-term perspective. The two-percent annual increases were not evenly distributed throughout the 1969–85 period. They were concentrated in the first six years of the project (1968–74). Moreover, these increases are remarkable only because cotton output had dropped sharply in the three seasons (1966–68) before the Project—the base figure. A longer historical perspective that takes account of the years before the drastic decline would give a different view on the 1968–73 statistics. In particular, under the Project production never reached the 1962 or 1965 output, and after several good years between 1969 and 1974,

Table 5.2.
Cotton Output in Metric Tons, 1959–83

Year	Tons	Year	Tons	Year	Tons	Year	Tons
1959	8,136	1966	8,682	1972–73	13,200	1979–80	10,200
1960	10,003	1967	6,510	1973–74	16,200	1980–81	10,500
1961	9,344	1968	5,100	1974–75	10,600	1981–82	7,900
1962	16,407	1968–69	11,500	1975–76	8,400	1982–83	7,500
1963	7,341	1969–70	15,600	1976–77	10,700	—	—
1964	12,000	1970–71	15,500	1977–78	10,700	—	—
1965	17,272	1971–72	16,200	1978–79	10,200	—	—

Notes and Sources: (1) Originals for 1959–63 are given in short tons (8,968, 11,026, 10,300, 18,085, and 8,092); see CCDP, Annual Cotton Statistics Report, 1972, 23–24. They were converted by the author. (2) Those for 1964–68 are from NADD, "A Report on Cotton Production Promotion Campaign Jointly Organized by Ngabu ADD and David Whitehead and Sons Limited in 1983/84 Season" (November 1987): 3–5. (3) Those for 1968–83 are from NADD, "Initial Stages in the Adaptation of Train and Visit Extension Approach System" (March 1984): 29. The table makes the important distinction between total production and ADMARC purchases, which other statistics do not do. See also NADD, "Historical Statistics" (March 1984): table 2.

it leveled off and began to decline. As table 5.2 shows, cotton agriculture entered the 1980s in a very weak state in spite of the investments that both the state and peasants had made in the spray technology.

The difference between targeted and actual output kept growing every year between 1972 and 1983, as table 5.3 shows. One dynamic in the discrepancy was the fact that the Project did not recruit many new producers. It may have in fact lost old ones. In 1925, 97.6 percent of all households in Nsanje District grew cotton. In Chikwawa it was 76.6 percent.[63] But by 1980, no one in Nsanje District outside the Mbenje subchiefdom grew cotton, and the percentage in Chikwawa had dropped to 66.[64] And the Project gave rise to no cotton specialists even in Chikwawa District.[65] Everywhere the cotton grower remained first and foremost a food cultivator, who happened to add the cash crop to one's farming enterprise.

Social, Political, and Economic Constraints

The busiest time of the year, and the most nerve-racking, was when we were gathering peanuts and cotton, our cash crops … The labor crunch came when all farmers were harvesting peanuts and cotton simultaneously … Beginning in mid-August, every able-bodied person in the community was needed for harvest.[66]

Table 5.3.
Differences between Target and Actual Production Figures in Metric Tons, 1968–83

Year	Target	Actual	Actual/ Target	Year	Target	Actual	Actual/ Target
1972–73	17,000	14,500	85	1978–79	21,000	10,625	50
1973–74	20,500	15,200	74	1979–80	21,750	12,059	55
1974–75	22,000	9,600	43	1980–81	23,250	10,716	46
1975–76	27,800	7,600	27	1981–82	24,000	16,451	68
1976–77	31,500	9,500	30	1982–83	12,650	6,652	52

Notes and Sources: (1) The above figures are from NADD, "Initial Stages in the Adaptation of the Train and Visit Extension Approach System" (March 1984): 7, 10. During 1968–73, the difference was always positive; see ibid., 5. (2) The "actual" figures for 1979–82 are suspect; they diverge too much from those given in table 5.2.

To me, my father seemed all-powerful, yet we knew that he shared with other farmers a sense of total impotence in the face of unpredictable weather conditions and the remote and mysterious economic system that set prices for hogs, timber, cotton, and peanuts.[67]

The F.M.B. is playing with money by employing so many staff. The work done by one man previously is today done by 3 or more people. *Why not reduce the number of employee* [*sic*] *and increase the price of cotton to farmers?*[68]

Cotton agriculture performed poorly in the valley partly because of the gap between its costs and rewards and partly because of political and social constraints. Ordinary villagers in the 1950s resisted the MFS on several grounds, the most important of which being the fear of losing their land to the emerging class of yeomen farmers. The relatives of Mr. Failosi—a potential master farmer in Port Herald—foiled the government's plan to give him 10 acres of "communal" land.[69] They successfully subverted the plan because they had the backing of their headmen, who also vehemently opposed the rise of private property rights in land. Peasants fought the scheme also because it formed an integral part of the hated new agricultural rules (see chapter 6).

Resistance to the colonial agricultural regulations merged with opposition to the MFS in the early 1950s. Strengthened by the violent uprisings in Thyolo District in 1953, peasants in Chikwawa openly flouted the government's drive for early stalk uprooting and burning.[70] The boycott disturbed the British not only because it signaled the beginnings of some organized resistance, but also because of its chilling effect on the master farmers. All "prospective master farmers," complained one official, "are just as behind in their work as everybody else."[71] The report goes on to explain the reasons master farmers were unable to meet the deadlines. They were afraid of popular resentment or, as one reporter put it: "Some probaly [*sic*] wished to carry on with their normal work, but as they realized it would not have been good for their health had they done so, in the face of such strong opposition."[72] The intimidation became particularly effective against mitumbira, which was the most reviled element of the government's rules in the valley (see chapter 6).

Uncertain about the reaction of their neighbors, real and potential master farmers did not ridge their gardens before planting. They were too frightened to comply with the conditions isolating them as a special group: "Due to intimidation, work on all holdings [belonging to master farmers] was at a standstill."[73] They were too "frightened to begin ridging"[74] because ordinary peasants did not limit their intimidation to verbal abuse; they also organized themselves in small bands, roaming the fields at night and destroying ridges master farmers had constructed with considerable labor, including hired workers.[75] Thus, on the eve of the country's political independence, those master farmers who stayed in the scheme worked their fields without mitumbira. As the 1963–64 report put it: "Ridging has been entirely dropped down and [master farmers] have been unwilling to associate themselves on [*sic*] ridging."[76] The scheme did not make it into the postcolonial era for the same economic reasons that undermined the SVADP. There was always a gap between the rewards and cost of cotton production.

Cotton growing was always an expensive undertaking, requiring considerable amounts of money and labor. As one large grower, Mr. Snake Mthepheya, bluntly put it: "The real problem with cotton is that it involves hard work, digging the land."[77] He was not completely right, because other villagers emphasize not only what they have to do to grow cotton, but also what they lose in so doing. They highlight, as some students of the crisis literature do, the diversion of labor from food production.[78] Hard to calculate, labor diverted from food weighs heavily in peasants' ideas about cotton as an unrewarding enterprise. Unlike their rulers and some of their interpreters, peasants think of cotton production as only one part of the daily routines of the growing season. Another part of the routines consists of food cultivation, whose labor demands conflict sharply with those of cotton.

As former president Jimmy Carter has shown for the Georgia of his youth, Allen Isaacman for colonial Mozambique, and Osumaka Likaka for the Democratic Republic of the Congo, cotton is a labor-intensive activity.[79] In the valley, it has soaked up peasants' energies from the beginning to the end of the growing season, especially under the SVADP, which sought to refashion rural work.[80] Project officials introduced completely new labor processes, like spraying, at the same time as they reinforced colonial rules on operations like land preparation, sowing, weeding, and harvesting. Only a few procedures escaped direct intervention, altering only in response to broader economic transformations.[81]

The following analysis discusses each operation separately for two principal reasons. The first is to draw attention to the fact that even under the SVADP each procedure forming part of the larger production system developed differently; the system could not have followed one particular direction. The second reason is to bring to the foreground the high labor demands of the growing season. Even those villagers who did not grow cotton spent their time in food gardens, performing broadly the same kinds of tasks as those of cotton cultivators. (For this reason, chapter 6 will not explicitly address the question of agricultural work schedules.) The wet season proved to be particularly nerve-racking for villagers who raised cotton as a "pure" culture in separate fields from food crops. Their workload increased as they moved between their fields of cotton and food crops. But even those who flouted the government's requirement for a pure cotton culture and interplanted the cash crop with their food crops also experienced labor bottlenecks. Some activities, like grading, were specific to cotton. From whatever angle one looks at it, under the existing technologies, cotton agriculture always raised peasants' workloads.

Garden preparation set the stage for the long-drawn-out struggle to become a cotton grower. Project officials did not introduce new rules on garden preparation, content on reinforcing colonial legislation, requiring peasants to make mitumbira ridges and uproot cotton stalks by 31 July and burn them by 15 August.[82] Most villagers continued to resist the campaign for ridging,[83] but accepted in principle the idea of uprooting and burning old stalks. Their ancestors had always uprooted and burned old crop residues in preparation for a new season; all they opposed were the official deadlines that denied them the flexibility to respond to emergencies and other forms of rural work. When pressed for time, villagers ignored the deadlines, as in 1972, when many gardens still contained old stalks in August, prompting the Project manager to urge all instructors to step up the early uprooting drive:

> It is essential ... that staff must, by example, demonstration and constant encouragement, uproot and burn cotton plants themselves, to show farmers how important and essential it is for this work to be completed. All Area Supervisors are required to submit a further special report direct to me on the 4th September, to report on the progress of uprooting and burning.[84]

When a similar drive failed to move peasants in 1974, the manager enlisted the support of the country's president-for-life himself, Dr. Banda.[85] This was in early October, but a quarterly report closing the year shows Project officials did not need to panic. Peasants were not against the idea of burning the old bushes; they only had other things to do, and once freed from their more pressing responsibilities, they began to burn the residues of the old growing season. Only five percent of the old crop remained standing and unburned by mid-October.[86] However, the majority continued to ignore the mitumbira drive and went straight from burning old bushes to sowing.

On sowing, the Project closely followed post–World War II colonial regulations, banning intercropping and promoting early planting. A major objective of the early planting drive was to discourage peasants from sowing munda cotton after they had harvested maize and millet in March–April in the same garden—a practice officials called "late-planting" and considered a major factor in the spread of the red bollworm. To break the pest's reproductive cycle, officials thought it necessary to establish a "dead" season, during which there would be no cotton on the ground; hence the rules requiring villagers to complete sowing, uprooting, and burning by certain deadlines.[87] Beginning in 1951, they required peasants to sow cotton with the first rains in November–December—to adopt an "early-planting" regime—and, to give teeth to the new rules, officials closed cotton markets early in the season so that villagers with late-planted cotton could not sell it.

Another component of the rules of 1951 turned Project officials to the battle against intercropping; cotton could only flourish as a pure culture, raised in a different field from food crops. The campaign against intercropping proved more successful in the hills than on the valley floor (see chapter 6), where it never became popular even among large cotton growers. The few who adopted the pure cotton culture on the valley floor did so partly because the Project made pure planting a condition for getting loans, partly because they feared cotton pesticides might poison their foodstuffs,[88] and partly because some believed in the "scientific" superiority of the pure over the intercropping system.[89] Mrs. Enifa Kwenje of Tomali Village, TA Lundu (Chikwawa), spoke for many converts when she related on 12 June 1996,

> In munda farming, we grow cotton in its own garden; maize in its own garden; sorghum in its own garden ... this is modern agriculture, not the traditional method, when they used to mix cotton with maize, groundnuts, and other food crops. Nowadays we follow the advice of agricultural instructors who are dead against intercropping and tell us never to mix crops ... we raise each crop in its own filed, be it cotton, maize, sorghum ... millet.[90]

Mrs. Kwenje is obviously simplifying the nature of rural responses to the pure planting that doubled the work of villagers who also grew their own food. Many growers not only continued to interplant their cotton with food crops, but those who tried to comply with the rules did so by combining elements of intercropping with the pure planting. One important variation in this practice was the "plot" system, dividing one and the same garden into several portions, with some dedicated to cotton and others to food crops.[91] Another variant was the "row" system of raising cotton in one row or several rows and food crops in another row or group of rows.[92] Peasants spoke of these variations and several others as forms of intercropping or pure farming, depending on the question. However, the one message that rings very loud from the many oral testimonies on the topic is that instead of streamlining, the drive for pure planting actually multiplied the forms of integrating cotton to food production. The ban on intercropping was significant not so much because it created its opposite—the ideal, pure cotton culture of agricultural experts—but mainly because it multiplied the ways of doing the intercropping system and its pure culture opposite.

Weeding (*kupalira*), which follows sowing, posed fewer intellectual hurdles for the peasantry and did not get to the list of operations the Project tried to teach peasants, drawing official attention only intermittently. Starting in December and ending in March, when the bolls of the early-planted cotton started to mature,[93] weeding is the longest operation in the entire cycle of cotton (as well as food) production. There are few breaks in this extended operation, for although rains are generally light in the valley, high humidity promotes rapid plant growth. Pure-planted cotton suffered the extra disadvantage of competing with food crops that peasants also weeded at this time. Villagers have had to weed each garden at least three times per season.[94] Everyone tried to keep the garden free of weeds on the understanding that weeds exerted the same retarding effect on cotton (and other crops) as waterlogging, drought, and pests.[95] As a result, weeding cotton in the valley often required the use of extra-household labor, much the same way it did in the Old South. These were moments when, according to former president Jimmy Carter, his father "would pace at night, scan the western skies for a break in the clouds, and scour the community, often far from our own farm, to recruit any person willing to hoe or pull up weeds for day wages."[96] Besides money, the well-to-do in the valley also used food to attract hungry villagers "to pull up weeds" in their gardens. As a result, officials were generally surprised with the thoroughness with which peasants controlled weeds in their gardens.[97] Only harvesting took more extra-family labor.

In the pre-Bomani era, the combination of dimba with munda cotton, planted between November and April, made harvesting a protracted affair stretching from May to September. Cotton buyers, who remained in the valley through-out this period, must have welcomed the changes of the post-Bomani era that ended dimba cotton and forced villagers to finish harvesting by June.[98] The next major change came with the Project, which tried to popularize picking bags to replace baskets people held on their heads with one hand while the other picked cotton.[99] Tied to the waist, bags were to free both hands for picking and speed up the process.[100]

Photo 5 Slinging bags allowed the use of both hands in cotton picking (1959). (Nyasaland Government, *Annual Reports of the Department of Agriculture 1960* [Zomba, Malawi: Government Press]: Part I)

As often happens, there is scanty evidence on how peasants responded to the campaign for picking bags. It is clear, however, that even if the new technique became popular, the problem of labor distribution between cotton and food production at this time of year remained unsolved. As before, villagers continued to be burdened by other tasks besides harvesting cotton.[101] Many had waited for this moment to stage major rites of passage, to harvest their sorghum, and to start their dimba gardens. As a result, cotton growers were always in need of extra help, especially during a bumper crop when, as one report put it, they would be "faced with the big problem of getting all cotton picked in time, and labour is scarce."[102] Thus, as in weeding, cotton growers resorted to all sorts of extra-household labor, including the dreaded but now disbanded MYP—the paramilitary wing of the MCP.[103] Under the SVADP, many farmers would have by this time spent their time and money spraying cotton.

Spraying cotton was a "dirty" and exhausting work.[104] Peasants had to draw water from wells that were not always close to their gardens, and after getting the water they had to mix it with pesticides. Then, as they sprayed, villagers had to walk at a certain speed and make sure they did so in the right direction in relation to the wind. After spraying, they had to clean the knapsack kits before storing them for the next day or next round of spraying. And these

Photo 6 Spraying cotton with pesticides in 1959, although the practice became popular only after the launching of the CCDP in 1968. (Nyasaland Government, *Annual Reports of the Department of Agriculture 1960* [Zomba, Malawi: Government Press]: Part I)

routines changed according to cotton's age. The typical spraying sequence ran roughly like this: start with carbaryl (to kill the elegant grasshopper, jassid, stainer, and red bollworm), then move to DDT (to eliminate the American bollworm), dimethoate (to kill colonies of red spider mites), and acaricides and aphicides (to stifle the outbreaks of aphid and spider mites).[105] In all, peasants had to spray their cotton every week, or about 12 to 14 times per season.[106] Owners of large gardens met these new labor demands by employing others, which created another category of direct costs besides the purchase of the technology itself.

The history of the spray technology in the valley highlights the obvious point that culture is not the only factor shaping African farmers' ability to adopt new technologies of production. In this, as in many other aspects of their lives, African peasants are also the children of their economic and political environments. Political history explains, in part, how peasants in southern Chikwawa embraced the spray technology more slowly and hesitantly than their neighbors in the northern part of the same district. Reporting on the differences between the two parts of the district, one irritated official sent the following memo to his superiors in Zomba:

> A black spot is the Ngabu area where it is proving extremely difficult to arouse interest in improved farming. No interest in cotton spraying has been shown in this area which is surprising as it is the main area of production ... In the Northern half of the district there is an awakening interest in improved farming. The services of instructors are in demand and relations between staff and villagers are good.[107]

This should not have come as a surprise. The campaign had an unpopular sponsor in the country's Department of Agriculture, which had until recently harassed the population with its campaign for new agricultural rules. Moreover, the southern rather than the northern part of the district had led the resistance to the regulations in the broader nationalist struggle for political independence. Only after the replacement of the vilified Department of Agriculture by the SVADP would southern Chikwawa join the northern section, which had taken up the new technology with enthusiasm from the beginning.

Barely affected by the colonial agricultural campaigns of the 1940s and 1950s, rich peasants in the northern part of the district welcomed the opportunity to spray their cotton. Most people, including the poor, understood the negative effects of various pests and diseases on their cash crop,[108] and the main limiting factor in the spread of the new technology was financial.[109] Otherwise, those with the means turned to spraying with little or no prodding. In 1963, they bought spraying machines and insecticides, which encouraged the district's Agricultural Department to form a Spraying Team for hire by those without machines.[110] The team continued to work until at least 1965, when officials of the FMB received more money from peasants eager to buy spraying machines.[111] Loans under the CCDP (and later SVADP) allowed more villagers to acquire sprayers and pesticides.

Starting from 759 in the 1968–69 financial year, the number of knapsack spraying machines doubled to 1,498 in the following year (1969–70), and the number of so-called spraying farmers increased at a similar rate, rising from 853 in 1968–69 to 1,819 in 1969–70.[112] By February 1972, there were 4,603 machines and 5,270 spraying farmers, representing 16.9 percent of all registered cotton growers in the Project area (Chikwawa and a small portion of northern Nsanje), and together they sprayed a total of 17,300 acres, or 21 percent of the area under cotton.[113] There was no lack of interest among the peasantry, who tried everything in their power to acquire the new technology, and in so doing raise the direct costs of cotton farming.

"Scientific" agriculture was a costly exercise under both the SVADP and MFS. In 1955 Chikwawa's two master farmers together hired tractors from a tractor pool for £90, which at the prevailing rate of six pence per pound of first-grade cotton amounted to nearly two short tons of cotton.[114] The spray technology was even more expensive. In the 1960s, a knapsack cost £12, and by the mid-1970s, farmers were paying up to K35 to purchase the same.[115] The cost of insecticides was even higher, and the amounts villagers cited as their expenditure on this aspect of production in 1995–96 ranged from K400 to K4,000.[116] Four thousand kwacha allowed one *bigifama* (big cotton farmer) to buy enough insecticides for his nine-acre cotton field.[117] Many relied on loans from the Project to purchase the new technology. In a three-month period, from October to December 1970, the Loans Committee held 12 meetings during which it approved 1,178 and rejected 72 applications for sprayers.[118] In all, peasants borrowed a total of K636,877 (about US$700,000 at the time) for spray technology during the first phase of the Project (1968–73) (see table 5.4).[119] As one perceptive grower confidently asserted: "Europeans introduced cotton varieties that require pesticides on purpose; they wanted to fleece us."[120] And fleeced they probably were.

I have tried in vain to obtain accounts of peasants' income and expenses in an attempt to assess their persistent claim that cotton has fleeced them. But

Table 5.4.
Prices of Pesticides during the 1974–75 Growing Season

Pesticide	Unit	Credit Price
DDT (wettable powder)	3.33 oz. sachet	K0.14
Carbaryl (WP sevin)	3 oz. sachet	K0.020
Dimethoate (WP)	1.2 oz. sachet	K0.07
DDT (ULV)	1 l.	K0.70
Carbaryl (ULV)	1 l.	K1.50
Dimethoate (ULV)	100cc.	K0.30

Notes: These are credit prices; cash prices allow a 10 percent discount.
Sources: SVADP, *Monthly Advice* (October 1974): 507. In 1983, K22.75 was the credit package cost of pesticides "considered to be enough for 8 to 12 sprays on 0.4 hectares." The package consisted of "30 sachets DDT, 11 sachets dimethoate, 50 sachets carbaryl/sevin plus 10% interest charge." The same package had cost K14.85 in 1976–77 (NADD, "Historical Statistics" [March 1984]: item 14), MNA. See also SVADP, Monthly Reports, March 1974 (14.1.2F/40364), MNA.

one can already speculate on the potential limitations of such an accounting exercise. It would most likely list direct costs—as some officials and progressive farmers have done anecdotally[121]—but not the value of household labor. There is practically no way to determine the time peasants spend on cotton and food under the popular intercropping system, and it is theoretically unfeasible to attach a figure to the losses the food system suffers as a result of the pure cotton regime. These are the incalculable losses that villagers do, however, take into account in their portrayal of cotton as an exploitative system.[122]

The notion that cotton is an unprofitable enterprise seems to rest on solid ground when one turns to long-term trends in producer prices, as table 5.5 does. After a steady rise in the first part of the 1950s, producer prices did not catch up with inflation during the second half of the 1950s and throughout the 1960s. The price rose slightly in 1971, when the kwacha, which has 100 tambala, replaced the British pound as the country's currency. At the going exchange rate, the 12.1 tambala peasants received for a kilogram of first-grade cotton amounted to nearly 17 pence. But prices stagnated again in the second half of the 1970s, and the last two decades of the twentieth century witnessed a significant slide in cotton growers' purchasing power. The devaluation of the kwacha ate up the apparent price hikes. In 1980, one U.S. dollar equaled approximately K0.80, so that the 28.5 tambala villagers received in that season for a kilogram of first-grade cotton had the same value as 34 U.S. cents. Five years later, one needed K1.2 to purchase a dollar, and by 1995, one U.S. dollar equaled K15. The villager who sold a kilogram for K4.50 realized only 30 U.S. cents. (Today, one needs K105 to buy one U.S. dollar; see table 5.1). Villagers are right in their criticism that cotton prices have not caught up with the general rise in consumer prices.

Besides fluctuations in the world demand for African products, lack of competition in the cotton trade and high freights rates were the main forces that helped keep cotton prices low in Malawi. The cost of transporting goods mattered because before the erection of David Whitehead's textile factory in the early 1970s, Malawi's cotton was grown exclusively for export. The country's primitive transport system (see chapter 4) suffocated the cotton trade as it did many other economic enterprises. In 1911 the African Lakes Company (ALC) charged a total of £11 3s. 7d. on transportation for a ton of cotton from Karonga on Lake Malawi to Liverpool. Only £3 7s. 11d., or 27 percent of the total, covered the cost of the longer but more competitive trip between Port Herald and Liverpool. The remainder was spent on internal haulage from Karonga to Port Herald, a distance of only 500 miles that involved a myriad of transport networks: lake steamers between Karonga and Fort Johnston (Mangoche), riverboats between Fort Johnston and Matope, a team of head carriers between Matope and Blantyre, and railroad between Blantyre and Port Herald.[123] The extension of the railway line to Lake Malawi and to Beira in Mozambique did not make much of a difference.

Table 5.5.
Prices Per Kilogram of First-Grade Cotton in British Pence (1950–70)
and Malawi Tambala (1971–95)

Year	Price (in Pence)	Year	Price (in Tambala)	Year	Price (in Tambala)
1950	6.6	1971–72	12.1	1979–80	23.0
1951	8.8	1972–73	12.1	1980–81	28.5
1952	11.0	1973–74	15.4	1981–82	32.5
1955	11.0	1974–75	17.6	1982–83	38.0
1957	13.2	1975–76	18.7	1983–84	42.0
1958	13.2	1977–78	23.1	1995	450.0
1959	13.2	1978–79	23.1	—	—
1960	13.2	—	—	—	—
1967	13.2	—	—	—	—
1970	13.2	—	—	—	—

Notes: (1) The original figures are in pounds (lbs.), and I have converted them to kilograms by multiplying by 2.2. (2) One should read this table in conjunction with table 5.1, which gives the changing value of the kwacha against the U.S. dollar.
Sources: Nyasaland Protectorate, *Annual Report of the Department of Agriculture* (Zomba, Malawi: Government Printer) for 1950 (p. 10), 1951 (p. 10), 1952 (p. 6), 1955 (p. 11), 1957 (p. 7), 1958 (p. 10), 1959 (p. 8), and 1960 (p. 9); "The Agricultural Meeting Called and Conveyed [*sic*] by Malawi Congress Party Leaders in Lower Shire on 29th December, 1967," Cotton File (17.16.2R/40370, Ag. 5); District Commissioner (Chikwawa) to All Chiefs (Chikwawa), 24 April 1970 (17.16.2R/40370, Ag. 5/162); SVADP, *Monthly Advice* (January 1975): 574; NADD, "Historical Statistics" (March 1984): item 13 (for the years 1972–84); Bonjesi Binzi Namizinga, J. V. Ngalu, Mandere Village, TA Ngabu, Chikwawa, 25 May 1996 (SM96/10).

Serving a tiny European sector and built by private funds,[124] the Nyasaland railway system (consisting of the Central Africa Railway, the Shire Highlands Railway, and the Trans-Zambesi Railway) charged higher rates than those prevailing in Southern Rhodesia or Uganda. A merchant using the railway system in Southern Rhodesia paid about 1.17 pence, and his counterpart in Uganda paid less than a penny, to transport a ton-mile. The corresponding figure in Nyasaland ranged between 4.05 and 4.60 pence.[125] And peasants paid for the higher transport costs. According to one estimate, Nyasaland's railways absorbed 40.66 percent of the money that Chiromo cotton growers would have received for their product in 1930.[126] Merchants always referred to the high transport costs in resisting any increase in producer prices.[127]

Buyers of Malawi's peasant-grown cotton did not face competition before the mid-1990s. After a few years when the trade was open to Indian merchants and European settlers, the British Cotton Growers Association (BCGA) won the right to become the country's sole buyer of peasant-grown cotton in 1923.[128] And the association's loss of the monopsony in the late 1930s did not promote competition. The BCGA gave way to the marketing boards of the post–World War II era. There was a Cotton Marketing Board, which became part of the Agricultural Produce and Marketing Board—the forerunner to the FMB and ADMARC.[129]

There was every reason for ADMARC to keep producer prices low. It was a business concern, committed to making profits,[130] and no other peasant produce surpassed cotton's value as an export crop. Surpluses from cotton helped ADMARC finance many businesses, including the estate tobacco economy.[131] Then the 1970s brought another reason for ADMARC to depress prices. The corporation had a financial stake in David Whitehead, the country's only textile manufacturer. Peasants rarely benefited from positive trends in the global demand for their product, but they shared every downward drift in world prices. The deficit-ridden government never subsidized producer prices, even as it collected part of the profits realized by cotton merchants.[132] Everyone except the growers seems to have made good money from cotton agriculture.

Peasants have consistently characterized the market as their structural enemy. In a meeting with leaders of the MCP in 1967, Headman Mafale spoke for many growers when he attacked the government for allowing the gap between income from cotton and prices of consumer goods to widen:

> My fellow friends and I are pleased of [*sic*] this sort of meeting and the speech of the Minister. From the time cotton was introduced in the country the price per lb [*sic*] was in accordance with the economy of the country and all other things on sale in Malawi. For example it was a penny per lb. and at the same time things in stores and anywhere were also very cheap. A person could buy a 2/- shirt. *Why then does the Government not raise price of cotton per lb [*sic*] since the standard of living has gone high and everything is also very high, we are tired of 6d per lb [*sic*] of our cotton.*[133]

Cotton prices were not keeping up with inflation. And about 20 years later, in 1996, one hears the same theme with one major addition. Low cotton prices made it difficult for producers to pay the new spray technology:

> But we have only one major complaint, only one. You may grow and harvest a lot of cotton. But look at the prices they offer; only K4.50 [per kilogram], which always comes as a surprise. No one expects such a [low] rate. People expect ten, eight, or fifteen [kwacha per kilogram], but we would always get K4.50 instead. And this would come after we had taken loans [to buy pesti-

cides] at something like K750 per pack or bottle ... Those who have many acres borrow up to four thousand, five thousand, and six thousand kwacha. How can these pay back the money they owe when they received only K4.50 [per kilogram]? How can we pay back our loans? This is our complaint and we pray they will raise the price ... that would give us strength ... that would encourage people to grow more cotton in the next season. We do not have another complaint besides this one.[134]

Scientific agriculture had raised the direct and invisible costs of cotton production. In the mid-1980s, for example, sprayer-owning and sprayer-borrowing farmers spent on the average 27 percent and 33 percent, respectively, of their total income from one acre of cotton on pesticides, as table 5.6 shows. The table assumes that all their cotton was first grade, which obviously could not have been the case. In 2002, villagers pointedly told officials from the government and the textile factory that the grow-more-cotton campaign could not succeed without narrowing the discrepancy between producer prices and the cost of inputs:

During the meeting farmers alleged that major cotton buyers, ADMARC and Great Lakes are exploiting them by offering low prices, saying there are no profits gained from their sales. The farmers also said they spend all the money realized from cotton sales in settling debts which they get from money lending institutions at high interest rates. This is what leads to the collapse of the farming industry, they said.[135]

Table 5.6.
Cost of Spraying as a Percentage of a Farmer's Income from One Acre of Cotton, mid-1980s

Farmer	Output	Income	Cost	Cost/Income
SR2 (borrowing)	432lbs.	K82.08	K22.3	27
SR3 (owning)	359lbs.	K68.21	K22.3	33

Notes and Sources: These figures are based on the following information:
(1) Every sprayed acre among sprayer-owning and sprayer-borrowing farmers yielded 359 pounds and 432 pounds respectively: SVADP, "Cotton Survey 1974/75," 49. (2) In 1983–84, the credit price for a complete package of pesticides for 0.4 hectares (0.98 acres) was K22.75 (NADD, "Historical Statistics" [March 1984]: item 14), and in that year the price for one kilogram of first-grade cotton was 42 tambala (or 19 tambala per pound): see ibid., item 13. The price of air-spraying was double this amount in the early 1970s: see CCDP, Project Manager (J.M. Hall) to DC (Chikwawa), Members and Chairman Liaison Committee, 11 May 1971 (14.1.2F/40365); CCDP, Monthly Reports, December 1970 (14.1.2F/40364), MNA.

Low producer prices discouraged not only the poor but also the rich, who should have been the government's allies in its project to "develop" the valley through cotton. Instead, rich growers have turned out as the most strident critics of the pricing regime, which does not allow them to acquire or effectively use new technologies of production.

Underutilization or Misuse of Spray Technology and Straddling

> Agricultural Staff are giving us good advice of farming and always we learn from our President that our money is in the soil and we really work hard *but our produces fetch less prices.*[136]
>
> Many farmers were continuing to depend on pensions as well as canteens, brick-making and other income generating activities to sustain agriculture.[137]

Financial constraints help explain the failure of many villagers in the valley to buy or effectively use the spray technology. And the key element here is, as all speakers quoted above make clear, the high cost of pesticides. Villagers were always cautious in their use of this aspect of the spray technology, afraid of losing money in the event of a drought, too much rain, and especially low producer prices. Thus, some bigifama did not use all the technology acquired from the Project. Instead, they traded it with their poorer neighbors, who could not meet the stringent loan conditions of the Project.[138] Bigifama leased their sprayers on easy terms,[139] so that up to 50 percent of the borrowing households did not have to pay for the machines, and many of those who had to were allowed to pay after harvest.[140] Bigifama were not, however, as liberal with their insecticides, which were the more expensive ingredient of the new technology.[141] They sold some of their pesticides, which may explain the astonishing finding of one survey: "Although both" sprayer-owning (SR3) and sprayer-borrowing (SR2) households "achieved mean yields above the non-sprayers' 210 pounds per acre, borrowing households' (SR2) yields averaged 432 pounds per acre compared with only 359 pounds per acre for SR3."[142] In other words, productivity was higher among those who borrowed than among those who owned the spray technology. Larger farmers (SR3) reaped more cotton only because their gardens were larger. They tried to spread risk by selling some of their pesticides to other villages. One could not put all one's eggs in the unreliable cotton market.

All growers used their pesticides sparingly, and many did not spray at all in the event of a drought.[143] Rain shortage not only augured the possibility of a bad harvest; it also raised the cost of labor by increasing the distances people had to walk to get water for spraying.[144] A large amount of the pesticides applied in 1995–96 came from 1994–95, which happened to be a drought season. It was not, however, only in times of drought that growers tried to minimize the cost of spraying. Farmers also resorted to less expensive spraying strategies on a regular basis. To save money, some villagers increased the water-to-pesticide ratio. They mixed one packet of carbaryl with six instead of the recommended three gallons of water, and some split one packet into two and mixed each with three gallons of water—which came to the same thing.[145] Other villagers sprayed two rows of cotton with the same dosage officials recommended for one row.[146] But the most common method of reducing the cost of the spray technology was to lower the frequency of spraying. According to one sample, peasants sprayed 5.15 times on the average instead of the recommended frequency of 12 to 14 applications per season.[147] Peasants did not earn enough money to apply the amount of dosages considered necessary to raise productivity, and those who continued to spray their gardens often did so with resources outside cotton agriculture itself. They did not become cotton specialists.

At the heart of the state-funded development project in the valley was the dream to create a yeoman or capitalist farmer, who would do nothing but raise cotton. As one director of agriculture put it in the mid-1950s: "The object must be to create a class of professional farmers with sufficient land to derive a reasonable standard of living." In the Tchiri Valley, this policy translated into attempts "to encourage the individual" cotton grower "to develop his initiative and to evolve a class of yeoman farmer."[148] The cotton cultivator thus became the archetypical peasant, with most government surveys designed to isolate those cotton growers who made progress toward their final destination as yeoman farmers from those who did not. Initially, those who were advancing according to plan came to be known variously as "type II" farmers, *mchikumbe*, or bigifama, and those who still lagged behind were "type I" or "backward-looking" peasants.

While some researchers sometimes found it difficult to draw a clear line between the two groups of cotton cultivators, those working under the SVADP did not face a problem: they found the "progressive" or type II farmer in anyone who purchased spray technology from the Project.[149] The subsequent finding that owning a sprayer did not automatically turn one into a spraying farmer, and that some peasants who did not own machines also sprayed their cotton, led to a refinement of what they called "Spraying Realities," or SR.[150] The refinement only changed the terms of the debate; it did not transform the paradigm itself. Officials and their theorists could not think of other routes to rural capitalism apart from the well-plotted path along cotton agriculture.

But while officials were myopically preoccupied with the search for specialists, something different was taking place on the ground. Many cotton cultivators engaged in nonagricultural activities like fishing, and almost all grew their own food. No segment of the cotton-growing population abandoned food production in what would have been a suicidal search for wealth through cotton.[151] Income from cotton was too low and unpredictable to support life. Moreover, even those who had money sometimes went hungry because there were no markets or food for sale in their areas.[152] Cotton farmers were first and foremost food growers, who happened to add the cash crop to their enterprise for a whole range of reasons. Some grew cotton because cotton growing had become a way of life,[153] because after each harvest they could earn money in one bundle,[154] because there was always a market for cotton (which was not the case with their other produce like groundnuts), and because there were no alternatives. There was not a single enterprise within and outside agriculture that could satisfy all rural needs. The SVADP entered its third phase in 1978 without cotton specialists, but with growers who participated in many enterprises; almost everyone straddled.

Cotton growers of every category partook in such activities as fishing, cattle keeping, and wage labor—enterprises that were also popular among non-cotton cultivators. But what is even more interesting is that some cotton growers took part in noncotton activities in order to finance their cotton operations. To become a successful cotton grower under both the MFS and SVADP often required capital from outside; the expensive high-tech cotton regime of the post-Bomani era often became parasitic on other sources of rural income.[155]

The lopsided official conception of development determined that only those who were already rich benefited from official rural improvement programs. Only those already with resources could become master farmers or qualify for loans under the MFS and SVADP. Thus, the list of even potential master farmers in the 1950s reads like who's who in the valley, featuring only influential politicians like Village Headman Gundani, enterprising farmers like Chakuamba, and resourceful professionals like the famous teacher Edwin Phiso. And the reason is simple. Master farmers needed money to work their large fields according to the government's labor-intensive rules, and those who joined the club of the elite without sufficient resources were often forced to drop from the program. Equally elitist in conception and operation was the SVADP.

The SVADP recruited its progressive farmers mostly from the ranks of the well-to-do. Well over 68 percent of the Project's type II peasants in the early 1970s had worked and saved some money outside the country as migrant workers.[156] They subsequently used their money and influence to procure sprayers and pesticides for their own fields and for resale or lease to type I cultivators. Indeed, as one writer correctly argued about the MFS, which preceded the SVADP, the scheme did not create rich peasants; it only assisted those who were already rich.[157] But the relationship is not only historical; once started, the new agriculture was too weak to generate funding for its own maintenance. Most growers started every new cotton season after spending their meager incomes from the previous harvest, and financed the new season with loans from the Project; money from the sale of beer, goats, and cattle; and especially wage employment.[158]

The data generated by the SVADP challenges us to think of the relationship between wage labor and cotton in new ways. It is not a matter of either cash cropping *or* wage employment, as I once formulated the issue on the basis of the pre-Bomani economy;[159] it can and sometimes needs to be a matter of *both*. One of the most common strains in the testimonies from the post-Bomani Tchiri Valley is that of a husband or son migrant worker who sends money home for cotton cultivation. With this money, the wife or parents would buy inputs and employ labor for the farm.[160] The evidence from Chikwawa also shows that not only the poor but also the rich become wage laborers, although for different reasons. Without education and other useful skills, those from poor households did not have much choice but sell their labor to anyone, including other peasants.[161] Few of them got government jobs, which in the mid-1970s offered the most stable and best-paying occupations in the region. Such jobs were instead dominated by members of wealthier households,[162] nearly half of whom came from nowhere but the Makande Plain—the country's epicenter of the cotton economy.[163] The richest cotton-growing area took a lion's share of the region's best-paying jobs.

The statistical data on wage employment referred to in the preceding paragraph embody two conflicting but complementary parts of the same tale, and they must to be understood together. The first part ought to give cause for celebration among government officials and other promoters of the project to develop the valley through cotton. The cash crop had indeed brought enough wealth to the Makande Plain for its residents to send their children to school; Rostow's "take-off" was just around the corner. But the second part of the same story should send alarm bells. After years of soaking up peasant, state, and international resources, cotton cannot generate enough income to reproduce itself or keep the best of its future growers. It would continue to rely for its long-term reproduction on the "backward-looking" and hungry peasants.

New Dependent Workers

The evidence from the valley also suggests the need to rethink the relationships among income, labor, and technology. Peasants in the area have underused or failed to acquire new technologies not because they have used their income to recruit social dependents.[164] The story of cotton agriculture suggests a different direction of causality. The cotton farmers of the valley were very much like pre-World War II landowners of Georgia, who "had little if any money for improvements or adequate fertilizer."[165] They were too poor to revolutionize their means of production. And without the new technologies, they responded to cotton's new labor demands by turning to the cheap labor of their fellow villagers. Thus, although it failed to generate specialists, cotton farming in the valley acted as an important catalyst in the emergence of wage-labor relations in the peasant sector.

Because they also grew their own food, all categories of cotton cultivators experienced the labor crunch at one point or another during the growing season. Even those who interplanted the cash crop with their food crops felt the labor bottleneck. People looked for help from their children, spouses, relatives, and other villagers. Cotton in the valley created new and strengthened old forms of oppression as cash cropping had done in other parts of the world: "second serfdom" in sixteenth-century Eastern Europe, slavery in the Americas, and novel types of servitude in late-nineteenth-century Africa. Without the benefit of machinery, dominant groups and individuals sought to maximize their trade links with the West by accumulating dependents, including wage laborers.

Like their employers, paid cotton workers in the valley were generalized laborers, raising food for themselves and for their employers and sometimes receiving their wages in food. Cotton employees were not, in other words, the specialized laborers of a typical capitalist firm; they were like most other rural laborers, including those working for large maize growers in the region's oases of plenty. What set off cotton employees from these other wage earners was, among other things, the fact that they worked for an industry that consumed a great deal of the region's labor force; the difference is quantitative.

Coinciding with the cycle of food production and seasonal hunger, the high labor demands of cotton transformed the peasant sector into an important arena of wage relations from the very beginning of the twentieth century. And these demands kept rising with each grow-more-cotton campaign. African zunde holders, who succeeded European settlers as the main agricultural employers of the 1920s and 1930s, may have owned big gardens, but their enterprise did not require as much work as its successors did in the post-Bomani era. Villagers began to struggle with the labor demands of the post-Bomani cotton regime in the 1940s already, when the government forced all cultivators to make mitumbira ridges. Then came the regulations of 1951, requiring those peasants who grew cotton to raise the cash crop in different fields from their food crops, which sharpened the conflict between the two cultures. A decade later, rural labor came to support a whole range of new activities, particularly spraying. Moreover, many farmers faced these mounting pressures on their time with little or no help from the traditional workers of the family "firm," like children. Children may not have become less obedient these days, as some elders allege,[166] but it is undeniable that families have lost their children to labor migration and schools. Even those schoolchildren who live with their parents—as most do before secondary school—can only be part-time field hands, working with their parents in the afternoons or on weekends.[167] No wonder, therefore, that a farm survey for the 1971–72 season found out that 88 percent of type II and 54 percent of type I cotton growers employed some extra-household labor.[168]

The demand for paid labor was highest during garden preparation, weeding, and harvesting. In 1971–72, garden preparation (between July and November) accounted for 20 percent of the hired labor hours of the year.[169] (One bigifama in 1996 engaged 15 workers to prepare his fields at the cost of K17,000.)[170] The same survey shows that 29 percent of the 1971–72 season's hired labor hours went into weeding and spraying (between December and March). (Another bigifama in 1996 engaged over 20 casual laborers during this part of the dzinja.)[171] The remaining 50 percent of hired labor hours went into the picking, grading, and transportation of cotton between April and June, with harvesting in May taking a lion's share of these hours.[172] Cotton then absorbed 83 percent and 79 percent of all the labor expenditures of type II and type I farmers, respectively.[173] A few years later, another study, which recognized many categories of spraying farmers, came to a similar conclusion.[174] Progressive cotton growers spent more money than their poor neighbors because they owned larger fields and devoted a larger portion of those holdings to cotton. All in all, wage laborers of the peasant sector in the late 1970s received K714,000 (six percent of the region's total income) per annum.[175]

Driven mostly by poverty and hunger, some employees in the peasant sector sold their labor as "casual" or *waganyo* and others as "regular" or *wanchito* workers.[176] Typically a young man in his mid-20s, a wanchito laborer received his wages on a monthly basis and tended to live with his employer during the period of service, which sometimes lasted up to six months.[177] Factoring the food he ate, one survey estimated that the monthly wage of a wanchito averaged between K7 and K8 in the early 1970s.[178] It was cheaper to employ a waganyo laborer who in the early 1970s averaged only between K3 and K4 per month.[179] Waganyo was the more common agricultural worker.

Cotton consumed more but not all paid labor hours of the peasant sector. Many, especially regular wanchito employees, also spent part of their time in the food gardens of their employers, who assigned up to 60 percent of their large fields to food production. (The comparable figure among the poor was 88.)[180] Wealthy cotton growers enjoyed an advantage as employers of labor not only because of their larger incomes from cotton, or remittances from their better-paid husbands and children in wage employment outside the peasant sector, but also because they grew more food than the poor. Their granaries were always full, allowing them to engage and feed their regular wanchito laborers, who sometimes received their wages in food.[181] In the 1920s, African farmers had won the competition for rural labor in part because, unlike their European rivals, they also grew food.[182] *Chakudya* (food) continues to support cotton agriculture in the valley today, although officials have never thought of it as an ally of cotton or as a potential route to the capitalist future of their imagination. Regardless of the ideas of their rulers, however, peasants have always thought of the Tchiri Valley as a terrain of other social processes besides cotton growing.

CONCLUSION

Impoverished and seemingly backward, the Tchiri Valley has not been one of Malawi's neglected regions; far from it: it has been the object of the so-called development project from the time of Dr. David Livingstone in the mid-nineteenth century onward. Individuals, organizations, and government officials sought to refashion it through cotton and, although different promoters of the project may have entertained different agendas, all shared a common vision that the region's future lay in the creation of a capitalist class of farmers who did nothing but grow cotton. Even the deficit-ridden state in Malawi was committed enough to this modernizing project to invest into it its scarce resources and those of international organizations. Thus, most surveys measuring social progress started and ended with the cotton grower as its universe.[183]

However, after an entire decade (the 1970s) of heroic efforts to create the valley in their own image, some investigators came to the conclusion that the search for a specialist cotton grower amounted to a search for chimera malt.[184] Cotton cultivators of every economic standing acted and defined themselves first and foremost as food cultivators, who just happened to do some cotton growing.[185] Thus, the different terms used to describe these growers, such as *poor* and *rich, small* and *large, backward-looking* and *progressive,* do not rise above the descriptive; they do not denote different types of producers. Rich growers probably eat better than their land- and labor-deficient neighbors. But that is all. Rich and poor, small and large growers form part of the same peasantry, each caught in a vicious circle of differing dimensions. By selling their labor in times of hunger, when wage rates are at their lowest, the poor get stuck in their poverty and hunger. Time's arrow may have enslaved officials and their theorists in their conceptions of the historical process, but it has not catapulted poor or rich peasants toward Hades or heaven. The rich are as trapped as the poor.

An unreliable climate, low productivity, and particularly low producer prices not only narrow the options of the rich, but they also disperse their energies into many directions, combining food production with fishing, cattle raising, and wage labor. And to further complicate the work and thought of their rulers, the independent producer would in one season respond to shifts in prices and other social forces by devoting more of their land to cotton than food (see chapter 6). But, just as officials would begin to celebrate the eventual birth of their dream child—the yeoman farmer—villagers would change course again, replacing cotton with maize, which is less expensive to grow than cotton.[186]

Annual cotton-production figures convey this frustrating backward and forward movement in no uncertain terms.

That the unlucky passengers of this defective and cranky cotton machine have not abandoned the vehicle along the bumpy road underscores the limited capacity of the other carriers to ferry the half-stranded travelers to their destination. Laborers cannot fully support themselves and their families with their wages, and food cultivators, including maize growers in the region's oases of plenty, face their own structural challenges besides contingent threats like drought. They do not have a reliable market partly because of the primitive transport system, but mainly because the people who need their product most are too poor to constitute a dependable source of income for others.[187] If they ever understood it, officials have yet to admit the fact that it is impossible to develop one section of the peasantry, one segment of the economy, or one part of the country when others languish in abject poverty. The beneficiary of official largesse, cotton cohabits the same world as, and its success is intrinsically tied to, the neglected food sector. The two compete for the daily routines of the same growing season. This and the next chapter are intrinsically connected because they are both about the intertwined orders of the season and day.

6

THE LOGIC OF THE PEASANT GARDEN

Villagers feel safer from drought and other hazards with their land divided into small plots distributed throughout the village. Having all one's land on a single soil type, in a single location and exposure, is considered risky.[1]

These dimbas are more than a second line of defence and their annual value to the populace & to the district cannot be overstressed.[2]

Sorghum and bulrush millet are still the staple crops in the southern part of the [Port Herald] District and ... Maize is grown more extensively in the Northern part of the district.[3]

Ridging has for several decades been a dominant theme of the extension service. It would be worthwhile to consider carefully just why so little is ridged after so much effort has been made to convince farmers that this practice will increase yields through the prevention of surface run off and the resultant retention of water in furrows. A long-term advantage is held to be the prevention of sheet erosion.[4]

Concentration upon cash crops, which occupy the most fertile land, leads to neglect of food crops.[5]

INTRODUCTION

Government attempts to create cotton specialists out of rural cultivators ran against the logic of the peasant garden. Peasants not only combine food production with fishing, cattle keeping, and wage labor, but, whenever possible, they maintain several fields, in different ecological zones, each garden carrying, at one and the same time, crops and crop varieties of differing characteristics. Officials also violated the logic of the peasant garden in their insistence on fixed schedules for the planting and harvesting of crops. Villagers stagger the planting process, sowing different crops or different strains of the same crop at different times during the same growing season. An ideal peasant garden replicates the natural landscape, with different plants in different stages of growth.

As producers, therefore, villagers create deserts of hunger and oases of plenty in multiple ways. They cultivate both munda gardens on the mphala drylands and dimba plots on the dambo floodplains. Drought turns munda gardens into deserts of hunger in contrast to the dimba oases of plenty on the dambo, and bad floods reverse the process. But peasants do not need to operate two different fields in two different niches to simultaneously generate deserts of hunger and oases of plenty. Every garden becomes both a desert of hunger and an oasis of plenty as it combines lower-yielding but drought-tolerant crops with higher-yielding but less drought-tolerant plants. Villagers both assume and avoid risk. Finally, because these crops carry different weights as use and as exchange values, the garden places the peasant community within the circuits of both time's arrow and time's cycle. As agricultural workers, villagers create history as a terrain of multiple tensions, whose ultimate resolution depends on the total historical context, which in the valley included ecological, demographic, political, and economic processes.

MAJOR FORCES BEHIND AGRICULTURAL CHANGE

The impact of any of the above-named pressures on the region's agricultural system was ambiguous and variable. None was strong enough by itself to project the food system in a particular direction. Government officials were rarely able to transform the region's farming methods according to their plans. Similarly unpredictable were the effects of population pressure and the cotton economy. Like government policy, demographic shifts and cotton created new opportunities and stresses without, however, predetermining the outcome of these tensions. Each assumed causal significance mostly in the context of other forces. And the same was true of ecological shifts. Although generally more effective than the other three factors, the changes brought about by variations in rainfall patterns and the flow of the Tchiri River can only be understood as part of the totality. Villagers sometimes exploited the same natural environment differently depending on their circumstances. Finally, while some of the resulting transformations have become permanent, many others were less durable and even reversible.

The Changing Levels of the Tchiri River

Long-term shifts in the flow of the Tchiri River have played a major role in the agricultural history of the valley. Starting in the 1880s, the Tchiri River began to drop sharply as a result of general climatic changes that also lowered Lake Malawi's levels. People in the valley began to experience the impact of this development toward the end of the 1880s, when, for example, John Moir of the ALC made the following observation: "I may state here my belief that the first years we were here in Africa, [18]78 to [18]85 were years of exceptionally [high?] rainfall and that subsequent years have been exceptionally dry."[6] Chief Katunga agreed, employing the discourse of the golden-age theory to make his point: "When you first came to this country, we had many years of much rain & plenty of mapira ... now we are having many years of little rain & poor crops. We never had it so before."[7] But neither Katunga nor Moir expected that this trend (figure 6.1), which was already adversely affecting munda agriculture, would also invigorate dimba farming and underpin the region's agricultural prosperity.

To appreciate how dryness could also have contributed to agricultural prosperity, one needs a dynamic approach to the ecological process, postulating a creative tension not only between society and the environment, but also within the ecological system itself. One and the same event—dryness—can lead different elements of the multifaceted ecological process into different trajectories. The same trend toward aridity, which exposed munda farming to frequent droughts, became the basis of a vibrant dimba regime during the five decades between 1890 and 1939. After fertilizing the marshes and allowing peasants to raise rice, good floods left as early as February and never returned to the land until December. The extended growing season allowed villagers to raise several early-maturing food crops consecutively besides slow-ripening plants like cotton. As a result, though measuring only 350 square miles—about 13.23 percent of the region's land area[8]—the dambo in the Dabanyi and Dinde came to assume great significance in the region, supporting (1) between 15,000 and 20,000 villagers living in and cultivating nothing but the dambo, (2) many occupants of the mphala drylands participating in dimba agriculture on a regular basis, and (3) and nearly everyone in the event of drought. Seasonal hunger was in principle impossible for the first group of growers in the period under discussion.

Figure 6.1 Lake Malawi water levels, 1900–1980 (Elias Mandala, *Work and Control in a Peasant Economy.* © 1990. Reprinted by permission of The University of Wisconsin Press)

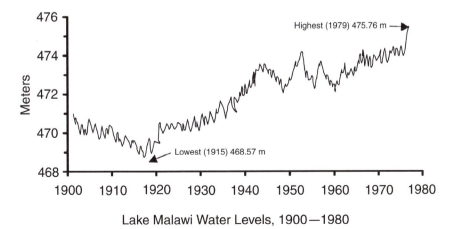

Lake Malawi Water Levels, 1900—1980

To highlight the agricultural prosperity of this period is not to deny the occurrence of major food deficits or conditions of general economic distress. Droughts, bad floods, and famines did occur, but in this period such events must be seen as having merely interrupted generally positive economic trends. This pattern of economic change started under Magololo rule in the northern section of the valley after the chaola of the early 1860s.[9] Once in place, the recovery did not stall with the onset of the dry spell in the 1880s. It instead spread to the southern section of the valley. The ivory and sesame trades of 1870–1900[10] and the cotton economy of 1900–1940 rested on a solid agricultural base, remarkable for its potential for further growth.

The region's tax record provides one kind of evidence for its general prosperity. The first to shoulder the British tax burden in Malawi, peasants of the then Lower Shire (later Port Herald or Nsanje) District paid £400 in taxes in 1893 and subsequently distinguished themselves for their excellent taxpaying habits.[11] That many defaulted during the Great Depression and in the aftermath of the Bomani floods shows that there was nothing "natural" in the rural population's taxpaying habits, as some commentators implied.[12] Peasants' ability to finance their oppression was directly related to the vitality of the agricultural sector, which also affected the region's demographics.

A vigorous agricultural sector between the 1880s and 1930s supported demographic processes very different from those generally identified for other parts of eastern Africa and Malawi itself. On the one hand, the valley exported few of its male population as migrant workers,[13] and on the other, it

Figure 6.2 The Tchiri water levels, 1909–1940 (Elias Mandala, *Work and Control in a Peasant Economy.* © 1990. Reprinted by permission of The University of Wisconsin Press)

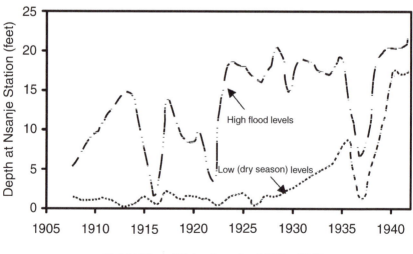

Tchiri River Water Levels, 1909—1940

experienced a dramatic growth in its population, as a result of natural increase and immigration. Oral history portrays the early years of British colonial occupation as a period of unprecedented immigration from Mozambique, and written sources largely confirm this picture. The country's first British administrator or governor, Sir Harry Johnston, wrote about the late nineteenth century in the valley as a time when "flourishing populations ... [were] springing up all along the west bank of the Shire."[14] In the north, some immigrants were "settling down under the Makololo chiefs" in what became the Chikwawa District.[15] But many more flocked to the economically more dynamic Lower Shire District. Its headquarters (or Boma) at Port Herald Township acted as a magnet for both Indian and European merchants:

> Indian and European traders have begun to settle, and land has gone up in value. Port Herald has been erected into a Township and laid out in Plots. One of these plots, about an acre in extent, has been sold to the African Lakes Trading Corporation for £70, and another plot of about 8 acres is to be sold for £140 to a Banyan, and there are numerous applications for other sites in the Township from Europeans and Indians.[16]

And this pattern continued until the floods of 1939, which marked a new phase in the history of dimba agriculture.

Peasants call the floods of 1939 *Bomani* after the Chisena verb *kuboma,* or "to push." A wall of water pushed through the Dabanyi and Dinde, sweeping away people and houses and flooding over 120,000 acres of cropland. However, Bomani has become an historical landmark not merely because of its one-time destructive power; many other floods were equally if not more devastating. Bomani has left an indelible mark on peasants' historical consciousness because it initiated a new era in dimba farming and the history of the region as a whole. With a few exceptions, the Tchiri River has maintained high water levels since Bomani, shortening the dimba growing season and making the differences between the wet- and dry-season levels relatively insignificant (figure 6.2).

Even light rains could force the river to overflow its banks, causing bad floods in 1940, 1943, 1944, 1946, 1947, and 1948.[17] Peasants in the Port Herald District, more dimba-dependent than Chikwawa, thus faced a new predicament. The 1943 annual report was typical:

> [1943] was one of the poorer seasons from an agricultural point of view. Grain crops planted in the southern half of the district failed owing to [too heavy rains followed by] long periods of drought ... The rice in the river plain was destroyed by floods.[18]

Four years later, in 1947, the author of the district's annual report had little to tell his superiors in Zomba besides his frustration with bad floods: "Floods in the district are now looked upon *as a normal annual event* and for the people living South of Port Herald in the area known as Nsuwa [Dinde], have become part of their *ordinary* existence."[19] Moreover, unlike their predecessors, the bad floods of the post-Bomani era tended to recede slowly, cutting down the period of cultivation on the usable portions of the marshes. In 1947, for example, villages in the Dinde were still under water in late May,[20] and sweet "potatoes ... had to be planted in a reduced acreage because large areas of the land were inundated until a late period by the floods of the previous year."[21] The subsequent trend toward aridity during the 1950s proved short-lived.[22] Floods became more common again in the closing years of the decade.

In the 1950s official attempts to control the river initiated yet another phase in post-Bomani dimba agriculture. The government completed building a barrage at Liwonde in 1957, which officials sometimes opened to prevent flooding in the area above Liwonde, and at other times closed to allow the construction of hydroelectric power stations and bridges below Liwonde. These controls sometimes coincided with the natural flow of the river, but very often they did not. The closing of the dam in February and March 1970 cut off the flow for rice producers, which led an infuriated chief Nyachikadza in the Dinde to write the following letter to the district commissioner:

> You close the River when we need water ... Rice needs water, but there is no water [in the fields] at this time—the fields are cracking. If the rice dies, we will also die. Forgive us, sir, we are not trying to be disrespectful or ordering you; we're just asking for your kindness. Now the rainy season is over, but you can help us ... Everyone should know that this is killing us. Every year we need water from January to April. Please, sir, we are asking you, by this letter, that you release the River so we can get water this month [March] ... we need it until next month.[23]

But opening the river before the rainy season sometimes led to early flooding, which is also a disaster for downstream peasants. Early floods kill dimba crops in their formative stages, and when such flooding coincided with drought, the results could be tragic, as in 1966. A drought led everyone to look to the dambo for relief. But that hope was dashed with the "opening of the barrage and the overflowing of the river."[24] Villagers have always blamed bad people or witches for withholding rain, but not for causing floods. Peasants had mostly accepted bad floods as "acts of God," but the harnessing of the Tchiri for the purposes of development has broadened the scope of political misfortunes.

Besides broadening the scope of socially constructed misfortunes, the combination of early and frequent floods with the permanent inundation of considerable parts of the marshes adversely affected the demographic process and the relative position of the dambo vis-à-vis the mphala. Villagers abandoned the dambo as a place of habitation, although some intermittently returned to the Dabanyi and Dinde whenever the water receded for extended periods, as in some years during the 1950s, 1970s, and 1980s. The 1990s reestablished the out-migration again, and there are only a few isolated communities in the Dinde today, and virtually no one in the Dabanyi.

The combination of the above ecological shifts with economic change has rearranged the demographic relationship between Chikwawa and Port Herald (Nsanje). While some people from the southern sections of the Dabanyi and from the Dinde migrated to Nsanje's mphala drylands, many more migrated to Chikwawa, leading to the district's emergence as the new demographic center of the valley.

The marshes have also assumed a new meaning in relation to the mphala drylands. The munda system now supports more people on a regular basis than it did in the pre-Bomani era. For many, particularly government officials, agriculture now means nothing but munda farming. The dambo contributes less to the region's economic livelihood in absolute terms. But precisely because of its reduced size, the dambo has become more precious today than it was in the pre-Bomani era. Peasants literally scramble for access to the few portions of the dambo that become cultivatable during the short growing season. Thus, in contrast to the relatively more abundant mphala, the dambo has become the focus of conflicts over land and, increasingly, monetary transactions.[25] It still retains its pre-Bomani position as a place for emergency farming and the first line of defense against chaola famine.[26]

Developments after the Bomani floods underscore the need to separate famine events from njala seasonal hunger. The inundation of the marshes did, without doubt, increase the victims of formal njala as a period without a fresh crop. In addition to the original munda-dependent farmers, there were now the former inhabitants of the marshes, who had no experience of formal njala between the 1880s and 1930s. Most of those who left the marshes for the mphala drylands ended up in the region's deserts of hunger, while those who remained on the dambo had to deal with the realities of a shortened growing season. Both groups of the former dimba-dependent cultivators had to learn to cope with the annual food gap. However, the mere increase in the number of hungry mouths did not automatically plunge the region into a cycle of chaola famines. Perennially hungry people can conquer famine. For example, the peasants who fled to Chikwawa's deserts of hunger were able to turn cotton agriculture into a useful tool against chaola. The cotton economy proved to be a double-edged instrument in the story of food security.

Cotton

Many garden owners considered it more profitable to scare birds from the sorghum crops than to pick and attempt to grade a messy crop of cotton.[27]

The old story of too much cotton grown and wasted and not enough food crops has been repeated.[28]

Evidence from the valley advances our understanding of the consequences of cash-crop agriculture in two ways. First, it suggests that cash crops may affect the production and distribution phases of the food economy differently. Although cotton diverted land and labor from food production, it also allowed villagers to acquire food from the market (see chapters 4 and 5). Second, and even more significant for this chapter on production systems, is the finding that the relationship between food and cash-crop production is a two-way process. Cash-crop agriculture has both shaped *and* been shaped by food production. In addition to the standard query about the impact of cash-crop agriculture on food crops, one needs to ask about the influence of the food economy on cash-crop farming. Thus, the working hypothesis of this book is that cash-crop agriculture created new tensions for food producers, sharpening their risk-taking and risk-avoiding tendencies without, however, predetermining the outcome of those tensions. Villagers have sometimes resolved the conflict in favor of commodity production and at other times in favor of food. The real challenge for historians, therefore, is to figure out exactly how and when food growers made and implemented those conflicting decisions.

Peasants have accommodated cotton into the existing systems of food production in four major ways. In the pre-Bomani era, some villagers in the congested Nsanje District grew cotton in the same garden and at the same time as their food crops—the famous intercropping method common on the Dinde. Other villagers without access to the dambo during the same period and area planted their cotton on the mphala drylands immediately after harvesting their mchewere millet around March—intraseasonal rotation. Then, some growers in the land-rich areas like Chikwawa confined cotton to their munda gardens and reserved the dambo exclusively for their maize, sweet potatoes, and other food crops. The fact that these villagers utilized the dambo differently than their counterparts in Nsanje District remains a powerful reminder of the limits of ecological imperatives. Finally, other villagers in the same land-abundant Chikwawa responded positively to the government campaign requiring them to raise cotton in a different field from, but at the same time as, their food crops on the mphala drylands—the "pure cotton culture."

The state-mandated pure cotton regime posed the greatest challenge to food growers, as the labor demands of the two regimes collided from the beginning to the end of the growing season. The conflict between the two engendered new domestic struggles, as Mrs. Elizabeth Anthuachino of Khembo Village (Nsanje) related in 1996:

Yes, there are usually intense fights, sir; people fight as they prepare their fields. A wife would say, asking the husband, telling him that we should start planting sorghum, because we want to start eating sorghum early. But the husband would not agree, saying he wants to start with the cotton fields. He would say, "look at what others are doing" and that is when [the wife would say], let's split, you go to the cotton field, and I go to take care of the sorghum; the two would go to different fields, without reaching an agreement.[29]

But the dilemma does not end after sowing; the two gardens continued to challenge the food-first principle up to harvesting time, as District Commissioner P. M. Lewis remarked in May 1958:

The clash in harvesting between sorghum and cotton is well illustrated this year either the cotton being harvested and the sorghum left for the birds to eat, or the foodstuffs being brought in and the cotton left to blow about the garden.[30]

The agricultural officer for Chikwawa South in 1965, Mr. Fabian Anthuacino, noted the same conflict a few years later: "There are a few problems why picking [cotton] is not going on well. Some of these are drinking beer, *sorghum harvesting* and necessary absence."[31] However, not only the pure cotton culture but all forms of cotton growing created labor bottlenecks, as there were operations specific to cotton under any cultivation system (see chapter 5). All producers had to make hard choices at each point in the agricultural cycle.

Peasants tried to resolve the tension in several ways, depending on their intradomestic relations and the general economic environment. They have sometimes invested more of their labor into cotton and at other times into food crops; they have sometimes assumed and at other times avoided risk; they have sometimes followed time's arrow to modernity and at other times recoiled under the logic of time's cycle. Directionality, which makes the crisis literature so appealing, has been conspicuous by its absence. Given particular economic conditions, many villagers resolutely defended the integrity of the food economy and avoided risk.

When and where peasants could generate income through other activities like maize growing, they sometimes defended the integrity of the food economy most radically by staying away from cotton. Many villagers did not grow cotton even at the height of its popularity in the 1920s and 1930s, and their disinclination grew even stronger as the government tried to impose modern agricultural techniques, increasing the direct and indirect costs of the cash crop. Thus, while only 10 percent of Nsanje's households did not grow cotton in the mid-1920s, by the 1960s this figure had jumped to nearly 100 percent in the district outside the Mbenje subchiefdom. Nor did all households grow cotton in Chikwawa District under the SVADP of the 1970s and 1980s. About a third of the district's households abstained from the cash crop.

Complete noninvolvement was not, however, the only or most popular way of defending the food-first principle against cotton. Many villagers grew cotton and tried to protect the integrity of the food economy at the same time. One strategy to accomplish this was to deny cotton the more valuable of their land resources. Thus, peasants who exploited the northwestern section of the Dabanyi in Chikwawa District confined cotton to the less fertile mphala drylands, while using the rich alluvial soils of the dambo exclusively for food crops. They succeeded doing this for a number of reasons. Land was relatively abundant on the mphala in Chikwawa District. Moreover, the conflict between dimba and munda work schedules was relatively mild at the beginning of this strategy in the pre-Bomani era. The labor demands of the two regimes merged mostly in November and December, when peasants harvested their dimba maize and prepared or planted their munda fields with cotton. But, as if to underscore the insignificance of the problem of labor distribution, peasants did not change their ways in the post-Bomani era, when the floods left the marshes more slowly and the opening of dimba gardens conflicted with the harvesting of cotton between May and June. Villagers continued to pay more attention to their food crops on the dambo than cotton on the mphala[32] largely because cotton was not the only cash crop in this region; it competed with maize, which had a ready market in the Blantyre and Limbe Townships. Cotton was not as important among these growers.

Cotton ranked so low in the household economies of this portion of Chikwawa District that villagers almost consistently resolved the problem of labor distribution in favor of the food economy. Thus, instead of preparing munda gardens, they spent their precious time in November and December harvesting maize on the dambo:

> It appears that they were late with [munda] garden preparation, because of the previous season's madimba crops, which they were busy harvesting when they should have been occupied with garden preparation and planting dry land gardens.[33]

Slowly receding floods brought more bad news for the promoters of the early cotton planting campaign: "Madimba gardens were entered late this year as a result of prolonged rains and this work was still behind on the 15th September. As a result cultivators were *reluctant* to withdraw from the dimbas to begin their garden preparation" on the mphala.[34] But officials would be equally distressed when the dambo became available for cultivation as early as May: "Madimba cultivation has commenced," complained one official, "much to the determent of cotton work."[35] Another report went even further: "People are over keen to get on with their Madimba cultivation, and leave their cotton falling off the plants."[36] Officials continued to complain about this halfhearted engagement in cotton right up to the time of independence and beyond.

"There was a considerable quantity of cotton lost in the main growing areas," noted one report in the early 1960s, "due to the failure of growers to pick all their cotton."[37]

Prices also weighed heavily in rural decisions to abandon their cotton in the fields. Merchants purchased first-, second-, and third-grade cotton at different rates and villagers harvested their cotton in several stages with those prices in mind. The first round of picking resulted mostly in first-grade cotton that fetched the highest rates, and subsequent operations ended with mostly unprofitable lower-grade cotton. Thus, even under healthy market conditions, the harvesting of low-grade cotton was not a high priority among growers, and interest in this cotton would fall even more sharply after receiving disappointing prices for first-grade cotton. Peasants would concentrate their efforts on other activities.[38]

Finally, villagers tried to subordinate the land and labor demands of cotton through intercropping and intraseasonal crop rotation. These were among the most popular strategies of defending the food-first principle in Nsanje before the Bomani floods of 1939. Intercropping and intraseasonal rotation highlight the complex relationship between food and cash-crop production in an economy without much land and with limited rural cash-earning opportunities. A technique almost as old and as widespread as the peasant world itself, intercropping allowed villagers to reduce both the land and labor demands of cotton agriculture as they raised the cash crop at the same time and in the same garden as their food crops on the dambo. Pressure on land also played a part in intraseasonal rotation, a form of staggering that allowed villagers to plant cotton in the same gardens as, but after, harvesting their munda maize and millet around March.

Crop rotation and interplanting satisfied British demand for cotton so effectively that that the colonial government quickly gave up its feeble campaign for the pure cotton culture in the first decade of the twentieth century.[39] The "backwardness" of the two techniques were to reignite British penchant for "modernity" only after the decline of cotton output in the Port Herald District in the post-Bomani era. The resulting campaign to revive the sagging economy through "scientific" methods of farming formed the background to the death of the industry in the district and the invigoration of other branches of the nonfood sector (see chapter 5).

But the above story formed only one paradox in the history of cotton among food producers. Another was the indivisibility between resistance and accommodation, risk avoiding and risk taking. The triumph of the food-first principle and failure of the government to create cotton specialists does not exhaust the history of cotton in the valley. If that were the case, the story of chapter 5 would have had a clear ending, which it does not. People still grow cotton because, among other things, living peasants both assume and avoid risk, create history along both time's cycle and time's arrow, and both prioritize and override the food-first principle.

Cash from cotton compromised the food-first principle in the region's major cotton-growing strata of pre-Bomani Nsanje South and post-Bomani Makande Plain. Pre-Bomani Nsanje South approximated the ideal of a monoculture better than the Makande Plain. Without many rural opportunities for earning cash, risk-averse peasants in the land-scarce Nsanje South had to give up something in order to sustain their resistance to the tyranny of cotton in a money economy. The boundaries between risk taking and risk avoiding become increasingly blurred.

Success at subordinating the demands of cotton through intercropping on the dambo came with its own price. To allow cotton to flourish alone in its later stages, peasants who popularized intercropping in the Dinde Marshes did not raise another maize crop after picking the initial one around May. They did not exploit the full potential of the dambo for food production, as their counterparts in Chikwawa did. Without competition from cotton, peasants in Chikwawa raised one maize crop after another during the same growing season.

A similar dilemma faced the farmers who sought to protect food security by rotating cotton with maize or millet on the mphala. They did so only by abandoning gonkho sorghum. The tall gonkho not only overshadows cotton, but is also a slow-maturing plant. As it competed with the cash crop for labor until it was harvested in May and June, villagers began to replace gonkho with the fast-ripening maize, which they harvested at the same time as millet before planting cotton in March–April. Peasants gambled. Gonkho was much more drought-resilient than maize. To meet the demands of cotton, villagers effectively exposed the food economy to the vagaries of the climate. Under certain conditions, to avoid risk in one respect demanded risk taking in another.

The interests of the British cotton lobby also triumphed in the post-Bomani Makande Plain. As in Nsanje South, peasants in Chikwawa's Makande Plain often grew cotton at the expense of food crops. Some of the dynamics were similar. There were few alternatives to cotton as a source of money, especially in the 1940s and 1950s. The subregion's most popular food crops—millet and sorghum—did not have a demand beyond the village community. To remain conservative as cultivators of subsistence crops, villagers needed to be progressive as cotton growers. But other forces in the post-Bomani Makande Plain were different from those dominant in pre-Bomani Nsanje South. Cotton producers of the post-Bomani era in the Makande Plain did not enjoy such delaying tactics as intraseasonal rotation. In 1951, the state imposed the early cotton-planting scheme, ordering all growers of cotton to sow the cash crop at the beginning of the rainy season in November and harvest it by May. To give teeth to the regulation, officials closed markets as early as August. There was no market for late-planted cotton. Munda cotton thus competed for household labor with food from the beginning to the end of the growing season. Labor-deficient, cotton-growing households often grew less food and/or failed to take adequate care of their food crops in pursuit of cotton money, which they could also use to procure food from the market. Cotton money had assumed a distinctly economic function besides the payment of the so-called hut tax. The food-first principle is negotiable and can lead to different actions under different conditions, although some of those diversions attracted official attention mostly in the event of a major food shortage.

One officer in 1955 feared that "food ... shortages may occur later due to people planting more cotton than food."[40] Whether his fears materialized is not clear from the sources, but three years later, his successor explained the food shortages of the year with reference to the fact that his subjects paid "more attention to their cotton crop first at the neglect of food crops."[41] Then, during a major food deficit in 1962, officials of the same district complained about the diversion of rural resources from food to cotton: "Food crops [are] generally very patchy and gardens weedy. People are tending to neglect food crops in favour of cotton."[42] And blaming the victim, one official explained the plight of the residents of the Kakoma Resettlement Scheme this way: "While cotton plots were clean weeded promptly the maize and mapira suffered from delayed weeding."[43] What this official wanted to forget was that the families were only trying to become modern according to the official definition of development that prioritized export crop production over subsistence. They followed the footsteps of Nsanje cotton growers who had pursued cotton money at the expense of food production:

> Much has been done to improve cotton growing but practically nothing with regard to the far more important food crops. When I came back to the District after four years of absence I was very much struck with the lack of progress in the production of food crops. In some respects things have changed for the worse.[44]

Many large growers in the Makande Plain diverted resources from food production also because they looked to cotton as a source of money for food. They wanted to become cotton specialists, placing the valley along the path of time's arrow.

The emergence of cotton specialists, using cotton money to purchase food from the market, has always remained a distinct possibility in the post-Bomani Tchiri Valley.[45] Even those growing cotton on the mphala and food crops on the dambo sometimes looked to cotton to finance their food needs: "Food, they will cultivate in Madimba when possible," wrote one official, "but mainly the idea appears to be that Boma will send food to strategic points where it will be on sale."[46] Another official made the connection between cotton and food more direct when he reported, "People appear to have got used to the idea of buying food with the money obtained from their cotton."[47] Other sources make it clear that this expanded notion of food security, which also takes account of food from the market, was not unique to the Makande Plain.

The entire country had started moving in that direction, according to the 1949 annual report of the Department of Agriculture:

> An interesting aspect of the emergency [replanting campaign because of drought] was a distinct tendency on the part of some African cultivators to believe that if they had money they could soon purchase food and, in consequence, to regard the production of economic crops such as cotton and tobacco as more important than the production of food.[48]

Some peasants were ready to become the specialists of the official imagination.

That most growers did not routinely try this risky venture speaks as much about the strengths of the food-first principle as about the weaknesses of the cotton economy itself. The gap between producer prices and the cost of inputs foiled the trend toward specialization. Growers could not live on cotton alone. They needed to grow their own food, subjecting the fate of cotton to seasonal fluctuations in food availability. In one season, villagers would concentrate on food, only to change course in the next season, which explains, in part, the upward and downward swings in cotton output and the fickleness of time's arrow (table 5.2). Every trend became reversible. It did not take a generation for the risk takers of Nsanje South to discover the wisdom of their ancestors. By the 1960s, the same growers who had abandoned gonkho sorghum in the 1920s in what turned out to be a spurious groping into modernity through cotton abandoned the cash crop and returned to sorghum. Cotton exerted as much pressure on food as food did on cotton, and the food-first principle was as tentative as the drive toward cotton money. The real challenge is to understand the context of the conflict, just as one needs the larger field of forces to appreciate the demographic process. Routinely blamed by scholars and policymakers for Africa's food problems, population pressure emerges from the history of the valley as one of the least important forces in setting the direction of agricultural production.

Population Pressure

The population of the valley grew rapidly in the late nineteenth and early twentieth centuries, rising from about 22,500 in 1895 to 319,206 in 1977, although this increase was not evenly distributed in space or time. In the pre-Bomani era, much of this growth occurred in the cotton-driven Nsanje (Port Herald or Lower Shire) District. The population of the 747-square-mile Nsanje District in 1922 was 63,294, an average of 94.8 per square mile, while the 1,897-square-mile Chikwawa District had only 27,954 persons—14.7 individuals per square mile. But developments after Bomani reversed the fortunes of the two districts. By 1945, Nsanje still led Chikwawa, but only by several thousand (66,746 people in Nsanje against Chikwawa's 59,644). In the following two decades, Chikwawa caught up with and left Nsanje behind. In 1966, Chikwawa

had a total population of 157,805 against Nsanje's 101,074.[49] Nothing stopped
Chikwawa's surge in the next decade, so that by 1977 Chikwawa's 205,873
people eclipsed Nsanje's 113,333, although Nsanje still had the higher population density.[50] Nsanje had run out of virgin land and Chikwawa had not.

Although there are no data on the relationship between population growth
and the expansion of cultivated land for much of the history of the valley, there
are interesting figures for the 12 years from 1960 to 1972. The population of
the entire valley grew at 2.3 percent per annum while cultivated land expanded
by 4.6 percent per annum (table 6.1). But like population growth itself, this
expansion of cultivated land did not occur at the same rate throughout the
region. To sharpen our understanding of the demographic process in the valley's
two administrative areas, we will focus on Nsanje South and the Gaga Hills
as representative of the general trends in, respectively, Nsanje and Chikwawa
Districts. The area of cultivated land in Nsanje South grew at only 1.9 percent
per year; there was simply no virgin land for further expansion. In contrast, in
the Gaga Hills newly cultivated land rose at the vigorous rate of 6.5 percent
annually. And the difference between the two strata becomes even sharper from
the perspective of their respective total growth rates in the 12 years. Overall,
cultivated land in the Gaga Hills grew by 112 percent in contrast to Nsanje
South's 26 percent. Finally, the two strata become two totally different worlds
when one compares their respective garden sizes, as one can see from table
6.2. Fifty-two percent of the holdings in Nsanje South were under one hectare,
compared to the Gaga Hills' 13 percent.

Table 6.1.
Cultivated Area by Stratum and Annual Rate of Change

Stratum	1960 (ha)	1972 (ha)	%Change	Annual Growth Rate (%)
Gaga Hills	6,800	14,400	112	6.5
Mwanza Valley	6,000	14,200	137	7.4
Tomali Plain	14,600	24,400	67	4.4
Makande Plain	37,300	78,600	111	6.4
East Bank	24,300	29,900	23	1.7
Nsanje North	14,500	14,400		−0.1
Nsanje South	12,000	15,100	26	1.9
Chididi Hills	2,800	12,000	329	12.9
All	118,300	202,900	72	4.6

Sources: NADD, "Garden Survey," chapter 3, p. 2, table 3.1. According to the surveyors, Nsanje
North "suffered a net reduction in cultivated area ... due to the permanent flooding of some
900 hectares by the rising level of the Shire River, which more than cancelled out an expansion
of cultivated area of 800 ha." (ibid.).

Table 6.2.
Size Distribution of Holdings (%)

| | *DESERTS OF HUNGER* | | | | | *OASES OF PLENTY* | | | |
Holding Size (ha)	Makande Plain	Mwanza Valley	Nsanje North	Nsanje South	Tomali Plain	Chididi Hills	East Bank	Gaga Hills	All Strata
0–1	24	33	19	52	26	69	63	13	38
1–2	34	42	34	35	39	26	26	37	33
2–3	21	14	30	8	17	6	5	28	15
3+	21	11	17	6	18	0	6	22	13
N	342	115	124	121	170	82	258	46	1258

Sources: Adapted from NADD, "Garden Survey," Chapter 1, p. 2, Table 1.2. The "*N*" stands for the number of surveyed households. Some columns add up to slightly more or less than 100.

For a whole range of reasons, table 6.2, which rearranges table 1.2 of the NADD's "Garden Survey Report" on the basis of the distinction between the region's deserts of hunger and oases of plenty (see chapter 3), may not say much, but it provides empirical evidence for beginning to question the almost instinctive assumption about the role of population pressure in agricultural performance. There is no intrinsic correlation between a region's landholding regime and its capacity to feed itself. Not all deserts of hunger are overcrowded, and not all oases of plenty are land-abundant. On the basis of landholding sizes alone, Nsanje South is different from the other deserts of hunger but closer to the Chididi Hills, which is an oasis of plenty.[51] Similarly, the Gaga Hills in Chapananga North are as different from the other oases of plenty as they are close to four of the five deserts of hunger (besides Nsanje South). One cannot, in short, separate regions of hunger from those of abundance on the basis of their respective garden sizes alone. Land pressure becomes a relevant force in the story of hunger and plenty only in the context of other factors, including government policy.

State Intervention

Starting in the 1940s, the colonial government embarked on many projects to transform the agricultural practices of the valley. Some of the pressures behind the initiatives were national in character, reflecting European attempts to rationalize peasant production during Africa's "second colonial occupation" following World War II. Others were local in origin, directly related to the region's population distribution and the third cotton campaign (see chapter 5). To revive the faltering cotton economy after the Bomani floods, officials banned

interplanting and promoted early cotton planting. The early-planting drive succeeded mainly because officials closed cotton markets too early in the season
for anyone to sell late-planted cotton. On the other hand, the prohibition on
intercropping ended up multiplying patterns of mixing cotton with food crops
instead of streamlining them, as officials wanted (see chapter 5). Then there
was the project to resettle peasants from the "congested" Nsanje South to the
"empty" Chikwawa chiefdoms of Chapananga and Ngabu. Villagers successfully resisted this scheme in the mid-1950s, when migrating to Chikwawa
required the settlers to adopt the government's new agricultural rules, known
collectively as malimidwe. However, as soon as the state dropped malimidwe
rules in the late 1950s, villagers started to resettle themselves in the land-
abundant Chikwawa areas of Chapananga and Ngabu. The only program
that continued to strain peasants' relations with the state was the nationwide
scheme, forcing villagers, under heavy penalties, to make mitumbira ridges in
their fields in preparation for planting.

Touted as the principal method of raising productivity and preventing soil
erosion, ridges were to rise between 12 and 18 inches above the ground and
run between one and three feet apart. In the hills, the mounds were to follow
natural contours at intervals of three to five feet.[52] Only dimba cultivators did
not have to make ridges, because annual floods could easily wash away the
mounds. Otherwise, all other growers had to ridge their fields, which was an
extremely labor-intensive operation. According to one estimate, a man could
make between 440 to 660 yards of mitumbira on a piece of land not ridged
before and between 660 and 880 yards on a previously ridged garden.[53] The
ridging campaign represented the most ambitious form of state intervention
in peasant agriculture, although, as was often the case outside cotton farming,
the state did not invest a single penny in the project. Peasants were to do all
the work and assume all the risks of the untested experiment.

First introduced in Nsanje District in the late 1940s, the campaign succeeded among mountain farmers, who had practiced a precolonial version of
mitumbira and who had no reason to oppose the drive (see below). Elsewhere,
the campaign did not make many converts, and succeeded only in strain-
ing peasant-state relations in a series of conflicts, popularly remembered as
nkhondo-ya-mitumbira (the war of the ridges). Nkhondo-ya-mitumbira drove
villagers to Mozambique and the Dinde, where they did not have to construct
ridges: "There has been a fair movement of population within the district and
to Portuguese East Africa;" wrote one official in 1949, "internal movement has
tended for people to move ... to the areas of Ngabu and Nyachikadza [Dinde],
both in search of better soil and to temporarily *escape the ridging rules.*"[54] The
campaign politicized agriculture, providing nationalist politicians with an effective platform around which to rally the peasantry against the colonial state.

Rural resistance to mitumbira remained stiff and consistent, spreading from
Nsanje to Chikwawa, where the British imposed the system only in 1950s.

And when the new political leaders of Malawi reneged on their promise to abolish mitumbira, peasants of both districts hardened their opposition, providing one line of continuity between the colonial and postcolonial agricultural histories of the two otherwise demographically different districts of Chikwawa and Nsanje. Failed programs did succeed in disturbing rural life.

As in Nsanje, peasants in Chikwawa had supported the MCP on the condition that once in power, the party would abolish malimidwe. But with Dr. Banda at the helm at the Ministry of Natural Resources, the newly elected government made only one concession. It would no longer use coercion to implement colonial land-utilization rules, trusting the force of persuasion. Thus, summarizing the developments of the previous 12 months since the general elections of August 1961, the district commissioner for Chikwawa welcomed the dawn of an "entirely new approach in our extension Methods."[55] British administrators who had remained in the country after independence in 1964 were generally happy, implementing the same agricultural rules they had formulated in the colonial era. Malawi's African rulers believed as firmly as their predecessors had done in the scientific superiority of mitumbira ridges, despite the serious reservations of some British experts about the suitability of the scheme in some parts of the country.[56]

The new government's unquestioning commitment to the colonial agricultural program in the valley took form in 1968 with the establishment of the CCDP—the precursor to the SVADP. In the days leading to the formation of the CCDP, the new leaders launched a two-pronged campaign. First, they mended fences with the Agriculture Department they had demonized since the 1940s, making it clear that they had no ideological quarrels with existing policies and that they needed the support of the department's personnel. There was, according to the contented compiler of the annual agricultural report for Chikwawa in 1961–62, "increasing contact and co-operation" between his department and "leaders in the political and economic fields." The old enemies had "shown that they are willing and anxious to support the Department" so that the morale of the staff, which had run low before the election, "has in most cases improved."[57]

As they tried to improve their relations with the Department of Agriculture, local MCP leaders pursued another agenda—to faithfully support Dr. Banda's call for peasants to adopt so-called progressive methods of farming. The newly elected member of Parliament for Nsanje South, the Honorable K. J. Malamba, spent the first part of 1965 promoting new agricultural methods.[58] To build a social infrastructure for the campaign, authorities encouraged villagers to organize themselves in "farmers' clubs"[59] and, in a forerunner to the government's strategy under the SVADP, made the adoption of "proper methods of farming"—the new euphemism for malimidwe—a precondition for peasants to get loans and pieces of land previously owned by the government.[60] Thus, an energetic minister of education organized "an educational visit for the farmers" of Chikwawa and Nsanje "to go and see cotton on ridges in Mlanje and Blantyre Districts."[61] His was a tough job.

The new MCP-controlled government did not succeed in generating new support for or breaking old rural opposition to mitumbira for many reasons, not the least of which was the party's previous success in galvanizing resistance to the scheme in the final days of British rule. With the support of local cadres, peasants had destroyed bunds and ridges in the gardens of collaborators, staging a general boycott against mitumbira.[62] According to the 1960 annual report for Nsanje:

> There is great hostility throughout the district to all forms of good husbandry and soil conservation as taught by the Department of Agriculture. Garden preparation started very late but most gardens have been cleared of weeds and trash. *There is, however, an almost complete refusal to make ridges.* A few persons, such as Agricultural Instructors, have made them and *gangs of persons have gone to the garden at night and flattened the ridges.* In some cases, the owner has to dig his garden all over, but has made no ridges. In others contour bunds have been damaged.[63]

Villagers continued their acts of defiance, intimidating progressive farmers so that they were "unwilling to associate themselves on [*sic*] ridging."[64] The valley entered the postcolonial era as an ungovernable place with regard to mitumbira, and the new government's attempts to reinforce the scheme did not make a difference, except that with the threat of penalties removed, villagers did not have to resort to hidden forms of resistance. Political independence meant nothing for many villagers besides freedom from mitumbira, and they challenged any official breaching the contract.

In the period immediately after independence, peasants availed themselves of every opportunity to voice their opposition to mitumbira openly. At a meeting with local political leaders, villagers "expressed the feeling that they were pretty reluctant to make ridges in their gardens."[65] Thus, reporting on the minister of education's meeting with peasants in May 1968, the district commissioner for Nsanje wrote, "In spite of the encouragement that cotton should be planted on ridges, both Nsanje and Chikwawa farmers bitterly attacked the policy and stated that they were going to continue planting cotton and all Agricultural Activities without the use of ridges."[66] No one could persuade the peasantry to make mitumbira, and, as one reporter once put it, "ridging has ceased."[67]

Then, in the late 1960s, there occurred a decisive break in the nature of reporting in Malawi, as the movement to formally crown Dr. Banda as president-for-life gained momentum and as the state became blatantly repressive. Voices of dissent began to disappear from the historical record, and agricultural reports started echoing the language of the annual party

conventions. Nothing could go wrong under Dr. Banda's brand of dictator-
ship. Thanks to his infinite wisdom and ability to convert backward-looking
villagers,[68] peasants were either ridging, showing greater interest in ridging, or promising to ridge more land.[69] He had opened the eyes of these
conservative villagers to the dangers of traditional farming methods and to
the benefits of modern agriculture and ridging.[70] One confident agricultural
officer in 1969 boldly predicted that 75 percent of all farmers in Chikwawa
would ridge their gardens.[71] Where does wishful thinking end and social
reality begin?

Thanks to the "Garden Survey Report" of 1977–80, it is possible to gauge
the level of peasants' conversion to mitumbira. Overall, only 22 percent (18
by hand, 1 by oxen, and 3 by other means) of the farmed land in the valley
was ridged in the late 1970s. Moreover, much of this ridged land was located
in three of the region's oases of plenty: the Chididi and Gaga Hills and the
East Bank.[72] But this represented another case of success by default. Peasants
in the three zones had not resisted mitumbira as fiercely as their counterparts
on the valley floor during the colonial era. Their ancestors had developed the
mathutu mound system, which was similar to mitumbira. Contour ridging
made a lot of sense in the undulating landscape; the government did not make
new converts out of these farmers. The only converts to the ridging campaign
in the postcolonial era were rich cotton growers of the Makande Plain and
Nsanje North (Mbenje subchiefdom), who constructed mitumbira in order to
qualify for loans under the SVADP. Otherwise, the campaign did not accomplish its stated objectives, as one survey for 1973–74 noted:

> Although ridging has been promoted by the Extension Service for many
> years there is a deep seated resistance amongst farmers to adopting the
> practice. Ridging is still associated with in the minds of many farmers with
> colonialist agricultural laws, and the political campaigns of the 1950s, in
> which disregard for the laws on ridging was a major focus.[73]

The "backward" peasant foiled the plans crafted by experts.

Promoters of mitumbira on the valley floor faced many hurdles. Some
peasants saw the campaign as a precursor to the emergence of master farmers,
who would take away their land.[74] Some argued that ridging would weaken
and expose the topsoils of the flat mphala to wind erosion, a position some
experts also expressed with respect to the Makande Plain. "In the special
case of the Makande Plain, where it is very difficult to maintain ridges on the
unstable black cotton soils, there are grounds for questioning the relevance of
ridging."[75] Then the leaders of the Mbona cult also joined the opposition on
both religious and ecological grounds.[76] And all protesters fought mitumbira
because of its heavy labor demands during the wet season of diminished food

Table 6.3.
Method of Ridging (% of area measured)

Method	CHIKWAWA						NSANJE		All Strata
	Gaga Hills	Mwanza Valley	Tomali Plain	Makande Plain	East Bank	Nsanje North	Nsanje South	Chididi Hills	
Not ridged	64	90	94	79	66	80	77	60	79
By hand	27	7	4	18	31	18	21	34	18
By Oxen	0	0	0	1	*	0	0	0	*
By other	9	3	1	2	3	2	2	6	3
N	107	205	321	732	271	258	148	64	2,106

Sources: NADD, "Garden Survey," chapter 8, p. 117, table 8.2. The *N* stands for area measured in hectares. The two asterisks were given in the original source with no explanation and are reproduced here; they appear to be inconsequential.

stocks. Needless to say, food availability played a direct and immediate role in how peasants worked in their gardens any season.

OLD AND NEW TENSIONS IN THE GARDEN

Through the Lower River the dimba gardens are in excellent condition and very much larger areas have been planted this year than ever before. From north end of Chikwawa to the south end of the Lower Shire maize, sweet potatoes, beans (Phaseolus and Vigna spp) and pumpkins ... are yielding well or give promise of doing so.[77]

The agricultural system of the valley has neither collapsed, as the crisis literature might have predicted, nor taken the region into the era of unlimited abundance, as the promoters of scientific agriculture might have imagined. Like cotton growers, food cultivators have created a system that challenges us to think of change according to the laws of both time's cycle and time's arrow. One can see irreversible change in the disappearance of *maere* finger millet (*Eleusine coracana*) and in the replacement of mapira sorghum or *kaffir* corn (*Sorghum vulgare*) with maize as the number-one cereal of the valley.

The triumph of maize as the most popular crop of the region tells the story of gamblers. More marketable and higher-yielding than any of the old cereals, maize guarantees a high standard of living when the weather cooperates, but, as one of the region's least drought-resistant crops, it can lead to disaster in the event of drought. Maize also suffers the distinct disadvantage that it is more vulnerable to attacks by vermin and pests than the old cereals under the existing storage systems. But gamblers are not the only producers in the valley; they form part of risk-averse peasants, who have maintained the old cereals, particularly mapira and mchewere (bulrush or pearl millet, or *Pennisetum typhoides*). The low-yielding but drought-resistant crops protect the risk-averse peasants of the deserts of hunger against the vagaries of the weather on a seasonal basis, without allowing them to raise their income in the long run. The coexistence of the two types of producers goes a long way to explain why the valley has been able to conquer chaola famine without eradicating seasonal hunger.

Although spatially distinct as enduring processes, the creation of deserts of hunger and oases of plenty amplify the same logic of the garden. Every day, peasants generate deserts of hunger and oases of plenty as they maintain plots in different microenvironments, as they combine in one and the same field crops and crop varieties of varying heat-resistance and yielding capacities, and as they stagger the sowing process. An ideal peasant garden, regardless of its location, remains an exercise in both risk avoidance and risk taking, and the risk-averse and risk-taking peasants are not necessarily two different types of growers. Every villager both assumes and avoids risks as he or she works in the field. Only a radical transformation, like the draining of the marshes or the irrigation of mphala drylands, in a new political and economic setting, can reorient the food system in one particular direction. In the absence of such a revolution, food producers continue to be drawn into contradictory directions, re-creating in their own gardens the biodiversity of their natural setting.

The Tchiri Valley is home to many kinds of domesticated plants, reflecting in part the region's diverse ecological systems. According to the "Garden Survey Report" of 1977–80, peasants in the region cultivate crops of 14 botanic families, as table 6.4 shows. Most members of the 14 families flourish as both dimba and munda crops. Maize is a good example of a crop that grows on both the dambo and mphala, and cotton was another example before it became an exclusively munda crop in the post-Bomani era. Some other crops grow in one but not in both ecological zones. For example, rice growing under the traditional system is only possible on the dambo floodlands, just as millet and sorghum are exclusively munda plants.[78] Then there are crops that can flourish on both the dambo and mphala, but do better in one than in the other. Sweet potatoes, kidney beans, and many kinds of vegetables belong to this group, doing better under dimba than munda conditions. Finally, some crops are more popular than others.

The "Garden Survey Report" ranked the region's crops according to the land area they occupied and the number of households growing them. On the basis of the latter criterion, a higher percentage of households (81%) grew maize than any other crop. Closely following maize were mapira sorghum (72%); *masamba* vegetables (68%); mchewere millet (55%); cotton (49%); *nyemba* beans, peas, and grams ("bpg" in table 6.5; 39%); guar beans

Table 6.4.
Major Crops Grown in the Lower Tchiri Valley

BOTANIC FAMILY	CROP	BOTANIC FAMILY	CROP
Amaranthacial	Blite	Gramineae	millet, maize, rice, sorghum, sugarcane
Bromeliaglae	Pineapple	Leguminosae	Beans, guar, peas, gram
Compositae	Sunflower	Malvaceae	Cotton, Okra
Convolvolaceal	Sweet Potatoes	Musaceae	Banana
Cruciftrae	Chinese Cabbage	Pedaliaceae	Sesame
Cucurbitaceae	Cucumber, gourd	Solanaceae	Chillies, Tomatoes
Euphorbiaceae	Cassava, Castor	Stercullaceae	Cocoa Sterculia

Sources: Adapted from NADD, "Garden Survey," chapter 4, p. 50, table 4.2.

Table 6.5.
Area Under Food Crops as Percentage of All Cropped Land

			CHIKWAWA				NSANJE	
Rank	Gaga Hills	Mwanza Valley	Tomali Plain	Makande Plain	East Bank	Nsanje North	Nsanje South	Chididi Hills
1	maize 58	veg 47	maize 32	veg 39	maize 44	veg 36	millet 34	maize 73
2	bpg 33	bpg 35	sorghum 27	sorghum 26	veg 19	millet 29	sorghum 26	veg 64
3	veg 29	maize 30	veg 23	maize 25	rice 9	sorghum 28	maize 14	bpg 38
4	sorghum 5	sorghum 19	bpg 8	millet 12	millet 8	bpg 25	veg 14	roots 10
5	rice 2	millet 9	millet 8	bpg 6	bpg 8	maize 16	bpg 8	sorghum 7
6	millet 1	roots 2	roots 1	roots 2	Sorghum 6	rice 0	rice 1	rice 0
7	roots (?)	rice 1	rice (?)	rice (?)	roots 1	roots 0	roots 0	millet (?)

Sources: Adapted from NADD, "Garden Survey," chapter 4, p. 66, table 4.13. The figure after each crop stands for the percentage of land it occupies in each stratum.

(14%); *mtedza* groundnuts (12%); mpunga rice (10%); root crops (10%); and *mzimbe* sugarcane (6%). This order differed slightly when the same crops were graded on the basis of the amount of land they occupied, as table 6.5 attempts to do. Maize occupied 30 percent of the cropped land; vegetables 29 percent; cotton 25 percent; sorghum 22 percent; beans, peas, and grams 17 percent; bulrush millet 14 percent; guar beans 4 percent; groundnuts 2 percent; rice 1 percent; and root crops 1 percent. Maize thus emerged as the most popular crop in terms of both criteria.

The report's attempt to assess the prevalence of the various crops on the basis of the land area they occupied (table 6.5) is both revealing and problematic. It is problematic mainly because villagers grew most crops as mixtures. The surveyors must have used a more complex set of assumptions to work out the area each crop occupied than to calculate the number of households. Thus, while one has to treat with care all the figures in this book, table 6.5 demands even greater caution. For example, vegetables, legumes, and roots probably occupied a larger area than the survey estimates. These crops could have easily escaped the attention of the surveyors partly because they were often grown as mixtures with major crops, and particularly because they were more popular on the dambo—an oasis of plenty that does not feature at all in the report. The SVADP, which sponsored most of the surveys in this book, was primarily interested in cotton—an entirely munda crop since the 1940s.[79] Despite these problems, however, table 6.5 points to at least two interesting agricultural realities.

The first was the discovery that vegetables had become "a very important crop both in terms of the number of growers and in terms of the area covered."[80] They ranked first in three strata, second in two, third in two, and fourth in only one zone. This is a remarkable finding for several reasons. Grown by 68 percent of the households, vegetables were more popular than cotton and guar beans that otherwise ranked first (73%) and second (17%) as the region's cash crops. That vegetables were as widely grown as cereals makes an interesting revelation from the perspective of the region's eating habits. An ideal meal includes nsima porridge and ndiwo stew, and most nsima and ndiwo dishes are made from cereals and vegetables, respectively (see chapter 7). In other words, vegetables are as important as cereals in the local dietary regime. Yet while there is a considerable amount of information on the region's cereals and its cash crops, no one has done any research on the vegetables. What are the main vegetables of the area and how are they grown? Did their popularity represent something new? And, if so what drove such a development? Table 6.5 raises more questions than it answers.

The second most significant information in table 6.5 is the close association of the old cereals (millet, sorghum) with deserts of hunger, and maize with the oases of plenty. Maize is the most popular crop in the mountains (Gaga Hills, East Bank, and Chididi Hills) and probably second only to sweet potatoes on the "unnoticed" dambo. Acting both as a food and as a cash crop, maize replaces and competes with cotton in the four zones. Maize's popularity only declines in the deserts of hunger, where millet and sorghum continue to dominate the munda system.

Old Cereals and the Deserts of Hunger

Like the dimba on the marshes, an ideal munda garden features some of the following crops: cassava (*chinahgwa*), groundnuts, legumes, sweet potatoes, vegetables, maize, millet, and sorghum. Some of these crops mature earlier than others, some yield more than others, and some can resist drought better than others. Every garden replicates nature's biodiversity, and what distinguishes the munda of the valley floor from that of the mountains as well as from the dimba was the dominance of millet and sorghum. Thus, although each munda in the deserts of hunger carries a plethora of domesticated plants, villagers typically refer to it as a mapira or mchewere garden. This is as true today as it was in the 1920s and 1930s, when their interest in cotton drew officials to the food crops of Nsanje District.

In the 1930s, peasants distinguished one mchewere variety from another on several criteria, including the length of time it took the crop to reach maturity.[81] Foremost among the late-maturing mchewere was *nachacha,* which became ready for eating five months from the time of planting.[82] Thus, though high-yielding and relatively immune from attacks by birds (*mbalame*), nachacha did not become popular with growers who defined mchewere as an early hunger breaker. It lost the competition to early-maturing varieties,[83] which, sown in November, began to swell by the end of January and became ready for consumption by February.[84] It was their capacity to end the hungry season at an early stage that on the one hand offset their generally low-yielding capacities,[85] and on the other gave mchewere its distinctive position in the agriculture system vis-à-vis the dominant mapira strains.

The histories of mapira and mchewere were intimately connected at the levels of cultivation techniques and their respective properties. It would, for example, be correct to view the two crops as mirror images of each other. The most popular mapira varieties were drought-resistant but slow-maturing, stretching from November to May, while the dominant mchewere strains were less drought-resistant but early-maturing. Moreover, some cultivation methods tended to temporarily obscure their particular identities. Villagers planted the two in the same garden at the beginning of the rainy season in November, and, as if to underscore the similarities between the two, people mixed their seeds before planting: "The usual native practice [is] to mix mapira and mchewere seed before planting and then to plant 20 to 30 seeds in a hole, the holes approximately 3 ft. apart."[86] Then villagers employed two other practices that also drew the contempt of British agricultural experts. First, peasants did not thin the resulting foliage, which, while running against the British ideal garden of a few healthy plants in a hole, satisfied rural notions of a successful garden enterprise. Villagers tried to protect every plant that managed to sprout from each hole. Second, growers did not uproot every mapira stalk, but left some that subsequently sprouted on their own after the first rains. No one apparently made an effort to understand the rationale of this practice—which the British called "ratooning"—but many agricultural officers roundly condemned it as the primary cause of some diseases and infestations afflicting mapira and mchewere every growing season.

The list of diseases and pests affecting one or both crops included the stem borer, witch weed, smut, and green ear or downy mildew.[87] But because government agricultural officials did not study the problem, there is little information on the nature or prevalence of these common threats to food crops.[88] The regular enemies of the munda system made news headlines only in the event of disasters, as when a combination of grasshoppers[89] and locusts ravaged mapira and mchewere in the early 1930s. The locust invasion exaggerated the impact of the more endemic attacks by birds.[90]

According to one estimate, birds devoured about 25 percent of mapira and mchewere every year.[91] Among the worst offenders were weaverbirds and waxbill finches.[92] Like weaverbirds, waxbill finches bred in large numbers on the Mozambique side of the Tchiri River twice a year, in March, when mchewere and maere millets were ripening, and in May, when people were beginning to harvest the slow-growing gonkho sorghum.[93] A monthly agricultural report for May 1933 summarized the resulting devastation this way:

Small seed eating birds have done an enormous amount of damage to the sorghum crop during this month. Reports have been received of gardens in which the grain has been entirely destroyed and everywhere where there is any crop the attack is heavy ... Natives have been busy all the month in their gardens trying to keep the birds off their grain and in many cases have built small temporary huts and slept there as well. Men, women and children have all been busily employed but the birds are hungry and several flocks come at a time so that the task of saving the crop is a very difficult and often disappointing one.[94]

The birds were unusually hungry that year because locusts had destroyed mchewere, leaving gonkho as the only food for the predators. The fate of one crop determined the fate of the other, although sharing common or complementary traits did not rule out differences. Mchewere has acted as a factor of stability in the munda system, consistently keeping one rank behind mapira in the valley outside Nsanje South. This was partly because, as fast-ripening plants, the dominant mchewere varieties did not compete with cotton, which gonkho sorghum did at its own peril during the heyday of munda cotton in Nsanje South.

As the readers of the foregoing pages will remember, sorghum embodies two instructive stories about the fate of the old cereals in a new economy. The first points to mapira's slow-maturing properties and the possibilities of short-term change. In the 1920s and 1930s, peasants in Nsanje South replaced the slow-ripening gonkho sorghum with maize in order to accommodate cotton. But, as if to underline the impermanence of some patterns of change, the same peasantry revived gonkho and introduced other sorghum varieties like *thengalamanga* after the collapse of cotton agriculture. Only in Nsanje South did mapira trail behind the more stable mchewere in the late 1970s (table 6.5); it had not yet regained the lost momentum.

Mapira's second story suggests one example of irreversible change in the munda regime. The crop has permanently lost to maize its mid-nineteenth-century position as the number-one cereal of the valley, partly because of its low-yielding qualities, partly because of its character as an exclusively munda plant, and mainly because of the absence of a demand for it outside the village sector. That is one instance of time's arrow in the munda system. Maere finger millet furnishes yet another example. The once popular maere has for all practical purposes disappeared from the valley mainly because, although useful as an ingredient for nsima and *mkate* bread, villagers had grown maere mostly for mowa beer. Some types of beer contained nothing else besides maere, so that when plentiful, as in 1932, no one in the valley went "thirsty ... through lack of beer."[95] But all brewers prized maere as a malt, mixed with the flour of millet, sorghum, or maize. Beer with a maere base was supposed to be highly intoxicating and tasteful.

However, as chapter 2 made clear, malt making was a painstaking process without any guarantees of a high-quality outcome. That represented one challenge to the survival of maere. The other was social. Much of the beer villagers brewed with finger millet satisfied ritual needs, serving people attending major rites of passage like funerals. But many villagers commemorate such moments differently today. Under Christian influence, some do not serve alcohol, and of those who do, many resort to factory-brewed liquor. Most importantly, peasants now choose sugar as a substitute for maere malt, which simplifies the brewing process, making it shorter, less risky, and more open to nonprofessional brewers (see chapter 7). Finally, like mapira and mchewere, maere did not enjoy a regular demand in the formal economy, forcing many producers to sell their surplus to Indian merchants at dismal prices. "It is a pity," whined one official in the 1930s, "that the only sale for it is to the Banyan traders locally."[96] The story of maize, the premier crop of the oases of plenty, was quite different.

Maize, Rice, and Sweet Potatoes in the Oases of Plenty

> Fresh low-lying dimbas are still being opened and unless something unforeseen happens to destroy these dimba gardens there can be no fear of famine on the Lower River. There will be shortage: that is inevitable as the dimba areas are limited and are not sufficient alone to keep the whole population.[97]

Ecological factors played a more decisive role than either government policy or population pressure in separating the agricultural histories of the oases of plenty from the deserts of hunger. Mountain and dimba growers enjoyed the distinct advantage of working soils of high moisture (*chinyontho*) content. The marshes are almost always moisture-laden, and flooding was the key determinant of dimba farming on a seasonal or long-term basis. More land was available for cultivation before than after the Bomani deluge of 1939, and the dimba system was in this regard more unstable than the mountain munda regime that owed its chinyontho to high rainfalls.[98] Whereas the valley as a whole averaged 32 inches of rain per year between 1964–65 and 1973–74, the hill areas of the East Bank, Chididi, and Gaga received, respectively, 36.76, 38.49, and 45 inches of rain per year during the same period.[99]

As a result of their higher moisture content, the mphala on the mountains and dambo in the marshes support different kinds of crops than those popular on the valley floor. Millet and sorghum, the chief crops of the deserts of hunger, have played a less significant part in the agricultural systems of the hills and no part at all in the dimba regime. Maize is the most important cereal in the mountains and marshes, supported by such secondary crops as *nandolo* pigeon peas in the mountains and sweet potatoes (*Ipomoea batatas*) on the dambo. Maize and sweet potatoes thrive together on the dambo, in the same way as maize and pigeon peas do on the hills and millet and sorghum do on the valley floor. Clearly, nature does set limits on the agricultural system.

But setting the outer limits of an agricultural system is not the same as determining it. Nature does not in particular tell people how to use the physical environment. Peasants can exploit one and the same ecosystem differently, depending on their economic, political, and demographic contexts. And under certain conditions, they can also misuse their ecosystem. For example, land-hungry villagers responded to the pressures of cotton agriculture by growing maize instead of sorghum in the drought-prone environment of Nsanje South. Other villagers in the same district grew cotton on the precious Dinde at the expense of maize, in contrast to their counterparts in the land-abundant Chikwawa, who used the northwestern section of the Dabanyi exclusively for food. Different economic conditions led to two radically different patterns of deploying the same dambo. Economic and political conditions also help to

explain the popularity of some crops and the disappearance or stunted development of others. Ecologically, the valley floor is a suitable location for finger
millet, but the crop has failed largely on economic and social grounds. Similar
pressures played a major role in the underdevelopment of wetland mpunga
rice (*Oryza sativa*) on the otherwise ecologically friendly dambo marshes.

One of the earliest written references to rice in the valley comes from the
diaries of Dr. David Livingstone's Zembezi Expedition. A severe food shortage at Thete in 1859 sent his party on a rice-buying mission that ended at
what is today Nsanje Township.[100] The "Cuama," a non-Mang'anja people,
now part of the Sena, were the main cultivators of mpunga rice. Livingstone
does not specify the kind of rice his party purchased, but colonial officials
in the 1930s identified about a dozen varieties, classified either as slow- and
early-maturing, or as of local and foreign origin.[101]

Faya and *india* were among the most popular foreign varieties, and both
were white, although faya was larger than india.[102] Agricultural officers frequently mentioned *nsingano* and *machewere* as examples of local varieties.
Both were large, but whereas nsingano was white, machewere was red.[103] It
seems that local varieties came in many more colors than their foreign counterparts, most of them invariably white.[104] The foreign-local distinction does not,
however, appear to have gone beyond the color issue; it did not, in particular,
seem to correlate with maturing times.

The list of late-maturing strains included both local and foreign varieties. Faya matured as late as some local varieties like *bungala, thyolakhosi,*
nsingano, and machewere.[105] In the 1930s, when most sections of the dambo
remained flooded for about three months only, late-ripening rice thrived
better in the lower drifts that stayed under water until May or June. Ripening
earlier than May,[106] short-term varieties fitted the general conditions of the
1880–1940 period better than their late-maturing counterparts.

Peasants seeded their rice gardens in two ways after harvesting their other
dimba crops between December and January. Some villagers planted the
entire field at once, while others started the process in small nurseries and
transferred the young plants later in the season.[107] The gardens received a first
hoeing and mulching before the floods.[108] Thereafter, people did not do much
work in the inundated rice fields until the time of scaring off birds, lasting
for about a month between February and May, according to the rice strain in
question.

Typically falling on children, protecting rice against birds was a difficult
task, especially when there was still water in the fields. Boys and girls would
go to the fields in a canoe early in the morning, stay there for about 12 hours,
and return home only after the birds had gone to rest. During the day, the children guarded from a specially constructed platform, *nsanja,* with a seat a little
higher than the rice. From the nsanja radiated a network of strings, crisscrossing the entire garden and supported at intervals by standing reeds or bamboo.

Peasants sometimes attached to these poles gourds or metal cans filled with stones and other clattering items. From their seat on the nsanja, the children would activate the network of strings and rattling cans upon spotting birds in the field. Most birds would get frightened and fly away, but stubborn ones would continue eating, forcing the poor guards to climb down from the nsanja and wade through the water to drive them away. Guarding slow-maturing rice like faya was a tough job, lasting several weeks during the cold season in May–June. Children eagerly looked forward to the end of the cycle.[109] Relatively easy at the beginning, rice growing required a lot of work and patience toward the end, when elders would join the children in harvesting and transporting the rice to the village still on the head. The threshing took place in the village in a manner not different from that described for mapira and sorghum in chapter 7. All this took place beyond the immediate purview of the state.

Preoccupied with cotton, officials in Malawi never paid much attention to wetland rice.[110] State intervention was sporadic and limited, as when officials sometimes imported and sold seeds to villagers after a bad flood. Such seeds normally came from Nkhota-Kota on Lake Malawi, where villagers grew rice more extensively than in the valley. Only in the 1950s did the state try to establish a steady market for rice through the creation of the Lower River Rice Co-operative Society.[111] But for reasons not entirely clear to this author, the experiment was short-lived, with the result that growers continued to dispose of their surplus in Indian shops, often in exchange for salt, cloth, and other goods.[112] This disincentive proved especially effective in the northern part of the valley, where villagers grew the crop mostly for sale and where it competed with maize.[113] In Chikwawa District maize triumphed at the expense of rice under the same economic environment as it ousted mapira sorghum throughout the valley.

The triumph of maize over mapira in the valley underscores the need to keep focus on both the economic and ecological dynamics of agricultural production. As suggested earlier in this chapter, mapira lost the competition to maize on four grounds. It is low-yielding in a densely populated region, and, as a slow-maturing plant, it can only grow on the mphala drylands. By contrast, maize can thrive under both mphala and dambo environments, and is one of the early hunger breakers. Finally, maize beats mapira as a crop with both use and exchange values beyond the village community. It has become the principal cash crop in the region's oases of plenty, with little or no cotton. In the late 1970s, mountain farmers devoted more land to maize than to any other crop. Maize received 73, 58, and 44 percent of all the cultivated land respectively in the Chididi and Gaga Hills and on the East Bank. Thus, though peasants of every stratum in the valley grew some maize, only in the mountains did it occupy the first position (table 6.5). None of the major crops of the deserts of hunger, such as cotton, sorghum, and millet, occupied more than eight percent of the cropped land in the mountains.

The finding that 65 percent of the maize gardens in Chididi and Gaga Hills did not carry other food crops[114] may reflect three overlapping realities at the same time. First, with their more reliable rainfalls, mountain farmers can be more confident about the outcome of their enterprise; they may not need to avoid risk through intercropping, as their counterparts on the valley floor do.[115] Second, growers of pigeon peas, the close associate of maize on the hills, often plant the crop after harvesting maize in March–April under the common intraseasonal rotation method. Finally, the surveyors may have simply overlooked the smaller or subsidiary companions of maize. In the hills peasants do not typically mix maize with the tall and easily detectable millet or sorghum, but with the less visible groundnuts, sesame, cucumbers, pumpkins, watermelon, vegetables, and grams. Regardless, however, of its exact position vis-à-vis other crops, there can be no doubt about the dominance of maize in the region's oases of plenty.

A large portion of Chikwawa's 500-ton maize "surplus" in 1952 came from the Gaga Hills of northern Chapananga and the East Bank.[116] Eight years later, in 1960, government officials tried everything to "encourage private enterprise to purchase maize from" Chapananga, where "there is plenty and to resell it in the southern parts of the District where it is short."[117] In the following year, maize from the hills helped to alleviate hunger in other parts of the district.[118] During the serious drought of 1980, maize did better in the East Bank chiefdoms of Makhwira and Mlolo than in any other place besides the Gaga Hills and the Thyolo Escarpment.[119] And there is every indication that the mountain farmers have not fully exploited their regions' potential for maize because they do not have good roads and markets (see chapter 4). Every year, the people of northern Chapananga sell their maize to traders and other villagers from Mozambique.[120] The farmers of Chapananga face the same predicament as the cultivators of the even more inaccessible Nyachikadza chiefdom in the Dinde.

Although important, mountain farmers contribute only one portion of the maize from the Tchiri Valley. The other comes from the Dabanyi and Dinde marshes, which together constitute the ninth forgotten stratum of the valley. That the otherwise intelligently done "Garden Survey Report" of 1977–80 took no account of this stratum testifies to the tyranny of cotton on the official imagination of the valley: for any place to exist, it has to grow cotton. But outside the official circles, no one can end a serious conversation with villagers about the region's farming systems without hearing something about dimba agriculture. The history of dimba farming has penetrated peasant thought so much that it has provided golden-age theorists with another turning point. The Bomani floods of 1939 separate the "before" from the "now" of the food system in general and the dimba regime in particular.

Though small in size, the dambo has always been a land of great agricultural potential. Prior to the 1880s, peasants worked their fields on the Dabanyi

Photo 7 With her short-handled hoe, a woman opens a dimba garden on the eastern shores of the Dabanyi Marsh between Chiromo and Mlolo (2002). (photo by author)

and Dinde for nearly six months, from June to December. But the growing season became shorter in the aftermath of the Bomani floods of 1939, when farming on the dambo can start as late as August.[121] Dimba agriculture flourished best during the middle period, from the 1880s to the 1930s, when a consistently low Tchiri River made it possible for peasants to cultivate the marshes between February and December, although, as already noted, villagers did not everywhere avail themselves of the new opportunities for maize growing. In the Dinde, peasants cut short the maize cycle to accommodate cotton. Only in the northwestern section of the Dabanyi did villagers realize the full potential of the marshes for food production, raising several maize crops consecutively during the same growing period. Therefore, to highlight the possibilities of maize agriculture on the dambo, the following account will mostly draw on examples from the northwestern section of the Dabanyi between 1880 and 1940 and only refer to other places and times that approximated those conditions.

A dimba plot actualized the logic of the garden in its full sense. On the one hand, maize competed with *mbwanda* kidney beans, *dzungu* pumpkins, *nkhaka* cucumbers, sweet potatoes, and vegetables, and on the other hand, the cultivation of these crops brought to perfection the art of staggering. Instead of waiting for the whole garden to become dry, villagers started clearing and planting maize (and other crops) on those portions of the field that emerged from the floods first. They would expand their operations as more parts of the marshes became available for cultivation. As a result, some parts of the garden carried more mature crops than others, and peasants immediately reseeded those portions of the garden from which they had just picked the earliest-planted crop. Thus, the missionary Horace Waller identified in one spot maize in five different stages of growth because, as he confided to his diary, "so rich is the soil [that when] one crop is taken up another [is] put in the same day the moisture filtering through the roots of the corn."[122] This was in 1862, and about seven decades later, in 1932, a colonial official confirmed Waller's observation: "Throughout the Lower River," he wrote, "there are, after March, always gardens being harvested or planted with maize some-where or other."[123] A year later, another Briton reported, "Fresh land is still being hoed and cleared for planting and further areas of maize, sweet potatoes & beans have been planted at the waters [*sic*] edge as the streams and rivers recede to their middle dry season channels."[124] Peasants stopped planting about two months before the advent of good floods in December. The floods closed most dimba activities besides rice.

In the absence of bad or early floods, dimba cultivators could not experience an extended food gap. In particular, they did not have to wait for a full year before getting a new harvest, as munda cultivators of millet and sorghum did. Moreover, whereas an acre of munda gave between 1,000 and 1,200 pounds of millet or sorghum, the same amount of land on dambo in the 1930s yielded between 2,000 and 3,000 pounds of shelled maize.[125] And while it has reduced the amount of land for farming, the permanent inundation of large tracts of the marshes after 1939 has not adversely affected the fertility of the dambo.

The usefulness of the dambo in the region's survival strategies becomes especially evident when one turns to sweet potatoes. No dimba garden was complete without sweet potatoes and maize; mention one, and you automatically imply the other. Moreover, if maize represented time's arrow in terms of the formal economy, sweet potatoes stood for time's cycle, without organized markets and mostly dominated by women as its principal cultivators, sellers, and buyers in small rural trading centers.

Villagers grew sweet potatoes on both the mphala and dambo, but the tubers thrived better under dimba than munda conditions. And, like dimba maize, the growing of sweet potatoes on the dambo started anytime the land became ready for cultivation. Thus, although the sweet potatoes cycle on the marshes always ended with the first rains in December, its beginning varied from season to season and from one epoch to another, depending on the withdrawal of the floods. Typically, villagers started digging the soil deep to plant potato vines around June during the 1860s–80s, around February in the 1880s–1930s, and around August from 1940 onward. These were the ideal dates that did not always coincide with reality even within the same epoch. Table 6.6 reproduces the ideal conditions of the middle epoch between the 1880s and 1930s. Growers of sweet potatoes were busiest during the six months from April to September, when they both planted and harvested the tubers.

The extended growing season underwrote a buoyant sweet potatoes culture in 1880–1940 that provided relief for everyone in the valley, including munda cultivators. In a serious drought, villagers without regular access to the dambo entered all sorts of arrangements with the inhabitants of the marshes to acquire a dimba plot. During every major drought there was a surge in dimba farming, as members of the SAGM noted several times after their arrival in the valley in 1901. In 1907 they noted how

> the people have taken advantage of the rains to plant other food-stuffs, such as sweet potatoes and arrowroot, which, it is hoped, will help them over the difficulty of the food question. Just now many of our women are staying at the river, having gone down to put in potatoes on the river bank; they naturally stay to hoe and look after their gardens.[126]

Many stayed in the marshes until the close of the dimba season in December, returning to the mphala with vines, which they subsequently used to launch a new potatoes cycle on munda gardens.

In the absence of bad floods, the dimba and munda potatoes regimes perfectly complemented each other, as growers started the munda cycle in December with cuttings from the dambo, and the dimba system around February with seeds from the mphala. But by delaying the commencement of the dimba regime to as late as August, bad and slow receding floods often destabilized the interdependence between the two systems. Work on the dambo would begin many months after the closure of the main potatoes season on the mphala. Though not unusual before 1940, this gap became common and systemic in the post-Bomani era. Dimba growers could not rely on the main munda cycle for seeds—though munda cultivators continued to obtain cuttings from dimba farmers in December.

Table 6.6.
Mbatata Cycle on the Dimba and Munda, 1880–1940

Month	Jan	Feb	Mar	Apr	May	Jun	Jul	Aug	Sep	Oct	Nov	Dec
Dimba	—	P	P	PH	PH	PH	PH	PH	PH	H	H	H
Munda	P	—	H	H	—	—	—	—	—	—	—	P

Note: P and *H* stand for planting and harvesting, respectively.

The seed problem elicited several responses that together gave rise to a slightly different potato culture in the post-Bomani era. One such measure, typical of the pre-Bomani era when bad floods still made news, involved the state. Officials often included potato cuttings as part of their relief to victims of a bad flood.[127] But dimba cultivators did not sit down, waiting for the government; they undertook their own initiatives, importing seeds from within and outside the country, particularly Mozambique. In the post-Bomani era, the searches focused on new, quick-ripening strains, capable of reaching maturity within the shortened dimba growing season. As a result, the post-Bomani era witnessed a phenomenal increase in the range of new potato varieties.[128] Not a regular concern among government planners, this development has played a crucial role in preventing njala from becoming chaola famine.[129]

But state officials are not alone in their inability to see the importance of sweet potatoes also escape the attention of rich and progressive farmers, who allow their cattle to roam the "empty" marshes during the dry season. The dambo exists as the land of the lifesaving sweet potatoes mainly for poor and risk-averse peasants, who plan their agricultural season around the tuber. In their search for wealth and modernity, the rich and powerful cannot see that there are not two but only one Tchiri Valley; that the fate of the poor is inseparable from their own; that under certain conditions—as on dimba plots—maize requires sweet potatoes for its cultural identity; and that time's arrow needs time's cycle to constitute time.

CONCLUSION

This chapter represents yet another effort to answer the question why, although a land of recurrent hunger, the valley is not at the same time a place of frequent chaola famine *and* why the conquest of chaola since 1923 has not led to the end of njala. This is obviously a complex question, drawing attention to both the production and exchange phases of the food system. Wage labor and other forms of production outside one's own garden created new opportunities in the fight against chaola (see chapters 4 and 5). This chapter and parts of chapter 3 address the same question from the vantage of the system of production.

The production-oriented explanation takes place at several levels. One directs our attention to spatial differentiation, particularly the distinction between munda and dimba farming, and between deserts of hunger and oases of plenty. In a regular hungry season, the oases of plenty on the hills and marshes turn into places of relief for the inhabitants of the deserts of hunger on the valley floor, while a serious drought drives every munda cultivator to the expanding niches of the dambo. But deserts of hunger and oases of plenty get connected at another level in the real lives of food growers. There is a nonspatial dimension to the relationship between the two spaces, as each embodies its own contradictions.

There can be no doubt that as growers of high-yielding maize, peasants of the oases of plenty enjoy a higher level of subsistence in the long run, but precisely this advantage increases their vulnerability to climatic variability in the event of a serious drought. The region's oases of plenty on the hills thus mimic southern Africa's predicament. Greater reliance on the New World cereal played a major role in southern Africa's food shortages between 2000 and 2003.[130] Equally vulnerable on a seasonal basis are the cultivators of the dambo, where bad and early floods can in a day wipe out a potentially rich harvest. Dimba and mountain cultivators are real gamblers, in contrast to their counterparts in the deserts of hunger, who have chosen a radically different path toward food security.

Heat-resistant mapira and millet protect the food system of the deserts of hunger against such terrors of history as drought. But, as in every other human action, this defense comes at a price. As cultivators of low-yielding crops, peasants of the deserts of hunger in today's land-scarce economies subsist at relatively low levels of income from one year to another. Moreover, to guarantee the survival of the old cropping patterns, directed mainly to the creation of use values in a money-driven economy, they divert their limited resources into activities like wage labor or cotton to earn cash. These producers replicate the conditions of many West African cultivators, who insulate their traditional food production regimes by investing their labor into pure export commodities that, like cocoa, have little or no use value in the domestic economy. Thus, while the oases of plenty pull the food system along time's arrow, exposing it to the vagaries of the climate and markets, the overwhelming power of the deserts of hunger places the same within the orbit of time's cycle and recurrent hunger.

This chapter suggests yet another level of analysis. The conflicting forces within each oasis of plenty and desert of hunger are always at work in one and the same garden, regardless of its specific location. By mixing in the same field crops and varieties of differing properties, and by staggering them during the same growing season, peasants routinely create the deserts of hunger and oases of plenty, making and implementing decisions that simultaneously transform them into risk-taking and risk-avoiding historical agents. The conquest of chaola famine and the reproduction of seasonal hunger do not require two different kinds of explanation or peasantry; they are complementary processes, converging on one and the same actor.

Finally, the histories of all major crops in the valley show that risk-taking and risk-avoiding tendencies did not operate in a vacuum. They were byproducts of shifts in state intervention, demography, ecology, and economic processes like cotton agriculture. This book has also shown that none of these pressures, either singly or as a grouping, placed the food system in any particular direction; they only created tensions that peasants resolved in differing ways according to their times and places. Time's arrow has not yet overtaken the system toward "feast" or "famine," partly because the new forces were too weak or contradictory, and partly because they were also subject to the logic of seasonal and daily fluctuations in food availability. Daily routines like eating can deflect time's arrow. One needs to understand these routines in their own right, as the next chapter will continue to do.

7

THE DAILY MEAL

Even the sick [and powerless] have a right to that which is in the pot.[1]
   [My daughter] ... take these bones,
   Give them to your husband.
   But come back
   To eat the steak.[2]
   [But] much of the food we [villagers] eat these days comes from the market; we depend on the market just like wage earners do.[3]

INTRODUCTION

   This chapter stands at the opposite end of chapter 1 in more than organizational terms. The first chapter deals with the news-making famine events that attract the attention of politicians, scholars, and the general public. One can vividly see the victims of famine on the television. The daily meal is, by contrast, a "nonevent"; no television camera captures those who complete the ritual with full or half-empty stomachs, and it leaves no trace even in the memory of its participants. The daily meal has thus escaped the attention of state officials, including those who zealously recorded their impressions of famine, cash-crop agriculture, and food production. It disappears from the intellectual radar of the students of the crisis literature as soon as they begin debating about food.[4] This chapter has had little to look to for theoretical inspiration or evidence, and had to generate its own sources based on contemporary eating habits.

   But the two chapters are different in other ways. Chapter 1 is about the irreversible. The famines of 1862–63 and 1922–23 were different from each other in their etiology and impact, and no one can revisit either. On the other hand, one meal is hardly different from another; today's meal more or less replicates yesterday's in its contents and organization. The meal is one of the most repetitive events of social life. Finally, famine is ultimately about disorder, particularly the manipulation of the rules of sharing, while the daily meal is one of the most orderly events of the day. Nothing about it is left to chance. Everyone knows in advance who will prepare it, which people will form the eating group, and which kinds of food women and men, children and the elderly will eat. The rules governing its processing and distribution rest on some of the most common and elementary variables of social organization: age and gender. So orderly is the meal that it assumes the appearance of a natural order.

One purpose of this chapter is to show that despite its apparent cohesiveness, the daily meal is a social construct, with its own dynamics for change. The chapter will identify these dynamics with the help of scattered written sources, oral history, and observations from the contemporary scene. The daily meal emerges from this data as a disorderly system that is amenable to historical analysis.

Oral history and contemporary evidence portray a stark contradiction between the rules of sharing food and the work going into food processing and preparation. Moreover, peasants eat in both formal and informal ways. But even the formal meal has its own tensions. On the one hand, villagers can eat as members of one or several independent households, and on the other hand, every meal denies the equality of consumers while promoting it. Every meal strengthens the position of those with interest in the status quo while encouraging the underprivileged to question and challenge the order. Order is not always far away from disorder.

This chapter argues, however, that structural tensions do not by themselves give rise to social change. It takes human actors to transform the disorder of today into the order of tomorrow. But the fact that human beings act within specific contexts, including those beyond their own creation, requires an understanding of the historical background. Since the nineteenth century, potential village rebels have taken advantage of the market, Sena immigration, and Christianity to challenge the old order and the methods of imparting knowledge about it.

THE GOLDEN-AGE THEORY AND THE ALTERNATIVE VISION

> If you do not willingly share your food, your hungry neighbor will snatch it from your mouth.[5]

Peasants conceptualize the food system and its history around at least two major theories: the golden-age theory and the alternative vision.[6] The golden-age theory makes access to cooked food and the fruits of the bush an entitlement of every member of the community, regardless of his or her position in material production, while the alternative vision underscores the limited nature of that right. The two theories are, however, similar in at least two respects. First, both underline the social character of food. Food is as much about people's relationships to things as it is about their ties to one another. To eat is to get connected to other members of the community; food is about sharing. Second, both theories form part of what the geologist, paleontologist, and zoologist Stephen J. Gould called "time's cycle" or "the intelligibility of timeless order and lawlike structure," in contrast to "time's arrow," or the view of history as "an irreversible sequence of events."[7] As aspects of Gould's time's cycle, the golden-age theory and the alternative vision address the problem of order and represent peasants' collective protest against what Mircea Eliade appropriately called the "terror" of history[8]—unpredictable events like drought.

As Gould has convincingly defended his bipolar theory, "time's arrow and time's cycle is ... a great dichotomy because each of its poles captures, by its essence, a theme ... central to intellectual (and practical) life."[9] In particular, the theory allows the student of food matters to explain simultaneously spectacular events like chaola famine and routines like eating. Time's arrow and time's cycle is a great dichotomy also because it provides a more effective method of addressing the problem of change than the common genuflection to "change and continuity," which typically allows historians to place in a timeless box the "continuity" part of the equation as they comfortably pursue "change" along time's arrow. Time's cycle is not simply about a changeless order; it is also about change, but change of a different order than the irreversible. No two seasons or days are exactly the same; they constitute the necessary ingredients of the irreversible. Time's cycle needs time's arrow to become time. The golden-age theory and alternative vision do not deny change; they only draw our attention to different *patterns* of change than the linear movement of the crisis literature.

The golden-age theory is remarkable for its inclusiveness and lack of specifics. It loudly declares the equality of every consumer before the meal. Villagers put this principle into practice on a daily basis through the chidyerano communal meal that brought together members of different independent households for the purposes of eating. Although important, kinship was not the only organizing principle; households came to share their meals primarily as neighbors. Chidyerano stood for the core ideals of the golden-age theory that defines food as an object for sharing. And while some traditions make it an outcome of hunger (see p. 236), many others locate chidyerano's origins in the indefinite past of abundance, as Mr. Tiwongolera Bayisi did on 13 April 1995:

> There is no chidyerano nowadays, but it ruled the day in the past, when rains were plentiful and there was no hunger. There was no reason for people to be stingy [umbombo]. Granaries were always full of food, and people were only too happy to share their food with others. No one was stingy those days and, indeed, it was difficult for anyone to be stingy because the granaries were always full.[10]

This classic statement of the golden-age theory presupposes the view of the sociopolitical system as a stable and fully developed regime, allowing no room for conflict. Rains always came as expected, the granaries were always full, and no one had reason to be greedy. People shared food with their neighbors almost instinctively: "When women from this *nyumba* house, that house, and another house cooked food, they ate together under a tree like this one; that's what they called ... [chidyerano]."[11] There was so much food in those days that even the meanest did not think twice before sharing it with their neighbors.[12] Chidyerano reproduced the generosity of the great feasts of the harvest season (see chapter 2) on a daily basis:

> It is true that in those days people shared their food and did not discriminate against others, as they do today. People ate together because they were united; there was no discrimination those days. And they also shared their beer, drinking together. When people brew beer, they would take the pots into the open, invite their neighbors, who would happily come to enjoy the brew as a community.[13]

This was a past without internal tensions and a time radically different from the present.

The golden-age theory is a two-part model, with the first extolling the past of abundance and the other deprecating the present of persistent hunger. Whereas the one era promoted chidyerano and sharing, the other did the opposite. There can be no mediating points between the two epochs.[14] Chidyerano could not have survived the transition from the past to the present. The persistent hunger of the present era brought an end to chidyerano. There is nothing to support it today.

Different oral historians draw the dividing line between the past of plenty and the present of hunger at different points. Some, like the former inhabitants of the Dabanyi and Dinde Marshes, make the Bomani floods of 1939 the turning point.[15] But in the more elaborate and established charters, the end of chidyerano coincides with the conquest of the Mang'anja by the Magololo immigrants (see chapter 1). The conquest put an end to the prosperous era of reliable rainfalls and food supplies under the lundu rulers and initiated the opposite—an era of hunger and umbombo meanness. Droughts have become part of daily life in the valley because, so golden-age theorists argue, the Magololo stopped listening to Mbona.[16] They have plunged the valley into an era of persistent food insecurity and meanness, when "everyone tries to survive on one's own, unmindful of the needs of others."[17] Meanness and hunger rule the day nowadays against the background of a new kind of decadence that pits children against their parents:

> The world has indeed changed. Even your own children will rebel against you soon after their wedding and you have given them the ability to live on

their own. As soon as they get their own *banja* household, they forget you. Gone forever were the days when people lived as a community. Nowadays people begin to lead independent lives soon after establishing their own banja. Sharing food the way they did in the past is a story you tell these children, but they do not appear to appreciate the story. They do not listen to elders.[18]

That these children do not follow parental advice is not, however, entirely their fault. They are the products of persistent njala, denying them the educational system and nkute leftovers of the past. Good morals cannot coexist with hunger.[19] Chidyerano has become a powerful metaphor of what peasants view as the past glories and current maladies of their food and political systems.

As an integral part of the region's political charters, the golden-age theory is loud, powerful, widespread, and overwhelming, proclaiming an impenetrable system that degenerated only because of external forces. To repair it, one needs to return to the past. Short on details, the golden-age theory has the coherence of all simplifying ideologies, and can easily lead the unsuspecting researcher to think of it as the only theory of sharing in the region. It is not. If one listens to the subaltern voices of the underprivileged one hears another voice, however indistinctly. This is what I call, for lack of better terms, the alternative vision.

Almost formless and never part of the dominant charters, the alternative vision is largely a female perspective on the food system. It does not divide time between the past of plenty and the present of hunger; rather, the theory rests on the distinction between nsima and ndiwo stew (the American "stew", English "relish" or some scholars' "side dish"). Without much to say about nsima—the principal if unspoken target of the golden-age theory—the alternative vision focuses on the sharing of ndiwo that did and continues to divide the community along the lines of age and gender.[20] Differential rights to ndiwo make male elders the more privileged members of the community during every meal.

The advocates of the alternative vision do not deny the existence of chidyerano in the past or the fact that only few people practice it today. All they assert is that, like any other social value, chidyerano was something people had to fight for because there were equally strong forces against it. Its decline results not from some long-term deterioration in food availability, as golden-age theorists argue, but from day-to-day tensions over ndiwo:

Chidyerano comes to a halt when some people eat meat alone in their houses at the same time as they enjoy other people's meat at the communal meal. When others find this out, they too begin eating their meat inside their houses, and that marks the end of chidyerano.[21]

Not so much the absence as the presence of food, in the form of ndiwo, led to the end of chidyerano. And ndiwo also strains intradomestic relations, pitting the male elder against his wives and children. Every day it repudiates the subsistence ethic of the golden-age theory and the equality of consumers.

Every meal, regardless of its format, emerges from the alternative vision, as "feast" for male elders with their rights to ndiwo and "better" portions of meat and fish, *and* as "famine" for women and children without those rights. One does not, therefore, have to look to the past for feast and to the present for famine. Feast and famine can coexist. The protein-delivering ndiwo transforms the daily meal into a terrain of social struggle and contestation and acts as a potent force of change. Every day, ndiwo creates potential rebels out of women as it denies them equality with men as workers in the garden and as it devalues their predominant role in transforming the social biography of food.

TRANSFORMING THE SOCIAL BIOGRAPHY OF FOOD

Dr. Platt's dictum was that save in a few specific respects the Nyasaland native ate the right sorts of food, but not enough of it, save at certain seasons.[22]
The belief among many Malawians both African and European that maize flour as prepared in the villages contains little else but starch is incorrect. This misconception probably arises from the standard grouping of foods into three classes, those containing mainly carbohydrates, proteins and fats. Maize is put in with sugar and cassava into the carbohydrate category and people conclude that maize contains only carbohydrates and no one tells them of the small but very important 8–14 per cent of protein (all cereals contain useful protein).[23]

As suggested in chapter 2, food assumes different social meanings on its journey toward the eating place, although the nature of the journey varies with the food in question. Most undomesticated foods start the journey as the property of the entire community before becoming the private asset of the hunter and collector. (Chaola famine inverts this logic when some of its victims use prowess to deny others access to the fruits of nature; see chapter 2.) Foods from the market have an analogous beginning from the perspective of the buyers. They are there for anyone with money or other exchange goods before they fall into the private domain of the buyer. By contrast, cultivated foods start their life as the private goods of the household. But regardless of their origins, most foods tend to become social assets of the community after going through fire. Cooking is a key event in the transformation of food.

At the center of this process are women, who assume more and more responsibilities soon after food has left the marketplace, the bush, and the fields. Each day rural women organize their lives around food processing. And though often ignored by historians, the pounding of grain, cooking, and related activities define what it is to be a village woman. Quite understandably, women have shown more willingness than men to embrace new food processing technologies that, like mechanical grinding mills, reduce their toil and indirectly compel husbands, as providers of money for the service, to share the work of transforming the social identities of food after harvesting.

From the Garden to the Granary

As part of garden work, food harvesting is largely gender-neutral, engaging, in varying degrees of technical equivalence, men and women, the old and the young.[24] People sometimes use knives to cut off heads from the stems of crops like millet and sorghum, but at other times they use their bare hands to sever cobs from the stem.[25] Those collecting cowpeas, kidney beans, and other types of legumes take special care not to break the pods, while the digging out of groundnuts and sweet potatoes with hoes is a dirty and arduous task.

The next most important operation after harvesting is threshing, which can take place in the garden itself or in the village. Because people harvest their rice when the ground is still wet or underwater, they almost invariably thresh the crop in the village. But the threshing of munda crops can take place in the garden itself, especially when the latter is far from the *mudzi* village. Threshing would in that sense represent an extension of the *dindiro* period, when villagers spend days and even nights in the fields guarding their crops against birds and wild animals.[26] Threshing crops in the garden cuts down the amount of load villagers carry to the village. When their gardens are close to the village, peasants normally take home their legumes, millet, and sorghum while still in the head.[27]

Peasants do not usually thresh their cereals and legumes immediately after bringing them to the village. Some crops leave the field still green or wet and have to be dried in the sun. Another reason for the delay is pressure of work, for the harvesting season happens to be an unusually busy period, coinciding with cotton harvesting, the opening of dimba gardens, and the beginning of the great celebrations of the year. There is great competition for household labor, leading many villagers to postpone threshing for several weeks or even months after harvesting.[28]

Threshing is not a gender- or age-specific operation, though women dominate the process. A wife chooses a threshing spot outside the house and plasters it with a special kind of soil to provide a solid surface. Once this preparatory work is done, other members of the family help her carry the crops from the granary to the threshing floor, where they could be left for several days to dry. Then, on an appointed day, people would employ long sticks to flail and loosen the grains from the heads. Women sift the chaff from the grains with winnowing baskets (lichero), which completes the threshing of millet, sorghum, and legumes.[29] Maize receives a different treatment.

Some growers thresh a large amount of maize by placing the cobs in a sack, which they subsequently beat with heavy sticks to separate the grains.[30] Others remove the grain from the cob with fingers in a slow and tedious process that can involve every member of the household. They employ this method mostly when preparing a small amount of grain for immediate processing (*mphale*).[31] And, as with millet and sorghum, they store the maize in bags, *mbiya* pots, and *chikwa* baskets.

More common among the Sena than among the Mang'anja, the chikwa is a huge basket, made from grass plaited with palms. Reaching a height of six feet, a chikwa has the shape of a wine barrel, with a small base and a small mouth but a very wide center.[32] To protect their contents against vermin, growers sometimes smear the chikwa with ashes in the same way as they treat large mbiya pots. Mbiya are very popular in the preservation of smaller-sized grain like finger millet (maere) and sesame.[33] Finally, peasants also store their grains in sacks, also valued as a means of transporting goods. Growers almost invariably place the sacks, pots, and chikwa containers in nkhokwe bins or on *khungulu* platforms.

Built inside the house, the khungulu flatbed stands about three feet above the ground, which helps protect its contents from crawling insects and other wingless creatures. The stored food also receives the smoke and soot from the hearth under the khungulu.[34] Such food can last more than a season without rotting. Villagers regard khungulu as a symbol of abundance, like the nkhokwe.[35]

Attached to each Mang'anja household, the nkhokwe is a small grass- or bamboo-plaited building that stands on a raised platform, four to six feet above the ground. It is similar to what the Sena call *chete,* but whereas the Mang'anja nkhokwe is circular (like all Mang'anja houses), the chete is rectangular (like all Sena houses). Otherwise, the nkhokwe and chete are functionally equivalent, and both share some resemblances and differences with the khungulu. One difference is that, built outside and often standing taller than most houses, the chete and nkhokwe constitute one of the most visible and striking features of the village infrastructure, unlike the khungulu inside the house.[36] But the nkhokwe or chete are similar to the khungulu in one important respect. They both preserve food by keeping it high off the ground. Many also keep their sweet potatoes on the khungulu and nkhokwe granaries.[37] And as long as the potatoes and other foods remain in storage, they are the exclusive property of the household as managed by the wife. Only the wife enjoys the right to remove the foodstuffs from storage and prepare the daily meal—to make food an asset of every member of the community.

From the Granary to the Eating Place

As elsewhere in southern Africa, the formal meal in Malawi has two components: the nsima porridge or its substitutes and ndiwo. Ndiwo is the more diversified and variable group, consisting of meat, fish, legumes, and vegetables,

Photo 8 A woman winnows the grain selected for processing into flour (2002). (photo by author)

which give each meal its distinctive character. By contrast, members of the nsima group are relatively few, featuring mostly cereals on a regular basis and roots and cucurbits during the hungry season. Finally, while villagers get nsima items mostly from their own gardens, the procurement of ndiwo often sends them to the bush and markets. Getting ndiwo for the next meal is not always an easy task, although its preparation is generally easier than the processing of grains into *ufa* flour for making nsima.

The nsima group features cereals, roots, and cucurbits. The preparation of roots and cucurbits demands less work than the processing of cereals,[38] which falls in two stages. In the first, the aim is to remove *deya* bran from the mphale, the name for the grain selected for flour making. Sometimes working in groups, women crush (*kusinja*) the mphale in a wooden mtondo mortar with a heavy wooden pestle. While strenuously pounding the mphale, women continually drop water in the mortar to soften the grain. After generating a considerable amount of bran in the mortar, they would sit down and separate the bran from the grains with a lichero winnowing basket. They would then return the purified mphale into the mortar and alternate between pounding and sifting until all the impurities are removed from the kernels.[39] They close this stage of producing flour by soaking the grain in hot or cold water, where it would remain for several days before the beginning of the second stage.

Photo 9 With both hands pressing hard and moving the top but smaller stone of the traditional grinding mill, a woman would turn grain into flour (1960s). (Matthew Schoffeleers's collection)

In the second and last stage, women pulverize mphale in two ways depending on its size. They would typically grind a small amount on the *mphero* grinding mill. This was by definition a single-person activity, in contrast to the pounding of a large amount of mphale in a mortar, which they sometimes do as a team of several women.[40] They would crush the softened grain the same way as during the first stage and dry the resulting white flour (*ufa woyera*) in the sun before storing it in earthen pots. One can understand why the so-called conservative peasant woman has led the silent rebellion against the traditional ways of doing the order of the day, and has enthusiastically embraced new technologies in the form of mechanical and electric *chigayo* mills.

Introduced in the area for popular use during the 1940s, chigayo machines are found everywhere in the valley today, penetrating even remote areas like the Dinde Marshes.[41] Originally gasoline-powered, some machines today run on electricity. In a clear indication of their dislike of old work habits, women travel long distances to reach the machines, wait in long lines for their turn, and spend the little money at their disposal for the service. Only poverty and custom explains the failure of the new technology to completely overtake the old pounding and grinding processes.

Photo 10 Women wait in line to get their grain processed into flour by this electrical grinding mill (2002). (photo by author)

Custom once stood against the spread of chigayo because they were partial technologies. They could not, in particular, separate the bran from the grain, as women did in the first stage of flour making. Peasants had two options, one more radical than the other. The radical option saw women taking their whole maize, millet, and sorghum to the chigayo before removing the bran. The result would be course flour and course nsima (*ngaiwa*), which men do not like, despite the teachings of educated Africans and Europeans about the benefits of such nsima. Men prefer nsima made with branless flour and would have welcomed the findings of one study of the 1950s, showing that the cleaning and soaking of maize to make branless flour releases certain nutrients that remain "locked" in whole grains.[42] They would insist on the second and less radical option, requiring women to do the first traditional stage in the manufacturing of ufa before taking their mphale to chigayo mills. Women must have therefore felt great relief with the introduction of chigayo that can both remove the bran and grind the resulting mphale into refined flour. Those living close to the new machines can, in a matter of a few hours, get from their mphale of unprocessed grains ufa woyera and start cooking nsima—the final stage in transforming food.

Photo 11 A young man operates an electrical grinding mill (2002). (photo by author)

It takes an experienced woman less than an hour to complete preparing nsima, which, like all forms of cooking, takes place inside the house. She begins by mixing cold water with flour in a pot (*mphika*) over fire and supported by three conical stands (*pfuwa*). As the mixture starts boiling, the cook adds more flour to the porridge, vigorously stirring it with a stick until it reaches the desired consistency. She serves the resulting nsima on traditional or factory-manufactured plates, one containing a lump for women and the other for men.[43] Starting as the property of the household in the garden, maize, mapira, and mchewere now assume the character of a public asset, available for every hungry member of the community.

Mpunga rice acquires a similar social identity after traveling a slightly different path. Women sometimes make nsima from rice, following more or less the same procedures as those described for other grains, but they commonly cook it whole after removing the bran in a mtondo mortar. They begin cooking the cleaned rice by heating water in a pot. After the water reaches a boil, they add rice, close the pot tightly, and allow the rice to cook for about 30 minutes. Then the woman drains the milky water from the pot, reduces the heat by removing all burning wood from the hearth, tightly recloses the pot, and lets it steam until it is ready for eating.[44] Women cook rice mostly in earthen pots because of their greater heat-preserving capacities, but they are not as particular about the pots for boiling cucurbits and roots.

Sweet potatoes, cassava, and Irish potatoes are the main root crops of the valley.[45] Irish potatoes, which mostly come from the Gaga Hills of Chikwawa and the Tchiri Highlands, are the least significant of the three, satisfying mostly the needs of a tiny minority of nonpeasants. Cassava, which again is grown more widely in the hills than on the valley floor, is more popular than Irish potatoes, but neither can compete with sweet potatoes, grown more extensively in the marshes than on the mphala drylands. Sweet potatoes act as the first line of defense, and their own competitor in this respect is the wild nyika water-lily bulbs, characterized by one scholar as a "store house" of minerals and vitamins.[46] Nyika may be a better food than cassava, which is made up mostly of carbohydrates with only insignificant amounts of protein, minerals, and vitamins.[47] Whatever their exact nutritional contributions, the preparation of roots does not require much work in the valley, where peasants eat them whole after boiling or roasting. Boiling is also the principal method of cooking cucurbits, which people sometimes eat as a substitute for nsima during the hungry season.

Pumpkins, loofah, and gourd are the popular cucurbits of the valley. These crops do not form part of regular meals in the area, which is probably good, given their low caloric and protein content.[48] Peasants value them mostly as hunger breakers because they mature much earlier than cereals, but quickly disappear with the end of the rainy season. The few that flourish during the dry season serve mostly as snacks and as ndiwo ingredients, suggesting how thin the line between nsima and ndiwo can sometimes be. Many villagers in the marshes live for days on end subsisting on fish as both nsima and as ndiwo.

For the purposes of simplification, one can divide the ndiwo group into four subcategories of meat, fish, beans (pulses), and vegetables. Collectively known as "leaves" or masamba among peasants, vegetables occupy the first rank among the four. Peasants consume a wide range of wild leaves, such as wild blite, mushrooms, cats' whiskers, and wild okra. Then there are the leaves of cassava, haricot beans, cowpeas, pumpkins, sweet potatoes, and sesame, grown for other uses besides their masamba.[49] Finally, villagers raise cabbage, rape, okra, and other plants exclusively for their leaves.

Nutritionists have noted with approval the popularity of vegetables because they are a valuable source of high-quality (though generally limited) protein, in addition to calcium, iron, and vitamins A, C, and B complex.[50] But these same scientists also think that villagers do not realize all the advantages of vegetables, partly because some cooking techniques destroy vitamins (see pp. 219) and partly because peasants do not regularly eat the leaves in large quantities. The supply of leaves fluctuates by the seasons, and villagers have not developed successful ways of preserving them besides the *mfutso* method. Women make mfutso from the leaves of plants like pumpkins, kidney beans, and cowpeas by boiling and drying them in the sun.[51] Cowpeas and other legumes are also important as members of the second ndiwo subgroup.

Popular ndiwo legumes include velvet (or Bengal) beans, cowpeas, kidney beans, groundnuts, pigeon peas, hyacinth beans, Bambara ground beans, and field peas. Not all of these pulses are grown in the valley; some, like Bambara nuts, come from the Tchiri Highlands, and disparities exist within the valley itself. Some parts grow no pulses, while those areas that do grow pulses tend to specialize in different types of legumes. For example, kidney beans do better under dimba than munda conditions. The supply of beans is as ecologically sensitive as that of vegetables, and the only major difference between the two is that as a group, beans last longer than vegetables under the current storage systems. As a result, there is a fair amount of trade in beans between the Tchiri Highlands and the valley and within the latter, making it possible for those with money to obtain legumes almost any time during the year, which is good news given that beans are a good source of vitamins A and B1 and are rich in protein. About 20 percent of the content of the dried bean is protein.[52] Meat and fish have more protein.

Fish is the third most common ndiwo ingredient after beans and vegetables. There are many kinds of fish in the Tchiri River, its tributaries, and marshes. Most popular among these is the *mlamba* catfish,[53] which one can catch in almost every river and dambo marsh. Besides mlamba, peasants also catch and eat a long list of fish for which I have found no English equivalents.[54] In some localities the term *ndiwo* is almost synonymous with fish. Meat (*nyama*) occupies a distant fourth position and features such items as goat meat, pork, chicken, duck, mice, and beef.

The flesh of meat is an important source of protein, varying amounts of fat, mineral salts, and vitamins A and B complex. Especially rich in both minerals and vitamins are internal organs like liver and kidney, whereas bones contain considerable amounts of calcium. Villagers who eat so little meat miss a valuable source of nutrients, although this may not necessarily mean that their diets are structurally deficient. The relative value of the protein derived from animal sources as compared with that from vegetables, beans, or cereals is a hotly debated issue among nutrition scientists.[55] Moreover, besides their natural content, the nutritional value of the ndiwo (and food in general) can also depend on cooking methods.

Women employ various techniques to prepare the numerous ndiwo items, but, as with many other aspects of rural life, this area too remains unexplored. One can only make a few general statements at this stage in our understanding. It is clear, for example, that while the procurement of ndiwo is a constant struggle for many women, the preparation of most items does not demand as much physical labor as the processing of cereals. Women can begin cooking beans, fish, and meat almost immediately after getting them from the bush, river, garden, or market. And they do this mostly by boiling; baking does not appear to be a popular method of preparing ndiwo in the valley. Besides boiling, women also fry their ndiwo with factory- and locally manufactured oils like those from groundnuts and sesame.

Peasants also apply many other condiments to make ndiwo more palatable. The list of condiments ranges from *mchere* salt to *tsabola* peppers, shallots, onion, tomatoes, and curry powder. Equally common is chutney, made from a mixture of peppers, onions, tomatoes, and sometimes limes. Besides flavor, products like tomatoes add vitamins and minerals to many ndiwo dishes.[56] Finally, women apply potashes to soften "hard" relishes, particularly okra and the leaves of pumpkins, hyacinth beans, cowpeas, field peas, and cassava. Some nutritionists think, however, that potashes destroy the vitamins in the leaves.[57] But this is only one view, and peasants may have their own perspectives on the problem. There can be little doubt, however, that even though it does not demand as much physical energy as pounding and grinding grains, the supply and preparation of ndiwo challenges the mental capacities of married village women on a daily basis. The so-called side dish of the academic world is not a side issue for village women. They have to be constantly creative to supply their families with this defining but variable component of the daily meal.

WEIGHING THE DIFFERENT COMPONENTS OF THE DAILY MEAL

To get an idea of the frequency and relative weight of different foods in the region's dietary regimen, this project conducted a survey of the daily meals of 17 households, each over a period of seven days. Five of the families lived in the Dinde Marsh, depending entirely on dimba farming, and the others occupied the mphala drylands, drawing their subsistence mostly from munda farming. Research assistants recorded the foods each of the families ate in the morning, at midday, and in the evening, although the following analysis only discusses the two main meals of lunch and dinner. But before analyzing the data, it is important to point out the shortcomings of the survey.

The first and most obvious limitation relates to the size of the sample. Seventeen families cannot accurately reflect the diverse eating habits of the region's nearly 90,000 households.[58] The second limitation, somewhat similar to the first, is that the survey did not cover all the substrata of the valley, missing important subregions like the Chididi and Gaga Hills. Inclusion of these zones might significantly alter the ndiwo map given, among other things, the virtual absence of the fishing industry in those areas. The third drawback is temporal. The survey took place during the last days of the hungry season (February–March) and the beginnings of the harvesting season (May) on the mphala drylands, leaving out the peak of the njala in December and January. (In the Dinde, peasants were harvesting their sweet potatoes and maize at the time of the survey.) Observations on munda-dependent households in

December and January could have significantly altered the picture, particularly the frequency of the cereal-based nsima.

Despite these shortcomings, the data have some value in that they at least confirm common observations about the region's eating patterns. They do, for example, highlight the problem of insufficiency. When asked whether they had enough nsima the previous night to leave some for their children to eat as nkute the following day, less than half of the respondents answered yes. Most families finished the nsima, confirming in some way the common complaint among both village women and nutritionists that many families are chronically undernourished (see p. 222–23). Malawians may not eat wrong foods, but they do not have enough of the right ones all the time. That such a finding shows up in a survey taken at harvest time is a powerful reminder of the problem of silent hunger in the region.

Another important but also not unexpected finding of the survey relates to the overwhelming role of nsima and, by implication, cereals in the local diet. As table 7.1 illustrates, the 12 munda-dependent households together ate nsima 166 times out of a possible 168. Nsima and food are nearly synonymous.[59] The inclusion of December and January (the height of the hungry season) could have probably lowered the frequency, without, however, altering the overall picture. One also doubts if data from the Chididi and Gaga Hills would have significantly modified the overall ndiwo picture in the region. Information from the two zones would have definitely lowered the rate of fish consumption among mphala dwellers; mountain farmers buy most of the fish they eat. But this fish deficit may not automatically translate into a meat surplus. In other words, inclusion of the two subregions may not have raised the present meat consumption rate of 13 among mphala dwellers. They may compensate the fish deficit by eating more legumes and vegetables. "Leaves" featured in 32 percent of the 168 meals,[60] while beans and fish vied for second position, with each appearing in 27 percent of the meals of munda-dependent farmers.

As table 7.2 shows, the nsima regimen of dambo dwellers does not differ significantly from that of their munda-dependent counterparts. As in table 7.1, cereals still dominate the nsima of dambo dwellers, though not as overwhelmingly as they do on the mphala. Maize—the only cereal of the marshes besides rice—competes with sweet potatoes that were being harvested at the time of the survey. And rice would modify the picture later on, in April and May. The real, though again not unexpected, difference between the two regions lies in their respective ndiwo. Fish featured in 72 percent of the Dinde meals against the mphala dwellers' 27. The last point of interest in table 7.2 is the "No Relish" column, suggesting that peasants do not take the availability of ndiwo for granted; ndiwo is the subject of struggle, an aspect of the food regime that hardly shows up in scientific surveys.

Table 7.1.
**Frequency of Particular Foods Eaten for Lunch and Dinner on the
Mphala Drylands**

Family	NSIMA GROUP		NDIWO GROUP				Month	Place
	Nsima	*Rice*	*Beans*	*Fish*	*Leaves*	*Meat*	*Month*	*Place*
1	13	1	6	5	3	0	May	Ndamera
2	14	0	8	2	2	2	February	Mbenje
3	14	0	5	3	4	2	May	Kasisi
4	14	0	4	6	4	0	May	Ndamera
5	14	0	3	3	4	4	May	Kasisi
6	14	0	2	3	6	3	March	Mbenje
7	13	1	5	5	2	2	March	Mbenje
8	14	0	5	3	3	3	May	Mlolo
9	14	0	2	3	7	2	February	Mbenje
10	14	0	5	3	6	0	February	Mbenje
11	14	0	0	5	8	1	March	Mbenje
12	14	0	1	5	5	3	May	Makhwira
TOTAL	166	2	46	46	54	22	—	—
%	99%	1%	27%	27%	32%	13%	—	—

Table 7.2.
**Frequency of Particular Foods Eaten for Lunch and Dinner in the
Dinde Marshes**

Family	NSIMA GROUP				NDIWO GROUP				
	Nsima	*Rice*	*Potato*	*Other*	*Beans*	*Fish*	*Leaves*	*Meat*	*No Relish*
1	7	0	3	0	0	10	0	0	0
2	6	0	4	0	1	7	1	1	0
3	6	0	4	0	2	7	1	0	0
4	8	1	0	1	0	8	1	0	1
5	7	0	3	0	0	4	4	0	2
Total	34	1	14	1	3	36	7	1	3
%	68	2	28	2	6	72	14	2	6

I am only aware of two scientific assessments of the nutritional status of Malawi's rural diets. The first, known as the Nyasaland Nutrition Survey, was conducted in 1939–43 and focused on three villages—Jere, Biwi, and Kasamba—in the Nkhota-Kota District of the Central Region.[61] After reviewing their data, the surveyors concluded that with the notable exception of cassava eaters, most villagers ate the right sorts of food.[62] They thought that the intake of fat qua fat was adequate, although the researchers wished peasants ate more of it to facilitate the absorption of vitamin A originating in carotene. The surveyors also believed that, with the exception of those subsisting on cassava, most villagers consumed adequate levels of iron and protein. The overall conclusion was that the inhabitants of the three villages ate balanced meals, but did not take enough calories during certain periods of the year. This was also the main finding of the Ngabu Nutrition Survey of 1970.[63]

Less elaborate than the Nyasaland Nutrition Survey, the Ngabu team studied 23 households, each for a week during the harvest season (April and May) in the Ngabu chiefdom of Chikwawa. After noting the principal limitations of their project, the surveyors went on to discuss both the strengths and weaknesses of the local diet regime. They considered the consumption of thiamin and niacin as adequate in all households. They also found that although people did not regularly eat tomatoes, eggs, and fruit, there were no obvious signs of vitamin-A deficiency because, in their view, people had eaten vitamin-A-producing foods, especially mangoes, earlier on and were still getting low doses of the vitamin stored in the liver. Physical signs of deficiency would show up only after prolonged deprivation.[64] The researchers did, however, raise some issues of real concern.

One concern was quality, noting in particular that some villagers did not consume enough foods rich in vitamin A, iron, and riboflavin. But, like the surveyors of the Nyasaland Nutrition Survey, the principal worry of the Ngabu researchers was that many people in the sample did not get enough calories. The energy intake of 11 of the 23 households (or nearly 50 percent) was too low to maintain weight or to promote growth and activity at the Food and Agriculture Organization "reference" level. One Malawian mother, Mrs. Sigresi Lingstonya Zachepa, whom we first met in the introduction, employed the medium of the golden-age theory to voice a similar concern:

> In the past people used to eat large quantities of nsima, but not today ... in this area these days one doesn't find nkute leftovers ... in the past people never finished their nsima ... but today our children do not know nkute ... because we don't have enough food. Our children grow as if they are in an initiation camp; when they wake up they don't ask for any leftovers; they just get up, wash their faces, and put on their clothes ... because they cannot ask for anything; there is no food ... That was not the case in the past ... they used to eat nkute regularly; there was a lot to eat; there were

always nsima leftovers because women used to cook nsima in large quantities ... and there were large quantities of nkute leftovers for the children to play with.[65]

Villagers also understand that the problem of quantity can become, after a certain point, one of quality. The connectedness between the two becomes clear when one tries to understand the technical and social dynamics of this ritual in their own right.

EATING

The joys of being a community come to an end when you have to share ndiwo stew.[66]

Students of the crisis literature may have a valid point in their argument that study of famine—their universe (see the introduction)—can provide useful insights into the everyday.[67] Moments of extreme and sudden disorder can indeed act as a powerful window on certain aspects of social life that remain under the cloud of routines. But it is reductionist to end the analysis at this level, as students of the crisis literature do. The crisis can only illuminate some struggles of daily life, and it will do so from a particular angle. Famine events cannot be a carbon copy of the routines because, among other things, chaola subverts the normal rules of sharing. In a chaola all foods have only one social life, as the private property of the powerful. The weak lose their rights, as the speaker of the first quotation of this chapter would put it. Moreover, these are not necessarily the socially powerful. Sheer physical prowess allows famine victims to claim as their own and to deny others access to food, including the fruits of the bush—the Hobbesian world of all against all. By contrast, the more endemic struggles over food get their logic from social conventions, which give food multiple social lives. These are undeclared tensions, covering for the most part the ndiwo portion of the meal. One cannot subsume all the routines under the crisis; indeed, one can, after a certain point, reverse the argument of the crisis literature: the routines act as a window on the crisis. But whatever the order of the argument, one cannot escape from the need to understand the routines in their own right and hope to appreciate food, which is about the everyday.

A supraseasonal event, the daily meal reenacts the ideal community of the golden-age theory as men and women, the young and the old find their place in it. A principal event of the day for most working adults, the meal is the only meaningful social ritual for children and the old who do not work in the fields. It is also a well-choreographed event. People know in advance who will cook it, which parts of the ndiwo are theirs, and who will be their partners, and their ears and noses are tuned to pick up the first signals from this quotidian ritual.

The aroma from steaming rice or the cracking sound of a *likombe* spoon scraping the inside of a nsima pot sends a clear message to those outside the house, who would respond in different ways. Casual visitors and children playing with the kids of the household would leave, if they expect their own meals at home. Those without such a hope would linger around, continue to play around, extend the conversation, and subsequently join the regular members of the eating group—after saying no to repeated requests. It is bad manners to accept the first invitation, which may not amount to anything more than a polite suggestion for nonmembers to leave. The cook would then call her children playing in the neighborhood in coded but well-understood messages. Finally, she would, again without specifically mentioning food, ask real guests to get inside the house in the company of a well-disciplined child, who would serve them with water and other needs.[68] The visitors would eat as much as possible, but would leave something in the *mbale* plate as a sign that they had their fill. Women and children would finish the leftovers, including those portions of the ndiwo not normally theirs. Visitors can be a windfall for children.

Only guests eat inside the house; regular members of the eating group take their meals in the open. Seated on mats, women eat as a group on the own, with children of both sexes five years and younger. In the past, unmarried boys of the puberty age ate separately in a communal dormitory.[69] But today, they mix with the married men, sometimes using tables and chairs. This is true whether or not people take the meal as members of the chidyerano communal meal.

Men usually take the midday meal (*chakudya-cha-masana*)[70] under a big tree, and they call this space *bwalo,* which serves other public purposes like meetings.[71] Peasants do not, however, pay much attention to the location of the evening meal (*chakudya-cha-madzulo*), so that in the absence of rain, any place becomes a potential "dining room" in the cool of the evening. Mobile dining rooms do not, however, imply the absence of "table" manners; the Mang'anja and Sena are very strict in this regard.

Participants in a meal wash their hands before and after eating, and each meal comes with water for that purpose. People wash both hands, although they only use the right hand (never the left) to do the actual eating, which has three steps. First, one breaks off an eating-size chunk (*mbamu*) of the hot nsima that comes to the eating-place in a clay, wooden, or factory-made plate (mbale). Then an individual would dip the mbamu into the common plate of ndiwo to absorb the *nsuzi* sauce and grab a small piece of the ndiwo. Finally he or she places the juicy mbamu and portion of the ndiwo into the mouth. It takes a matter of seconds for a seasoned eater to accomplish all these operations. A well-trained participant knows how to adjust his or her speed to the rhythm established by others.

The ability to coordinate one's movements and speed is not the only requisite skill at these meals. Eating also tests and reinforces the good habits children are supposed to have learned from their mothers during the first five years of life. It is an exercise in discipline, and well-behaved children neither gobble nor talk during meals (just as they are not generally supposed to speak in the presence of their elders). In fact, there is no need to silence smart children, knowing they need to keep pace with everyone else, including their more experienced elders. Finally, every child knows which parts of the ndiwo to leave for the elders. The organized meal reproduces the social order with all its contradictions. The same villagers who, through the pervasive idiom of the golden-age theory, loudly proclaim the equality of all members of the community before the meal also endorse an unequal system of sharing, centered on ndiwo.

Three principles guide the unequal distribution of ndiwo between male adults vis-à-vis women (and the young). The first bars women from certain types of ndiwo, but the list of such foods is very short, limited under most conditions to eggs.[72] Nowadays, Mang'anja and Sena women eat almost everything that men do, and the more pervasive discriminatory practices follow the second and third principles. The second places ndiwo in different grades, starting with the meat group on top, and followed, in descending order, by fish, vegetables, and salt (mchere). Villagers expect women to eat the lower grades in the event the more desirable cannot feed everyone. The third and probably most common form of differentiation categorizes some parts of fish and meat as distinctively "female" and "male."[73]

The rules regulating the division of beef—a newcomer to the valley—are almost the same as those applied to wild and domesticated animals.[74] The men who kill the animal boil its blood together with the kidneys, heart, and the smaller intestines to make *nsiya,* which they may share with women, who cook the other parts of the meat in preparation for the regular meal. After cooking, women allocate the choicest portions of the meat, such as the liver, as part of the men's ndiwo.[75] But even more intricate is the distribution of fish and chicken.

Considered a delicacy more so than fish, chicken is the standard meat villagers use to entertain guests, serving it whole in the case of special visitors like strategic friends, a suitor, and the relatives of a bride or bridegroom. Otherwise, they cut the chicken in pieces, giving men the "best" portions: gizzard, liver, thighs, and the fatty "pope's nose."[76] Women get these parts mostly in their capacity as guests, doctors, or as other officeholders; otherwise, tradition assigns to them the less desirable lower breast and similar portions. (Children are supposedly happy to receive wings, the neck, legs, and feet.)

Equally stratified is fish—the most common source of protein in the valley. According to the gender-driven classification, there are three parts to the mlamba and other large fish. A well-trained peasant wife loads the ndiwo plate going to women and their children with fleshy, fat-free, and "tasteless" section between the head and the upper part of the belly.[77] Men claim as theirs the entire head, the tail, and the blubbery section of the belly with reproductive organs and eggs. These are the "tastier" and fat-bearing portions of fish, and men closely guard their prerogatives to these. Some greedy husbands count the best portions of fish, chicken, and meat in the cooking pot to make sure that their wives do not eat or give them away.[78] Every meal becomes "feast" for men and elders with their established rights to better portions of the ndiwo, and "famine" for the women and children without those rights. Feast and famine can coexist, and hunger is never too far away from abundance.

A centerpiece of the alternative vision, the above account represents the perspective of elderly women and raises two questions—one easier to answer than the other. It is not difficult to see why ndiwo, rather than nsima, should stand as the focus of attention. On the one hand, ndiwo gives any meal its distinctive character, and on the other, it is the more erratic element, with its availability varying according to season and location. Moreover, unlike the ingredients of nsima, most items forming ndiwo are perishable; it is the more scarce resource. Peasants have to be continuously creative to provide stew for their families.

Then comes the second and more difficult question. Behind the second question is the recognition that, like the golden-age theory, the alternative vision is also an ideal, proclaiming a model of behavior whose materialization requires social action. How, in particular, have men reinforced it, and how have women complied with these dictates on a daily basis? This question becomes especially pertinent in view of the fact that the model's conditions of reproduction are in a flux (see pp. 228–33), and women, who are supposed to implement these discriminatory rules, are also the primary providers of ndiwo.

The task of procuring ndiwo routinely falls on women, although there are temporal and spatial variations to the theme. In areas with all-season rivers, like the Tchiri, men share a considerable amount of that responsibility with their wives, maintaining *mono* snares in the river that they inspect for fish every morning.[79] Furthermore, husbands in wage employment use their money to purchase ndiwo on the market. This is one side of the story of ndiwo procurement. The other side shifts the burden to women. Regardless of their ideas about the proper division of labor in this respect, villagers expect the woman who prepares the meal to come up with ndiwo and to respect the dictates of the alternative vision. Beneath its apparent order, the daily meal is a disorderly terrain, breeding its own potential rebels.

It is unfortunate, therefore, that going into this project with the misguided questions about "crises" (see the introduction), this book was not prepared to learn from the women how they cope with these contradictions on a daily basis. The most one can say with certainty at the moment is that, as in other aspects of their lives, women have not acted as hapless victims. They must have negotiated and even fought against the wholesale application of the ideals of the alternative vision.

Three kinds of evidence point to the need to view the ndiwo as a subject for contestation. First, while their male counterparts would spend hours on end on the virtues of the golden-age theory without the slightest hint of the dark world of the alternative vision, elderly women responded to almost every question about food with answers detailing the taboos and conventions regulating ndiwo. And even when they laugh, one can also detect a sense of resentment and dissent in their voices.[80] Second, not every woman in the valley is knowledgeable about the intricate rules of sharing ndiwo. The issue divides the peasant community not only along the lines of gender but also age. Some young women are not conversant with these rules or openly flout them. Finally, women have shown they can embrace change in other matters relative to the daily meal, including the technologies of food processing, as noted earlier in this discussion. The charter regulating ndiwo may be more relevant as an aspect of the region's belief systems than as a reflection of real practices under all conditions. The greedy husband of the alternative vision may be as much of an abstraction as the generous peasant of the golden-age theory. The real world is as complex today as it was in the past.

THE DAILY MEAL IN HISTORY

On the whole native diet is getting steadily worse ... The many fruits, vegetables, and insects which used to be found in the bush and which added so
much variety to the diet are disappearing as the amount of bush grows less
and poorer in quality ... In addition refined imported foodstuffs are becoming popular ... Even raw natives can be seen licking at handfuls of sugar
which they have bought in the store.[81]

It may never be possible to sketch the evolution of the golden-age theory, the alternative vision, and many other aspects of the daily meal. But with the help of oral history and scattered documentary sources, it is possible to identify some shifts not only within the system itself but also in the institutions of formal education that supports it. Transformations in both aspects of the food regime flowed from their own internal contradictions as well as the general field of their operation. As food processors and as consumers, peasants in the valley have had to contend with three major forces of change over the past century or so: modern food markets, Sena immigration, and Christianity. The three have strengthened the hand of the rebel and risk taker, weakening and even eradicating some elements of the old regime, while introducing new foods, practices, and, as critically, new ways of imparting knowledge and skills necessary for the reproduction of the system. People are not born with the arts of provisioning; they learn them, so no account of the food system can pretend to be complete without some outline of the educational system and its history.

Teaching Order

Among the Mang'anja original inhabitants of the valley, food conventions formed an integral component of *mwambo,* which signifies social practices, skills, taboos, and knowledge. Mang'anja boys and girls learned some aspects of this mwambo informally, but the teaching of many others was institutionally organized. They call the formal process of teaching mwambo *kubvinira,* which literally means, "to dance for."[82] Elders "danced for" members of their respective communities during the famous rites of passage that punctuated the life of individuals on their way from the cradle to the grave.

Coming around the time of puberty, *chinamwali* was the first important rite of passage in the life of a Mang'anja woman. It declared her capacity to re-create the community in a physical sense. Then there was nsembe—the last funerary rite sending the departed into the powerful world of ancestral spirits. In between these two, there were many other rituals, marking different stages in the social biography of human beings. These included chikwati wedding ceremonies and rituals associated with the birth of the first child. The latter simultaneously welcomed the newborn into the community of human beings and provided a forum for the elders to dance for the new parents. At every important turn in their lives, the Mang'anja learned new skills necessary for their survival as members of the community.

The community took an active part in teaching mwambo. As we have seen in chapter 2, to hold a successful chinamwali, chikwati, or nsembe, peasants deployed the food and labor of their friends, relatives, and neighbors. The community invested its resources in the formal institutions of learning. Besides food and labor, one also looked to the community for teachers. *Nankungwi* female elders, who ran chinamwali schools, were often political appointees, chosen by the chief or headperson for their proved knowledge and commitment to tradition. Finally, some chinamwali ceremonies were coordinated events, involving all the girls of a neighborhood or group of villages who reached puberty in a particular year. These were the more elaborate forms of chinamwali.

The existence of more elaborate chinamwali rituals did not, however, exclude simpler forms like those organized for one girl. The Mang'anja enjoyed options in the way they danced for their children. Just as they grew, threshed, stored, and ground their food in different ways, the Mang'anja also enjoyed many and equally legitimate approaches to dancing for the young. There were, for lack of better terms, both "small" and "big" methods of imparting mwambo. The elaborate and expensive rites of passage of chapter 2 did not exclude less costly techniques. The options were especially numerous for those staging the essential rites of chinamwali, chikwati, and nsembe.

A common thread running through all small versions was the absence of beer, drumming, and nyau masked dancers.[83] Tradition in this regard was inflexible only to the extent that it demanded some kind of celebration when a member of the community attained adulthood, married, or died. Otherwise, it never determined which approach to adopt. The peasant world was not, in other words, the procrustean bed of popular imagination; it was large enough to accommodate the poor and rich, and the thrifty and the big spender. Social and political context becomes critical.

Villagers adopted particular methods of organizing chinamwali, chikwati, and nsembe according to their circumstances. Lack of cooperation from their living wives sometimes foiled attempts by generous and wealthy polyga- mous husbands among the matrilineal Mang'anja to stage big nsembe for their dead wives.[84] But a different context often drove even poor and stingy parents to spend lots of food in dancing for their daughters in a "big" way. At the height of Magololo rule in the late nineteenth and early twentieth centuries, peasants could not avoid sending their children to the communally organized chinamwali featuring nyau masked dancers, beer, and drumming. Participation in such rituals formed an integral part of being a Magololo subject.[85] None of the ceremonies described in chapter 2 were preordained reflexes of some cultural imperatives; they were all negotiated events, with the capacity to absorb and promote change.

Mang'anja institutions of formal education have, during the past 150 years, changed in several directions as a result of the money economy, Christianity, and Sena immigration. These pressures both undermined and enriched the region's institutional framework for introducing the young to social adult- hood. Just as the preexisting institutions did not constitute a homogenous or closed system, the new pressures were not powerful or consistent enough to transform the cultural map into one particular direction. One needs both time's arrow and time's cycle to understand change at this level also.

It is clear, of course, that if the missionaries had their way, one would be writing a different history than that which has actually transpired in the valley. Like all zealots imbued in the sense of the superiority of their mission, European preachers wanted nothing but total victory. Soon after their arrival at the beginning of the twentieth century, members of the SAGM launched a vigorous campaign against the region's many "dark" forces, starting with Mbona, the Prince of Devils (see chapter 1). Then, as the cotton economy gathered momentum, they discovered yet another agent of evil in the form of the *nomi* youth labor associations.[86] This was in the 1920s, when the newly arrived Roman Catholic missionaries joined the Protestants' fight against the region's devils, concentrating their efforts on chinamwali female rituals and the all-male nyau secret societies of masked dancers. Their encounters with nyau sometimes turned brutal and violent.[87]

Missionaries did score some victories, with the help of new economic pressures. The collapse of the cotton economy in Nsanje District after the Bomani foods of 1939 drove the male members of the nomi into wage labor and ultimately weakened the associations.[88] Similarly, the modernization of Chikwawa's economy after the district's emergence as the new demographic and cotton center sapped some energy from nyau societies. Christian missionaries won indirectly in both cases, and the real losers were elders and pragmatic British administrators who had defended these "pagan" institutions for their capacity to create effective cotton growers and obedient taxpayers.[89] Moreover, the fact that the attacks on the old schools of education became effective in the post-Bomani era, when many families depended on the market for their food supplies, strengthened the hand of the thrifty spender. Big methods of dancing for the young became an unaffordable luxury for many villagers.

Nyau societies are not as popular today as they were in the 1920s and 1930s. *Mabzyoka,* a ceremony that featured beer and drumming and that was organized to heal Sena women suffering from physical and mental illnesses, has met a similar fate.[90] A common spectacle at the turn of the twentieth century, mabzyoka dances are today conspicuous by their absence.[91] Nor can one find any trace today of the extravagant *magoneko,* which rich Sena parents used to perform for their daughters and sons in addition to the common puberty rituals. Magoneko rituals have disappeared together with the finger millet that had provided a critical ingredient in the mowa beer for entertaining participants at the celebrations.[92] Some parents do not simply organize dances for their children nowadays. The world has indeed changed, as Mr. Washeni Khembo admitted on 8 June 1995, with a sense of resignation:

> Things have changed ... People should expect change; everything has its time. Change is part of real life; real life changes every day. You will fight a useless battle teaching your children to behave the way you did; they live in different times. They will act according to their times.[93]

But it would be simplistic to understand these changes exclusively from the logic of time's arrow implicit in Mr. Khembo's testimony. Mang'anja institutions also survived and even prospered despite and sometimes because of these external pressures.

Heterogeneous and always open to outside influences, Mang'anja institutions of formal education have changed in complex ways over the past century and a half. At the risk of oversimplification, one can say that the story of decline is largely the narrative of the "big" institutions, too conspicuous to escape the attention of intrusive missionaries and too costly to survive the money economy. The "small" schools have faced a different fate. They have withered the winds of change to become the basis of a new kind of syncretism that one sees everywhere in the valley.

There are, for example, two parts to the story of the Sena impact on the Mang'anja. One part celebrates the triumph of the Sena patrilineal and patrilocal system over the Mang'anja matrilineal and matrilocal regime. A larger section of the peasantry in the valley now organizes itself along the patrilineal than the matrilineal system.[94] The second part of the story draws our attention to the ability of the Sena to enrich the region's repertoire of teaching order. The immigrants brought new institutions that have not replaced but instead thrive alongside similar rites of Mang'anja origin. Rites of passage for girls, known as maseseto, provide one example of the Sena innovations. Maseseto has become popular for the same reason that that small Mang'anja ways of dancing for the young have done. Organizers of maseseto do not need to employ drummers, brew beer, and spend scarce resources of the community. Not surprisingly, therefore, these small schools have attracted the attention of Christian innovators, keen on introducing modernity by inventing tradition.

Christian missionaries must have learned to live with the devil for many reasons, including their failure to inflict a knockout punch against him. There must have always been voices for moderation among the belligerent modernizers. But, for a long time, only lonely individual missionaries acknowledged the need for reconciliation; accommodation was not part of official policy. Modernization through the invention of tradition became a guiding principle only from the 1960s onward.

Political independence in the mid-1960s played a part in this awakening. Independence required the celebration of tradition. Even Dr. Banda, sometimes more committed to the "civilizing" mission of the West than some of the missionaries themselves, brought into the open some pagan ways of life like the nyau. Then there were the groundbreaking reforms of the Second Vatican Council—now under fire from an aging and increasingly intolerant hierarchy—counseling Roman Catholics to recognize the validity of certain aspects of pagan life. Catholics thus started looking for those elements of tradition they could co-opt and make part of their teaching and formal liturgies. Local languages began to substitute for the mysterious Latin, and, once condemned as the living bells inviting Satan from his uncomfortable abode in hell, drums became part of the Mass. A new era of religious reconciliation had dawned in the valley.

As in most adaptive processes, however, missionaries did not accommodate everything pagan. They were selective, as they continued to rally their troops against the more "repugnant" pagan practices like mabzyoka. Missionaries have also been equally discriminating in their choice of rites of passage for adoption. In general, they have kept an arms' length from the big institutions, while welcoming into their own liturgies elements of the small methods of dancing for the young, which got a new lease on life in a double sense. There were few open wars against most traditional institutions after the 1960s, and the once barely noticeable small methods of transmitting knowledge came to inspire new Christian rituals.[95] To the old Mang'anja list of small schools, one must now add not only Sena but also Christian versions, all easily executable in the market-dependent food economy. For most villagers, therefore, it is not a question of either doing or not doing something for the young; rather, it as a question of choosing between competing strategies, some of which may not be as effective in imparting mwambo as the less popular big schools.

There can be little doubt that the big versions of nsembe, chikwati, and chinamwali were, if only in theory, more effective methods of introducing the young to adulthood. With plenty of food after harvest, female initiates under-going a communally organized chinamwali stayed in the bush up to a month, subjected to rigorous tests in endurance and capacity to absorb mwambo under their female nankungwi teachers.[96] Through such pedagogical devices as riddles and proverbs, elders drove home the ideals of the golden-age theory and the alternative vision. Then after this seclusion, the entire group emerged from the bush for the public and final phase of chinamwali. Performed at the court of the headman or chief, the last part of chinamwali served to welcome the initiates into the community of adults. The Mang'anja solemnized the occasion with the drumming, beer drinking, and nyau dancing that attracted the attention of outsiders.[97]

By contrast, the small versions are crash courses, lasting one or two days and supervised by teachers with no public credentials and, in the case of mis-sionary alternatives, by individuals whose primary qualification is their alien-ation from tradition. Moreover, the small versions are isolated events, without much input from the community or intrinsic connection to other rites of pas-sage. In the past, parents who could not stage a big feast for their children at one point were expected to do so at the next occasion. A small chinamwali would typically be followed by a big chikwati, compensating for the inad-equacies of the first. But this spreading of resources does not normally occur today. Most people go through only one small rite of passage or a succession of similarly abbreviated exercises.[98] Change can be costly.

Today, many boys and girls start their married lives after only an incom-plete exposure to the old mwambo. But even more disturbing for many elders is the fact that many of these imperfectly educated children also aspire to and espouse modern ways, which they do not sufficiently understand either. The result is confusion and intellectual uncertainty. When elders speak of a "breakdown" in morals, they are not simply concerned about the absence of the old, but they are also worried about the presence of something: the unholy mixture of old with new half-truths. This is the state of maladjustment many elders refer to in their explanation of many problems their children face today. Thus, unlike some state officials and NGOs—the West's consulates in this era of informal empire—elders in the valley do not see the coherence of tradition as the principal cause of the AIDS pandemic; for them, AIDS logically follows from the breakdown of tradition that has left the young in a wilderness, insufficiently grounded in either the old or new ways of life.[99] This state of confusion and uncertainty also reflects and shores up old tensions in the daily meal and eating habits.

New Foods, Drinks, and Practices

A market survey, designed to establish the range of foods peasants sell and buy in the valley, made three discoveries. First, it shows the food regime of the region is an open system, with peasants eating more types of foods than they grow themselves. The survey provides clear evidence of the significance of money in peasants' survival strategies. There is now a wide gap, which also existed in the precolonial era, between what Amartya Sen refers to as production-based and exchange-derived entitlements to food.[100] One's garden work, fishing, and food-collecting activities supply only one portion of the foods eaten in the villages. Peasants are dependent on the market not only for cereals during the hungry season, but also for ndiwo on a more or less regular basis. Second, the list reveals that people consume more foods than what they do in organized meals. Narrow and monotonous, the formal daily meal exists only as part of informal ways of eating. Third, informal eating exhibits the same kind of flexibility as the small rites of passage in terms of their capacity to absorb foreign foods and to give rise to new eating habits.

For the purposes of simplicity, one can divide informal foods into three subcategories. The first and most variegated features foods like fruits, alcoholic beverages, and soft drinks. The second and third subgroups are to be treated as extensions or mirror images of the ndiwo and nsima of formal meals. Ndiwo extensions make up the narrowest subgroup of the three. Peasants do not often eat vegetables, beans, fish, or meat outside the formal meal. These are scarce commodities that, moreover, require cooking before peasants can eat them, and soon after going through fire, they almost automatically fall into the realm of the formal meal as ndiwo, available for all members of the community.[101] Fried meat or fish one buys on the market has a tenuous existence as a candidate for snacking; it often ends up as part of the organized meal.[102] Nsima extensions have a longer lifespan as informal foods.

Many extensions of the nsima thrive better as informal foods largely because people can eat them raw or roasted. Peasants snack on raw or roasted sweet potatoes, maize, mapira, mchewere, and their byproducts, such as the stiff *chigodo* and soft *mperera* paste, made from a mixture of water with the wet flour of the cereals. Women also eat the tiny fragments of broken grains before they become ufa flour. When boiled, such fragments turn into *mitama,* which peasants sometimes take as a substitute for nsima. In their ambiguous position as both informal and formal foods, mitama compete with several kinds of bread (mkate) and bread-like items.[103]

Women manufacture bread from maize, millet, sorghum, and rice by baking but, more commonly, by boiling the dough, with each loaf wrapped in banana leaves. Dimba growers sometimes make large quantities of maize bread in response to the flooding of the marshes. Forced to harvest their crop before maturity, women preserve the young grain by turning it into mkate bread.[104] On the market one also finds many types of baked cakes that compete with fruits and other members of the third subcategory of informally eaten foods. Rarely do fruits constitute part of the formal meal.

Peasants eat a broad range of fruits, such as *malambe* (of the baobab tree), tiny masau, guava, passion fruit, lemon, grapefruit, pineapple, oranges, papaws, avocado pears, and especially mangoes and bananas (*nthochi*). People on the valley floor get some of these fruits from the Tchiri Highlands, partly because they do not grow them at all and partly because local demand exceeds supply. Bananas and mangoes furnish good examples of the second scenario. Nearly every village on the valley floor grows mangoes, but these mature as early as November and disappear by January. (Hunger often forces villagers to eat their mangoes while still green.) Thus, after exhausting their own supplies, peasants of the valley floor turn to the mangoes of the local mountains and the Tchiri Highlands, which ripen much later in the season. Similarly, most bananas one finds on local markets in the valley hail from the Tchiri Highlands, especially the Thyolo District, the banana capital of Malawi. Trade with the ecologically different Tchiri Highlands allows villagers in the valley with money to obtain bananas and other nutritionally rich foods throughout the year.

Focus on informal eating thus opens a window on the importance of money in rural survival strategies, the wide variety of items people eat, and the food regime's openness to "foreign" influences. Informal eating does in this respect replay the story of the small institutions of formal education. Unlike formal meals, informal eating releases the risk-taking capacities of the villager. Peasants have experimented with new beverages, new brewing practices, and even new eating routines. But because most of these trials require money, they have also illuminated the problem of social inequality in the food sector. Only the well-to-do are able to take advantage of the new opportunities—often to the disadvantage of the poor. People do not share with their neighbors food from the market as easily as they do with provisions from their own granaries, although such behavior is not necessarily new. The modern breakfast may be new in its content, but it closely parallels certain versions of the old in its social dynamics.

Some villagers eat and many others crave the modern breakfast, featuring such factory-made foods as bread, scones, tea, coffee, sugar, milk, jam, and margarine. This new meal succeeds three kinds of traditional breakfast taken informally in the past. The first is nkute, a portion of nsima from the previous night's meal, eaten mostly by children with salt as ndiwo. Second was the freshly cooked soft porridge or roasted sweet potatoes, available to every member of the household, regardless of age or gender. The third and the one that most sharply countered the ideal of cooked food as provision for everyone presented a freshly cooked nsima and the choice portions of fish or meat from the previous night. This was the privilege of well-to-do men who ate it with their wives inside the house.[105] The modern breakfast has its social roots in this traditional meal. Like the old, the new breakfast stands for wealth and, although sometimes available to all members of the household, it never forms part of the chidyerano communal meal. Some kinds of drinks have traveled a similar route, leaving the domain of the great communal celebrations while integrating foreign items.

New foods and drinks have transformed the drinking habits of the valley in two major ways, highlighting the process of social differentiation in a money economy. First, factory beverages now challenge their homemade rivals. Soft drinks of such brand names as Coca-Cola and Fanta have penetrated both the urban and rural areas, rivaling traditional drinks like the thobwa sweet beer, and a similar competition takes place in the field of alcoholic beverages. The old hard liquors, like kachasu gin, have had to contend with factory-brewed gin, brandy, and beer, most of which were originally imported but are now manufactured in the country.[106] Whatever their origin, however, all the new liquors serve the needs of the upper echelons of the wage laborers. Those in menial jobs look to the cheaper Chibuku, a factory-brewed concoction similar to the old mowa. When not entertaining themselves with Chibuku, these same poor workers join villagers drinking homemade mowa beer and kachasu, whose processing has, however, undergone significant changes as a result of sugar. Innovations stimulated by sugar constitute the second factor in the transformation of the country's drinking patterns.[107]

Sugar has revolutionized both the social and technical conditions of the traditional brewery, as the stories of *kabanga* beer and kachasu gin illustrate. Before sugar, peasants had made kachasu mostly with mzimbe sugarcane and masau fruit,[108] both of which are dry-season plants. Sugar has solved this seasonal limitation at the same time as it has rivaled and even replaced traditional malts made from maize, millet, and particularly maere finger millet. Sugar has made the distilling process easier and less risky, allowing a woman to prepare kabanga beer in a matter of days.[109] Women do not need the support of others these days to brew kabanga or kachasu. Thus, notwithstanding colonial attempts to ban the practice, kachasu brewing has become a very popular enterprise among poor women in both rural and urban areas.[110]

Drinking has also come to lose some of the social functions it used to serve in the past. On the one hand, women distill kabanga and kachasu almost exclusively for economic purpose. On the other hand, their customers in the bars and other drinking places meet not to celebrate any particular social event, and they interact without the kind of constraints characteristic of chinamwali or nsembe partying (see chapter 2). Moreover, after leaving the drinking sessions, most would take their meals as members of an individual household rather than as members of a chidyerano group.

The End of Chidyerano?

A nonscientific survey of 158 meals eaten in different parts of the valley between 1995 and 1996 confirms the golden-age theory's representation of chidyerano as an institution of the past. In 70 percent of the meals, people shared food strictly as members of the nuclear family, while the non-household members participating in the next 29 percent of the meals did so as visitors. There were only two instances, representing about one percent of the total, fitting the description of chidyerano as a grouping of independent households. If it was ever a widespread institution, as all the evidence (including that from the Tchiri Highlands) suggests, then golden-age theorists are right in their portrayal of the past and present in terms of chidyerano and its demise.

Stories about the origins and decline of chidyerano underscore the connectedness and duplicity of social life. They highlight some of the major implications of the fact that human beings exercise their freedom in a world they were not free to make. This is a world in which even knowledge of the cause does not necessarily allow us to prejudge the effect of human action. One and the same set of initial forces can lead to differing outcomes, just as different results can flow from the same conditions. Chidyerano could have originated in times of plenty as well as in times of hunger. Mr. Bernard Demba dramatized the dual origins of chidyerano on 10 May 1995 when, after linking it to abundance in one part of the interview, he went on to stress the role of hunger in another part of the testimony:

> According to the testimonies of our grandparents and parents, people started communal meals in the past because of hunger. When one family has nothing, it can look to neighbors who have food to eat. They would invite the women and children. Women and children would get food from other households participating in a communal meal. Some families could not survive on their own ... people were wise in the past; those who did not have their own food were able to live with the support of others. People who did not have food were not reluctant to tell others about their situation.[111]

Both hunger and abundance can lead to generosity, one because there is so little to share and the other because there is so much. Hunger and abundance exist as two separate things only for the students of the crisis literature, whose single-minded preoccupation with one blinded them from the other. A tunnel vision of the peasant world would also make it difficult if not impossible to understand that even in the best of times, chidyerano faced a precarious existence as an alternative to other ways of organizing the daily meal.

Chidyerano was similar to other rituals in that it never won the day to the exclusion of other forms of taking the meal. Thus, while they consistently extol chidyerano as the embodiment of Mang'anja generosity in the glorious days of unlimited abundance, village elders do not treat the single-household meal as an illegitimate competitor; it was as institutionalized as chidyerano. Most instructions women received during their initiation and wedding ceremonies centered on how to take care of the husband as head of the household. Lectures on how to apportion ndiwo emphasized the validity of the household as a unit of consumption. Participants at a chidyerano meal would not be surprised to find that some parts of a chicken were missing from the dish. Wives had retained such portions to eat with their husbands in the "secrecy" of their households before or after the communal meal.[112] However desirable, chidyerano remained nothing but one method of doing the order; its disappearance does not bring down the social system.

There was, however, nothing inevitable about its demise. Like all other living institutions, chidyerano could cope with its internal contradictions, and its failure to do so demands an explanation. One needs to insert the ritual in its context, particularly the confluence among new market relations, religious ideologies, and new strategies of reproducing social values. The resulting transformations, which sometimes manifested themselves in conflicts over the definition of the ideal, generated a fertile terrain for risk takers, who challenged chidyerano from many angles. They could exploit the fact that, like any meal, chidyerano both promoted and undermined the virtues of social equality. Chidyerano could disintegrate from within, with or without long-term deteriorations in the system of food production. According to proponents of the alternative vision, individual chidyerano groups grounded when rebels abused their neighbors' generosity with their ndiwo:

> Yes, chidyerano came to an end because people's hearts changed. People's hearts changed this way. Some people would always share their good ndiwo with their neighbors at the communal meal. But there were others who would not take their good ndiwo to the public. They would take masamba vegetables to the communal meal and eat the meat alone in their houses. Now when others discover this behavior they get disappointed and decide to end chidyerano.[113]

This is a story about the presence of food. Some people were stingy with their ndiwo. And the intervention of market relations only broadened this struggle over sharing and meaning. The end of chidyerano is as much about the absence as about the presence of food. It folded against the backdrop of new forms of breakfasting, new brewing techniques, and new ways of partying that every day brought hunger to some and abundance to other members of the same community. And if it indeed existed close to the way oral history paints it, then chidyerano's demise came with a price. Not all forms of eating are as effective in promoting good diets.

One of the most attractive features of chidyerano, a benefit for which peasants were ready to give up part of their autonomy, was that, tapping on the resources of many independent households, each chidyerano meal brought to the table a great variety of foods, especially ndiwo. In some chidyerano groupings, people realized this variety in succession, as when one household cooked the meal for the entire group at a time. This kind of arrangement increased the chances of different ndiwo from one meal to another. The other arrangement, according to which all participating households brought prepared dishes at the same time, raised the possibility of different foods at each and every meal.[114] (This also appears to have been the kind of chidyerano that Mrs. Williamson witnessed in the Tchiri Highlands in the late 1930s and early 1940s.)[115] Regardless, however, of the exact system of rotation, it is clear that chidyerano once brought to the table a greater variety of foods than the single household meal, most remarkable for the narrowness of its food items and monotony. Peasants are right when they make the end of chidyerano a metaphor for the maladies of the contemporary meal and society at large. Stories about chidyerano's ending are more relevant than accounts about its origins for golden-age theorists, for whom the past is only meaningful in terms of the present; hence the title of this book. Chidyerano must have had a glorious past precisely because there is no such a thing as a glorious present.

It would be overly simplistic, however, to equate the disappearance of chidyerano with the end of the subsistence ethic that seeks to protect the more vulnerable members of the community. Chidyerano was only one vehicle of this ethic, and people can act generously even in its absence. It seems that kinship, which only acted as one factor in the life of chidyerano groups, has now emerged as the main organizer of the new communal meals. The non-nuclear family members, taking part in 29 percent of the meals in our survey, were relatives of the households that prepared the meals. In the predominantly matrilineal Chikwawa and patrilineal Nsanje, it was mostly the relatives of the wife and husband, respectively, who joined these household-based meals as outsiders.[116] The disappearance of chidyerano has not necessarily brought an end to food sharing; peasants still define food with reference to its dual character as a relationship between people and things and between people with reference to things. They still share, although under different rules, including those that were already there.

Outsiders still find a place in the household-based meal, which takes them more as dependents than as owners of independent households. The relatives participating in the communal meals of our survey did not bring their own nsima or ndiwo, as neighbors would have done under chidyerano. On this count, one may argue that today's peasants are more generous than those practicing chidyerano. The end of chidyerano has compromised the Sfood security of the poor mainly by narrowing the range of protected people and foods available at each formal meal. The absence of chidyerano has not, however, revoked the principle behind the old adage that "even the sick [and powerless] have a right to that which is in the pot."[117] The food system of the valley has been, like most other institutions, a terrain of possibilities, requiring an appreciation of the dynamics of both time's arrow and time's cycle.

CONCLUSION

African historians have shunned the daily meal as a subject for research partly because there is little if any historical information on the subject, but mainly because our training requires that we tell stories of cumulative change. Failure to demonstrate a linear progression amounts to falling into the maligned trap of the ethnographic present or, even worse, validating the racist ideologies denying history to Africa. Consequently, Africanists have placed in the timeless box of "continuity" some topics, which allows them to pursue, with ease, other aspects they can plot along time's arrow. To write the history of states, slavery, peasants, and the food system is to trace their development from "simpler" to more "complex" forms, although the ultimate "goal" of these linear processes shifts from one ideological persuasion to another.

Starting from the same view of so-called precapitalist famines as "crises" of "absolute shortage," modern Whigs and liberals hold capitalism responsible for two radically different outcomes. Time's arrow propels the continent toward the capitalist paradise of unlimited abundance for modern Whigs, but toward an apocalyptic disaster for their liberal rivals. There is no possibility of a deviation from either path. Neither school can understand that the journey toward hell or paradise is made up of pieces of time: the second, the minute, the day, and the season, each with its own laws of motion and the capacity to slow down and complicate the direction of time's arrow. As a social artifact, the daily meal represents a convergence between time's arrow and time's cycle and has a history despite its orderly appearance.

Villagers could take their meals in both organized and informal ways, as members of one or multiple households, and every meal, regardless of its format, both promoted and undermined the equality of consumers. The ideals extolling the right of every member of the community to food, and the limited nature of that right, constituted the principal source of the daily meal's strength and weakness. The other source of disorder points to the reproduction of the ideals themselves. Peasants have employed different methods to impart the technical, social, and ideological fundamentals of provisioning, with small rites of passage thriving alongside big ones. The peasant world has been a dynamic terrain, with room for both the conformist and the rebel. The real question, therefore, is not whether the meal did change; one can take that for granted. The real challenge for the historian is to understand the conditions favoring or restraining the forces of rebellion.

This chapter has identified Christian and Sena influences and shifts in the economy as the effective context for the transformation of the meal regime since the nineteenth century. Some crops, foods, and eating practices have declined and even disappeared, while others have emerged. But, equally significant has been the reconstitution of the conditions of reproducing the knowledge and skills necessary for doing the order of the meal. The past century has indeed been a period of great change, confusion, and intellectual uncertainty. Village elders, especially nankungwi teachers responsible for the teaching of mwambo, have had to share the podium with new evangelists the first day that Sena and Christian modernizers set foot in the region. But this was not the first time they have done so. There were always internal debates in the village, with both the rebels and defenders of the status quo often oblivious to the fact that time's arrow and time's cycle ride the same spaceship, not without discomfort or argument.

Conclusion: Order and Disorder Copilot the Same Spaceship

Any scholar immersed in the details of an intricate problem will tell you that its richness cannot be abstracted as a dichotomy, a conflict between two opposing interpretations. Yet, for reasons that I do not begin to understand, the human mind loves to dichotomize—at least in our culture, but probably more generally, as structuralist analyses of non-Western systems have demonstrated. We can extend our own tradition at least to the famous aphorism of Diogenes Laertius: "Protagoras asserted that there were two sides to every question, exactly opposite to each other."[1]

INTRODUCTION

This project has landed many miles away from its original destination: to faithfully execute the program of the "crisis literature," with only one modification. Right from the beginning, I wanted to inject the debate about "famine" with rural notions of hunger that seemed to me only proper if I were to understand how peasants plan their farming activities and respond to food deficits. Otherwise, this book started with no agenda. But, as the reader of the foregoing pages must know by now, the project has stopped a long distance from its original target, raising questions about both the crisis literature and the practice of history itself.

The book advances food studies in two ways. First, it turns to peasants as theoreticians, and not merely as a source of raw data needed to fill in the gaps left by archival evidence. It accords peasants' ideas about food the same analytical status as the theories of academics and other Western thinkers—thus implicitly calling for an end to the familiar division of labor that sends academics to libraries for "theory" and to the village for "information." One needs the village as much as the library for theory and for information.

The second major contribution of this book follows directly from the first. The expanded theoretical base, incorporating peasants' and academic ideas about the past, has allowed this book to pursue the history of food along *multiple* timescales. In their debates, peasants and academics place emphasis on different time signatures: while academics conduct their debates mostly in terms of linear time, peasant intellectuals articulate theirs along cyclical time and the repetitive. But since the cyclical and linear carry differing weight in the real past of any food system, one needs to be clear about their distinctiveness and interdependence if one is to avoid the kind of conceptual limitations like those that characterize the crisis literature.

MULTIPLE HISTORICAL TRAJECTORIES

A defining characteristic of the crisis literature is its single-minded preoccupation with linear time or central tendency. Much of African history shares that preoccupation. Eager to debunk imperialist myths denying history to Africa, scholars have asserted the power of time's arrow behind every conceivable development in the African past. Thus, despite their other disagreements, all students of the crisis literature proceed under the same assumption: that there was a "transition" from "precapitalist" to "capitalist" forms of social organization. For modern Whigs, the switch carried Africa from so-called precapitalist famines toward capitalist abundance or famines of boom; for the liberals, the great transition placed the continent on an inexorable path toward its destruction. Every hunger turns into a famine, and one famine represents greater devastation than its predecessor. After the "take-off," the story becomes one of either food *or* hunger, but never the two together. This is the "arrow" signature, which promotes the fallacious extrapolation of a supposed trend toward either the conquest of so-called precapitalist famine *or* the progressive absence of food.

The arrow signature does not promote attention to the presence of food. What is more, it in effect shunts attention away from highly pertinent historical questions raised by that presence. So we see that what begins only as a metaphor, originating in the historian's mind, can stride into the midst of the world the historian is trying to understand. The damage it can then do is plain. Whenever the evidence does not justify the identification of a trend, that should be the end of it—the same as one would do with the notion of "average," a measure of central tendency, if the numbers vary so widely that there is no central tendency to measure.

If one insists on measuring a spurious central tendency, what is really happening disappears forever under generalizations that say nothing about it. The crisis literature has had little to say about food largely because the most significant food-related processes occur during the day, tsiku, and season, nyengo, none of which has analytical space in their debates. As elements of the cyclical, tsiku and nyengo obey their own laws of motion, which sometimes weaken, diffuse, and even bend the forward march of the arrow. Thus, new social and ecological pressures for change produced not one but many outcomes of varying strengths and durability.

Beginning in the late 1850s, an army of disorder descended upon the valley, riding such vehicles as the shifting levels of the Tchiri River, the slave trade, the colonial state, Christianity, and the all-powerful but faceless engine they call money. The alliances between the new and old enemies of order created a situation of revolutionary potential. But the actual results were mixed, with only a few developments satisfying the definition of central tendency.

High on the list of the irreversible were developments that brought about new crops, new institutions of formal education, new food-processing tools, the colonial state, and chaola famines. It is impossible to revisit the developments leading to the advent of new crops, new schools of education, the colonial regime, or the chaola of the early 1860s or 1920s. They all carried the imprint of their historical times. Every chaola formed an aspect of time's arrow. Villagers therefore give every chaola a proper name—something they do not do to cyclical events like seasonal hunger.

To argue that seasonal hunger belongs to cyclical time is not to remove it from history. The cyclical is not a timeless residual like the "continuity" subset of the familiar "change-and-continuity" formula. The cyclical is as much part of the historical process as the linear, only the two obey different laws of historical motion. Seasonal hunger could not escape the challenges of the new economy and politics. Today's peasants experience seasonal hunger in significantly different ways than their ancestors did in the mid-nineteenth century. But neither the new economy nor the halfhearted government measures for hunger relief have made a dent in the status of njala as a predictable and perfectly intelligible event among a sizable population of the rural poor. While it only takes political will on the part of the ruling class to end chaola famine, the conquest of seasonal hunger requires the daunting task of reconstituting productive forces and their political context. Many households today continue to suffer a food gap every season, as their ancestors did in the 1860s.

Unlike seasonal hunger, many other food events were irreversible in the short run but proved to be transitory in a long historical perspective. The histories of dimba farming, cotton, and maize in Port Herald District exemplify this pattern of change. Each started the twentieth century as a central tendency, heading toward a progressive future, only to falter and even point in the opposite direction after the Bomani floods of 1939, transforming, in the meantime, the innovators and risk takers of the earlier years into the conservatives and risk avoiders of the post-Bomani period. (Golden-age theorists are in this respect correct in representing the periods before and after the Bomani floods as, respectively, the "past" and "present" of the food system.) Developments that were cumulative in one era lost that characteristic in another. A long-term historical perspective also changes our view of the ability of the new army of disorder to expand or contract rural options.

It would be valid to argue, from a certain point in time, that the enemies of the old order helped increase rural options. The enemies introduced new institutions of formal education, new crops, and new branches of production like wage employment, cattle keeping, and cotton agriculture. One can treat these developments as evidence for a movement toward the multiplication of opportunities in the economic, religious, and agricultural fields. But such a view of the historical process would run against many problems. One can, for example, legitimately consider some accumulations as mere replacements for lost opportunities. Cotton agriculture, wage labor, and the cattle economy emerged in an economy that had lost such enterprises as ivory hunting, cloth making, and the salt industry. Moreover, some initiatives, like those in formal education, often formed another side of the story of the disappearance of old ways of "dancing for" the youth. Finally, the idea of expanding or diminishing options becomes very difficult to defend in qualitative terms. One cannot, in particular, always be certain about the efficiency of the new ways of doing the order. New schools of formal education are not necessarily more efficient than the old ones. Similarly questionable is the ability of the new branches of production to satisfy rural needs. Very often peasants straddle many enterprises not to improve the quality of their lives; many straddle because not a single enterprise gives them enough income. One cannot always be sure about the qualitative effects of those transformations. Cumulative change was rare.

This book explains the scarcity of cumulative developments with reference to the (a) structural tensions within the food system itself (see next section) and (b) the fragility of the agents of disorder. Not every carrier transporting the modernizers was well constructed. Some vehicles, like official agricultural policy, were so badly built that they never made it off the ground, becoming part of history only to the extent that they did occur in the minds of their planners. Other machines were too noisy and intrusive to win the hearts and minds of even the old enemies of order. Cotton failed to reinforce preexisting pressures toward specialization not only because of the vagaries of the climate, but mainly because of the wide discrepancy between the cash crop's rewards and inputs. The gap strengthened the resolve of the many friends of the old order, defending their positions behind the habits of the day and season.

One battalion of defenders upheld the old order behind the unresolved contradiction that makes the growing season a perfect season only to the extent that it promises a future of plenty against the backdrop of the present hunger. Another group rallied behind the logic of the garden, requiring villagers to locate their fields in different ecological zones, planting many crops in the same field, and staggering the sowing process. Finally, others fought the agents of disorder valiantly under the protective umbrella of the conflicting ideals of the golden-age theory and the alternative vision. Very few arrows went through the old wall uncontested.

A SYSTEM OF TENSIONS

As mentioned earlier, this book locates the second group of reasons for the paucity of linear developments in the social character of food. Food is about sharing and, as such, it exists only as part of the social relations of those who eat it. This is the central message of both the golden-age theory and the alternative vision, which establish the ideals of sharing nsima porridge and ndiwo stew, respectively. To the extent that it takes ndiwo and nsima to compose a balanced meal, the two theories affirm not only the relationships of equality and inequality among consumers but also their inseparability. Every meal becomes both feast and famine, whether or not it assumes the form of a chidyerano communal meal of independent households. A living testimony to the golden-age theory's spirit of generosity, chidyerano also acts as a powerful metaphor for the ambiguities of social life. Oral historians place its origins as well as ending in times of both hunger and abundance. Moments of hunger do not have an independent life apart from periods of abundance. Nor do locations of food deficits have meaning apart from areas of surplus.

Although notorious for its droughts, floods, and seasonal hunger, the Lower Tchiri Valley is not at the same time a place of frequent chaola famines, mainly because it features both deserts of hunger and oases of plenty. Deserts of hunger on the valley floor support mostly low-yielding but drought-resilient millet and sorghum. Villagers who depend on such crops subsist at low levels of income in the long run, but are in the short run better protected against the vagaries of the climate than the inhabitants of the oases of plenty.

Part of the hill areas and marshes, the oases of plenty are the principal producers of the high-yielding but less heat-tolerant maize that allows peasants to maintain higher levels of income in the long run but exposes them to the omnipresent dangers of drought or floods on a yearly basis. In very general terms, therefore, the Tchiri Valley combines the vulnerabilities of the maize-dependent southern Africa with the strengths of the traditional cropping patterns of West Africa. Under normal conditions, the deserts of hunger survive on the "surpluses" from the oases of plenty, but this relationship gets reversed under drought or flood conditions. There is a temporal dimension to the relationship between the deserts of hunger and oases of plenty, which also finds expression at the level of daily practice.

Every day, villagers create deserts of hunger and oases of plenty as they cultivate fields in different microenvironments, such as the dambo and mphala; as they raise different crops in the same garden; and as they stagger the sowing process during the same season. They materialize the logic of the garden, which is to reproduce the biological diversity of the natural terrain in the face of strong tendencies toward specialization. As cultivators, villagers both assume and avoid risk with regard to what they grow, the land they exploit, and the techniques they employ. Risk taking and risk avoiding are not the traits of two different species of historical agents. That these labor processes take place in multiple but interconnected time frames provides yet another set of tensions crucial to an understanding of some food events like chaola and njala.

In contrast to the students of the crisis literature, peasants in the valley do not see chaola famine as the universe of the food system; they treat it as a subset of food deficits, the other being njala seasonal hunger. Njala and chaola direct our attention to different time frames, such as the rare and the routine, the irreversible and the repetitive, and time's arrow and time's cycle. Whereas every chaola becomes part of irreversible time, njala falls into the group of repetitive events, afflicting the village poor on a regular basis. It exerts greater pressure on rural practices and behavior than the news-making chaola. Villagers plan and execute their garden work and other activities with njala on their minds. Moreover, during every wet season the poor re-create njala when, in order to survive, they spend a good portion of their time away from their own fields. They generate future disasters in the image of the present. Njala unites the present with the future in the same way as it brings together the rare and the routine. Seasonal hunger becomes chaola—a rare event—when its victims subvert the *quotidian* rules of sharing. The rare and the routine are not always far away from each other, and even migrant workers go through the disorderly process of adjusting to new environments in an orderly fashion. In life, order and disorder reconstitute each other.

GLOSSARY

(1) To reduce the number of African terms in the text, I relegate most Sena terms and many other words for which I have no English equivalent to the endnotes. Such words do not appear in the glossary. (2) Except for the scientific equivalent for the Seha word *bande,* all botanical terms are from Jesse Williamson, *Useful Plants of Malawi* (Zomba, Malawi: Government Printer, 1972 [1954]).

anapache   tiny human beings people believe rich villagers use to steal food from the granaries of other villagers. The singular form is *mwanapache.*

bande   thick grass that lines the Tchiri River and its marshes, identified as *Echinochloa haploclada.*

banja   family, household.

bigifama   "big" or "modern" farmer; same as *mchikumbe* (see mchikumbe) or "type II" farmer.

bungala   late-maturing rice of local origin.

bwalo   meeting or eating place, usually under a tree.

bwemba   tamarind (*Tamarindus indica*).

bwenzi   friend.

chakudya   food.

chakudya-cha-madzulo   dinner or evening meal; the Sena call this *siyali,* from the Portuguese terms *ceia* (supper) or *cear* (to have supper).

chakudya-cha-masana   lunch; the Sena call this *zyantari,* from the Portuguese term *jantar.*

chale   brew one stage before it is ready for drinking.

chaola   famine; from the verb *kuola,* or "to get rotten."

chete   Sena term for granary; same as Mang'anja *nkhokwe* (see nkhokwe).

chidyerano   communal meal of independent households; same as what the Sena call *thando* as in the phrase *kudya-pa-thando*.

chigayo   grinding mill; also known as *mchino* (engine).

chigodo   paste made with undried flour of maize, millet, or sorghum; the Sena call this *chinkhodo*.

chikwa   barrel-like food container made with plaited grass.

chikwati   wedding; family.

chilala   drought; this is also called *dzuwa,* which means "sun."

chilimwe   dry season; the Sena call this *malimwe.*

chimanga   maize (*Zea mays*); the Sena call this *mapiramanga.*

chimera   malt.

chinamwali   female puberty rites.

chinangwa   cassava, manioc (*Manihot esculenta*); in Chisena this is *mfalinya.*

chinyontho   moisture; the Sena term is *mtota.*

chitowe   sesame (*Sesame orientale*).

dambo   floodplain, marsh.

deya   bran.

dimba   garden on *dambo* marshes (plural *madimba*).

dindiro   period when peasants live in their gardens scaring birds or guarding their crops against animals.

dzinja   rainy season or growing season on the *mphala* drylands; this is *mainza* in Chisena.

dzoma   initiation ritual, dance.

dzungu   pumpkin (*Cucurbita maxima*); the plural is *maungu.* The Sena call this *thanga* and use the term *dzungu* to refer to chaff.

faya   a very popular late-maturing white rice variety of foreign origin.

goli   slave stick; forked wood used to tie captives together as they walked to their destinations.

gonkho   slow-ripening sorghum variety.

gugu   a wild sorghum or millet people eat during the hungry season.

india   early-maturing rice of foreign origin.

kabanga   a kind of home-brewed beer.

kachasu   locally made gin; the Sena call this *nipa.*

kachisi   shrine.

kapepe   a wild sorghum or millet people used to collect and eat during the hungry season.

khasu short-handled hoe; the Sena call this *phadza*.

khundi early-maturing rice variety; also the name for wild millet or sorghum people used to eat during the hungry season.

khungulu raised platform inside the house used for storing food; it stands over the cooking hearth. Also known as *thandala*.

kuboma to push or move; hence Madzi-a-Bomani, or the Bomani Floods, which pushed and scattered people in all directions.

kubvinira to "dance for," to instruct in a formal way. Hence, the terms *mwana-wobvinidwa* (which literally means "a child who has been danced for," a phrase they apply to someone of good behavior) and the opposite, *mwana wosabvinidwa* ("a child who has not been danced for," which refers to anyone of bad manners, regardless of age; they also call such persons *mwana wopanda mwambo*).

kupalira to weed; the Sena call the process *kusakula*.

kupambula to separate or thin plants in a hole; same as *kutengula* and *kuzulira*.

kusinja to pound grain in a wooden mortar.

kusuma to search for food from relatives or friends; the Sena call the same process *kuzunsa*. *Kusuma* in Chisena means to file charges against someone.

kutengula to separate or thin plants in a hole; same as *kupambula* and *kuzulira*.

kuthawa madzi to flee from floodwaters.

kuzulira to separate or thin plants in a hole; same as *kupambula* and *kutengula*.

lichero winnowing basket; same as *chisero* in Chisena.

likombe shell used as a spoon.

lundu title of kings who ruled the Lower Tchiri Valley and adjacent highlands as a centralized state between the sixteenth and late eighteenth centuries.

mabzyoka ceremony conducted for sick women, featuring beer and drums.

machewere early-maturing rice variety; also the Sena term for millet or what the Mang'anja call *mchewere* (see mchewere).

machila hammock used to carry Europeans.

madzi water, floods.

maere finger millet (*Eleusine coracana*); the Sena call this *murumbi*.

magala term used to denote large fields belonging to (Magololo) chiefs; also called *maplazi*.

magoneko a special initiation ritual performed for the sons and daughters of rich Sena peasants in addition to the normal puberty rites.

makhuli-a-nthochi roots of a banana plant eaten in times of severe food shortage; same as *zibowa-za-nthochi* (see zibowa-za-nthochi).

makumbi tiny or miniature houses children build outside the village and use when playing as married couples with their own children. The singular form is *khumbi*.

malambe   fruit of the baobab or *mlambe* tree (*Adansonia digitata*).

malimidwe   generic term for colonial agricultural rules, derived from the word *kulima,* which means to cultivate or to hoe.

maphupu   sweet potatoes people leave (usually inadvertently) in the garden or that shoot on their own after the harvesting period. Children, and sometimes ruminants like goats, have free access to such roots; they belong to the community.

mapira   sorghum (*Sorghum vulgare*) or *kaffir* corn.

masamba   leaves; vegetables.

masau   tiny fruit of the dry season (*Ziziphus mauritiana*); people snack on these, and in the past they used the fruits to make strong *kachasu* liquor.

maseseto   girls' initiation ritual among the Sena.

masika   harvest season; season of plenty; cold season (May–July). Same as *khoni* among the Sena.

matanthi   beer before it reaches the stage of *chale.*

mathutu   mound.

matondo   African plum; fruits of the tree *Codyla africana.*

mbalame   bird or birds.

mbale   plate.

mbamu   lump or morse of *nsima.* The Sena call it *nsuwa,* which is also the term (with a different tone) for "island" in their language.

mbatata   sweet potatoes (*Ipomoea batatas*); the Sena call this *bambaya.*

mbatatesi   Irish potato; also known as *kachere* (*S. tuberosum* L.).

mbiya   pot. The Sena call it *nkhali* and reserve the word *thenthe* for a pot used almost exclusively for storing food.

mbudzi   priestess in rain-calling ceremony.

mbwanda   kidney or haricot bean (*Phaseolus vulgaris*); same as *chimbamba* among the Sena.

mchape   witchcraft eradicator or eradication movement (from the verb *kuchapa,* which means to wash or clean.).

mchere   salt; same as *munyu* in Chisena.

mchewere   bullrush or pearl millet (*Pennisetum typhoides*); the same as the Sena term *machewere.*

mchikumbe   "Modern," "big," or "type II" farmer; also known in the Lower Tchiri Valley as *bigifama.*

mdzukulu   grandchild.

mfiti   witch.

mfutso   dried vegetables (leaves).

mgwetsa   rain-calling ceremony.

minyanya   wild tubers villagers used to eat during the hungry season.

mitama   Boiled fragments of maize women produce as they pound the grain to make flour; eaten as a snack or as a replacement for *nsima*. When boiled, the fragments are called *mphunje* among the Sena.

mitumbira   ridges.

mkate   traditional bread made from maize, millet, rice, or sorghum.

mlamba   catfish. The Sena call it *nsomba,* a term which in Chimang'anja refers to any kind of fish.

mlangizi   instructor; agricultural extension worker. The plural form is *alangizi.*

mono   fish trap—the *khonga* of the Sena.

mowa   beer. The Sena call it *bwadwa*—the *badwa* of Gamitto in the quotation that opens the first section of chapter 2.

mpama   wild yam (*Dioscorea* spp.) peasants eat during the hungry season.

mperera   a soft dough made from cereals.

mphala   drylands where farming depends on the rains.

mphale   grain selected for pounding; same as Chisena *njera.*

mphambadza   water-lily bulb villagers eat during the hungry season.

mphero   grinding mill made of a large stone at the bottom and a smaller one on top; the Sena call this *libwe.*

mphika   pot; the Sena call this *chikalango.*

mphunga   wild rice villagers eat during the hungry season.

mpunga   rice (*Oryza sativa*).

msasa   temporary dwelling place. The plural form is *misasa,* which Europeans sometimes rendered as *msasas.*

mtedza   groundnuts, peanuts (*Arachis hypogaea*). The Sena call them *mandui.*

mtenga-tenga   system of carrying goods on the head.

mtondo   wooden mortar for pounding grain; the same as *banda* among the Sena.

mtunda   drylands, ridge.

mudzi   village.

mulusu   initial brew resulting from mixing *chimera* malt with *phala* on the third day of the second phase of the beer-brewing process.

munda   rain-dependent field on *mphala* drylands.

mwabvi   poison ordeal.

mwambo   knowledge, skills, customs, etc., one learns especially through initiation rituals; also the rituals themselves.

mzimbe   sugarcane; the Sena call this *msale.*

nachacha   a late-maturing millet (*mchewere*) variety that is ready to eat five months after being planted.

nandolo   pigeon pea (*Cajanus cajan*); the Sena call this *mbweti.*

nankungwi   female instructor.

ndiwo   American stew; British relish; academics' "side dish"; same as Sena *chisai* or *mlio.*

ngaiwa   course flour ground by mechanical or electrical machines before removing bran; also *nsima* made with such flour. Known as *ngaira* among the Sena.

ngalawa   canoe; the Sena call it *mwadiya.*

njala   hunger.

nkhaka   cucumber; the plural form is *makaka.*

nkhokwe   circular granary. This is similar to what the Sena call *chete;* the only major difference is that the *chete* is rectangular.

nkhondo-ya-mitumbira   the war of the ridges, a reference to the stiff resistance peasants staged against the official campaign for ridges.

nkhoswe   marriage surety; guardian.

nkute   leftovers from the previous night; children's breakfast; same as *nkhuche* among the Sena.

nomi   youth labor societies.

nsanja   a specially constructed platform in a millet, sorghum, or rice field. From the nsanja radiates a network of strings, crisscrossing the entire garden and supported at intervals by standing reeds or bamboo. A child guarding the crops against birds would stay on a seat a bit higher than the crops and activate the network of strings and rattling cans upon spotting birds in the field.

nsembe   sacrifice; second funerary rites.

nsima   stiff porridge made from cereals and a principal component of the daily meal.

nsingano   late-maturing rice of local origin.

nsiya   a mixture of the blood, intestines, heart, and other small internal organs of cattle, goats, pigs, or wild game men boil and eat after killing an animal.

nsomba   fish. *Nsomba* is a generic term for fish in the Chichewa and Chimang'anja languages, but in the Chisena language it only refers to catfish, which the Mang'anja and Chewa call *mlamba.*

nsuzi   *ndiwo* sauce.

ntchenjezi   water-lily bulb villagers used to eat during the hungry season.

ntheme   wild orange (*Strychnos spinosa* Lam.).

nthochi   banana (*Musa sapientum* L.); the Sena call this *mfigu.*

ntholera   medicine the rich use to entice other people's food into their garden or granaries.

nyama   meat.

nyatchenka   a woman who leads the beer-brewing process.

nyau   all-male association of masked dancers.

nyemba   beans of any kind.

nyengo   season.

nyenzi   roots of a water lily villagers eat during the hungry season; probably the same as *nyezi*.

nyika   roots of a water lily of the botanical family *Nymphaeaceae*, the most popular water root of the hungry season.

nyumba   house.

pfuwa   conical blocks (three of them) of earth used to support a pot on fire; the plural is *mafuwa*.

phala   porridge; a mixture of water and flour.

phiri   mountain, hill.

phumbi   frothing brew; beer ready for people to drink.

salima   title of a woman dedicated to serve as Mbona's "wife"; the term literally means "the one who does not hoe."

shamwali   "strategic" friend; one level higher than an ordinary friend or *bwenzi*.

thedzi   a kind of grass, found mostly in the marshes, that people use for thatching roofs and constructing dikes.

thengalamanga   an early-maturing sorghum.

thobwa   sweet beer.

thonje   cotton.

thyolakhosi   a late-maturing rice of local origin.

tsabola   hot peppers (*Capsicum annuum* and *Capsicum frutescens*); same as *mphiripiri* in Chisena.

tsabwila   funeral friend; *nyalumbi* in Chisena.

tsiku   day; the Sena call this *nsiku*.

ufa   flour.

ufa woyera   refined flour produced after the bran had been removed.

ufiti   witchcraft.

umbombo   meanness.

waganyo   hired laborer; from the Portuguese term *ganhar*.

wanchito   regular worker; from the noun *nchito*, which means "work."

zibowa-za-nthochi   roots of a banana plant; same as *makhuli-a-nthochi* (above).

zunde   large garden, belonging to a polygamous husband or large cotton grower.

NOTES

INTRODUCTION: PEASANTS DEBATE ACADEMICS ON FOOD, HUNGER, AND TIME

1. S.J. Gould, *Time's Arrow Time's Cycle: Myth and Metaphor in the Discovery of Geological Time* (Cambridge: Harvard University Press, 1987): 15–16 (emphasis added).

2. E. Durkheim, *The Elementary Forms of Religious Life,* trans. Karen E. Fields (New York: Free Press, 1995): 67. Thanks to Dr. Fields for directing my attention to this text.

3. As a native of the Tchiri Valley, I enjoy some advantages when studying the region. One of the clearest of these is knowledge of the languages of the region (see pp. 25–26). However, one should not exaggerate this advantage. Not all European or American scholars analyze their respective societies with similar depth; nor can one distinguish between different scholarly productions about Africa purely on the basis of the origins of their authors. And some of the reasons are quite obvious. Both African and non-African scholars go through the same kind of academic training. Moreover, neither African peasants nor their governments have the resources to fund projects in African studies. They cannot propose the areas for research or frame the issues as rich Western institutions, including nongovernmental organizations (NGOs), do. (Michael Watts has rightly characterized some of this NGO-funded and inspired work as having "been of the most primitive quality." See his *Silent Violence: Food, Famine and Peasantry in Northern Nigeria* [Berkeley and Los Angeles: University of California Press, 1983]: 571, n. 7). The fact that one is an African does not guarantee a uniquely African perspective.

4. Peasants lost a good part of their crops in 1994, after my first research trip to the area in connection with this project.

5. Shire Valley Agricultural Development Project (SVADP), *An Atlas of the Lower Shire Valley, Malawi* (Blantyre, Malawi: Department of Surveys, 1975), under "Meteorology."

6. Ibid.

7. Ibid.

8. Horace Waller papers, MSS Afr s. 16, 10 vols. (hereafter cited as Waller papers); Horace Waller diaries, 11 vols. (1860–64) (hereafter cited as Waller diaries), Rhodes House, Oxford University; J. M. Schoffeleers, *River of Blood: The Genesis of a Martyr Cult in Southern Malawi, c. A.D. 1600* (Madison: University of Wisconsin Press, 1992): 144, 164–65, where the exact place in the Chididi area is identified as Matundu Hills.

9. Port Herald District Annual Reports (Administration), 1948 (NSP3/1/18); see also ibid., 1946, Malawi National Archives, Zomba (hereafter cited as MNA).

10. The botanical name for this kind of palm tree is *Borassus aethiopum.* The Nchalo Sugar Estate and Factory cover much of this territory today.

11. The botanical name for bande grass is *Echinochloa haploclada.*

12. For some of those scholars who did not shift gears into the crisis mode, see note 30 below.

13. S. Berry, "The Food Crisis and Agrarian Change in Africa: A Review Essay," *African Studies Review* 27, 2 (June 1984): 89 (emphasis added).

14. Some scholars have characterized their analyses as "internalist" in opposition to "externalist" arguments that emphasize the role of colonialism and capitalism: R. Cummings, "Internal Factors That Generate Famine," in *Drought and Hunger in Africa: Denying Famine a Future,* ed. M.H. Glantz (Cambridge: Cambridge University Press, 1987): 111–26; M. Lofchie, "The Decline of African Agriculture: An Internalist Perspective," in *Drought and Hunger in Africa: Denying Famine a Future,* ed. M.H. Glantz (Cambridge: Cambridge University Press, 1987): 85–109. This makes their analyses close to the World Bank's position (World Bank, *Accelerated Development in Sub-Saharan Africa* [Washington, D.C.: World Bank, 1981]) although Cummings and Lofchie do not deny, as the World Bank does, the role of external forces. In powerfully argued political-economic approaches, like those of H. Bernstein and Michael Watts, the distinction between the externalist and internalist loses force. See H. Bernstein, "African Peasantries: A Theoretical Framework," *Journal of Peasant Studies* 6, 4 (July 1979): 421–43; M. Watts, "Drought, Environment and Food Security: Some Reflections on Peasants, Pastoralists and Commoditization in Dryland West Africa," in *Drought and Hunger in Africa: Denying Famine a Future,* ed. M.H. Glantz (Cambridge: Cambridge University Press, 1987): 171–211.

15. J.R. Dias, "Famine and Disease in the History of Angola, c. 1830–1930," *Journal of African History* 22 (1988): 349–78; J. Miller, "The Significance of Drought, Disease and Famine in the Agriculturally Marginal Zones of West-Central Africa," *Journal of African History* 23 (1982): 17–61; M.D.D. Newitt, "Drought in Mozambique, 1823–1831," *Journal of Southern African Studies* 15, 1 (1988): 15–35.

16. J. Goody, *Technology, Tradition, and the State in West Africa* (Cambridge: Cambridge University Press, 1971); idem, *Production and Reproduction: A Comparative Study of the Domestic Domain* (Cambridge: Cambridge University Press, 1976); J. Iliffe, *Africans: The History of a Continent* (New York: Cambridge University Press, 1995); J.B. Webster, "Drought and Migration: The Lake Malawi Littoral as a Region of Refuge," in *Proceedings of the Symposium on Drought in Botswana, National Museum, Gaborone, Botswana, June 5th to 8th, 1978,* ed. M.T. Hinchey (Gaborone, Botswana: Botswana Society in collaboration with Clark University Press; Hanover, NH: distributed by University Press of New England, 1979): 148–57; idem, "Noi! Noi! Famines as an Aid to Interlacustrine Chronology," in *Chronology, Migration and Drought in Interlacustrine Africa,* ed. J.B. Webster (New York: Africana Publishing Company, Dalhousie University Press, 1979): 1–37.

17. E.L. Jones, *The European Miracle: Environments, Economics and Geopolitics in the History of Europe and Asia* (Cambridge: Cambridge University Press, 1981, 1987): 154–56 (emphasis added). I am grateful to Ms. Melita Thomas, a student in my History 201 course ("The Third World") in 2003, for directing my attention to this book.

18. H. Ruthenberg, *Farming Systems in the Tropics,* 3rd ed. (London: OUP, 1980); M. Thomas and G. Whittington, eds., *Environment and Land Use in Africa* (London: Methuen, 1969).

19. J. Iliffe, *The African Poor: A History* (Cambridge: Cambridge University Press, 1987); idem, *Famine in Zimbabwe, 1890–1960* (Gweru, Zimbabwe: Mambo Press, 1990).

The white-controlled press now blames President Robert Mugabe's land-redistribution program for Zimbabwe's food crisis in 2000–2003, while it isolates drought as the principal cause of the deficits in the other countries of Southern Africa. D.F. Bryceson also thinks that colonial relief programs saved Tanzanians from starvation; see her "Changes in Peasant Food Production and Food Supply in Relation to the Historical Development of Commodity Production in Pre-Colonial and Colonial Tanganyika," *Journal of Peasant Studies* 7 (April 1980): 281–311.

20. See, among others, E.A. Eldredge, "Drought, Famine and Disease in Nineteenth-Century Lesotho," *African Economic History* 16 (1987): 61–94; B. Rau, *From Feast to Famine: Official Cures and Grassroots Remedies to Africa's Food Crisis* (Atlantic Highlands, NJ, and London: Zed Press, 1991); T. Shaw, "Towards the Political Economy of the African Crisis: Diplomacy, Debates, and Dialectics," in *Drought and Hunger in Africa: Denying Famine a Future*, ed. M.H. Glantz (Cambridge: Cambridge University Press, 1987): 126–47; M. Vaughan, *The Story of an African Famine: Gender and Famine in Twentieth-Century Malawi* (Cambridge: Cambridge University Press, 1987); Watts, *Silent Violence.*

21. R. Bates, *Markets and States in Tropical Africa* (Berkeley and Los Angeles: University of California Press, 1981); Cummings, "Internal Factors That Generate Famine"; Lofchie, "The Decline of African Agriculture"; World Bank, *Accelerated Development.* Vaughan, who is critical of this position, has dubbed it the "marketing-board" theory (*Story of an African Famine,* 11–14, 86–101).

22. M. Crowder, *West Africa under Colonial Rule* (London: Hutchison, 1968): 348; J. De Castro, *The Geopolitics of Hunger* (New York: Monthly Review, 1976); P. O'Keefe and B. Wisner, "African Drought: The State of the Game," in *The African Environment,* ed. P. Richards (London: International African Institute, 1975): 31–39; J. Suret-Canale, "The Economic Balance Sheet of French Colonialism in West Africa," in *African Social Studies: A Radical Reader,* ed. P. Gutkind and P. Waterman (New York: Monthly Review, 1977): 125–34.

23. Berry, "Food Crisis," 96. Berry elaborates this view in her *No Condition Is Permanent: The Social Dynamics of Agrarian Change in Sub-Saharan Africa* (Madison: University of Wisconsin Press, 1993). If valid, Berry's position seems to indicate that the unevenness in the development of the forces and relations of production is not a peculiarly precapitalist phenomenon, as Goran Hyden assumes in his *Beyond Ujamaa in Tanzania: Underdevelopment and an Uncaptured Peasantry* (Berkeley and Los Angeles: University of California Press, 1980): 245–46. Berry provides a history to the divergence between the two structures of a social formation.

24. World Bank, *Accelerated Development.*

25. Watts, "Drought, Environment and Food Security," 207.

26. R. Palmer, "The Agricultural History of Rhodesia," in *The Roots of Rural Poverty in Central and Southern Africa,* ed. R. Palmer and N. Parsons (Berkeley and Los Angeles: University of California Press, 1977): 221–54; L. Vail, "Ecology and History: The Example of Eastern Zambia," *Journal of Southern African Studies* 3, 2 (1976): 129–55.

27. Bernstein calls this the "simple reproduction squeeze"; see his "African Peasantries."

28. Watts, *Silent Violence,* 147.

29. This is the title of a book by Peter Gill: *A Year in the Death of Africa: Politics, Bureaucracy and the Famine* (London: Paladin Grafton Books, 1986).

30. I am here thinking of such important works as G. Clark, *Onions Are My Husband: Survival and Accumulation by West African Market Women* (Chicago: Chicago University Press, 1994); J. Guyer, "The Food Economy and French Colonial Rule in Central Cameroon," *Journal of African History* 19 (1978): 577–97; idem, "Food, Cocoa, and the Division of Labor by Sex in Two West African Societies," *Comparative Studies in Society*

and History 22, 3 (1980): 355–57; idem, *Family and Farm in Southern Cameroon* (Boston: Boston University African Studies Center, 1984); idem, *An African Niche Economy* (Edinburgh: Edinburgh University Press and the International African Institute, 1997); idem, *Marginal Gains: Monetary Transactions in Atlantic Africa* (Chicago: University of Chicago Press, 2004); H.L. Moore and M. Vaughan, *Cutting Down Trees: Gender, Nutrition, and Agricultural Change in the Northern Province of Zambia, 1890–1990* (Portsmouth, NH: Heinemann, 1994); T. Spear, *Mountain Farmers: Moral Economies of Land and Agricultural Development in Arusha and Meru* (Berkeley and Los Angeles: University of California Press, 1997); A.I. Richards, *Hunger and Work in a Savage Tribe* (London: Oxford University Press, 1932); idem, *Land, Labour and Diet in Northern Rhodesia: An Economic Study of the Bemba Tribe* (London: Oxford University Press, 1952, 1961 [1939]); B. Weiss, *The Making and Unmaking of the Haya Lived World: Consumption, Commoditization, and Everyday Practice* (Durham, NC: Duke University Press, 1996).

31. There might have been other famines before Mwamthota.

32. Mrs. Sigresi Lingstonya Zachepa, Vinancio Zachepa, Njereza Village, TA Kasisi, Chikwawa, 8 July 1995 (TCM95/7).

33. *Discovery* is not the right word because some students of rural Africa, particularly early anthropologists like Audrey Richards, have explored the problem of seasonality. But few in the crisis literature have taken it as a serious problem. Even Megan Vaughan—a very cautious writer—is disturbingly silent on njala; Deborah F. Bryceson allocates only half a page to the problem in her *Food Insecurity and the Social Division of Labour in Tanzania, 1919–85* (New York: St. Martin's Press, 1990): 46; and in his nearly 700-page *Silent Violence,* Watts devotes no more than 9 pages (441–48) to the problem, which does not, moreover, structure the argument of the book. Failure to see seasonal hunger as a major problem has led some scholars to declare Banda's Malawi a hunger-free country: J.G. Liebenow, "Food Self-Sufficiency in Malawi: Are Successes Transferable?" in *Drought and Hunger in Africa: Denying Famine a Future,* ed. M.H. Glantz (Cambridge: Cambridge University Press, 1987): 369–92.

34. See, for example, Bryceson, *Food Insecurity,* 3–18.

35. This is a liberal translation of "Ali awiri si mantha, kuipira kutha ndiwo m'mbale."

36. Gould, *Time's Arrow Time's Cycle,* 16.

37. Mircea Eliade, *The Myth of Eternal Return: Or, Cosmos and History,* trans. Willard R. Trask (Princeton, NJ: Princeton University Press, 1991 [1949]).

38. For some interesting literature on this subject, see R. Horton, *Patterns of Thought in Africa and the West: Essays on Magic, Religion and Science* (Cambridge: Cambridge University Press, 1993); J.S. Mbiti, *African Religions and Philosophy* (New York: Anchor Books, 1970 [1969]).

39. Some kind of eschatology seems to be a key element of the witchcraft-eradication (or *mchape*) complex. While officially sponsored religions like the Mbona rain cult project villagers to one well-defined future, namely a future that was already realized in the "golden" age, some mchape specialists operating on the fringes of or outside established order could have promised a future with a goal. For a parallel with modern millenarian movements, see K.E. Fields, "Antinomian Conduct at the Millennium: Metaphorical Conceptions of Time in Social Science and Social Life," in *The Political Dimensions of Religion,* ed. Said Amir Arjomand (Albany: State University of New York Press, 1993): 157–68. Time's arrow may not have dominated African cosmologies; but it often showed up, as an uninvited guest, in times of trouble to highlight the meaning of the ordinary.

40. Vaughan's analysis (*Story of an African Famine*) is different in this respect; she does briefly speak about eating in chapter 5. But she comes to this from the perspective of crisis (e.g., p. 119); chapters 1–4 present the history of food in terms of the different debates

about the causes of famine. For an interesting analysis not informed by the crisis literature, see, among others, Weiss, *Making and Unmaking.*

41. Watts, *Silent Violence,* 119–27.

42. For my response to this classification, see chapters 1 and 2.

43. Vaughan, *Story of an African Famine,* 119; Watts, *Silent Violence,* 146.

44. Watts, *Silent Violence,* 124.

45. Ibid., 436, 446.

46. Iliffe, *Famine in Zimbabwe.* In this book, Iliffe elaborates on the theme of his *The African Poor.* Poverty during the continent's dark precolonial era coincided with physical disability; it assumed political and economic dimensions only under European colonial enlightenment.

47. See, for example, Berry, "Food Crisis," 61–63.

48. Ibid., 89. In his more theoretical discussion, Watts does suggest that capitalism may not have been powerful enough to consign Nigeria's precolonial economy to the dustbin of history: "All this makes for complicated if not convoluted dialectical developments, not simple unilinear change" (*Silent Violence,* 24–25). But without centering on the repetitive, he cannot check the long march of time's arrow, which structures the book.

49. See Martin Chanoch's stimulating essay "Development and Change in the History of Malawi," in *The Early History of Malawi,* ed. B. Pachai (London: Longman, 1972): 429–46.

50. There is, for example, not a single chapter dedicated to women as food processors in one of the seminal collective works on women in Africa: M. J. Hay and S. Stitcher, eds., *African Women South of the Sahara* (London and New York: Longman, 1984).

51. J. Vansina, *The Tio Kingdom of the Middle Congo, 1880–1892* (London: IAI, 1973); idem, *Living with Africa* (Madison: University of Wisconsin Press, 1994): 151–52.

52. I see in Eugene Genovese's twin concepts of "resistance in accommodation" and "accommodation in resistance" an attempt to tame time's arrow: *Roll, Jordan, Roll: The World the Slaves Made* (New York: Vintage, 1976 [1972]).

53. Gould, *Time's Arrow Time's Cycle,* 8.

54. Most of their diaries and letters have been published, but there are still many unpublished works, including those in the National Library of Scotland in Edinburgh and the Rhodes House at Oxford University. For published works on the Zambezi Expedition, see, among others, G. W. Clendennen, ed., *David Livingstone's Shire Journal, 1861–1864* (Aberdeen, Scotland: Scottish Cultural Press, 1992); D. Livingstone and C. Livingstone, *The Narrative of an Expedition to the Zambesi and Its Tributaries and of the Discoveries of Lakes Shirwa and Nyassa* (London: Murray, 1865); R. Foskett, ed., *The Zambesi Journal of Dr. John Kirk, 1858–1863,* 2 vols. (London: Oliver and Boyd, 1965); T. Holmes, ed., *David Livingstone: Letters and Documents, 1841–1872* (Livingstone, Zambia: Livingstone Museum in association with Lusaka: Multimedia Zambia; Bloomington and Indianapolis: Indiana University Press; London: James Currey, 1990); E. C. Tabler, ed., *The Zambezi Papers of Richard Thornton: Geologist to Livingstone's Zambezi Expedition,* 2 vols. (London: Chatto and Windus, 1963); J.P.R. Wallis, ed., *The Zambesi Expedition of David Livingstone, 1858–63,* 2 vols. (London: Chatto and Windus, 1956). And for a guide to the National Library of Scotland holdings, see G. W. Clendennen and I. C. Cunningham, comps., *David Livingstone: A Catalogue of Documents* (Edinburgh: National Library of Scotland, 1979). For the records of the UMCA, see N. R. Bennett and M. Ylvisaker, eds., *The Central African Journal of Lovell Procter, 1860–64* (Boston: Boston University Press, 1971); H. Rowley, *The Story of the Universities Mission to Central Africa* (New York: Negro Universities Press, 1969 [1867]); J.P.R. Wallis, ed., *The Zambesi Journal of James Stewart, 1862–1863* (London: Chatto and Windus, 1952); Waller diaries.

55. These were the managers of the African Lakes Company (ALC), popularly known as the Mandala Brothers. They arrived in the country in 1876, and their unpublished papers are housed in the University of Witwatersrand Library in Johannesburg. The diaries (1882–87) of Frederick T. Morrison constitute another important source for this period; they are in the University of Edinburgh Library. For published accounts, see, among others, J. Buchanan, *Shire Highlands (East Central Africa): As a Colony and Mission* (London: Blackwell and Sons, 1885); H. B. Cotterill, ed., *Travels and Researches among the Lakes and Mountains of Eastern and Central Africa* (London: Cass, 1968); J. A. Coutinho, *Memorias de um Velho Marinheiro Soldado de Africa* (Lisbon: Livraria Bertrand, 1941); H. Faulkner, *Elephant Haunts* (London: Hurst and Blackett, 1868); A. Hetherwick, *The Romance of Blantyre: How Livingstone's Dream Became True* (London: Clarke, n.d. [1931]); H. H. Johnston, *British Central Africa: An Attempt to Give Some Account of a Portion of the Territories under British Influence North of the Zambesi* (London: Methuen, 1897); W. M. Kerr, *The Far Interior: A Narrative of Travel and Adventure from the Cape of Good Hope across the Zambezi to the Lake Regions of Central Africa,* 2 vols. (London: Sampson Low, Marston, Searle and Rivington, 1887); W. P. Livingstone, *Laws of Livingstonia: A Narrative of Missionary Adventure and Achievement* (London: Hodder and Stoughton, n.d.); D. Macdonald, *Africana: The Heart of Heathen Africa* (London: Dawson of Paul Mall, 1969); F.L.M. Moir, *After Livingstone: An African Trade Romance* (London: Hodder and Stoughton, n.d.); D.J. Rankin, *The Zambesi Basin and Nyasaland* (London: Blackwell and Sons, 1893); E. D. Young, *The Search after Livingstone: A Diary Kept during the Investigation of His Reported Murder* (London: Letts, 1868); idem, *Mission to Nyassa* (London: John Murray, 1877).

56. This was especially true of the ALC and planters. See my "Feeding and Fleecing the Native: How the Nyasaland Transport System Distorted a New Food Market, 1890s–1920s," *Journal of Southern African Studies* (forthcoming).

57. The Lower Tchiri Valley was originally divided into three administrative districts: the West Shire in the north, Ruo (or Chiromo) in the center, and the Lower Shire in the south. Ruo was declared a subdistrict of the Lower Shire in August 1920, only to be reverted to its former status under the name Chiromo in 1922. Chiromo was finally abolished in 1925, with two of its chiefdoms (Makhwira and Ngabu) merged into the West Shire District (now called Chikwawa), and the other two chiefdoms (Mlolo and the Mbenje subchiefdom of Tengani) joining the Lower Shire (now renamed Port Herald) (*Nyasaland Government Gazette* 32 [Notice 281 of 1925]). Then, in 1949, the British united Chikwawa with Port Herald, calling the new entity the Lower River District. But after a year the two units reverted to their old status as the Chikwawa and Port Herald Districts. The latter came to be known as Nsanje after political independence in 1964.

58. A good example of such men was Mr. P. M. Lewis, who headed Port Herald in the late 1940s and early 1950s.

59. Ngabu Agricultural Development Division (NADD), "Garden Survey Report: Results of a Garden Survey Conducted 1977/8, 78/9, 79/80" (Evaluation Section, October 1981), SVADP. This project was known by different names over time: the Chikwawa Cotton Development Project (CCDP) in 1968–73, and the SVADP in 1973–78. NADD is the term used to refer to the project since 1978 (see chapter 5). Some of these reports are in the MNA in Zomba, but many others are still at Ngabu (in Chikwawa), which has been the project's headquarters.

60. H. Kjekshus once called this the "maximum population disruption" hypothesis. See his *Ecology Control and Economic Development in East African History: The Case of Tanganyika, 1850–1950* (London: Heinemann, 1977).

61. Chikwawa District Annual Reports (Administration), 1922–23 (NSC2/1/1), MNA.

62. Ibid.

63. Local authorities may have succumbed to their own or their superiors' need to suppress news about the suffering of the people; but, as tax collectors, they had to explain to their superiors the serious shortfalls in tax revenues during the famine (chapter 2).

64. Vaughan, *Story of an African Famine.*

65. J.N. Kotre, *White Gloves, How We Create Ourselves through Memory* (New York: Norton, 1995): 88–89.

66. J. McCracken in *American Historical Review* 97, 6 (February 1992): 261–62; L. White, "Working Lives in the Lower Shire," *Journal of African History* 34, 1 (1993): 158–59.

67. As Sir Harry Johnston noted in 1894: "'Shire' I would say is absolutely unknown as a native name." H. Johnston, Report of the First Three Years' Administration of BCA, 31 March 1894, Foreign Office (hereafter cited as FO) 2/66, Public Record Office (hereafter cited as PRO), London.

68. White, "Working Lives." Note that this critique comes from someone who, as an English teacher in Malawi, rightly insisted that his students learn to spell, pronounce, write, and speak English "correctly."

69. Ibid. See also R. Pelissier in *Revue francaise d'histoire d'outre-mer* 81, 302 (1994): 117–18.

70. For a brilliant response to academics who think they do not need to know African languages, see P.T. Zeleza, *Manufacturing African Studies and Crises* (Dakar, Senegal: CODESRIA, 1997): 498–99.

71. See my review "Gold-Seekers, *Prazo*-Holders and Capitalists in Mozambique: A Review," *Canadian Journal of African Studies* 18 (1983): 545–47.

72. Any Chichewa speaker would tell you I had to do a lot of jiggling to render the Chewa proverb "Ali awiri si mantha, kuipira kutha ndiwo m'mbale" the way I did (see note 35 above). A literal translation would run something like this: "To be two is not fear; too bad only because it finishes stew in the plate."

PART I: CHAOLA ABOLISHES HISTORY

CHAPTER 1: POLITICAL CRISES AND FAMINE, 1862–1923

1. Chimbeli, the councillor of Lundu Mankhokwe (whose wife was given by the chief to become Mbona's "wife" at Khulubvi), as quoted by Rowley, *Story,* 348.

2. UN Integrated Regional Information Networks (distributed by AllAfrica Global Media), August 6, 2002, http://allafrica.com/stories/printable/200208060509.html.

3. Livingstone and Livingstone, *Narrative,* 456.

4. Foskett, *Kirk,* 2:500.

5. Bennett and Ylvisaker, *Procter,* 346.

6. Livingstone and Livingstone, *Narrative,* 400; Rowley, *Story,* 341.

7. The term *mgwetsa,* which literally means "that which makes it [rain] fall," is a generic term for any rain ritual. See Rowley, *Story,* 226–27; Schoffeleers, *River of Blood,* 55.

8. The following account summarizes Schoffeleers's writings, especially "The Political Role of the Mbona Cult of the Mang'anja," in *The Historical Study of African Religion,* ed. T.O. Ranger and I. Kimambo (London: Heinemann, 1972): 73–94; idem, "The Chisumphi and Mbona Cults in Malawi: A Comparative History," in *Guardians of the Land: Essays*

on Central African Territorial Cults, ed. J. M. Schoffeleers (Gwelo, Zimbabwe: Mambo, 1978): 147–85.

9. Rowley, *Story,* 224.

10. Ibid., 224–25. They first approached Tengani, who was the most senior chief in the southern part of the valley (the Malawi section). However, for reasons that we do not know, the Tengani of the time was unwilling to assume what the sources refer to as his "traditional" responsibility. The chief was probably too busy trying to defend his territory against the slave raiders, especially Matekenya, who finally killed the chief in 1863: Bennett and Ylvisaker, *Procter,* 383; G. W. Clendennen, ed., "The Shire Journal of David Livingstone, 1861–1864" (unpublished MS): 150; Waller diaries, 4:19 (September 8, 1863). Whatever the exact reason, by refusing to work with Khulubvi officials this Tengani set a precedent to be followed by other Tengani incumbents during the colonial era (see next section).

11. On 6 August 1862, James Stewart and Horace Waller slept at Mankhokwe's village (Mbewe-ya-ku-Madzi) on their way to Thyolo Mountain. The missionaries, who had been at Chikwawa since May, were looking for a healthier place to move to, and the nearby Thyolo Escarpment seemed ideal. They went through Mbewe-ya-ku-Madzi to ask Mankhokwe's permission, since people recognized his authority over the area. Mankhokwe did not apparently object to the plan. The missionaries went to the top of the mountain only to face strong opposition from the people there, saying they could not allow white people to live near the shrine of Mbona and his wife, the salima (Bennett and Ylvisaker, *Procter,* 308–9; Wallis, *Stewart,* 93–94; Schoffeleers, *River of Blood,* 94; Waller diaries, 4:12 [August 6, 1862]).

12. Waller diaries, 4:12 (August 6, 1862).

13. "At night we heard an outcry and soon men dropped into the village at which we were sleeping relating now that a poor woman had been caught no less than CMbeli's [*sic*] wife—he by the bye is out of favour at court just now" (Waller diaries, 4:12 [August 6, 1862]; see also Rowley, *Story,* 225; Wallis, *Stewart,* 93–94).

14. There are many such accounts for the twentieth century.

15. Rowley, *Story,* 226–27.

16. According to Rowley, *Story,* 227, rains fell immediately after the nsembe.

17. A. Sen, *Poverty and Famines: An Essay on Entitlement and Deprivation* (Oxford: Clarendon Press, 1981).

18. The picture of the Tchiri Valley I present here (a more peaceful place in the 1850s, followed by a period of open violence and devastation) closely follows Livingstone's. Other observers, particularly James Stewart, thought Livingstone had idealized the pre-1861 period (Wallis, *Stewart*). But I find little in the critics' arguments or experiences that invalidates Livingstone's portrayal in its broad outlines. See my *Work and Control in a Peasant Economy: A History of the Lower Tchiri Valley in Malawi, 1859–1960* (Madison: University of Wisconsin Press, 1990): xvi–xvii, 68–69.

19. Foskett, *Kirk,* 1:164. He went on to say, "The men are strong fellows, the women good natured and not the scraggy things of the Zambezi" (ibid.).

20. Foskett, *Kirk,* 1:209; Wallis, *Livingstone,* 1:104–5.

21. Waller diaries, 4:12 (August 6, 1862).

22. Rowley, *Story,* 87.

23. Ibid., 358. Rowley had made a similar observation about the people of Mankhokwe's village (ibid., 87).

24. Waller diaries, 4:18 (June 20, 1863); see also 4:12 (August 26, 1862); Livingstone and Livingstone, *Narrative,* 102; Foskett, *Kirk,* 1:173; Wallis, *Livingstone,* 1:92.

25. Bennett and Ylvisaker, *Procter,* 82–83; Foskett, *Kirk,* 2:351–53; Livingstone and Livingstone, *Narrative,* 355; Rowley, *Story,* 103–4.

26. Rowley, *Story,* 339.

27. Waller diaries, 4:12 (September 18, 1862).

28. Bennett and Ylvisaker, *Procter,* 382.

29. Bennett and Ylvisaker, *Procter,* 321–31; Foskett, *Kirk,* 2:364; Rowley, *Story,* 316–17; Wallis, *Stewart,* 107.

30. Foskett, *Kirk,* 2:500.

31. Livingstone and Livingstone, *Narrative,* 457.

32. Rowley, *Story,* 384.

33. *South African Pioneer* 26 (July 13): 105 (hereafter cited as *SAP*).

34. Interview with Matthias Chimtanda Mlilima (former Chief Mlilima), Mlilima Village, TA Kasisi, Chikwawa, 23 January 1976 (M/CK1).

35. See the introduction, note 57.

36. Lower Shire District Monthly Reports (Administration), 1920–21, May, April 1921 (S1/486/20), MNA.

37. Southern Province Annual Reports (Administration), 1921–22 (S1/1110/22); Ruo District Monthly Reports (Administration), May 1921 (S1/300/21), MNA.

38. Chikwawa District Annual Reports (Administration), 1918–19 (S1/781/19), MNA. The only bad spot in this season was Maseya's chiefdom, whose population survived on food from other parts of the district (Chikwawa District Monthly Reports [Administration], April 1919 [S1/1052/20], MNA). For evidence on the availability of food in other parts of the district, see Meeting with Chiefs, 21 December 1919, Chikwawa District Monthly Reports (Administration), April 1919 (S1/1052/20), MNA.

39. Chikwawa District Monthly Reports (Administration), 1920–21, 14 May 1920 (S1/474/20), MNA.

40. District Council Meetings, 13 August, 10 November 1920, Chikwawa District Monthly Reports (Administration), 1920–21 (S1/474/20), MNA.

41. District Council Meetings, 22 February 1921, Chikwawa District Monthly Reports (Administration), 1920–21 (S1/474/20), MNA.

42. Chikwawa District Annual Reports (Administration), 1920–21 (S1/474/20), MNA.

43. Thus, at a district council meeting on 16 February 1922, Ruo's District Resident made an emotional appeal, asking chiefs to step up the campaign against the export of food and the brewing of beer, and to encourage their people to grow "catch" or emergency crops. And, in a move that highlighted the seriousness of the situation, he expressed his desire to see people devote more of their time to food than cotton production (District Council Meeting, 16 February 1922, Ruo District Book II, MNA). He estimated that only the Makhwira and Mlolo sections had enough food to last them 12 months (*ibid.*). He apparently ignored the fact that the two chiefdoms would lose their food to the hungrier parts of the district, the Lower Shire, and even the Tchiri Highlands. As a result, the people of Makhwira and Mlolo suffered from hunger nearly as much as the other parts of the valley in 1922–23.

44. Southern Province Annual Reports (Administration), 1921–22 (S1/1110/22), MNA.

45. According to the district commissioner, the epidemic killed 101 people by March 1920. A medical officer thought that many more people succumbed to the disease because of the poor quality of the lymph administered in the inoculation campaign (Lower Shire District Annual Reports [Administration], 1919–20 [S1/1077/19], 1920–21 [S1/486/20], MNA). For Chikwawa District, see West Shire District Annual Reports (Administration), 1918–19 (S1/781/19), 1919–20 (S1/1052/19), 1920–21 (S1/474/20),

MNA. For Ruo, see Ruo District Annual Reports (Administration), 1919–20 (S1/1041/19), 1920–21 (S1/487/20), MNA. For the beginning and end of the smallpox epidemic, see Ruo District Monthly and Annual Reports (Administration), September 1919, 1919–1921 (S1/1041/19); Ruo District Council Meetings, 29 November 1920, Ruo District Book II, 1918–23; Lower Shire District Monthly and Annual Reports (Administration), October 1919, 1919–1921 (S1/1077/19), November 1920, 1919–1921 (S1/486/20), MNA; *SAP* 33 (1920): 17, 45; interviews with Jackson Kwaibvamtowe, Tursida Village, STA Mbenje, Nsanje, 10 September 1980 (TVES5/6); Rampi Masamba, Tizola Village, TA Chimombo, Nsanje, 11 September 1980 (TVES5/9).

46. Chikwawa District Annual Reports (Administration), 1922–23 (NSC2/1/1), MNA. The Resident was being less than candid when he told his superiors that as a result of government "assistance in the form of Liquid Quinine and Kerosene Oil and sugar … the mortality from the epidemic appears to be very small" (ibid.). Every other evidence suggests that the concoction did not make much of a difference: Chikwawa District Annual Reports (Administration), 1922–23 (NSC2/1/1); Chikwawa District Monthly and Annual Reports (Administration), April, July, August, September, October 1919, 1919–20 (S1/1052/19), MNA.

47. That some of these accusations were related to famine, see Ruo District Annual and Monthly Reports (Administration), April 1921, 1919–21 (S1/1041/19), MNA.

48. Ruo District Council Meetings, 13 January 1919, Ruo District Book II, 1918–23, 25 September 1919; Ruo District Monthly and Annual Reports (Administration), 1919–1921 (S1/1041/19), MNA. The fact that official reports from the Lower Shire District are silent on witchcraft accusations does not necessarily mean that the district escaped the phenomenon; it may simply mean that the officers there did not pay much attention to it or that the pro-Mbona chiefs suppressed information on the movement.

49. In some cases, the accused were only women (West Shire District Monthly and Annual Reports [Administration], April 1919, 1919–20 [S1/1052/19], August 1920, 1920–21 [S1/474/20], MNA); in some it was only men (West Shire District Monthly and Annual Reports [Administration], April 1919, February 1920, 1919–20 [S1/1052/19], MNA); but in many others, men were accused together with their women (Ruo District Annual and Monthly Reports [Administration], May 1919, 1919–21 [S1/1041/19], MNA).

50. As in the case of the two half-brothers in Chikwawa who accused each other of "being mfiti" after the deaths of their relatives; see West Shire District Monthly and Annual Reports (Administration), February 1920, 1919–21 (S1/1052/19), MNA.

51. Ruo District Annual and Monthly Reports (Administration), May 1919, 1919–21 (S1/1041/19), MNA.

52. West Shire District Monthly and Annual Reports (Administration), May 1919, 1919–20 (S1/1052/19), MNA.

53. Ruo District Annual and Monthly Reports (Administration), June 1919, 1919–21 (S1/1041/19), MNA.

54. Ruo District Annual and Monthly Reports (Administration), May 1919, 1919–21 (S1/1041/19), MNA.

55. Ruo District Annual and Monthly Reports (Administration), May 1919, 1919–21 (S1/1041/19), MNA. Others were given a 15-year jail sentence even after traditional tests had proven them innocent; see West Shire District Monthly and Annual Reports (Administration), May 1919, 1919–20 (S1/1052/19), MNA.

56. The chiefs then used mchape to eliminate their political rivals. For some of the tales about Magololo cruelty as reported by European observers, see Buchanan, *Shire Highlands*; Livingstone, *Laws of Livingstonia*; Macdonald, *Africana*; A. Werner, *The*

Natives of British Central Africa (New York: Negro University Press, 1969); Young, *Mission to Nyassa.*

57. Schoffeleers, "Chisumphi and Mbona." This is one of two recorded cases of Magololo military operations against the Mbona shrines. In the second story it was Chiputula who allegedly destroyed and looted the Mbona shrine at Khulubvi in Nsanje. (The spirit retaliated by sending a severe drought into the country, and Chiputula was forced to repent and recall the shrine functionaries he had dispersed.) For this story, see J. M. Schoffeleers, "Mang'anja Religion and History" (a collection of oral testimonies), 10:3. In this case, the Chiputula of oral history may have been the notorious pillager Matekenya, who in 1863 did indeed destroy the Khulubvi shrine (see Foskett, *Kirk,* 2:521; Wallis, *Livingstone,* 2:288). The two names, Chiputula and Matekenya, are interchangeable in many oral accounts.

58. Schoffeleers, "Mang'anja Religion," 49:230.

59. *Central Africa: A Record of the Work of the Universities Mission* (1895), 13:66–67; Schoffeleers, *River of Blood,* 100.

60. Foskett, *Kirk,* 2:521; Wallis, *Livingstone,* 2:288.

61. E. C. Mandala, "The Tengani Chieftaincy and Its Relations with Other Chieftaincies in Nsanje District" (Final Year Students Seminar Papers, Chancellor College, University of Malawi, 1973–74).

62. Chikwawa District Annual Reports (Administration), 1935 (S1/79B/36); Annual Reports for the Southern Province (Administration), 1934 (S1/88/35); Lower Shire Chiefs to District Commissioner (DC), Port Herald, 21 January 1936; DC (Port Herald) to Provincial Commissioner (PC) (Southern Province [SP]), 4 March, 6 May 1936 (NSP1/15/1), MNA.

63. According to Rowley, *Story,* 224–25, the Tengani family used to supply Mbona with salima wives.

64. Mchape reappeared in its public form in the Lower Shire District only during the Great Depression of the early 1930s: Port Herald District Annual Reports (Administration), 1931 (S1/60F/32), 1932 (S1/43A/33); Lower Shire District Book 4, 1928–32, MNA; *SAP* 46 (August–September 1933): 105.

65. *SAP* 29, 8 (August 1916): 113. This theme had already started in 1913 (*SAP* 26, 7 [August 1913]: 105–6).

66. Schoffeleers, *River of Blood,* 103; J. M. Schoffeleers, "Crisis, Criticism, and Critique: An Interpretative Model of Territorial Mediumship among the Chewa," *Journal of Social Science* 3 (1974): 74–80. Mollen Tengani, who ruled between 1936 and 1961, perfected this "modernist" strategy; see my "Tengani." Their determination to keep distance from the cult may have also been reinforced by the popular belief that anyone over whose head people built the roof "would die within a year or so after the first or second occasion" (Schoffeleers, *River of Blood,* 65).

67. Only Mwita, who in 1911–13 ruled over only four villages near today's Chikwawa District headquarters (West Shire District Book II, 1910–13, MNA), lost his position.

68. Mandala, "Tengani."

69. Interviews with Moshtishu, Chiphwembwe Village, TA Malemia, Nsanje, 9 and 14 August 1973 (T73/8/2); David Makoko, Subchief Ostrich Makoko, Makoko Village, TA Chimombo, Nsanje, 16 August 1973 (T73/8/5); Headman Mphamba, Mphamba Village, TA Malemia, Nsanje, 19 August1973 (T73/8/8).

70. Port Herald District Annual Reports (Administration), 1933 (NSP2/1/4), MNA. The existence of public pressure for nsembe to Mbona is suggested by the following report: "Faith in the God Mbona was so influential that [people were] fortified against

progress. They almost believed that nothing is worth doing to make their crops success-ful than the use of native medicines and charms and offerings to Mbona. Everything that happens is supposed to be done by him, so if he can be humoured sufficiently, he will bring rain and produce good crops in the land. So the welfare of the natives is in pleas-ing Mbona." (Department of Agriculture [DA], March 1922 [A3/2/157], MNA, quoted in Schoffeleers, "Chisumphi and Mbona," 176). The drought revived the beliefs but not action.

71. Schoffeleers, "Mang'anja Religion," 47:138–39.

72. Rowley, *Story,* 297. See also Foskett, *Kirk,* 2:512, 585–86; Bennett and Ylvisaker, *Procter,* 248.

73. Rowley, *Story,* 277. See also Bennett and Ylvisaker, *Procter,* 216, 248 (where the Magololo are said to have owned between 200 and 300 goats); Wallis, *Stewart,* 92, 124–25; Foskett, *Kirk,* 2:493, 507, 584–86.

74. Interview with Matthias Chimtanda Mlilima (former Chief Mlilima), Mlilima Village, TA Kasisi, Chikwawa, 23 January 1976 (M/CK1).

75. According to a 1910–11 census, the combined population of the six Magololo chiefdoms did not exceed 10,000. Not included in the census was the more populous Makhwira chiefdom, which then belonged to the Ruo District: West Shire District Book II, 1910–13, MNA.

76. This was Rowley's (*Story,* 371) prediction in 1863. For an elaboration of the same theme, see some of the literature cited in note 58 above, especially *Mission to Nyassa.*

77. Mathias Chimtanda Mlilima (former Chief Mlilima), Mlilima Village, TA Kasisi, Chikwawa, 23 January 1976 (M/CK1).

78. I develop this theme in a separate paper, "Feeding and Fleecing the Native."

79. *Central African Times,* October 6, 1900 (hereafter cited as *CAT*). The paper changed its name to the *Nyasaland Times* in 1906, when British Central Africa became Nyasaland.

80. *CAT,* October 15, 1904.

81. *Nyasaland Times,* July 25, 1912 (hereafter cited as *NT*; see also *NT,* August 29, 1912). The actual figures given in the paper are two pounds of flour per day, two pounds of beans per week, and four ounces of salt per week. The Public Works Department needed 750 tons to feed its 3,000 workers in six months in 1919 (*NT,* December 17, 1919).

82. *CAT,* March 18, 1905.

83. Ibid., July 22, 1905.

84. Ibid., March 5, 1905.

85. *SAP* 26 (July 1913): 105.

86. See, for example, A. G. Hopkins, "Economic Imperialism in West Africa: Lagos, 1880–92," *Economic History Review* 21 (1968): 580–606.

87. For Chiromo, see, for example, *CAT,* March 4, 1905; *NT,* October 5, 1911; and the figures given at the beginning of this section.

88. Mandala, "Feeding and Fleecing the Native."

89. Lower River (Chikwawa and Port Herald) District Annual Reports (Administration), 1949 (NS3/1/18), MNA.

90. Interview with Karota Tsaibola, Chikhambi Village, TA Katunga, Chikwawa, 30 August 1994 (TCM94/2).

91. Interview with Chief Joseph Maseya, TA Maseya, Chikwawa, 30 January 1976 (M/CK4).

92. In this book, by John Iliffe, every food crisis is "famine," and there is no suggestion that European settlers might have been responsible for some of the crises, which are uncritically labeled "precapitalist" famines. Like his award-winning *The African Poor*, *Famine in Zimbabwe* is a powerful exposé of the benevolence of European settlers, who succeeded in saving Africans from the tyranny of their natural environment. See also Bryceson, "Changes in Peasant Food Production."

93. Lower Shire District Monthly Reports (Administration), February 1919 (S1/430/19), MNA.

94. This was true, although officials never asked themselves why Africans did what they did.

95. PC for SP to Chief Secretary (CS), 27 January 1922 (S1/244/22), MNA.

96. Famine Conditions Anticipated in Nyasaland (S1/244/22), MNA.

97. Director of Agriculture (DA), Progress Report on Native Food Supplies (A3/2/111), MNA.

98. CS to District Residents, Central and Southern Provinces, Telegram, 28 January 1922; CS to Nyasaland Chamber of Commerce and Agriculture, 1 February 1922; DA to CS, 1 February 1922 (S1/244/22), MNA.

99. DA, Progress Report on Native Food Supplies, February 1922 (A3/2/113), MNA. The director was quoting the District Resident's report, which says, "A great many people are leaving the district." See Resident Lower Shire District to PC (SP), 31 January 1922 (S1/296/22), MNA.

100. Governor of Nyasaland to Governor of Tanganyika, Telegram, 28 January 1922 (S1/244/22), MNA.

101. Governor of Tanganyika to Governor of Nyasaland, Telegram, 6 March 1922 (S1/244/22), MNA.

102. PC (SP) to Governor, 14 March 1922; Governor of Nyasaland to Governor of Tanganyika, 17 March 1922 (S1/244/22), MNA.

103. DA to CS, 13 March 1922 (S1/244/22), MNA.

104. Governor of Nyasaland to Governor of Tanganyika, 24 April, 5 May 1922 (S1/244/22), MNA.

105. Governor of Tanganyika to Governor of Nyasaland, 18 May 1922 (S1/244/22), MNA. According to this letter, the chief transportation officer (CTO) had made another order for food. It was not clear to Tanganyika's governor whether the order made by his counterpart in Nyasaland was in addition to that made by the CTO. But see CTO to CS, 17 July (S1/244/22), MNA, where the CTO denies having made such an order.

106. Governor of Tanganyika to Governor of Nyasaland, 25 May, 20 July 1922; Political Officer (Mahenge, Tanganyika) to CTO, 19 June 1922 (S1/244/22), MNA.

107. Governor of Nyasaland to Governor of Tanganyika, 26 July 1922; see also CS to Political Officer (Mahenge, Tanganyika), 19 July 1922; DA to Acting CS, 25 July 1922 (S1/244/22), MNA.

108. DA to CS, 27 July (S1/1852/22), MNA. The new estimate resulted from financial considerations and the shrinking of the Tchiri River that allowed people to raise "catch" crops on the river's bed.

109. DA to Acting CS, 27 July 1922 (S1/1852/22), MNA. It is not clear from the sources whether it was peasants or planters who produced the maize.

110. According to the DA, the entire relief operation, involving the purchase of 1,070 tons, would cost the government a total of £11,547 17s. (£6,657 17s. for the 500 tons from Beira

and £4,890 for the 570 tons to be purchased within the country: DA to Acting CS, 27 July 1922 (S1/1852/22), MNA.

111. Minute: Governor, 15 August 1922 (S1/1852/22), MNA.

112. Ibid. See also CS to Governor, 14 August 1922; DA to CS, 22 August 1922; Resident (Chikwawa) to PC (SP), 2 September 1922 (S1/1852/22), MNA.

113. Ranald Macdonald (Acting PC) to Governor, 24 August 1922 (S1/1852/22), MNA. Macdonald had tried the credit system when he was Resident of the Lower Shire District; about 50 percent of the peasantry repaid their debts.

114. Minute: Governor, 15 August 1922 (S1/1852/22), MNA.

115. Minute: Governor, 23 August 1922 (S1/1852/22), MNA.

116. On 27 July 1922 the DA estimated that the northern section of Chikwawa would only need 100 tons of maize (DA to Acting CS, 27 July 1922 [S1/1852/22], MNA). We do not know, however, whether this was the actual amount of food distributed from Mpemba.

117. Interview with Mathias Chimtanda Mlilima (former Chief Mlilima), Mlilima Village, TA Kasisi, Chikwawa, 26 February 1980 (TVES2/3). Africans called him "Bwana Male," so that in this part of the valley the famine is sometimes referred to as "Njala-ya-Bwana-Male" (see chapter 2).

118. This is the "Kherekhe" of oral history, which is why Mwamthota is also known as Kherekhe in much of the old Ruo District (see chapter 2).

119. Lower Shire District Annual Reports (Administration), 1922–23 (NSP2/1/1); Annual Report for the Southern Province (Administration), 1922–23 (S1/1748/23), MNA.

120. Summary of Conditions of Native Food Crops, n.d. (c. January 1922) (S1/296/22), MNA.

121. N.D. Clegg to DA, 9 March 1923 (A3/2/111), MNA.

122. DA to CS, 25 November 1922 (S1/1852/22), MNA.

123. Clegg to DA, 31 December 1922; see also Clegg to DA, 8, 20 January 1923 (A3/2/111), MNA. And as demand increased, Clegg decided at the beginning of January 1923 to dispense 9.21 instead of the usual 6.05 tons a day: Clegg to DA, 1 January 1923 (A3/2/111), MNA.

124. Clegg to DA, 13 January 1923 (A3/2/111), MNA. The idea that peasants could feed themselves in two or three weeks following the rains is another example of how, unable or unwilling to feed the hungry, officials were ready to trust another system to come to their rescue. It is sometimes peasant generosity, which would not, according to the British, allow one's neighbor to die of hunger, and at other times it is the bountiful nature. Few if any cereals sown with such rains could ripen in three weeks. Only the maize, millet, and sorghum that had already taken root but shriveled as a result of drought could reestablish themselves and bear fruit within three weeks. But the largest group of plants that fitted the official schedule consisted of wild plants and roots.

125. Clegg to DA, 22 January 1923 (A3/2/111), MNA.

126. Clegg to DA, 26 January 1923 (A3/2/111), MNA.

127. As Clegg noted: "To buy here, necessitates them working to get the amount required, and anything to do with 'work' these natives intensely dislike" (Clegg to DA, 29 January 1923 [A3/2/111], MNA). It was not, of course, *any* type of work that villagers did not like.

128. Clegg to DA, 25 February, 9 March 1923 (A3/2/111), MNA.

129. Watts, *Silent Violence*, 147 (emphasis in original).

130. Ibid., xxiii.

131. Ibid., 147. But see n. 135 on p. 550, some parts of the introduction, and the book in general, where the author rightly insists on the social character of famine. This inconsistency

results mainly from the tyranny of time's arrow (disclaimers to the contrary, e.g., pp. 24–25). If food availability is not necessarily the problem under capitalism, then it must be under the precapitalist order.

132. Iliffe, *Famine in Zimbabwe.*

CHAPTER 2: IN TIMES OF RENEWAL AND IN TIMES OF DISASTER

1. Rowley, *Story*, 386.

2. This poem was recorded by Dr. Samuel Safuli, to whom due acknowledgment is made.

3. See the EPT91 series of interviews in the bibliography.

4. This may in part explain the failure of the British to create "communal" granaries in the 1930s.

5. Martin Seemungal, "Long Road to Relief: American Food Being Sent to Africans Who Are Forced to Eat Dirt," ABC World News, July 1, 2002, http://printerfriendly.abc-news.com/printerfriendly/Print?fetchFromGLUE=true&GLUEService.

6. A.C.P. Gamitto, *King Kazembe and the Marave, Cheva, Bisa, Bemba, Lunda, and Other Peoples of Southern Africa: Being the Diary of the Portuguese Expedition to That Potante in the Years 1831 and 1832,* 2 vols., trans. I. Cunnison (Lisboa: Junta de Investigacoes do Ultramar, 1960): 1:106–7.

7. I am using the word in its Chimang'anja version because among the Sena, *shamwali* simply means "friend," like *bwenzi* among the Mang'anja.

8. E. W. Chafulumira, *Mbiri ya Amang'anja* [A History of the Mang'anja] (Zomba, Malawi: Nyasaland Government, Department of Education, 1948): 21–22.

9. Unlike the more restricted Sena term *bwadwa* (or Gamitto's *badwa*), mowa among the Mang'anja denotes almost any kind of beer, such as the local gin (kachasu or *nipa*) as well as what the Sena would call *derunde* and *kabanga*. Kabanga and derunde are the "Europeanized" forms of bwadwa in that they used sugar instead of malt. Kabanga is different from derunde mainly in that it is made from maize bran (*deya,* or *goche*). For more details on these beers, see interviews with Windo Kampira, Antonio Mwanaleza, Antonio Nyakanyanza, Chanazi Nyakanyanza, Tambo Village, STA Mbenje, Nsanje, 4 July 1995 (TCM95/2); Damison Kulima Tambo, Kolina Chipondeni Tambo, Tambo Village, STA Mbenje, Nsanje, 5 July 1995 (TCM95/4).

10. Windo Kampira, Antonio Mwanaleza, Antonio Nyakanyanza, Chanazi Nyakanyanza, Tambo Village, STA Mbenje, Nsanje, 4 July 1995 (TCM95/2).

11. Ibid.

12. The Sena used to have an expensive rite of passage, featuring both drumming and beer, known as *magoneko*. They staged magoneko for both boys and girls before their wedding, and before or after the specifically female maseseto puberty rites for girls. Magoneko was a lavish ritual, which only the rich could afford. The initiate received a new name or title on the last day (Windo Kampira, Antonio Mwanaleza, Antonio Nyakanyanza, Chanazi Nyakanyanza, Tambo Village, STA Mbenje, Nsanje, 4 July 1995 [TCM95/2]).

13. Nsayi Bira Mbesa, Tambo Village, STA Mbenje, Nsanje, 5 July 1995 (TCM95/3); Elena Chagwa, with Asiteva Faifi, Calista Mikaeli, Tsapa Village, TA Kasisi, Chikwawa, 7 July 1995 (TCM95/6).

14. J.M. Schoffeleers, "Social and Symbolic Aspects of Spirit Worship among the Mang'anja" (Ph.D. thesis, Oxford University, 1968): 365–87.

0268 *Notes*

15. They call this *kusumisa chimera kwa azimu,* or to dedicate the malt to the spirits: Windo Kampira, Antonio Mwanaleza, Antonio Nyakanyanza, Chanazi Nyakanyanza, Tambo Village, STA Mbenje, Nsanje, 4 July 1995 (TCM95/2).

16. It appears that beer brewing at this stage was more sensitive to geographical variability, especially altitude and temperature, than to ethnic differences; see V. Berry and C. Petty, eds., *The Nyasaland Survey Papers, 1938–1943: Agriculture, Food and Health* (London: Academic Books, 1992).

17. Windo Kampira, Antonio Mwanaleza, Antonio Nyakanyanza, Chanazi Nyakanyanza, Tambo Village, STA Mbenje, Nsanje, 4 July 1995 (TCM95/2).

18. Interviews with Village Headwoman Malita Chimtedza, Chimtedza Village, STA Mbenje, Nsanje, 6 July 1995 (TCM95/5); Windo Kampira, Antonio Mwanaleza, Antonio Nyakanyanza, Chanazi Nyakanyanza, Tambo Village, STA Mbenje, Nsanje, 4 July1995 (TCM95/2).

19. The following timetable is an adaptation of Chafulumira, *Mbiri ya Amang'anja,* 17, which is sometimes at odds with information from non-Mang'anja areas.

20. Ibid. This procedure is described differently by Windo Kampira, Antonio Mwanaleza, Antonio Nyakanyanza, Chanazi Nyakanyanza, Tambo Village, STA Mbenje, Nsanje, 4 July 1995 (TCM95/2); Elena Chagwa, with Asiteva Faifi, Calista Mikaeli, Tsapa Village, TA Kasisi, Chikwawa, 7 July 1995 (TCM95/6).

21. According to some sources (e.g., Gregorio Usseni, telephone conversation, 13 May 1998 [TCM98/1]), the last chimera was always made from millet, sorghum, or, preferably, finger millet, but never maize. Thus, if the chimera used for *kugogodera* was made from millet, sorghum, or finger millet, women did not have to prepare more chimera for chale.

22. Chafulumira, *Mbiri ya Amang'anja,* 17.

23. Windo Kampira, Antonio Mwanaleza, Antonio Nyakanyanza, Chanazi Nyakanyanza, Tambo Village, STA Mbenje, Nsanje, 4 July 1995 (TCM95/2).

24. Ibid.; Mrs. Sigresi Lingstonya Zachepa, Vinancio Zachepa, Njereza Village, TA Kasisi, Chikwawa, 8 July 1995 (TCM95/7); see also chapter 7.

25. See Chimbeli's comment on how the chief spent his days drinking his mowa instead of organizing nsembe to Mbona: Rowley, *Story,* 348.

26. Interviews with Windo Kampira, Antonio Mwanaleza, Antonio Nyakanyanza, Chanazi Nyakanyanza, Tambo Village, STA Mbenje, Nsanje, 4 July 1995 (TCM95/2); Damison Kulima Tambo, Kolina Chipondeni Tambo, Tambo Village, STA Mbenje, Nsanje, 5 July 1995 (TCM95/4); Village Headwoman Malita Chimtedza, Chimtedza Village, STA Mbenje, Nsanje, 6 July 1995 (TCM95/5); Helemesi Pepala, Mwalija Village, TA Kasisi, Chikwawa, 18 April 1995 (SM95/4); Tayipi Alfred, Mafumbi Village, TA Makhwira, Chikwawa, 17 May 1995 (SM95/11); Tsamdoka Renso, Mrs. Renso, Dreva Chibonga, one other informant, Chikunkhu Village, TA Tengani, Nsanje, 4 June 1995 (SM95/15); Henry Genti, Maere Village, TA Mbenje, Nsanje, 8 June 1995 (SM95/17). There were some *nyakwawa* and *mfumu* who did not, as a matter of custom, eat at these rites: see Frederick Lebala and Albert Mvula, Mpangeni Village, TA Kasisi, 18 April 1995 (SM95/3); Mchelengi Nkhambala, Malemia II Village, TA Ngabu, Chikwawa, 21 April 1995 (SM95/7); Tayipi Alfred, Mafumbi Village, TA Makhwira, Chikwawa, 17 May 1995 (SM95/11); Magireni Theka, Chikunkhu Village, TA Tengani, Nsanje, 6 June 1995 (SM95/16). They would instead get uncooked meat: Frederick Lebala and Albert Mvula, Mpangeni Village, TA Kasisi, 18 April 1995 (SM95/3); Lendison July Gawani, Mphamba Village, TA Ngabu, Chikwawa, 21 April 1995 (SM95/5); Mchelengi Nkhambala, Malemia II Village, TA Ngabu, Chikwawa, 21 April 1995 (SM95/7).

Tsabwila funeral friends were especially aggressive in asserting their privileges at funerals: see Village Headman Tambo, Tambo Village, STA Mbenje, Nsanje, 3 November 1991 (EPT91/8); Mrs. Kolina Tambo, Tambo Village, STA Mbenje, Nsanje, 3 November 1991 (EPT91/9); Tsamdoka Renso, Mrs. Renso (?), Dreva Chibonga, one other informant, Chikunkhu Village, TA Tengani, Nsanje, 4 June 1995 (SM95/15). See also Laisoni Musaika and Mrs. Musaika, Mtambo Village, TA Makhwira, Chikwawa, 26 May 1995 (SM95/13).

27. Interviews with Village Headwoman Malita Chimtedza, Chimtedza Village, STA Mbenje, Nsanje, 6 July 1995 (TCM95/5); Elena Chagwa, with Asiteva Faifi, Calista Mikaeli, Tsapa Village, TA Kasisi, Chikwawa, 7 July 1995 (TCM95/6).

28. Organizers of maseseto female initiation also fed their female guests with a wide range of foods. Parents' failure to provide such foods jeopardized a daughter's chances to fully participate in other girls' maseseto. No girl was allowed to eat at another girl's maseseto an item not offered at her own initiation: interview with Nsayi Bira Mbesa, Tambo Village, STA Mbenje, Nsanje, 5 July 1995 (TCM95/3). See also Windo Kampira, Antonio Mwanaleza, Antonio Nyakanyanza, Chanazi Nyakanyanza, Tambo Village, STA Mbenje, Nsanje, 4 July 1995 (TCM95/2); Damison Kulima Tambo, Kolina Chipondeni Tambo, Tambo Village, STA Mbenje, Nsanje, 5 July 1995 (TCM95/4).

29. Gregorio Usseni, telephone conversation, 13 May 1998 (TCM98/1); Windo Kampira, Antonio Mwanaleza, Antonio Nyakanyanza, Chanazi Nyakanyanza, Tambo Village, STA Mbenje, Nsanje, 4 July 1995 (TCM95/2); Damison Kulima Tambo, Kolina Chipondeni Tambo, Tambo Village, STA Mbenje, Nsanje, 5 July 1995 (TCM95/4).

30. Gregorio Usseni, telephone conversation, 13 May 1998 (TCM98/1).

31. Nsayi Bira Mbesa, Tambo Village, STA Mbenje, Nsanje, 5 July 1995 (TCM95/3).

32. Interviews with Windo Kampira, Antonio Mwanaleza, Antonio Nyakanyanza, Chanazi Nyakanyanza, Tambo Village, STA Mbenje, Nsanje, 4 July 1995 (TCM95/2); Nsayi Bira Mbesa, Tambo Village, STA Mbenje, Nsanje, 5 July 1995 (TCM95/3); Mchelengi Nkhambala, Malemia II Village, TA Ngabu, Chikwawa, 21 April 1995 (SM95/7); Laisoni Musaika and Mrs. Musaika, Mtambo Village, TA Makhwira, Chikwawa, 26 May 1995 (SM95/13).

33. Rowley, *Story,* 384.

34. Clendennen, "Shire Journal," 124; see also Livingstone to Russell, 28 January 1863, MS. 10715, no. 1316, National Library of Scotland (hereafter cited as NLS).

35. Bennett and Ylvisaker, *Procter,* 396.

36. Interview with Mrs. Leni Pereira, Chitsa Village, TA Tengani, Nsanje, 5 November 1991 (EPT91/13); Unidentified Nsanje Tradition, Bangula (?), Nsanje, October–November 1991 (EPT91/16). See also interviews with Mrs. Kolina Tambo, Tambo Village, STA Mbenje, Nsanje, 3 November 1991 (EPT91/9); Mrs. Patrishu, Mbande Village, TA Lundu, Chikwawa, 5 November 1991 (EPT91/12).

37. Interviews with Anthony Bankamu Chipakuza, Chipakuza Village, TA Lundu, Chikwawa, 17 October 1991 (EPT91/2); Kamondo Suliali, location unknown, 19 October 1991 (EPT91/3).

38. One can treat these accounts as presenting what Kjekshus termed the "maximum population disruption" theory—the view among European visitors to eastern Africa in the nineteenth century that "Arab" slave trading led to the depopulation of entire regions; see his *Ecology Control and Economic Development,* 1–25.

39. Two of the best examples of these structured accounts are Livingstone and Livingstone, *Narrative*; and Rowley, *Story.* For the diaries, see, among others, Bennett and Ylvisaker, *Procter*; Clendennen, "Shire Journal"; Foskett, *Kirk*; Tabler, *Zambezi Papers*; Wallis, *Stewart*; Waller papers; Waller diaries.

40. For example, James Stewart, who came to the valley at the height of the famine and slave raids in 1862–63, accused Livingstone of having painted an overly optimistic picture of the region and of having exaggerated the depth of its cotton economy in the 1850s: see Wallis, *Stewart,* 83, 87–89, 100–103, 210–11, 222–23, 225, 227.

41. Livingstone and Livingstone, *Narrative,* 450.

42. Livingstone and Livingstone, *Narrative,* 457–58. Dr. Kirk had no trouble finding specimens of Mang'anja skulls; they were everywhere: see Foskett, *Kirk,* 2:516.

43. Waller diaries, 4:17 (March 4, 1863).

44. Rowley, *Story,* 384. See also Wallis, *Livingstone*, 2:230.

45. Rowley, *Story,* 384 (emphasis added).

46. Livingstone and Livingstone, *Narrative,* 457, 456.

47. Foskett, *Kirk,* 1:595.

48. Rowley, *Story,* 384.

49. Chikwawa District Annual Reports (Administration), 1922–23 (NSC2/1/1), MNA.

50. Chafulumira, *Mbiri ya Amang'anja,* 5.

51. Chikwawa District Annual Reports (Administration), 1922–23 (NSC2/1/1), MNA.

52. Ibid.

53. Lower Shire District Monthly Reports (Administration), April–May 1921 (S1/299/21), MNA.

54. Port Herald District Annual Reports (Administration), 1922–23 (NSP2/1/1), MNA.

55. Chikwawa District Annual Reports (Administration), 1922–23 (NSC2/1/1), MNA. The report for 1924–25 dismissed emigration as a factor in the shortfall of tax revenues; it explained the drop with reference to "the removal of numerous duplicated names." Chikwawa District Annual Reports (Administration), 1924–25 (NSC2/1/1), MNA.

56. Interview with Mrs. Leni Pereira, Chitsa Village, TA Tengani, Nsanje, 5 November 1991 (EPT91/13).

57. Sen, *Poverty and Famines.*

58. Damison Kulima Tambo, Kolina Chipondeni Tambo, Tambo Village, STA Mbenje, Nsanje, 5 July 1995 (TCM95/4).

59. Waller diaries, 4:16 (January 20, January 21, February 6, 1863).

60. Interviews with Mrs. Kolina Tambo, Tambo Village, STA Mbenje, Nsanje, 3 November 1991 (EPT91/9); Mrs. Leni Pereira, Chitsa Village, TA Tengani, Nsanje, 5 November 1991 (EPT91/13); Mfumu Zimola, Zimola Village, Chikwawa, October–November 1991 (EPT91/15).

61. Livingstone and Livingstone, *Narrative,* 457. In the more seriously affected areas like Mathiti, to the north of Chikwawa, fully matured grain fell to the ground and rotted because there was no one to pick it. Waller diaries, 4:18 (May 27, 1863).

62. Bennett and Ylvisaker, *Procter,* 359, 360, 366, 372, 379, 396, 410.

63. Ibid., 366.

64. Ibid., 379. Some victims, like the woman who had a poisoned arrow lodged deep in her liver, did survive (Livingstone and Livingstone, *Narrative,* 462–63). But others did not. See also Rowley, *Story,* 306.

65. The sources are especially rich on this subject. See, among others, Chasasa Nyang'ombe Fole, Odriki Village, TA Chapananga, Chikwawa, October 1991 (EPT91/6); Nadumbo Kanthema, Mangulenje, Chikwawa, October 1991 (EPT91/7); Village Headman Tambo, Tambo Village, STA Mbenje, Nsanje, 3 November 1991 (EPT91/8); Mrs. Patrishu, Mbande Village, TA Lundu, Chikwawa, 5 November 1991 (EPT91/12); Mrs. Leni Pereira, Chitsa Village, TA Tengani, Nsanje, 5 November 1991 (EPT91/13); Dafleni Chimatiro, Mafale Village, TA Lundu, Chikwawa, October–November 1991 (EPT91/14); Mfumu

Zimola, Zimola Village, Chikwawa, October–November 1991 (EPT91/15); Unidentified Nsanje Tradition, Bangula (?), Nsanje, October–November 1991 (EPT91/16); N. D. Clegg to DA, 2, 7 February 1923 (A3/2/111), MNA.

66. Mrs. Leni Pereira, Chitsa Village, TA Tengani, Nsanje, 5 November 1991 (EPT91/13).

67. Famine also exaggerated the plight of the *kapolo* "slaves." Some masters used their kapolo to test unknown roots and plants, which killed some kapolo; other owners sold their kapolo dependents for food: Waller diaries, 4:16 (January 20, 1863); Clendennen, "Shire Journal," 124; Livingstone to Russell, 28 January 1863, MS. 10715, no. 1316, NLS. But famine also afforded some kapolo the chance to buy their freedom. Portuguese masters at Thete lost nearly 75 percent of their slaves, who bought their freedom as they went to the bush looking for food (Livingstone and Livingstone, *Narrative*, 448–49).

68. Vaughan, *Story of an African Famine.*

69. In these villages, married men were for all intents and purposes mere "guests," with their natural allegiances to the communities of their mothers and their female siblings. Those who escaped murder at the hands of the marauders (Rowley, *Story*, 106) fled to their natal communities, leaving behind them their wives and children to fend for themselves (see Vaughan, *Story of an African Famine*, chapter 5).

70. Clendennen, "Shire Journal," 15, 101; Livingstone and Livingstone, *Narrative*, 106–7, 406, 593–94. See also Foskett, *Kirk*, 2:411, 414.

71. For the story of these women in the context of Magololo rise to power, see, for example, Bennett and Ylvisaker, *Procter*, 216, 248; Foskett, *Kirk*, 2:493, 507, 584–86; Rowley, *Story*, 106, 277; Wallis, *Stewart*, 92, 124–25.

72. Vaughan, *Story of an African Famine*, chapter 5.

73. Waller diaries, 4:16 (January 11, 1863); see also ibid., 4:16 (February 4, 1863).

74. Ibid., 4:16 (February 4, 1863).

75. Ibid., 4:16 (February 2, 1863).

76. Interview with Mrs. Patrishu, Mbande Village, TA Lundu, Chikwawa, 5 November 1991 (EPT91/12).

77. For the famine of the early 1860s, see, among others, Bennett and Ylvisaker, *Procter*, 176; for that of 1922–23, see interview with Mrs. Leni Pereira, Chitsa Village, TA Tengani, Nsanje, 5 November 1991 (EPT91/13).

78. Interview with Mrs. Leni Pereira, Chitsa Village, TA Tengani, Nsanje, 5 November 1991 (EPT91/13). Traditions of the northern part of the valley present the Nyungwe, or people from the Thete region, mainly as beggars and settlers, while oral accounts from the south make the same people and others from Mozambique as the buyers of children, particularly girls. One may explain the difference with reference to the dominance of the matrilineal system and ideology in the north and its patrilineal counterpart in the south.

79. I suspect that the shortages of 2000–2002 qualified as chaola in some parts of southern Africa.

80. Mrs. Margaret Phiri had been abandoned by her "philandering" husband three years earlier. One of her children had died of malnutrition, and she wanted to sell "three of" the remaining five children to get money to feed the others. Social workers gave her the equivalent of US$15 to buy food. See Brian Ligomeka and Raphael Mweninguwe, "Hungry Women Tries [*sic*] to Sell Children for Food," *Africa Eye News Service (NELSPRUIT)*, February 28, 2002, http://allafrica.com/stories/printable/200202280465.html.

81. Not many people remember the famine of 1862–63 as a distinct event, separate from the general chaos that led to the end of the lundu state and the emergence of Magololo rule. They do not have a specific name for the famine, and the few who specify it simply call it

the great chaola. On the other hand, peasants call the food shortage of 1901 Makanandula, although there are no detailed oral or documentary accounts on it. By contrast, there are many reports on the hunger of 1949, which in the southern part of the valley is sometimes referred to by the name "Thodi," a reference to Mr. Todd, who was an agricultural officer involved in food distribution. This was a serious shortage, especially in the southern or Port Herald district, but it did not become a chaola mainly because villagers were able to do emergency farming in the marshes and to leave the area for Mozambique. See Port Herald District Annual Reports (Administration), 1949 (NSP3/1/18), MNA.

82. Other terms that were popular in the past but which have largely disappeared from the general vocabulary include *magoneko*. The meaning of other terms has changed. For example, *mzinda* used to refer to centralized initiation schools under the control of chiefs. Today, the word simply means "town."

83. Although most officials used the term *famine* indiscriminately, some tried to restrict it to what I call *chaola*. Declaring a food shortage as famine would have required them to give aid: Secretary for Natural Resources and Surveys (Dr. H.K. Banda) to General Manager, Farmers Marketing Board, 17 October 1962 (10.1.9R/32150), MNA.

PART II: PRESENT HUNGER AGAINST THE FUTURE OF PLENTY

CHAPTER 3: DROUGHT, FLOODS, AND SEASONAL HUNGER

1. Richards, *Land, Labour and Diet*, 36.
2. UN Integrated Regional Information Network, October 5, 2001, http://allafrica.com/stories/printable/200110050269.html. Thanks to Dr. Cromwell Msuku for directing my attention to this report.
3. Bennett and Ylvisaker, *Procter*, 408.
4. Port Herald DC to PC (SP), 23 August 1962 (10.1.9R/32150, Foodstuffs 2/4, 1961–73), MNA.
5. See, among others, Lower Shire Division (including CCDP area), October 1972 (14.1.2F/40364), MNA.
6. Port Herald DC to PC (SP), 23 August 1962 (10.1.9R/32150, Foodstuffs 2/4, 1961–73), MNA.
7. Chikwawa District Monthly Reports (Administration), March 1964 (ADM 12/III); Port Herald District Monthly Reports (Agriculture), March 1958 (8.7.5F/7306), MNA.
8. NADD, "Garden Survey," chapter 7, identifies November–February as the height of the hungry season.
9. Port Herald District Monthly Reports (Agriculture), December 1954, December 1957 (8.7.5F/7306), MNA.
10. ADMARC, Maize Sales and Stocks, Monthly Reports in Short Tons, April 1976–March 1977 (C200/3A), MNA.
11. Port Herald District Monthly Reports (Administration), November 1962 (10–1.9F/32154), MNA. See the next chapter for more sources on this subject.
12. Port Herald District Monthly Reports (Administration), October 1957 (8.7.6F/7310); Port Herald District Monthly Reports (Agriculture), January 1958 (8.7.5F/7306), MNA.
13. Chikwawa District Monthly Reports (Agriculture), February 1963 (3.6.10R/16559, Ag. 3); Chikwawa District Monthly Reports (Administration), March 1962 (ADM 12/II), MNA.

14. Chikwawa District, Project Officer's Monthly Report, February 1981 (11.4.9F/40352), MNA. See also Chikwawa District Monthly Reports (Administration), February 1956 (no reference or location), MNA.

15. Port Herald District Monthly Reports (Agriculture), January 1957 (8.7.5F/7306), MNA. People would not have eaten their crops green if they had the money to buy maize or rice (Chikwawa District, Project Officer's Monthly Report, February 1981 [11.4.9F/40352], MNA). See also Port Herald District Monthly Reports (Administration), January 1958 (8.7.6F/7310), MNA.

16. Port Herald District Monthly Reports (Administration), March 1961 (10.1.9F/32154), MNA. See also ibid., March 1966; Port Herald District Monthly Reports (Agriculture), March 1958 (8.7.5F/7306); SVADP, March 1976 (11.4.9F/40352, Ag. 5/2), MNA.

17. Port Herald District Monthly Reports (Agriculture), February 1957 (8.7.5F/7306), MNA. For a drop in market dependency, see, among others, Chikwawa District Monthly Reports (Administration), February 1956 (no reference or location); Port Herald District Monthly Reports (Administration), March 1958 (8.7.6F/7310), March 1977 (DAM 30703); Lower Shire Division including CCDP, February 1972 (14.1.2F/40364); SVADP, Monthly Reports, March 1976 (11.4.9F/40352, Ag. 5/2); Chikwawa District, Project Officer's Monthly Reports, March 1981 (11.4.9F/40352); CCDP, February 1971 (14.1.2F/40364), MNA.

18. Port Herald District Monthly Reports (Administration), March 1958 (8.7.6F/7310), March 1975 (DAM 30722), MNA.

19. SVADP, Monthly Reports, March 1974 (14.1.2F/40364), MNA; see also Nsanje District Monthly Reports (Administration), March 1975 (DAM 30722); Chikwawa District Monthly Reports (Administration), March 1973 (14.1.2R/40362), MNA.

20. Lower River Annual Reports (Administration), 1948 (NSP3/1/18), MNA.

21. In 1957, the district commissioner for Chikwawa thought the food situation had worsened in the district: "The constant pre-occupation with the food situation in a district which, a few years ago, produced a handsome surplus is most worrying and the true cause most difficult to solve" (Chikwawa District Annual Reports [Administration], 1957 [no reference or location], MNA.)

22. See the introduction.

23. Cotton agriculture and cattle keeping did indeed exert a negative impact on food production in Nsanje South and Chikwawa South (see chapters 4, 5, 6). Similarly, the rise of a new food market did increase the levels of njala in some parts of the country, especially in what was known as the Ruo or Chiromo District. See my "Feeding and Fleecing the Native."

24. Lower Shire Division (including CCDP area), January 1973 (14.1.2F/40364); Nsanje District Monthly Reports (Administration), March 1977 (DAM30703), MNA.

25. Lower River Annual Reports (Administration), 1948 (NSP3/1/18); Lower Shire Division (including CCDP Area), January 1973 (14.1.2F/40364), MNA.

26. Lower River Annual Reports (Administration), 1948 (NSP3/1/18), MNA.

27. Lower River Annual Reports (Administration), 1949 (NSP3/1/18); Port Herald District Monthly Reports (Agriculture), January 1956 (8.7.5F/7306), MNA.

28. Lower River Annual Reports (Administration), 1950 (8.7.6F/7310), MNA. See also Chikwawa District Monthly Reports (Administration), November 1960 (ADM 12/1); Nsanje District Monthly Reports (Administration), November 1976 (DAM 30703), MNA.

29. Port Herald District Monthly Reports (Agriculture), November 1955, October 1957 (8.7.5F/7306), MNA.

30. Port Herald District Annual Reports (Administration), 1940 (NSP2/1/9), MNA. See also ibid., 1941, 1943 (NSP2/1/9), 1949 (NSP2/1/18), MNA.

31. Port Herald District Annual Reports (Administration), 1947 (NSP2/1/18), MNA.

32. Port Herald DC to PC (SP), 23 August 1962 (10.1.9R/32150, Foodstuffs 2/4, 1961–73), MNA.

33. CCDP, Monthly Crop Reports for the Lower Shire Division, April 1971 (14.1.2F/40365, Ag. 5/2), MNA.

34. Port Herald District Monthly Reports (Agriculture), October 1957 (8.7.5F/7306), MNA.

35. Port Herald DC to PC (SP), 23 August 1962 (10.1.9R/32150, Foodstuffs 2/4, 1961–73), MNA.

36. Port Herald District Monthly Reports (Agriculture), December 1957 (8.7.5F/7306), MNA.

37. Port Herald District Annual Reports (Administration), 1949 (NSP2/1/18), MNA.

38. Port Herald District Monthly Reports (Agriculture), March 1958 (8.7.5F/7306), MNA.

39. Chikwawa District Monthly Reports (Agriculture), February 1954 (1DCCK2/2/5), MNA. Also included in the 1954 report are the hill areas of Mlilima on the east bank of the Tchiri River.

40. Chikwawa District Monthly Reports (Agriculture), November 1954 (1DCCK2/2/5); Chikwawa District Monthly Reports (Administration), December 1958 (no reference or location), MNA.

41. Chikwawa District Monthly Reports (Agriculture), November 1954 (1DCCK2/2/5); SVADP, Monthly Reports, December 1973 (14.1.2F/40364), MNA. Between 1 October and 21 December 1973, ADMARC sold 2,598 tons of maize in this area (Chikwawa District Monthly Report [Administration], December 1973 [14.1.2R/40362], MNA), which includes three of the country's most important cotton markets of Tomali in the north, Ngabu or Makande in the center, and Dolo in the south (Chikwawa District Monthly Reports [Administration], October 1962, 1968 [ADM 12/II, ADM 12/III]; Chikwawa District Monthly Reports [Administration], June 1970 [14.1.2R/40362], MNA.)

42. Chikwawa District Monthly Reports (Agriculture), November 1954 (1DCCK2/2/5), MNA.

43. In 1965 the Ngabu Town Council sold maize at 38s. per bag (Chikwawa District Monthly Reports [Administration], January 1965 [ADM 12/III], MNA). Only 25 percent of the population of Chikwawa South had enough food to take them to the next harvesting season; the rest depended on the markets (Chikwawa District Monthly Reports [Administration], January 1967 [ADM III], MNA). See also Monthly Reports for Chikwawa South (Agriculture), December 1966 (3.6.10R/16559, Ag. 3), MNA.

44. Chikwawa District Monthly Reports (Agriculture), February, June, August, October 1954 (1DCCK2/2/5); Chikwawa South Monthly Reports (Agriculture), June 1966 (3.6.10R/16559, Ag. 3); Chikwawa District Monthly Reports (Administration), May 1960 (ADM 12/1), January 1964, July, September 1965 (ADM 12/III); Chikwawa District Monthly Reports (Agriculture), June 1969 (14.1.2R/40362), MNA.

45. Chikwawa District Monthly Reports (Administration), January 1977 (14.1.2R/40362), MNA.

46. Chikwawa District, Project Officer's Monthly Reports, January 1981 (11.4.9F/40352), MNA. The comparable figure for 1967 was 75 percent (Chikwawa District Monthly Reports [Administration], January 1967 [ADM 12/III], MNA). But, as I will show in the last section of this chapter, some of these figures were mere guesses.

47. Chikwawa District Monthly Reports (Administration), August 1975 (14.1.2R/40362), MNA. See also Chikwawa District Monthly Reports (Administration), December 1966, January 1967, August, September 1968 (ADM 12/III); May, June 1970, June, September 1973 (14.1.2R/40362); Chikwawa South Monthly Reports (Agriculture), December 1966 (3.6.10R/16559, Ag. 3); April, May, June, August, September 1968 (14.1.2F/40365, Ag. 5/2); January 1976 (11.4.9F/40352), MNA. For the area's reliance on maize sold by the district council, see Chikwawa District Monthly Reports (Administration), January 1964 (ADM 12/III); and on relief from the central government, see Chikwawa District Monthly Reports (Administration), January 1957 (no reference or location), MNA.

48. Chikwawa District Monthly Reports (Administration), December 1966 (ADM 12/III), MNA. The same bag sold for 50 shillings in Sub Native Authority (later Paramount) Lundu's area.

49. In May, the weather also proved ideal for all crops, particularly the picking of cotton. The days were warm and sunny, and only 0.31 inches of rain fell in 4 days. But early in June, the conditions began to deteriorate. Temperatures were constantly low and *chipironi* (or cold-season rain that came in June-July) delayed cotton picking and damaged cotton that had already broken. The situation began to improve toward the end of the month.

50. SVADP, *Atlas of the Lower Shire Valley.*

51. Bishop Charles F. Mackenzie, as quoted in Livingstone and Livingstone, *Narrative,* 500. Mackenzie died of fever and diarrhea on 31 January 1862 on Malo Island near the Tchiri-Ruo confluence: Bennett and Ylvisaker, *Procter,* 196–98.

52. Livingstone and Livingstone, *Narrative,* 400–402, 405.

53. Rowley, *Story,* 227. For the dream and date, see Bennett and Ylvisaker, *Procter,* 175, 178. See, for instance, *SAP* 40, 8–9 (August–September 1927): 103–4 for the claim that Christian prayers, said in competition with the region's established rain-calling ceremonies, always led to rainfall.

54. Bennett and Ylvisaker, *Procter,* 195. Procter calls Kankhomba variously "Kankomba" and "Kankamba" (ibid., 174, 195).

55. Rowley, *Story,* 226. See also Bennett and Ylvisaker, *Procter,* 195. For the impact of these latter droughts on maize yields, see Nsanje District Monthly Reports (Administration), February 1977 (DAM 30703B), MNA.

56. Rowley, *Story,* 294–97, 313–14, and 341 (August 1862), where he writes, "There had been no rain in the valley sufficient to moisten the surface of the earth for nearly eight months."

57. Ibid., 294.

58. Ibid., 295–97.

59. Ibid., 313–14.

60. Ibid., 363–64. In the early 1860s, they called the showers that come while the sun is shining *mvura a mpongo* (*mvula-ya-mphongo*) or "male rains." (Bennett and Ylvisaker, *Procter,* 401).

61. For the end of the drought with the planting rains late March 1863, see Bennett and Ylvisaker, *Procter,* 415; see also ibid., 423. There had been some showers in late February, but these were not enough (ibid., 403, 408).

62. Ibid., 208.

63. Ibid., Chikwawa District Monthly Reports (Agriculture), February, April 1980 (11.4.9F/40352, 1973–1985), MNA.

64. Chikwawa District Monthly Reports (Agriculture), February, March 1964 (3.6.10R/16559), MNA.

65. Ibid., January 1980 (11.4.9F/40352, 1973–1985), MNA.

66. Ibid., February 1964 (3.6.10R/16559), MNA.

67. Ibid.

68. Watts, *Silent Violence*, 428.

69. *SAP* 21 (August 1908): 130; and also 25 (October 1912): 162.

70. Port Herald District Annual Reports (Administration), 1944 (NSP2/1/9), MNA.

71. Lower River Annual Reports (Administration), 1949 (NSP3/1/18), MNA.

72. Ibid.

73. Chikwawa District Monthly Reports (Agriculture), February 1980 (11.4.9F/40352, 1973–1985), MNA. In fact, I had to interview many villagers in their dimba fields in 1979–80. For more evidence on this theme, see also Chikwawa District Monthly Reports (Administration), October 1960 (ADM 12/1), October 1962 (ADM 12/II), MNA. For these exchanges, see also Port Herald District Monthly Reports (Agriculture), December 1955, 1958, January 1957, 1960 (8.7.5F/7306); Nsanje District Monthly Reports (Administration), December 1970 (DAM 30722); SVADP, Monthly Reports, December 1975 (11.4.9F/40352, Ag. 5/2), MNA. And for sweet potatoes, see, among others, Port Herald District Monthly Reports (Agriculture), January 1956, 1960 (8.7.5F/7306), MNA.

74. Rowley, *Story,* 341 (emphasis added).

75. Chikwawa District Monthly Reports (Administration), March 1958 (no reference or location), MNA.

76. Lower River Annual Reports (Administration), 1949 (NSP3/1/18), MNA.

77. Ibid.

78. Ibid. (emphasis added).

79. But even when a chilala destroys some dimba crops, which it sometimes does, the result cannot be a complete wreck, as the story of Nyachikadza's people in 1973 shows. After losing their wetland rice, villagers quickly dug out the shriveled crop and replaced it with maize and sweet potatoes: Nsanje District Monthly Reports (Administration), February 1973 (DAM 30722), MNA.

80. There is another Thangadzi from the Kirk Range on the west, which flows into the Tchiri on the northern boundary of Bangula Township.

81. Field Supervisor (P. Terry), Chiromo, Report on Damage Done by Thangadzi Flood at Mlolo 1953 (1DCNE 1/2/5); Native Agricultural Instructor (Paulo Basiyao), Report on Floods, 5 February 1953 (1DCNE 1/2/5), MNA.

82. Port Herald District Monthly Reports (Administration), March 1967 (10.1.9F/32154); Area Supervisor (Nsanje North), Special Report on Ruo Flood, March 1967 (10.1.9R/32151, Soil Conservation, 1962–72, Ag. 9/2/6), MNA.

83. Beinart, "Agricultural Planning and the Late Colonial Technical Imagination: The Lower Shire Valley in Malawi, 1940–1960," in *Malawi: An Alternative Pattern of Development,* ed. K.J. McCracken (Edinburgh: Centre of African Studies, Edinburgh University, 1984): 95–148.

84. Port Herald District Monthly Reports (Agriculture), September 1957, November 1958 (8.7.5F/7306); Port Herald District Monthly Reports (Administration), September 1957 (8.7.6F/7310); Nsanje District Monthly Reports (Administration), September 1971 (DAM 30722); SVADP, Monthly Reports, November 1974 (14.1.2F/40364), MNA. In 1957, they destroyed about 630 short tons of maize in Chikwawa District (Chikwawa District Monthly Reports [Administration], October 1957 [no reference or location], MNA).

85. Peasants have left and returned to the Dinde and Dabanyi at different points after the 1939 floods, depending on the overall condition of the marshes.

86. These were not the only bad floods of the five decades between 1918 and 1971. There were others in, for example, 1946, 1966, and 1970; but there is very little documentation on these. Best known among the nine are Duladula or Mmbalu (1918), Sinapolotali (1925), Chinkhalamba or Fezaniuko (1926), Bomani (1939), Madzai-a-Padri (1952), and Msasila (1957). For names and dates, see also Malawi Congress Party, "Nsanje Calendar of Events" (unpublished, 1966).

87. Chikwawa District Monthly Reports (Administration), 16 February–15 March 1952 (19458II), MNA.

88. To delay or even prevent this, villagers filled up streams that cross the ridge with earth and reinforced the embankments with *thedzi* grass: Nyachikadza to Port Herald DC, 8 February 1952 (1DCNE 1/2/5), MNA.

89. Nyachikadza to Port Herald DC, 2 February 1953 (1DCNE 1/2/5), 18 March 1967 (10.1.9R/32151, Ag. 9/2/6); Nyachikadza to Government Agent (same as DC), 11 March 1966 (10.1.9R/32151, Soil Conservation, 1962–72, Ag. 9/2/6), MNA.

90. Nyachikadza to Port Herald DC, 2 February 1953 (1DCNE 1/2/5), MNA.

91. Nyachikadza to Government Agent, 28 January 1964 (10.1.9R/32151, Soil Conservation, 1962–72, Ag. 9/2/6); Port Herald DC, Report on Lower Shire Floods, 22 February 1952 (1DCNE 1/2/5), MNA. A member of the SAGM had put it this way: "At such times the people, instead of escaping from their villages, foolishly remain on the roofs of their huts, or erect some kind of platform in the water where they stay day and night, until the posts are loosened by the water, and the platform collapses with its occupants, loss of life often resulting" (*SAP* 38, 6 [June 1925]: 71).

92. William Halcrow and Partners (Shire Valley Project), Air Inspection of Flooded Area in the Lower Shire, 1952 (1DCNE 1/2/5), MNA. The 1952 flood was equal in intensity only to that of 1918: see Port Herald DC to PC (SP), 22 February 1952 (1DCNE 1/2/5), MNA.

93. William Halcrow and Partners (Shire Valley Project), Air Inspection of Flooded Area in the Lower Shire, 1952 (1DCNE 1/2/5), MNA.

94. *SAP* 38, 6 (June 1925): 71.

95. Port Herald DC to S.L. Bhagat, 23 February 1952 (1DCNE 1/2/5); Nyachikadza to Port Herald DC, 3 December 1969 (10.1.9F/53), MNA. On women and children as the people who leave the marshes first, see Nyachikadza to Port Herald DC, 2 April 1967 (10.1.9R/32151, Ag. 9/2/6); Nyachikadza to Port Herald DC, 8, 29 February 1952 (1DCNE 1/2/5); Chimombo to Port Herald DC, 18 January 1970 (10.1.9F/53), MNA.

96. Port Herald DC to PC (SP), 14 April 1952 (1DCNE 1/2/5); CS to PC (SP), 23 April 1952 (1DCNE 1/2/5), MNA.

97. Ibid.

98. This flood was particularly devastating in Mozambique, where a Roman Catholic priest drowned; hence the term *Madzi-a-Padri,* which literally means "the floods of the priest."

99. Port Herald District Monthly Reports (Administration), March 1958 (8.7.6F/7310), MNA.

100. Port Herald DC, Report on Lower Shire Floods, 22 February 1952 (1DCNE 1/2/5); Port Herald DC to PC (SP), 3 March 1952 (1DCNE 1/2/5); Port Herald District Monthly Reports (Administration), February 1963 (10.1.9F/32154); Ndamera to Port Herald DC, 8 February 1971 (10.1.9F/53); Nsanje DC to Regional Minister, 4 March 1971 (10.1.9F/53); Nsanje District Monthly Reports (Administration), August 1974 (DAM 30722), MNA.

101. Chikwawa District Monthly Reports (Administration), 16 February–15 March 1952 (19458II); Port Herald DC, Report on Lower Shire Floods, 22 February 1952 (1DCNE 1/2/5); Port Herald District Monthly Reports (Administration), February, March 1958 (8.7.6F/7310), MNA.

102. In peaceful times, distance played a significant role in influencing people's decision to settle in Malawi or Mozambique. Peasants on the northern end of the Dinde were closer to the Malawi's mphala drylands, while those on the southern end were closer to Mozambique's drylands: Port Herald DC, Report on Lower Shire Floods, 22 February 1952 (1DCNE 1/2/5); Port Herald District Monthly Reports (Administration), March 1958 (8.7.6F/7310); Port Herald District Monthly Reports (Administration), February 1963 (10.1.9F/32154); Nyachikadza to Port Herald DC, 2 April 1967 (10.1.9R/32151, Ag. 9/2/6); Ndamera to Port Herald DC, 8 February 1971 (10.1.9F/53), MNA.

103. Port Herald DC to PC (SP), 22 February 1952 (1DCNE 1/2/5); Port Herald District Monthly Reports (Administration), February 1963 (10.1.9F/32154), MNA. Antonio Lopez and Manuel Domingo owned much of the land Nyachikadza's people occupied.

104. Port Herald District Monthly Reports (Administration), March 1958 (8.7.6F/7310), MNA.

105. They sometimes fell easy prey to infectious diseases like smallpox: Medical Officer (?) to Medical Aide I/C Rural Dispensary, Makoko, 15 March 1952 (1DCNE 1/2/5), MNA.

106. This was why some villagers were always reluctant to return to the marshes: Port Herald District Monthly Reports (Administration), April 1958 (8.7.6F/7310), MNA.

107. Port Herald DC, Report on Lower Shire Floods, 22 February 1952 (1DCNE 1/2/5); Southern Province Monthly Reports, 16 February–15 March 1952 (19458II); Port Herald District Monthly Reports (Administration), March 1958 (8.7.6F/7310); Port Herald District Monthly Reports (Agriculture), February 1958 (8.7.5F/7306); Nsanje DC to Regional Minister (Southern Region), 4 March 1971 (10.1.9F/53), MNA. Peasants in Port Herald lost the entire maize crop in 1958: Port Herald District Monthly Reports (Administration), February 1958 (8.7.6F/7310), MNA.

108. Port Herald DC, Report on Lower Shire Floods, 22 February 1952 (1DCNE 1/2/5), MNA.

109. Port Herald DC to PC (SP), 23 August 1962 (10.1.9R/32150, Foodstuffs 2/4, 1961–73), MNA. See also chapter 6.

110. Port Herald District Annual Reports (Administration), 1941 (NSP2/1/9), MNA. See also ibid., 1940, 1942 (NSP2/1/9), 1947, 1948 (NSP2/1/18), MNA This area was sparsely populated in 1941.

111. Chikwawa District Monthly Reports (Agriculture), October 1955 (1DCCK2/2/5), MNA.

112. Chikwawa District Monthly Reports (Administration), September 1961 (ADM 12/I), MNA. See also ibid., August 1975 (14.1.2R/40362), MNA.

113. Port Herald DC to PC (SP), 23 August 1962 (10.1.9R/32150, Foodstuffs 2/4, 1961–73), MNA (emphasis added).

114. Chikwawa District Monthly Reports (Agriculture), October, November 1980 (11.4.9F/40352), MNA.

115. Chikwawa District Monthly Reports (Administration), June 1967 (ADM 12/III), MNA.

116. Chikwawa North Monthly Reports (Agriculture), July 1967 (3.6.10R/16559, Ag. 3); Chikwawa District Monthly Reports (Administration), May, July, November 1960, April, September 1961 (ADM 12/I); Chikwawa District Monthly Reports (Agriculture), September 1973, August 1975 (14.1.2R/40362), MNA.

117. Port Herald DC to G.M. Boby, 12 December 1952 (1DCNE 1/2/5); Port Herald DC to PC (SP), 12 December 1952 (1DCNE 1/2/5); Chikwawa DC to Port Herald DC, 30 December 1952 (1DCNE 1/2/5); Meteorological Office (Blantyre) to Water Development Engineer (Blantyre) (with copy to Port Herald DC), 9 January 1953 (1DCNE 1/2/5);

Port Herald DC to Hydrological Assistant, Chikwawa, 17 January 1953 (1DCNE 1/2/5); Hydrological Assistant (Chikwawa) to Port Herald DC, 27 January 1953 (1DCNE 1/2/5); DC to Boby, 30 January 1953 (1DCNE 1/2/5); Chief Nyachikadza to Port Herald DC, 2 February 1953 (1DCNE 1/2/5), MNA.

118. Chikwawa District Monthly Reports (Administration), March 1960 (ADM 12/1), MNA.

119. NADD, "Garden Survey Report."

120. CCDP, "Farm Survey, 1972/73" (Evaluation Section, December 1974).

121. Ibid. In 1989–90, 1990–91, 1991–92, 1992–93, 1993–94, and 1994–95, ADMARC sold the following metric tones of maize throughout the valley: 9,156.13, 11,109.3, 6,077.32, 17,043.18, 2,945.89, and 13,647, respectively (ADMARC, Annual Progressive Maize Purchases Comparison [OP/M/3B]), MNA. These figures do not, of course, represent the totality of the food people procured to supplement what they grew. I collected a considerable amount of data on maize sales by ADMARC with a view to measuring the food gap at different moments of the agricultural season, but I had to discard much of that data because of the huge gaps in the information.

122. Chikwawa District Monthly Reports (Agriculture), January 1976 (14.1.2R/40362), MNA. The corresponding figure for January 1984 was 90. See Chikwawa District, Project Officer's Monthly Reports, January 1984 (11.4.9F/40352), MNA.

123. Chikwawa District, Project Officer's Monthly Reports, December 1983 (11.4.9F/40352); Chikwawa District Monthly Reports (?), December 1976 (14.1.2R/40362), MNA. The same report gives 85, 70, and 85 as the dependence rates for Chikwawa in December of 1976, 1981, and 1984, respectively. According to a Chikwawa District Project Officer's Monthly Report (December 1984 [11.4.9F/40352], MNA), there were 45,200 peasant households in the area.

124. March 1962, 1976, 1977, 1984: Chikwawa District Monthly Reports (Administration), March 1976, 1977 (14.1.2R/40362); Chikwawa (excluding Port Herald) District Monthly Reports (Agriculture), March 1963 (3.6.10R/16559, Ag. 3); Chikwawa District, Project Officer's Monthly Reports, March 1984 (11.4.9F/40352), MNA. Reports for 1963 and 1984 give self-sufficiency (70 and 60) instead of dependency rates. A whopping 70 percent of the chiefdom's households were dependent on the market as early as March 1982 (Chikwawa District Project Officer's Monthly Report, March 1982 [11.4.9F/40352], MNA). Over 90 percent of the district's population depended on the market for survival in December 1983: Chikwawa District, Project Officer's Monthly Report, December 1983 (11.4.9F/40352), MNA.

125. The reports were to include those who could and those who could not buy food: Special Duties Officer (SDO), Office of the President and Cabinet (OPC) to all DCs, 26 June 1970 (17.16.2R/40370, Food Situation, 1964–70, Ag. 5); Secretary for Natural Resources and Surveys to General Manager, Farmers Marketing Board (FMB), 17 October 1962 (10.1.9R/32150, Foodstuffs 2/4, 1961–73), MNA.

126. Chikwawa District Monthly Reports (Administration), March 1960 (ADM 12/1), MNA. It is not clear whether this actually happened.

127. Port Herald District Monthly Reports (Administration), March 1961 (10.1.9F/32154), MNA.

128. For evidence that some DCs did not take their job seriously, see the exchanges between Nsanje DC and the OPC: Nsanje District Maize Situation as at 30 November 1970 (10.1.9R/32150); Chikwawa DC to SDO, OPC, 10 July 1970 (17.16.2R/40370, Food Situation, 1964–70, Ag. 5). Another factor that undermines the usefulness of even the more detailed predictions is that they often remain "hanging in the air." One can rarely

find information on the season for which the prediction is made; this problem is very common in the *Nyasaland Times.*

129. While maize "accounts for a little over 20% of domestic food production in Africa," in Malawi it occupies 80 percent of the cultivated land, and the per-capita consumption is 160 kilograms per annum. "Only in Mexico and Guatemala ... do people consume" as much maize as in Malawi: D. Byerlee and P. Heisey, "Evolution of the African Maize Economy," in *Africa's Emerging Maize Revolution,* ed. D. Byerlee and C. K. Eicher (Boulder, CO: Lynne Rienner, 1997), 16.

130. Some surveys recognized the limitations of their efforts; see NADD, "Garden Survey Report"; Lower River Monthly Reports (Agriculture), December 1962 (3.6.10R/16559, Ag. 3), MNA.

131. But because he had to send a figure, he thought that about 50 percent of his people would be short of food: Lower River Monthly Reports (Agriculture), December 1962 (3.6.10R/16559, Ag. 3), MNA.

132. Richards, *Land, Labour and Diet,* 37.

133. See chapter 4 for ways to break the annual cycle of njala in poor households.

CHAPTER 4: COPING WITH AND REPRODUCING HUNGER

1. Secretary for Natural Resources and Surveys (Dr. Hastings K. Banda) to General Manager, FMB, 17 October 1962 (10.1.9R/32150, Foodstuffs 2/4, 1961–73), MNA.

2. UN Integrated Regional Information Network, October 5, 2001, http://allafrica.com/stories/printable/200110050269.html.

3. Chikwawa District Monthly Reports (Administration), October 1955 (DCCK2/2/5), MNA.

4. DC (Port Herald) to PC (SP), Port Herald General Monthly Reports, January 1958 (8.7.6F/7310), MNA.

5. Richards, *Land, Labour and Diet,* 36.

6. Interviews with Mrs. Leni Pereira, Chitsa Village, TA Tengani, Nsanje, 5 November 1991 (EPT91/13); Anthony Bankamu Chipakuza, Chipakuza Village, TA Lundu, Chikwawa, 17 October 1991 (EPT91/2); Mrs. Kolina Tambo, Tambo Village, STA Mbenje, Nsanje, 3 1November 1991 (EPT91/9).

7. Port Herald District Annual Reports (Administration), 1940 (NSP2/1/9), MNA.

8. Port Herald District Monthly Reports (Administration), January 1958 (8.7.6F/7310), MNA.

9. The following analysis of Malawi's food laws has benefited from C.H.S. Ng'ong'ola, "Statutory Law and Agrarian Change in Malawi" (Ph.D. dissertation, London University, 1983): 296–321.

10. This was left unspecified in the legislation and had to be settled by the High Court: Ng'ong'ola, "Statutory Law," 296–321.

11. PC (SP) to DCs, 4 September 1952 (1DCNE 1/2/5), MNA.

12. Maize Export Ordinance of 1926; Maize Control Ordinance of 1946, 1949; Farmers Marketing Ordinance of 1962; and the Agricultural and Livestock Marketing Ordinance of 1963 (Ng'ong'ola, "Statutory Law," 296–321).

13. Acting PC to DCs, 10 April (and also 22 May) 1963 (10.1.9R/32150, Foodstuffs 2/4, 1961–73), MNA. But no one needed a license to buy or export cassava or maize *madeya* bran (ibid., especially 22 May memo).

14. Secretary to the President and Cabinet to DCs, etc., 19 June 1970 (10.1.9R/32150); Secretary for Natural Resources and Surveys to PCs, 23 May 1962 (10.1.9R/32150, Foodstuffs 2/4, 1961–73), MNA.

15. See, for instance, DC (Chikwawa) to FMB Divisional Supervisor (Ngabu), 14 June 1967 (17.16.2R/40370, Food Situation, 1964–70, Ag. 5); Chikwawa North District Monthly Reports (Agriculture), December 1966 (3.6.10R/16559, Ag. 3); ibid., March 1971 (14.1.2R/40362); Chikwawa District Project Officer's Monthly Reports, October 1982 (11.4.9F/40352), MNA.

16. DC (Chikwawa) to FMB Divisional Supervisor (Ngabu), 14 June 1967 (17.16.2R/40370, Food Situation, 1964–70, Ag. 5); PC (SP) to Maize Control Board, April–May 1951 (1DCNE 1/2/5); FMB Divisional Supervisor (Ngabu) to DC (Chikwawa), 21 June 1967 (17.16.2R/40370, Food Situation, 1964–70, Ag. 5), MNA. Otherwise, officials generally treated the rest of the valley as a net importer and subject only to the rules of internal trading. For exceptions, see, among others, Chikwawa District Project Officer's Monthly Reports, October 1982 (11.4.9F/40352), MNA. ADMARC purchased 95 metric tons of sorghum in Chikwawa.

17. PC (SP) to DCs 12 October 1962 (10.1.9R/32150, Foodstuffs 2/4, 1961–73), MNA.

18. See Mandala, "Feeding and Fleecing the Native."

19. Ng'ong'ola, "Statutory Law," 296–321.

20. PC (SP) to DC (Port Herald), 19 December 1951; DC (Port Herald) to PC (SP), 21 December 1951 (1DCNE 1/2/5); DC (Mulanje) to DC (Port Herald), 23 January 1952 (1DCNE 1/2/5); R. Mahomed and Sons (Malosa, Mulanje) to DC (Port Herald), 21 January 1970 (17.16.2R/40370, Food Situation, 1964–70, Ag. 5), MNA.

21. These were the Maize Export Ordinance of 1926 and Maize Control Ordinance of 1946, 1949 (Ng'ong'ola, "Statutory Law," 296–321).

22. Ibid.

23. J. Kydd and R. Christiansen, "Structural Change in Malawi since Independence: Consequences of a Development Strategy Based on Large-Scale Agriculture," *World Development* 10, 5 (1982): 355–75.

24. FMB Regional Manager (Limbe) to DC (Nsanje), 19 December 1969 (10.1.9R/32150, Foodstuffs 2/4, 1961–73); DC (Chikwawa) to FMB Divisional Supervisor (Ngabu), 14 June 1967 (17.16.2R/40370, Food Situation, 1964–70, Ag. 5). The FMB purchased maize from the peasantry, independent traders, and other sources: FMB General Manager to Secretary for Economic Affairs, 20 July 1968 (17.16.2R/40370, Food Situation, 1964–70, Ag. 5), MNA.

25. On Limbe to Bangula, see FMB Bangula to DC (Nsanje), 14 December 1968 (10.1.9R/32150, Foodstuffs 2/4, 1961–73); ADMARC Executive Chairman to DC (Nsanje), 9 February 1973 (10.1.9R/32150, Foodstuffs 2/4, 1961–73), MNA. On Bangula to Nsanje, see FMB Regional Manager to Depot Supervisor, 13 January 1970 (10.1.9R/32150), MNA. And on Limbe to Nsanje, see ADMARC Chiromo Area Supervisor to DC (Nsanje), 7 February 1973 (10.1.9R/32150, Foodstuffs 2/4, 1961–73); ADMARC Executive Chairman to DC (Nsanje), 9 February 1973 (10.1.9R/32150, Foodstuffs 2/4, 1961–73), MNA.

26. FMB General Manager to DC (Nsanje), 22 August 1970 (10.1.9R/32150), MNA. See also ADMARC Regional Manager (South) to Secretary to President and Cabinet, 15 June 1973 (10.1.9R/32150, Foodstuffs 2/4, 1961–73), MNA. Maize was also sold at all cotton markets: FMB Limbe to DC (Chikwawa), 19 August 1970 (17.16.2R/40370, Food Situation, 1964–70, Ag. 5), MNA. For sale at Native Authorities' Courts, see DC

(Blantyre) to Secretary for Economic Affairs, 6 August 1968 (17.16.2R/40370, Food Situation, 1964–70, Ag. 5), MNA.

27. ADMARC Regional Manager (South) to Secretary to President and Cabinet, 15 June 1973 (10.1.9R/32150, Foodstuffs 2/4, 1961–73), MNA.

28. Secretary for Natural Resources and Surveys to FMB General Manager, 17 October 1962 (10.1.9R/32150, Foodstuffs 2/4, 1961–73), MNA.

29. Secretary for Local Government to All Clerks of District Councils, 27 October 1962 (10.1.9R/32150, Foodstuffs 2/4, 1961–73), MNA.

30. Acting Secretary for Local Government to Clerks of Council, 19 May 1970 (10.1.9R/32150), MNA.

31. FMB General Manager to Regional Manager, 2 September 1970 (10.1.9R/32150 or 17.16.2R/40370, Ag. 5), MNA. According to the FMB Regional Manager: "The contract will be drawn up at the Regional Headquarters in Limbe and will be prepared in triplicate, one copy each being held by the trader and the Board, the third copy will be passed to the District commissioners" (FMB Regional Manager to Markets and Depots, Southern Region, 29 August 1970 [10.1.9R/32150 or 17.16.2R/40370, Ag. 5], MNA); see also FMB General Manager to DCs, 21 August 1970 (10.1.9R/32150 or 17.16.2R/40370, Ag. 5); SDO, OPC, to DCs, 20 August 1970 (17.16.2R/40370, Food Situation, 1964–70, Ag. 5), MNA.

32. FMB Limbe to Regional Manager (South and North), 14 December 1968 (10.1.9R/32150, Foodstuffs 2/4, 1961–73), MNA.

33. FMB Regional Manager to Markets and Depots, Southern Region, 29 August 1970 (10.1.9R/32150 or 17.16.2R/40370, Ag. 5); FMB Limbe to DC (Chikwawa), 19 August 1970 (17.16.2R/40370, Food Situation, 1964–70, Ag. 5), MNA.

34. FMB, Circular Letter on Maize Prices, 30 May 1970 (10.1.9R/32150); FMB General Manager to DCs, 22 August 1970 (10.1.9R/32150); FMB Regional Manager to Markets and Depots (Southern Region), 29 August 1970 (10.1.9R/32150 or 17.16.2R/40370, Ag. 5), MNA.

35. FMB General Manager to DCs, 21 August 1970 (10.1.9R/32150 or 17.16.2R/40370, Ag. 5), MNA.

36. Ibid.

37. Secretary for Natural Resources and Surveys to FMB General Manager, 17 October 1962 (10.1.9R/32150, Foodstuffs 2/4, 1961–73), MNA.

38. Secretary for Natural Resources to DC (Nsanje), 26 November 1968 (10.1.9R/32150, Foodstuffs 2/4, 1961–73); FMB Limbe to Regional Managers (South and North), 14 December 1968 (10.1.9R/32150, Foodstuffs 2/4, 1961–73); FMB Bangula to DC (Nsanje), 14 December 1968 (10.1.9R/32150, Foodstuffs 2/4, 1961–73), MNA.

39. FMB Regional Manager (Limbe) to DC (Nsanje), 19 December 1969 (10.1.9R/32150, Foodstuffs 2/4, 1961–73). See also FMB, Authority to Buy Maize, 1 May 1970 (10.1.9R/32150); FMB General Manager to DCs (Confidential), 6 April 1970 (17.16.2R/40370, Food Situation, 1964–70, Ag. 5), MNA. Traders often had to wait for weeks before they could get their discounts from FMB's regional headquarters in Limbe: FMB, Circular Letter on Maize Prices, 30 May 1970 (10.1.9R/32150), MNA.

40. FMB General Manager to DCs, 21 August 1970 (10.1.9R/32150 or 17.16.2R/40370, Ag. 5), MNA.

41. DC (Chikwawa), Circular Letter, 22 August 1970 (17.16.2R/40370, Food Situation, 1964–70, Ag. 5), MNA.

42. Secretary for Natural Resources and Surveys to DCs (as Licensing Officers under the Produce Marketing Ordinance), 10 September 1962 (10.1.9R/32150, Foodstuffs 2/4, 1961–73), MNA.

43. FMB Regional Manager to Markets and Depots, Southern Region, 29 August 1970 (10.1.9R/32150 or 17.16.2R/40370, Ag. 5), MNA. See the same circular for penalties on "excessive" buying.

44. The board would, for example, dump maize (selling at cost price) in the affected areas with a view to lowering consumer prices: PC (SP) to DCs (SP), Food Shortages, 15 September 1958 (1DCNE 1/2/5), MNA.

45. ADMARC Divisional Supervisor (Ngabu) to Regional Manager (South), 13 June 1973 (10.1.9R/32150, Foodstuffs 2/4, 1961–73), MNA.

46. FMB, Circular Letter on Maize Prices, 30 May 1970 (10.1.9R/32150), MNA.

47. One of the new cotton buyers is Cotton Ginnery Limited: Arnold Kukhala (an employee of Cotton Ginnery Limited), Jambo Village, TA Mbenje, Nsanje, 2 July 1995 (TCM95/1).

48. In 1995, some cotton growers were already complaining about the new marketing arrangements, particularly the fact that they have to purchase cottonseeds, which they did not do under ADMARC. I also suspect that the new dispensation unleashed forces that aggravated the food shortages of 2000–2002 in the country.

49. Today, Malawi has the highest traffic-accident rates in southern Africa (if not the whole continent), largely because of its bad or nonexistent roads. "The country has a total road network of 15,541 km, of which only 3,600 km is tarred" (UN Integrated Regional Information Networks, "Malawi: OPEC Gives $5m for Road Upgrade," May 13, 2004, http://www.irinnews.org/report.asp?ReportID.41032).

50. UN Integrated Regional Information Networks, "WFP's Efforts Hampered by Poor Rail Infrastructure," August 1, 2000, http://allafrica.com/stories/printable/200208010510.html. The rail line in question is a new one, built in the 1970s, from Liwonde to the Mozambican port of Nacala on the Indian Ocean. It was destroyed during Mozambique's civil war in the 1980s.

51. For the anger and frustrations that this road caused to European settlers, see my "Feeding and Fleecing the Native."

52. Chikwawa District Monthly Reports (Administration), February 1976 (14.1.2R/40362), MNA.

53. In 1965 the government built a cheap tarmac road from Chikwawa to Bangula, but the road started cracking even as Banda opened it. Recently, they repaired the Chikwawa-Nchalo but not the Nchalo-Bangula section, which is in a worse shape today than it was before they tarred it in 1965.

54. Chikwawa District Monthly Reports (Administration), October 1968 (ADM 12/III); Lower Shire Division (including CCDP area), Monthly Reports, October 1972 (14.1.2F/40364), MNA.

55. For rains that paralyze the food-distribution system, see CCDP, Monthly Reports, December 1970 (14.1.2F/40364); Lower Shire Division (including CCDP area) Monthly Reports, January 1973 (14.1.2F/40364), MNA.

56. Chikwawa District Monthly Reports (Administration), December 1966 (ADM 12/III); Chikwawa North District Monthly Reports (Agriculture), December 1966 (3.6.10R/16559, Ag. 3), MNA.

57. Nsanje District Monthly Reports (Administration), November 1962 (10.1.9F/32154), MNA.

58. To solve this problem, some administrators proposed to establish ADMARC agents in these inaccessible areas and to stock large quantities of maize during the dry season for sale during the rainy season. But Malawi Congress Party (MCP) officials turned down the proposal, fearing that agents might overcharge poor villagers: Nsanje District Monthly Reports (Administration), December 1974 (and see also October 1973, November 1974) (DAM 30722); Port Herald District Monthly Reports (Agriculture), October 1957 (8.7.5F/7306), MNA.

59. Port Herald District Monthly Reports (Administration), April 1956, March 1958 (8.7.6F/7310), MNA. For the hope of improvements in the marshes, see Nsanje District Monthly Reports (Administration), August 1974 (DAM 30722); DC (Nsanje) to Regional Minister (Southern Region), 4 March 1971 (10.1.9F/32154), MNA.

60. Nsanje District Monthly Reports (Administration), December 1974 (and see also October 1973) (DAM 30722), MNA.

61. Nsanje District Monthly Reports (Administration), February 1963 (10.1.9F/32154), MNA. In another serious food shortage seven years later, relief agencies had difficulty reaching Nyachikadza's people because the district administration did not have its own motorized boats. A relief team had to rely on the boat of the Fisheries Department, which was not always available when needed. In the end they had to turn to the barges of a Portuguese farmer from Mozambique (Chairman, Flood Relief Committee, 12 May 1970, [10.1.9F/32154], MNA). And nothing came out of the Ministry of Works and Supplies' proposal to make the district commissioner's boat serviceable and to purchase a flat-bottomed boat for use in shallow waters (Minutes on Flood Relief Held on 6 January 1970 [10.1.9F/32154], MNA).

62. No one knew the extent of hunger in the country in 2001–2 because the government did not have money to commission a study of the problem (see the conclusion to this chapter).

63. ADMARC (Limbe) to DCs (Southern Region), 6 March 1970 (17.16.2R/40370, Food Situation, 1964–70, Ag. 5), MNA.

64. Secretary for Natural Resources and Surveys to DCs, 2 July 1962; Mr. Malamba (a Member of Parliament for Nsanje) to DC (Nsanje), 7 December 1970 (10.1.9R/32150, Foodstuffs 2/4, 1961–73), MNA.

65. ADMARC (Chikwawa) to A.R. Thomson (Livunzu), 20 February 1970 (17.16.2R/40370, Food Situation, 1964–70, Ag. 5); ADMARC General Manager to DCs, 21 August 1970 (10.1.9R/32150 or 17.16.2R/40370, Ag. 5), MNA.

66. Traders could only sell maize in the following quantities (pounds): 200, 100, 50, 20, 10 or their multiples. Odd amounts were not allowed: FMB General Manager to DC, 22 August 1970 (10.1.9R/32150 or 17.16.2R/40370, Ag. 5); FMB, Authority to Buy Maize, 1 May 1970 (10.1.9R/32150); FMB Regional Manager (South) to FMB Divisional Supervisors, 26 October 1970 (10.1.9R/32150), MNA.

67. B. Pachai, *Malawi: The History of the Nation* (London: Longman, 1973), 185–86.

68. PC (SP) to DCs (SP), Food Shortages, 15 September 1958 (1DCNE 1/2/5), MNA.

69. Ten tons would come from the Maize Control Board: DC (Port Herald) to Maize Control Board, 15 February 1952 (1DCNE 1/2/5), MNA; 60 tons of maize and 15 tons of rice would be obtained in the Mlolo and Ngabu chiefdoms of Port Herald and Chikwawa Districts, respectively: DC (Port Herald) to PC (SP), 3 March 1952 (1DCNE 1/2/5), MNA.

70. DC (Port Herald) to PC (SP), 3 March 1952 (1DCNE 1/2/5), MNA.

71. CS to PC (SP), 16 April 1952 (1DCNE 1/2/5), MNA.

72. CS to PCs, DCs, etc., Famine Relief Funds, 25 November 1954 (1DCNE 1/2/5), MNA.

73. PC (SP) to DCs (SP), Food Shortages, 15 September 1958 (1DCNE 1/2/5), MNA.

74. Ibid.

75. Secretary for Natural Resources and Surveys to FMB General Manager, 17 October 1962 (10.1.9R/32150, Foodstuffs 2/4, 1961–73), MNA.

76. Secretary for Local Government to Clerks of District Councils, 27 October 1962 (10.1.9R/32150, Foodstuffs 2/4, 1961–73); Secretary for Natural Resources and Surveys to FMB General Manager, 17 October 1962 (10.1.9R/32150, Foodstuffs 2/4, 1961–73), MNA.

77. Chikwawa District Monthly Reports (Administration), January 1964 (ADM 12/III), MNA.

78. Mandala, "Feeding and Fleecing the Native."

79. Agricultural Assistant (Port Herald) to Soil Conservation Officer (Blantyre), 20 August, 5 September 1949 (2.29.10R/2565); PC (SP) to DA, 24 September 1941; Provincial Agricultural Officer to PC (SP), Food Situation: Lower River, 11 May 1941 (5.16.3R/2565); Port Herald District Annual Reports (Administration), 1944 (NSP2/1/9), MNA.

80. Secretary to the President and Cabinet to DCs, etc., 19 June 1970 (10.1.9R/32150), MNA.

81. SDO, OPC, to DCs, September 1970 (10.1.9R/32150), MNA.

82. Nsanje District Monthly Reports (Administration), January 1971 (DAM 30722), MNA.

83. Nsanje District Council to Secretary for Local Government, 6 January, 12 February 1971 (10.1.9R/32152). See also Chief Tengani to DC (Nsanje), 12 January 1971 (10.1.9R/32152); Malemia to DC (Nsanje), 13 January 1971 (10.1.9R/32152), MNA.

84. This represented a balance from the original £2,000 for the road construction project: Ministry of Local Government to Clerks of Council and DCs, 20 January 1971 (10.1.9R/32152); Secretary to the President and Cabinet to DC (Nsanje), 23 January 1971 (10.1.9R/32152); Chakuamba to District Council (Nsanje), 27 January 1971 (10.1.9R/32152), MNA.

85. Nsanje District Council to Secretary for Local Government, 12 February 1971 (10.1.9R/32152), MNA. The documents do not indicate the pay for one week of work.

86. DC (Nsanje) to Regional Minister (Southern Region), 15 February 1971 (10.1.9R/32150), MNA. And the following day the clerk of council told the district's chiefs he was unsure if he would have enough money to pay those employed after 20 February: Clerk of Council to Native Authorities, 16 February 1971 (10.1.9R/32152), MNA.

87. Nsanje District Monthly Reports (Administration), February 1971 (DAM 30722), MNA. They would have used the baskets to carry the food they would have bought after earning their wages.

88. Nsanje District Council to Secretary for Local Government, 17 May 1970, 3 June, 9 July 1971 (10.1.9R/32152); Clerk of Council to DC (Nsanje), 4 June 1971 (10.1.9R/32152); Secretary for Local Government to Clerk of Council, 22 May, 8 June 1971 (10.1.9R/32152), MNA.

89. Minutes of a Meeting on Flood Relief Held on 6 January 1970 (10.1.9F/53); Nsanje District Monthly Reports (Administration), January 1970 (10.1.9F/32154), MNA.

90. Ibid., Chairman (Tom S. Colvin), Flood Relief Committee, 12 May 1970 (10.1.9F/53), MNA.

91. Ibid.

92. Ibid.; Telegram from Flood Control to Regional Minister, etc., 23 January 1970 (10.1.9F/53), MNA.

93. Chairman (Tom S. Colvin), Flood Relief Committee, 12 May 1970 (10.1.9F/53), MNA.

94. Ibid. The Church World Service had received this food from the U.S. government under Public Law 480.

95. Ibid.

96. DC to Chairman of the Red Cross Society, Southern Division (Blantyre), 30 May 1967 (10.1.9R/32151, Ag. 9/2/6), MNA.

97. Minutes of the Final Meeting of the Red Cross, 13 April, 1970 (10.1.9F/53); Chairman (Tom S. Colvin), Flood Relief Committee, 12 May 1970 (10.1.9F/53), MNA.

98. Throughout this highly politicized operation, the police maintained public order with the help of the district commissioner's messengers, chiefs, and the local cadre of the omnipotent MCP.

99. Chikwawa District Annual Reports (Administration), 1922–23 (NSC2/1/1), MNA. See also Nsanje District Monthly Reports (Administration), February 1971 (DAM 30722), MNA; and listen to this incredible assessment: "The timing of the distribution of this maize has proved most opportune, enabling many people to find food for the last two or three weeks before the machewere became available in the gardens" (Nsanje District Monthly Reports [Administration], February 1958 [8.7.6F/7310], MNA).

100. See, for example, Lower River District Annual Reports (Administration), 1949 (NSP3/1/18), MNA. The colonial regime then sold maize at three pence per pound, which many local officials considered too high. As District Commissioner P. M. Lewis noted in anger: "The Africans of this district were put on the same footing as the wage-earner in the Towns."

101. The Agricultural Produce and Marketing Board sold a 200-pound bag of maize at £1 15s., and the District Council at 2 1/2d. per pound, or approximately £2 1s. 7d. per bag of 200 pounds: DC (Port Herald) to PC (SP), Port Herald General Monthly Report (Administration), January 1958 (8.7.6F/7310); Port Herald District Monthly Reports (Agriculture), January 1958 (8.7.5F/7306), MNA. See also Chikwawa District Monthly Reports (Administration), January 1958 (no reference or location), MNA.

102. Chikwawa North Monthly District Reports (Agriculture), January 1965 (3.6.10R/16559, Ag. 3), MNA.

103. Vaughan, *Story of an African Famine*, chapter 5.

104. DC (Nsanje) to SDO, OPC, 10 July 1970 (17.16.2R/40370, Food Situation, 1964–70, Ag. 5); Nsanje District Maize Situation as at 30 November 1970 (10.1.9R/32150), MNA.

105. Chief Ndamera to DC (Nsanje), 8 February 1971; Chief Chimombo to DC (Nsanje), 21 February 1971; DC (Nsanje) to Regional Minister (South), 4 March 1971; to Secretary to President and Cabinet, 9 July 1971; Secretary to President and Cabinet to Accountant General, 17 September 1971 (10.1.9F/32154), MNA.

106. Port Herald District Monthly Reports (Administration), January, February 1958 (8.7.6F/7310), MNA.

107. Chief Ndamera to DC (Nsanje), 8 February 1971; Chief Chimombo to DC (Nsanje), 21 February 1971; DC (Nsanje) to Regional Minister (South), 4 March 1971; Secretary to President and Cabinet, 9 July 1971; Secretary to President and Cabinet to Accountant General, 17 September 1971 (10.1.9F/32154), MNA.

108. Mandala, "Feeding and Fleecing the Native."

109. Chikwawa District Monthly Reports (Administration), January 1958 (no reference or location), MNA.

110. Port Herald District Monthly Reports (Agriculture), February 1958 (8.7.5F/7306) (emphasis added); Chikwawa District Monthly Reports (Administration), January 1958 (no reference or location), MNA.

111. Lower River Annual Reports (Administration), 1949 (NSP3/1/18), MNA (emphasis added).

112. Speaking of villagers in Nyasaland's Central Province in the late 1930s, one British daydreamer put it this way: "Villagers are short now as they short-sightedly ate their seed stocks [beans] due to *njala*. It is always trusted that the Government will provide; they make little effort to help themselves" (Berry and Petty, *The Nyasaland Survey Papers*, 251).

113. Watts, *Silent Violence*, 371.

114. UN Integrated Regional Information Network, October 5, 2001, http://allafrica.com/stories/printable/200110050269.html.

115. Lower River Annual Reports (Administration), 1949 (NSP3/1/18), MNA.

116. Ibid.

117. *SAP* 25 (October 1912): 162.

118. Lower River Annual Reports (Administration), 1949 (NSP3/1/18), MNA.

119. See Mandala, "Feeding and Fleecing the Native."

120. On *mvumo* (*Borassus aethiopum*), which they used to make *uchema* wine, see interviews with Dafleni Chimatiro, Mafale Village, TA Lundu, Chikwawa, October–November 1991 (EPT91/14); Mfumu Zimola, Zimola Village, Chikwawa, October–November 1991 (EPT91/15). For salt distilling in the 1860s, see, among others, Bennett and Ylvisaker, *Procter,* 299.

121. Mrs. Kolina Tambo, Tambo Village, STA Mbenje, Nsanje, 3 November 1991 (EPT91/9).

122. Interviews with Nsayi Mbalanyama Thabwa, Beleu Village, TA Lundu, Chikwawa, 13 October 1991 (EPT91/1); Chasasa Nyang'ombe Fole, Odriki Village, TA Chapananga, Chikwawa, October 1991 (EPT91/6); Nadumbo Kanthema, Mangulenje, Chikwawa, October 1991 (EPT91/7); Village Headman Tambo, Tambo Village, STA Mbenje, Nsanje, 3 November 1991 (EPT91/8); Unidentified Nsanje Tradition, Bangula (?), Nsanje, October–November 1991 (EPT91/16); Lower River District Annual Reports (Administration), 1949 (NSP3/1/18); Port Herald District Monthly Reports (Agriculture), September 1957, October 1958 (8.7.5F/7306), MNA.

123. Lower River Annual Reports (Administration), 1949 (NSP3/1/18), MNA.

124. Village Headman Tambo, Tambo Village, STA Mbenje, Nsanje, 3 November 1991 (EPT91/8); Mrs. Kolina Tambo, Tambo Village, STA Mbenje, Nsanje, 3 November 1991 (EPT91/9); Mrs. Leni Pereira, Chitsa Village, TA Tengani, Nsanje, 5 November 1991 (EPT91/13). But, according to Mrs. Pereira (ETP91/13) and the unnamed lady I have called the "Unidentified Nsanje Tradition" (ETP91/16) some of these foods caused serious digestive problems, especially for children.

125. Chikwawa District Monthly Reports (Administration), December 1954 (1DCCK2/2/5); Nsanje District Monthly Reports (Administration), December 1970 (DAM 30722); SVADP, Monthly Reports, December 1975 (11.4.9F/40352, Ag. 5/2), MNA. But in drought years, nyika was available throughout the hungry season.

126. On ntheme (*Strychnos spinosa* Lam.), see interview with Dafleni Chimatiro, Mafale Village, TA Lundu, Chikwawa, October–November 1991 (EPT91/14). Other sources characterize ntheme as a "large green spherical fruit with an extremely hard shell": J. Williamson, *Useful Plants of Malawi* (Zomba, Malawi: Government Press, 1972 [1956]): 114. On masau (*Ziziphus mauritiana*), see interview with Nadumbo Kanthema, Mangulenje, Chikwawa, October 1991 (EPT91/7); and on matondo, see Village Headman Tambo, Tambo Village, STA Mbenje, Nsanje, 3 November 1991 (EPT91/8); Dafleni Chimatiro, Mafale Village, TA Lundu, Chikwawa, October–November 1991 (EPT91/14); Mfumu Zimola, Zimola Village (?), Chikwawa, October–November 1991 (EPT91/15). According to one oral source (Frederick Lebala and Albert Mvula, Mpangeni Village, TA Kasisi, 18 April 1995 [SM95/3]), people owned matondo trees (*Codyla africana*), and in times of hunger, villagers had to work for the owner to get them. On bwemba (*Tamarindus indica*), see interview with Helemesi Pepala, Mwalija Village, TA Kasisi, Chikwawa, 18 April 1995 (SM95/4); Port Herald District Monthly Reports (Agriculture), September 1956 (8.7.5F/7306), MNA.

127. Port Herald District Monthly Reports (Agriculture), January 1958 (8.7.5F/7306), MNA.

128. On gugu, see Nadumbo Kanthema, Mangulenje, Chikwawa, October 1991 (EPT91/7); Mfumu Zimola, Zimola Village, Chikwawa, October–November 1991 (EPT91/15); Unidentified Nsanje Tradition, Bangula (?), Nsanje, October–November 1991 (EPT91/16); Frederick Lebala and Albert Mvula, Mpangeni Village, TA Kasisi, 18 April 1995 (SM95/3); Helemesi Pepala, Mwalija Village, TA Kasisi, Chikwawa, 18 April 1995 (SM95/4); N. D. Clegg to DA, 2 February 1923 (A3/2/111), MNA. Clegg gives other fruits (or different names of the same fruits) such as "Lole," "Kiepe," "nsanje," and "kauka." "Kiepe" is probably the same plant as what Africans call *kapepe*; see Nadumbo Kanthema, Mangulenje Chikwawa, October 1991 (EPT91/7); Mrs. Patrishu, Mbande Village, TA Lundu, Chikwawa, 5 November 1991 (EPT91/12); Mrs. Leni Pereira, Chitsa Village, TA Tengani, Nsanje, 5 November 1991 (EPT91/13). It could also have been the "kayepe" referred to in interview with Frederick Lebala and Albert Mvula, Mpangeni Village, TA Kasisi, 18 April 1995 (SM95/3). For the more popular khundi, see interviews with Kamondo Suliali, location unknown, 19 October 1991 (EPT91/3); Chasasa Nyang'ombe Fole, Odriki Village, TA Chapananga, Chikwawa, October 1991 (EPT91/6); Mrs. Leni Pereira, Chitsa Village, TA Tengani, Nsanje, 5 November 1991 (EPT91/13). And for mphunga, see Mfumu Zimola, Zimola Village, Chikwawa, October–November 1991 (ETP91/15), who also gives the time these became available for consumption. *Nsanje* was another popular wild plant people used to eat: Helemesi Pepala, Mwalija Village, TA Kasisi, Chikwawa, 18 April 1995 (SM95/4). Mr. N. D. Clegg was so impressed with the variety of grasses people ate as food that he collected samples and sent them to the director of agriculture (N. D. Clegg to DA, 7 February 1923 [A3/2/111], MNA.)

129. Port Herald District Monthly Reports (Agriculture), January, February 1958 (8.7.5F/7306), MNA. According to the January report, one official saw a group of "about twenty people, mainly children" collecting "grass seeds" near Bangula.

130. N. D. Clegg to DA, 2 and 7 February 1923 (A3/2/111); Lower River Annual Reports (Administration), 1949 (NSP3/1/18), MNA.

131. On minyanya, see Chasasa Nyang'ombe Fole, Odriki Village, TA Chapananga, Chikwawa, October 1991 (EPT91/6); Nadumbo Kanthema, Mangulenje, Chikwawa, October 1991 (EPT91/7); Mrs. Leni Pereira, Chitsa Village, TA Tengani, Nsanje, 5 November 1991 (EPT91/13); Dafleni Chimatiro, Mafale Village, TA Lundu, Chikwawa, October–November 1991 (EPT91/14); Mfumu Zimola, Zimola Village, Chikwawa, October–November 1991 (EPT91/15). On mpama (*Dioscorea* spp.), see Kamondo Suliali, location unknown, 19 October 1991 (EPT91/3). On nyenza, see Chasasa Nyang'ombe Fole, Odriki Village, TA Chapananga, Chikwawa, October 1991 (EPT91/6); Mfumu Zimola, Zimola Village (?), Chikwawa, October–November 1991 (EPT91/15); Unidentified Nsanje Tradition, Bangula (?), Nsanje, October–November 1991 (EPT91/16). Peasants also speak of *nyenje* (Village Headman Tambo, Tambo Village, STA Mbenje, Nsanje, 3 November 1991 [EPT91/8]). *Nyenje* is probably the same plant as what other villagers call *nyenza* or *nyenzi*, which they used to turn into sweet beer: Chasasa Nyang'ombe Fole, Odriki Village, TA Chapananga, Chikwawa, October 1991 (EPT91/6); Mfumu Zimola, Zimola Village (?), Chikwawa, October–November 1991 (EPT91/15); Unidentified Nsanje Tradition, Bangula (?), Nsanje, October–November 1991 (EPT91/16). They also made sweet beer with minyanya: Chasasa Nyang'ombe Fole, Odriki Village, TA Chapananga, Chikwawa, October 1991 (EPT91/6); Nadumbo Kanthema, Mangulenje, Chikwawa, October 1991 (EPT91/7); Mrs. Leni Pereira, Chitsa Village, TA Tengani, Nsanje, 5 November 1991 (EPT91/13); Dafleni Chimatiro, Mafale Village, TA Lundu, Chikwawa, October/November 1991 (EPT91/14). Minyanya, which people say is similar to sweet potatoes, seems to have been

quite different from nyenzi: see especially Chasasa Nyang'ombe Fole, Odriki Village, TA Chapananga, Chikwawa, October 1991 (EPT91/6); Mfumu Zimola, Zimola Village, Chikwawa, October–November 1991 (EPT91/15). For makhuli-a-nthochi, see interviews with Nadumbo Kanthema, Mangulenje, Chikwawa, October 1991 (EPT91/7); Mfumu Zimola, Zimola Village, Chikwawa, October–November 1991 (EPT91/15). For zibowa-za-nthochi, see interview with Helemesi Pepala, Mwalija Village, TA Kasisi, Chikwawa, 18 April 1995 (SM95/4); and also *SAP* 26 (January 1913): 11; *SAP* 36 (April 1923).

132. *SAP* 25 (March 1912): 37.

133. Port Herald District Monthly Reports (Agriculture), December 1954 (8.7.5F/7306), MNA.

134. Chasasa Nyang'ombe Fole, Odriki Village, TA Chapananga, Chikwawa, October 1991 (EPT91/6). For similarities with mowa beer brewing, see chapter 2.

135. *SAP* 21 (August 1908): 130.

136. Port Herald District Monthly Reports (Agriculture), May 1935 (A3/2/201), MNA. Most of these people had lost their munda crops to a locust invasion earlier in the season.

137. Interview with Frederick Lebala and Albert Mvula, Mpangeni Village, TA Kasisi, 18 April 1995 (SM95/3); Chikwawa District Monthly Reports (Administration), October 1960 (ADM 12/I); October 1962 (ADM 12/II), MNA.

138. See *SAP* 31 (August–September 1918): 71; 32 (March 1919): 20.

139. Lower Shire District Monthly Reports (Administration), April–May 1921 (S1/299/21), MNA.

140. Port Herald District Monthly Reports (Agriculture), January 1958 (8.7.5F/7306), MNA. According to this report peasants were slaughtering an average of eight goats per day to sell at Mbenje market in Makoko's area.

141. Chikwawa Cotton Development Project, "Farm Survey, 1971/72: A Report on a Sample Survey Conducted in the 1971/72 Crop Growing Season on Cotton Growing Farming [sic] Households in the CCDP Area."

142. Interview with: Magireni Theka, Chikunkhu Village, TA Tengani, Nsanje, 6 June 1995 (SM95/16).

143. CCDP, "Farm Survey, 1971/72: A Report on a Sample Survey Conducted in the 1971/7In 1974/75, for example, 9 percent of non-spraying households, 31 percent of sprayer-borrowing households, and 60 percent of sprayer-owing households, employed other villagers after March, see Shire Valley Agricultural Development Project (Evaluation Section), "Cotton Survey 1974/75: A Report of a Sample Survey Conducted in the 1974/75 Crop Growing Season in Households in the SVADP," 44.

144. The plan did not succeed, however: See my Work and Control in a Peasant Economy: A History of the Lower Tchiri Valley in Malawi, 1859-1960 (Madison: University of Wisconsin Press, 1990), Chapter 3.

145. Chikwawa District Monthly Reports (Administration), January 1958 (no reference or location); January 1962 (ADM 12/II), MNA.

146. This magic takes the form of "little people" (*anapache*), certain types of snakes, and so on, which transport the food at night. See also Bennett and Ylvisaker, *Procter,* 322.

147. Interviews with Windo Kampira, Antonio Mwanaleza, Antonio Nyakanyanza, Chanazi Nyakanyanza, Tambo Village, STA Mbenje, Nsanje, July 4, 1995 (TCM95/2); Peter K. Mandala, telephone conversation, 27 December 2003 (TCM03/1). In June 1859, Khwama immigrants near today's Nsanje Township had to sell their surplus rice to members of the Livingstone expedition at night for fear of being harassed and ostracized by the Mang'anja "owners" of the land: Wallis, *Livingstone,* 1:105; Foskett, *Kirk,* 1:209–10. See also Bennett and Ylvisaker, *Procter,* 322.

148. Richards, *Land, Labour and Diet,* 37.

149. Lower Shire District Annual Reports (Administration), 1922–23 (NSP2/1/1), MNA.

150. For the deplorable condition of children during the famine of 1862–63, see chapter 2.

151. Port Herald District Annual Reports (Administration), 1930 (NSP 2/1/3), MNA.

152. DC (Port Herald) to PC (SP), Port Herald General Monthly Reports, January 1958 (8.7.6F/7310), MNA.

153. Chikwawa District Monthly Reports (Administration), October 1955 (DCCK2/2/5), MNA.

154. Malawi government officials alleged that the IMF forced them to sell the maize so they could pay their debts, but the IMF denied the charge.

155. Penelope Paliani, "No Money to Assess Hunger," *Daily Times* (Blantyre), March 7, 2002, http://allafrica.com/stories/printable/200203070302.html.

156. Richards, *Land, Labour and Diet,* 36.

157. Chikwawa District Monthly Reports (Administration), September 1954, 1955 (1DCCK2/2/5), MNA.

158. Chikwawa District Monthly Reports (Administration), January 1958 (no reference or location), MNA. See also Chikwawa North District Monthly Reports (Agriculture), December 1964 (3.6.10R/16559, Ag. 3), MNA.

PART III: THE QUIET DAYS BEHIND THE NOISY TRANSITIONS

CHAPTER 5: IN THE LONG SHADOWS OF COTTON, 1860–2002

1. J. Carter, *An Hour before Daylight: Memories of a Rural Boyhood* (New York: Simon and Schuster, 2001): 178. Thanks to Dr. Karen Fields for directing my attention to this important and fascinating account of rural life in the Old South.

2. Mr. Balandao of TA Ngabu (Chikwawa) at "The Agricultural Meeting Called and Conveyed [*sic*] by Malawi Congress Party Leaders in Lower Shire on 29th December, 1967," Cotton File (17.16.2R/40370, Ag. 5), MNA (emphasis added).

3. Minister of Agriculture (Gwanda Chakuamba) to All Field Staff of the Ministry of Agriculture, August 1969 (17.16.2R/40370), MNA.

4. "Farmers Revive Cotton Growing," *Nation,* January 10, 2002, http://www.nationmalawi.com/print.asp?articleID=3054.

5. One such campaign was launched in 1983–84: NADD, "A Report on Cotton Production Promotion Campaign Jointly Organized by NADD and David Whitehead and Sons Limited in 1983/84 Season" (November 1987), SVADP. They launched both the 1983–84 and 2002 drives because David Whitehead and Sons Limited—the country's only textile factory—did not get enough cotton for processing.

6. I use the term *food sector* very narrowly to refer to the process of growing food for oneself and in one's own garden (see chapter 6). Consequently, what I call the *nonfood sector* is a very broad category and includes the growing of food in other people's gardens, which I classify as an element of wage labor. I also treat the cattle industry as a branch of the nonagricultural sector, though some analysts categorize it as agriculture.

7. E. Mandala, *Black Englishmen: The Magololo Chiefs of Malawi and the Europeans, 1855–1913* (forthcoming): chapter 5.

8. Cotton was different from the ivory trade, which was the monopoly of the Magololo rulers. It involved more people also in absolute terms: there were more people in the valley during the cotton era than before.

9. NADD, "Garden Survey Report," 25, table 2.13. The NADD succeeded the SVADP: see pp. 141.

10. SVADP, "Farm Survey 1973/74 [Part I]: Sample Villages" (Evaluation Section, July 1976): 13–17, SVADP; D.R. Colman and G.K. Garbett, "The Labour Economy of a Peasant Community in Malawi" (Second Report of the Socio-Economic Survey of the Lower Shire Valley, unpublished MS, March 1976).

11. NADD, "Garden Survey," chapter 2, p. 23.

12. Kydd and Christiansen, "Structural Change in Malawi," 373, n. 13. See also J.G. Kydd and N.J. Spooner, *The World Bank's Analysis of Malawian Agriculture: Changing Perspectives, 1966 to 1985* (Washington, D.C.: World Bank, 1987); Ng'ong'ola, "Statutory Law."

13. Malawi was taking advantage of the international sanctions against Rhodesia.

14. LONRHO, the original owner, sold the plantation and refinery to the ILLOVO Group of South Africa in the 1990s.

15. The Project classified its employees according to whether they were "time-scale" or "non-time-scale" workers, and the figures I give here are for the latter or nonsalaried workers: NADD, "Garden Survey," chapter 2, p. 21, table 2.11. It is important to keep in mind, however, that not all the workers employed by the Project or SUCOMA came from the valley.

16. This calculation is based on NADD, "Garden Survey," table 2.13.

17. Initially, most laborers found work in Nsanje District, but after the Bomani floods of 1939, the district emerged as a net exporter, with some of its people going to Chikwawa. In the 1973–74 season, Nsanje exported more than twice as much (21.5%) of its de jure male population in the 15–49 age group as Chikwawa did (9.3%): SVADP, "Farm Survey 1973/74 [Part I]," 14. This survey refers to Nsanje District, which became part of the Project only in 1973 (see pp. 141), as the Phase II (or Incorporated) area.

18. For the figure 550, see Nyasaland Protectorate, *Annual Report of the Department of Agriculture 1939* (Zomba, Malawi: Government Press): 12–15 (hereafter cited as *ARDA*). According to this report, there were 367 head owned by Africans and 847 owned by non-Africans in Port Herald District, and 183 head owned by Africans and 617 owned by non-Africans in Chikwawa District. For the 1980s, see NADD, "Initial Stages in the Adaptation of the Train and Visit Extension Approach System" (March 1984): table 7, SVADP. The exact figure for 1982 is 82,337. The government was encouraging owners to kill or sell their herds to stabilize the total herd at 60,000–65,000, which was supposed to be the region's carrying capacity. For other computations, see F. Kavinya, "An Appraisal of Crop Production Constraints in the Shire Valley Agricultural Development Project" (M.A. thesis, University College of Wales, Aberystwth, 1979): 21.

19. Kavinya, "Appraisal," 21.

20. Ibid.

21. CCDP, "Cattle Census and Sample Survey, 1971–72" (conducted by B.R. Mankhokwe and K.R.A. Oblitas of the Evaluation Section, September 1973): 59, SVADP.

22. They were given the initial herd in 1863 by Dr. David Livingstone: Bennett and Ylvisaker, *Procter*, 419; Wallis, *Livingstone*, 2:241.

23. It took officials of the CCDP in Chikwawa a long time to realize the importance of dimba agriculture.

24. Left with no legal options, the poor have retaliated by killing, stealing, and selling the animals across the border in Mozambique. The thefts became so serious in the late 1990s that they are thought to have reduced the region's cattle herd and forced owners

to form vigilante groups (Fabian Anthuacino, telephone conversation, November 2001 [TCM01/1]).

25. Yohane Mzanji, Mtchenyera Village, Sub Traditional Authority Mbenje, Nsanje, 1 April 1980 (TVES3/1); ibid., 3 April 1980 (TVES3/9).

26. Christino Chibanzi, Nsayi Kanting'u, Joakina Sekeni, Nyathando Village, TA Ndamera, Nsanje, 8 September 1980 (TVES5/3). See also Yohane Mzanji, Mtchenyera Village, Sub Traditional Authority Mbenje, Nsanje, 3 April 1980 (TVES3/9); Kapusi Chimombo, Chimombo Village, TA Chimombo, Nsanje, 11 September 1980 (TVES5/8).

27. Also known as the "cluster bean" or *Cyanopsis* spp. A nitrogen fixer, it can grow up to four feet high, producing hairy pods three to four inches long. "In India, the tender pods are eaten as a curry vegetable" and are an important cash crop because "the beans contain a valuable water-soluble gum which has wide applications in modern industry" (SVADP, *Monthly Advice* [November 1974]: 525, SVADP).

28. NADD, "Garden Survey," 60. See also ibid., 11.

29. SVADP, *Monthly Advice* (November 1974): 525.

30. Fabian Anthuacino, telephone conversation, November 2001 (TCM01/1). Another problem confronting producers today is the lack of an organized market for the crop. Like groundnuts in the 1930s, the beans are purchased mostly by Indian traders and their representatives.

31. Because my *Work and Control* covers the earlier period, this chapter concentrates on developments after World War II.

32. Minister of Agriculture (Gwanda Chakuamba) to All Field Staff of the Ministry of Agriculture, August 1969 (17.16.2R/40370), MNA. Chakuamba wanted to create 3,000 *chikumbe* farmers in the country before the end of 1969: 500, 1,500, and 1,000 in the Northern, Central, and Southern Regions, respectively. The Ministry's field staff were to identify the persons and submit their names to District Development Committees, who would select and send their final lists for approval by the minister. Only those who followed "basic rules" of "modern agriculture" could get selected (ibid.). Excluded from the list were people on the CCDP's list of delinquent borrowers: CCDP (Senior Credit Officer) to Regional Agricultural Officer, etc., 14 March 1970 (17.16.2R/40370), MNA. The nonsense went on until Banda had to intervene, ordering that the targets should "be dropped at once." See Secretary for Agriculture and Natural Resources, April 1970 Extension Circular No. 1/70 (17.16.2R/40370), MNA.

33. Livingstone and Livingstone, *Narrative*, 112; Wallis, *Stewart*, 83, 87–89, 100–103, 210–11, 222–23, 226–27.

34. Rowley, *Story*, 344.

35. Details about this can be found in my *Work and Control,* chapter 6.

36. This phrase, which means "light in darkness," graced the country's coat of arms during the colonial era.

37. The following discussion on the MFS in the country relies on O.J.M. Kalinga, "The Master Farmers' Scheme in Nyasaland, 1950–1962: A Study of a Failed Attempt to Create a 'Yeoman' Class," *African Affairs* 92 (1993): 367–87. To cultivate a smaller amount of land (in no case less than four acres), a master farmer had to receive permission from the provincial agricultural officer (PAO).

38. The PAO could also waive the stringent rotations requirements; see Kalinga, "Master."

39. DA (Zomba) to PCs, Soil Conservation Policy, 21 September 1948 (2.17.7F/879), MNA.

40. Port Herald District Monthly Reports (Agriculture), May 1955, 1956, June 1960 (8.7.5F/7306), MNA.

41. In November 1953, there were three master farmers in Chikwawa: Benjamin Chimbuto, R. Dala, and B. Goba (Chikwawa District Annual Reports [Agriculture], 1954–55; Chikwawa District Monthly Reports [Agriculture], November 1953 [1DCCK2/2/5], MNA). But one of the three drowned in February 1954 (Chikwawa District Monthly Reports [Agriculture], February 1954 [1DCCK2/2/5], MNA). And by 1961–62, there was only one practicing master farmer—Village Headman Mphamba—who apparently became a master farmer after 1954. In Port Herald District, there were only three master farmers left by 1961–62 (Chikwawa District Annual Reports [Agriculture], 1961–62 [3.6.10R/16559], MNA).

42. Governor G.F.T. Colby to Sir Godfrey Huggins, 13 November 1954 (2.17.5R/3335), MNA. This was in reference to the "Shire Valley Project" of the 1950s, which never took off because of lack of funds.

43. Project Manager (J.M. Hall) to District Inspector of Schools, Chikwawa and Nsanje, 1 August 1972 (14.1.2F/40365, Ag. 5), MNA.

44. CCDP, Monthly Reports, May 1971 (14.1.2F/40364), MNA.

45. A total of 4,970 such handouts and 13,366 leaflets and reports were prepared and distributed for local use in March 1971: CCDP, Monthly Reports, March 1971 (14.1.2F/40364), MNA.

46. In January 1971 the unit showed 10 films that attracted an audience of 12,170 villagers: CCDP, Monthly Reports, January 1971 (14.1.2F/40364), MNA. About two years later, five films and 26 puppet shows attracted an audience of 8,886 in the Project area: CCDP, Monthly Reports, April 1972 (14.1.2F/40364), MNA.

47. CCDP, Monthly Reports, January 1974, August 1971 (14.1.2F/40364), MNA.

48. To break rural opposition to unpopular techniques like ridging, extension officers worked closely with village headmen and officials of the MCP: CCDP, Minutes of CCDP Liaison Committee Held at Ngabu Training Center, 10 December 1970 (14.1.2F/40365), MNA; see also NADD, Crop Report for January, 1983 (11.4.9F/40352); SVADP, Monthly Reports, October 1974 (14.1.2F/40364), MNA.

49. SVADP, Chief Extension Officer (Fabian Anthuacino) to all Field Staff, 11 March, 5 May 1976 (11.4.9F/40352), MNA.

50. CCDP, Project Manager (J.M. Hall) to Agricultural Extension Staff, 1, 28 August 1972 (14.1.2F/40365), MNA. In his 28 August memo, Mr. J.M. Hall wrote, "It is essential that staff must, by example, demonstration and constant encouragement, uproot and burn cotton plants themselves, to show farmers how important and essential it is for this work to be completed." See also CCDP, Monthly Reports, August 1972 (14.1.2F/40364); CCDP, Project Manager (J.M. Hall) to Secretary for Agriculture and Natural Resources, 3 October 1974 (14.1.2F/40365), MNA.

51. CCDP, Monthly Reports, December 1970 (14.1.2F/40364), MNA.

52. Ibid., August 1971 (14.1.2F/40364), MNA.

53. Ibid., October 1971 (14.1.2F/40364), MNA.

54. CCDP, Minutes of CCDP Liaison Committee Held at Ngabu Training Center, 10 December 1970 (14.1.2F/40365), MNA.

55. CCDP, Monthly Reports, January 1971 (14.1.2F/40364), MNA.

56. CCDP, Project Manager (J.M. Hall) to DC (Chikwawa), Members and Chairman Liaison Committee, 11 May 1971 (14.1.2F/40365); CCDP, Monthly Reports, December 1970 (14.1.2F/40364), MNA.

57. CCDP, Monthly Reports, January 1971 (14.1.2F/40364), MNA.

58. Ibid., March 1973 (14.1.2F/40364), MNA. See also SVADP, "Cotton Survey 1974/75," 8.

59. CCDP, Monthly Reports, December 1970 (14.1.2F/40364), MNA.

60. Regional Agricultural Officer, Southern Region (J.F. Gower) to Regional Minister for Southern Region (Blantyre), 26 April 1968 (10.1.9F/54); CCDP, Minutes of CCDP Liaison Committee Meeting Held at Ngabu Training Center on 11 December 1970 (14.1.2F/40365), MNA.

61. U. Lele, N. van de Walle, and M. Gbetibouo, *Cotton in Africa: An Analysis of Differences in Performance,* MADIA Discussion Paper 7 (Washington, D.C.: World Bank, 1989).

62. Ibid.

63. Department of Agriculture, Production Per Capita of Export Crops, 1925 (3/2/233), MNA.

64. NADD, "Garden Survey," 57–58.

65. Ibid., 56.

66. Carter, *Hour,* 55.

67. Ibid., 199.

68. Mr. Nkhunzi of TA Ngabu (Chikwawa) at "The Agricultural Meeting Called and Conveyed [*sic*] by Malawi Congress Party Leaders in Lower Shire on 29th December, 1967," Cotton File (17.16.2R/40370, Ag. 5), MNA (emphasis added).

69. Monthly Reports for Port Herald District (Agriculture), July 1955 (8.7.5F/7306), MNA.

70. As one frustrated officer put it: "With all the political nonsense which has been going on throughout the District I consider that we are now 6 weeks behind with garden preparation" (Chikwawa District Monthly Reports [Agriculture], September 1953 [1DCCK2/2/5], MNA).

71. Ibid.

72. Ibid.

73. Port Herald District Monthly Reports (Agriculture), August 1960 (8.7.5F/7306), MNA.

74. Ibid., September 1960 (8.7.5F/7306), MNA. Even those classified as "small holders" (in opposition to master farmers) became the target of the anti-malimidwe movement. They too were described as being "too frightened to ridge." See Port Herald District Monthly Reports (Agriculture), November 1960 (8.7.5F/7306); Chikwawa District Annual Reports (Agriculture), 1963–64 (3.6.10R/16559), MNA.

75. Chikwawa District Annual Reports (Agriculture), 1952–53 (1DCCK2/2/5); Chikwawa District Monthly Reports (Agriculture), August, September, October 1953 (1DCCK2/2/5); Port Herald District Monthly Reports (Agriculture), September 1957 (8.7.5F/7306), MNA.

76. Chikwawa District Annual Reports (Agriculture), 1963–64 (3.6.10R/16559), MNA.

77. Snake Mthepheya, Kankhomba Village, STA Mbenje, Nsanje, 24 May 1996 (SM96/8).

78. Today, villagers have to buy seeds, which they did not do when ADMARC was the only buyer of cotton: interviews with Chiponyola Tomali, Tomali Village, TA Lundu, Chikwawa, 10 June 1996 (SM96/14); Mrs. Winalesi Kanyinji, Ndakwela Village, TA Chapananga, Chikwawa, 16 June 1996 (SM96/20).

79. Carter, *Hour;* A. Isaacman, *Cotton is the Mother of Poverty: Peasants, Work, and Rural Struggle in Colonial Mozambique* (Portsmouth, NH: Heinemann, 1996); O. Likaka, *Rural Society and Cotton in Colonial Zaire* (Madison: University of Wisconsin Press, 1997).

80. For a graphic representation of the huge labor demands of cotton, see NADD, "Garden Survey," chapter 2, p. 5.

81. Important changes have taken place in the way peasants market their crop: (1) there are now only two instead of three grades of cotton; (2) besides carrying their crop on the head, villagers also haul it in wheelbarrows, ox-drawn *ngolo* carts, and trucks (Naphiri Chikhambi [headman's wife] and Mrs. Elizabeth Lusiano Mwachumu, Chikhambi Village, TA Kasisi, 13 April 1995 [SM95/2]; Lendison July Gawani, Mphamba Village, TA Ngabu, Chikwawa, 21 April 1995 [SM95/5]; Washeni Lazaro, Malemia I Village, TA Ngabu, Chikwawa, 21 April 1995 [SM95/6]; Mrs. Farensa Makaniso, Chazuka I Village, TA Chimombo, Nsanje, 10 May 1995 [SM95/10]; Tayipi Alfred, Mafumbi Village, TA Makhwira, Chikwawa, 17 May 1995 [SM95/11]); and (3) probably the most significant change came in 1995 when ADMARC lost its monopsony over cotton and the market was thrown open to other buyers. Many traders now purchase cotton in the villages so that growers do not have to travel to or spend days and nights at ADMARC markets, as was the case in the past: CCDP, Monthly Reports, May 1969 (14.1.2R/40362), September, 1972 (14.1.2F/40364); Southern Chikwawa District Monthly Reports (Agriculture), May 1965 (3.6.10R/16559); Northern Chikwawa District Monthly Reports (Agriculture), May 1970 (3.6.10R/16559), MNA.

82. SVADP, *Monthly Advice* (July 1974): 454; Project Manager (J.M. Hall) to Agricultural Extension Staff, 1 August 1972 (14.1.2F/40365), MNA.

83. After four years of aggressive campaigns under the Project, only 13 percent of cotton growers ridged their fields in Chikwawa District in 1973–74: SVADP, Progress Report, September–December 1974 (14.1.2F/40365), MNA. See chapter 6 for a more detailed discussion of the resistance.

84. CCDP, Project Manager (J.M. Hall) to Agricultural Extension Staff, 28 August 1972 (14.1.2F/40365), MNA.

85. CCDP, Project Manager (J.M. Hall) to Secretary for Agriculture and Natural Resources, 3 October 1974 (14.1.2F/40365), MNA. Another factor that explains this urgency was the discovery of large colonies of the pink bollworm, which, unlike even the dreaded red bollworm, could not be killed by any of the existing pesticides. The destruction of cotton bushes was the only remedy. Only 20 percent of the gardens in the Ngabu chiefdom had been cleaned by August: CCDP, Monthly Reports, August, 1974 (14.1.2F/40364), MNA. The Project management enlisted the support of MCP leaders as well as the regional minister to get the stalks uprooted and burned before Dr. Banda's visit to the area: CCDP, Monthly Reports, September, 1974 (14.1.2F/40364), MNA. And when this did not have the desired effect, officials had no choice but to inform Dr. Banda about the situation: SVADP, Project Manager (J .M. Hall) to Secretary for Agriculture and Natural Resources, 3 October 1974 (14.1.2F/40365), MNA.

86. SVADP, Progress Report, September–December 1974 (14.1.2F/40365), MNA.

87. SVADP, *Monthly Advice* (July 1974): 454; Project Manager (J.M. Hall) to Agricultural Extension Staff, 1 August 1972 (14.1.2F/40365), MNA.

88. Interviews with Wikika Mbayenderana, Mbayenderana Village, TA Kasisi, Chikwawa, 16 May 1996 (SM96/2); Daison House, Willasi Kacholola, David Nsabwe, Mbaenderana Village, TA Kasisi, Chikwawa, 17 May 1996 (SM96/4); Landison July Gawani, Mphamba Village, TA Ngabu, Chikwawa, 20 May 1996 (SM96/5).

89. Mrs. Namaluza Bonongwe, Mbaenderana Village, TA Kasisi, Chikwawa, 17 May 1996 (SM96/3); A.M. Ndapasowa Banda, Mphamba Village, TA Ngabu, Chikwawa, 21 May 1996 (SM96/7); Snake Mthepheya, Kankhomba Village, STA Mbenje, Nsanje, 24 May 1996 (SM96/8); Bonjesi Binzi Namizinga, J.V. Ngalu, Mandere Village, TA Ngabu, Chikwawa, 25 May 1996 (SM96/10); Master Hafulaini, Khembo Village, STA Mbenje, Nsanje, 27 May 1996 (SM96/11); Elizabeth Anthuachino, Selina Kanyezi, Elina Mchawa, Khembo Village, STA Mbenje, Nsanje, 30 May 1996 (SM96/13).

90. Mrs. Enifa Kwenje, Mrs. Atafinu Petulo, Magret Jimu Mpheka, Tomali Village, TA Lundu, Chikwawa, 12 June 1996 (SM96/16). See also Mrs. Magret Jongesi, Mphamba Village, TA Ngabu, Chikwawa, 20 May 1996 (SM96/6).

91. Keyala Jailosi, James Jimu Kupheka, Baloni Yohane, Tomali Village, TA Lundu, Chikwawa, 10 June 1996 (SM96/15); Magira Daka, Joseph Edward Muyambitsa Ndakwera, Ndakwera Village, TA Chapananga, Chikwawa, 16 June 1996 (SM96/19).

92. Interviews with Timoti Davide, Ling'awa Village, TA Kasisi, Chikwawa, 16 May 1996 (SM96/1); Mrs. Namaluza Bonongwe, Mbayenderana Village, TA Kasisi, Chikwawa, 17 May 1996 (SM96/3); Landison July Gawani, Mphamba Village, TA Ngabu, Chikwawa, 20 May 1996 (SM96/5); A.M. Ndapasowa Banda, Mphamba Village, TA Ngabu, Chikwawa, 21 May 1996 (SM96/7); Keyala Jailosi, James Jimu Kupheka, Baloni Yohane, Tomali Village, TA Lundu, Chikwawa, 10 June 1996 (SM96/15); Msambachulu Muyambutsa Ndakwera, Ndakwera Village, TA Chapananga, Chikwawa, 16 June 1996 (SM96/21).

93. Southern Chikwawa District Monthly Reports (Agriculture), March 1965 (3.6.10R/16559), MNA.

94. Some villagers also thinned their cotton during the initial phase in weeding: Wikika Mbayenderana, Mbayenderana Village, TA Kasisi, Chikwawa, 16 May 1996 (SM96/2); Elizabeth Anthuachino, Selina Kanyezi, Elina Mchawa, Khembo Village, STA Mbenje, Nsanje, 30 May 1996 (SM96/13); Chiponyola Tomali, Tomali Village, TA Lundu, Chikwawa, 10 June 1996 (SM96/14); Elizabeth Jeke, Falena Keyala, Matinesi Laitoni, Victoria Mdzondo, Tomali Village, TA Lundu, Chikwawa, 12 June 1996 (SM96/17). Many claim that they started thinning only in response to official propaganda: Timoti Davide, Ling'awa Village, TA Kasisi, Chikwawa, 16 May 1996 (SM96/1); Wikika Mbayenderana, Mbayenderana Village, TA Kasisi, Chikwawa, 16 May 1996 (SM96/2); Mrs. Namaluza Bonongwe, Mbayenderana Village, TA Kasisi, Chikwawa, 17 May 1996 (SM96/3); Daison House, Willasi Kacholola, David Nsabwe, Mbayenderana Village, TA Kasisi, Chikwawa, 17 May 1996 (SM96/4); Elizabeth Anthuachino, Selina Kanyezi, Elina Mchawa, Khembo Village, STA Mbenje, Nsanje, 30 May 1996 (SM96/13); Chiponyola Tomali, Tomali Village, TA Lundu, Chikwawa, 10 June 1996 (SM96/14); Mrs. Enifa Kwenje, Mrs. Atafinu Petulo, Magret Jimu Mpheka, Tomali Village, TA Lundu, Chikwawa, 12 June 1996 (SM96/16); Elizabeth Jeke, Falena Keyala, Matinesi Laitoni, Victoria Mdzondo, Tomali Village, TA Lundu, Chikwawa, 12 June 1996 (SM96/17). However, the plurality of African terms (*kupambula, kutengula, kuzulira*) referring to the practice raises questions about this claim.

95. Chikwawa District Monthly Reports (Agriculture), March 1963 (3.5.10R/16559), MNA.

96. Carter, *Hour,* 200.

97. CCDP, Monthly Reports, January 1971 (14.1.2F/40364), MNA.

98. Peasants started picking their cotton as early as March: Southern Chikwawa District Monthly Reports (Agriculture), March 1965 (3.6.10R/16559); Northern Chikwawa District Monthly Reports (Agriculture), March 1970 (3.6.10R/16559), MNA.

99. SVADP, Chief Extension Officer (Fabian Anthuacino) to All Field Staff, 11 March 1976 (11.4.9F/40352), MNA.

100. Ibid., 11 March, 5 May 1976 (11.4.9F/40352), MNA.

101. Southern Chikwawa District Monthly Reports (Agriculture), April, May 1965 (3.6.10R/16559); Northern Chikwawa District Monthly Reports (Agriculture), April 1980 (11.4.9F/40352), MNA.

102. SVADP, *Monthly Advice* (June 1974): 434–35; Southern Chikwawa District Monthly Reports (Agriculture), May 1965 (3.6.10R/16559), MNA.

103. Southern Chikwawa District Monthly Reports (Agriculture), April, June 1965 (3.6.10R/16559), MNA. People normally paid the MYP after selling their cotton.

104. For similar struggles against cotton pests in the Old South, see Carter, *Hour,* 179–80.

105. CCDP, Monthly Reports, February 1972 (14.1.2F/40364), MNA; SVADP, *Monthly Advice* (January 1975): 570–71.

106. SVADP, *Monthly Advice* (February 1975): 3, 582; see also ibid. (January, April 1974): 311, 417.

107. Chikwawa District Monthly Reports (Agriculture), March 1963 (3.5.10R/16559), MNA; see also Chikwawa District Annual Reports (Agriculture), 1963–64 (3.6.10R/16559), MNA.

108. Most villagers also believed both in the need for and effectiveness of spray technology: Timoti Davide, Ling'awa Village, TA Kasisi, Chikwawa, 16 May 1996 (SM96/1); Mrs. Namaluza Bonongwe, Mbayenderana Village, TA Kasisi, Chikwawa, 17 May 1996 (SM96/3); Daison House, Willasi Kacholola, David Nsabwe, Mbayenderana Village, TA Kasisi, Chikwawa, 17 May 1996 (SM96/4); Keyala Jailosi , James Jimu Kupheka, Baloni Yohane, Tomali Village, TA Lundu, Chikwawa, 10 June 1996 (SM96/15); Elizabeth Jeke, Falena Keyala, Matinesi Laitoni, Victoria Mdzondo, Tomali Village, TA Lundu, Chikwawa, 12 June 1996(SM96/17). So complete was their faith in the technology that if things did not work, they were ready to blame the process rather than the technology itself: Mrs. Atafinu Petulo, Magret Jimu Mpheka, Tomali Village, TA Lundu, Chikwawa, 12 June 1996 (SM96/16). Peasants call the American bollworm variously *America bowiramu*; just *bowamu, buwamu,* or *bowemusi*: Landison July Gawani, Mphamba Village, TA Ngabu, Chikwawa, 20 May 1996 (SM96/5); A.M. Ndapasowa Banda, Mphamba Village, TA Ngabu, Chikwawa, 21 May 1996 (SM96/7); Snake Mthepheya, Kankhomba Village, STA Mbenje, Nsanje, 24 May 1996 (SM96/8); Bonjesi Binzi Namizinga, J.V. Ngalu, Mandere Village, TA Ngabu, Chikwawa, 25 May 1996 (SM96/10); Keyala Jailosi , James Jimu Kupheka, Baloni Yohane, Tomali Village, TA Lundu, Chikwawa, 10 June 1996 (SM96/15); Magira Daka, Joseph Edward Muyambitsa Ndakwera, Ndakwera Village, TA Chapananga, Chikwawa, 16 June 1996 (SM96/19). Still some call it *meribrahamu* (Elizabeth Anthuachino, Selina Kanyezi, Elina Mchawa, Khembo Village, STA Mbenje, Nsanje, 30 May1996 (SM96/13), and the stainer has become *stinale* (ibid.; Mrs. Dina Sabe, Mary Sabe, Khembo Village, STA Mbenje, Nsanje, 27 May 1996 [SM96/12]). The names of many pesticides have also been Africanized.

109. "The Agricultural Meeting Called and Conveyed [*sic*] by Malawi Congress Party Leaders in Lower Shire on 29th December, 1967," Cotton File (17.16.2R/40370, Ag. 5), MNA.

110. This was the Lundu-Tomali area: Chikwawa District Monthly Reports (Agriculture), April, July, November 1963 (3.5.10R/16559), MNA.

111. Northern Chikwawa District Monthly Reports (Agriculture), January, June 1965 (3.6.10R/16559), MNA. The board also received another installment from the southern part of the district six months later; see Southern Chikwawa District Monthly Reports (Agriculture), November 1965 (3.6.10R/16559), MNA.

112. "So-called" because farmers who did not own machines or buy insecticides from the Project did spray their cotton.

113. CCDP, Monthly Reports, February 1972 (14.1.2F/40364), MNA.

114. Nyasaland Government, *ARDA 1955,* 11.

115. SVADP, *Monthly Advice* (October 1974): 507. (The price of a ULV Sprayer was K11, and a ULV battery K0.90.) A farm cart bought on credit cost K195, and a plough K22 (ibid.).

116. Timoti Davide, Ling'awa Village, TA Kasisi, Chikwawa, 16 May 1996 (SM96/1); Wikika Mbayenderana, Mbayenderana Village, TA Kasisi, Chikwawa, 16 May 1996 (SM96/2); Mrs. Namaluza Bonongwe, Mbayenderana Village, TA Kasisi, Chikwawa, 17 May 1996 (SM96/3); Snake Mthepheya, Kankhomba Village, STA Mbenje, Nsanje, 24 May 1996 (SM96/8); Bonjesi Binzi Namizinga, J. V. Ngalu, Mandere Village, TA Ngabu, Chikwawa, 25 May 1996 (SM96/10); Master Hafulaini, Khembo Village, STA Mbenje, Nsanje, 27 May 1996 (SM96/11).

117. Interview with Snake Mthepheya, Kankhomba Village, STA Mbenje, Nsanje, 24 May 1996 (SM96/8). For other pesticide price ranges, see Magret Jongesi, Mphamba Village, TA Ngabu, Chikwawa, 20 May 1996 (SM96/6); Elizabeth Anthuachino, Selina Kanyezi, Elina Mchawa, Khembo Village, STA Mbenje, Nsanje, 30 May 1996 (SM96/13).

118. CCDP, Monthly Reports, December 1970 (14.1.2F/40364), MNA.

119. SVADP, Monthly Reports, March 1974 (14.1.2F/40364), MNA.

120. Interview with Magira Daka, Joseph Edward Muyambitsa Ndakwera, Ndakwera Village, TA Chapananga, Chikwawa, 16 June 1996 (SM96/19).

121. I have in mind losses like those incurred by the two master farmers who hired tractors for £90 in 1955, or the men who spent K17,000 and K4,000 on pesticides and labor in 1996.

122. Magret Jongesi, Mphamba Village, TA Ngabu, Chikwawa, 20 May 1996 (SM96/6); Snake Mthepheya, Kankhomba Village, STA Mbenje, Nsanje, 24 May 1996 (SM96/8); Mrs. Dina Sabe, Mary Sabe, Khembo Village, STA Mbenje, Nsanje, 27 May 1996 (SM96/12).

123. Report on Nyasaland Cotton, 24 April 1909 (A2/1/3); see also ALC Report, 1 March 1911 (?); McCall to Deputy Governor, 3 March 1911 (A2/1/4); British Cotton Growers Association (BCGA) to (?), 3 December 1912 (A1/1/3), MNA.

124. See L. Vail, "Railway Development and Colonial Underdevelopment: The Nyasaland Case," in *The Roots of Rural Poverty in Central and Southern Africa,* ed. R. Palmer and N. Parsons (Berkeley and Los Angeles: University of California Press, 1977): 365–95.

125. BCGA Manager to Chief Secretary, 21 July 1930 (S1/956/30); BCGA Manager, the Native Cotton Industry, Nyasaland, 1931 (A3/2/56), MNA.

126. BCGA Manager, the Native Cotton Industry, Nyasaland, 1931 (A3/2/56), MNA. The subsequent liberation and civil wars in Mozambique between the late 1960s and early 1990s only worsened the situation for Malawi's exporters, who had to send their goods through Tanzanian and South African (through Zambia and Zimbabwe) ports.

127. See, for example, BCGA to DA, 19 April 1911 (A1/1/2); BCGA to (?), 3 December 1912 (A1/1/3); Acting Chief Secretary to BCGA, 3 January 1913 (A1/1/4); BCGA to DA, 26 April 1934 (A3/2/53); Director, Liverpool-Uganda Cotton Company, to Chief Secretary, 7 June 1934 (S1/269/34), MNA.

128. Agreement with the BCGA, 1922 (A3/2/55); Development of the Native Cotton Industry, 9 May 1923 (A3/2/68), MNA. The initial contract was for five years and was to be renewed every three years afterward.

129. Nyasaland Government, *ARDA 1955,* 11; *1960,* 9. See also chapter 4.

130. Ng'ong'ola, "Statutory Law."

131. Kydd and Christiansen, "Structural Change in Malawi"; Kydd and Spooner, *The World Bank's Analysis of Malawian Agriculture*; Ng'ong'ola, "Statutory Law."

132. According to its contract with the BCGA in 1923, the government was to receive 50 percent of the association's annual profits, arguing that it needed a fund to subsidize producer prices in the event of a market crash. But officials never used the money for this purpose, even during the Great Depression, which caused a lot of suffering among peasants

who had come to depend on the cash crop: DA to British Central Africa Company, 6 June 1922 (A3/2/67); Report on the African Cotton Industry, 1923 (S1/481/24), MNA. For the opposition, see Acting Governor to Secretary of State for the Colonies, 2 February 1924 (S1/481/24); Churchill to Governor, 21 October 1922 (A3/2/55), MNA. Passfield was for a price-stabilization fund: Secretary of State for the Colonies to Governor, 10 April 1931 (552/40), MNA.

133. Headman Mafale of TA Lundu (Chikwawa) at "The Agricultural Meeting Called and Conveyed [*sic*] by Malawi Congress Party Leaders in Lower Shire on 29th December, 1967," Cotton File (17.16.2R/40370, Ag. 5), MNA (emphasis added).

134. Bonjesi Binzi Namizinga, J. V. Ngalu, Mandere Village, TA Ngabu, Chikwawa, 25 May 1996 (SM96/10), MNA. The same complaint was voiced by Daison House, Willasi Kacholola, David Nsabwe, Mbayenderana Village, TA Kasisi, Chikwawa, 17 May 1996 (SM96/4); Landison July Gawani, Mphamba Village, TA Ngabu, Chikwawa, 20 May 1996 (SM96/5); Magret Jongesi, Mphamba Village, TA Ngabu, Chikwawa, 20 May 1996 (SM96/6); A. M. Ndapasowa Banda, Mphamba Village, TA Ngabu, Chikwawa, 21 May 1996 (SM96/7); Master Hafulaini, Khembo Village, STA Mbenje, Nsanje, 27 May 1996 (SM96/11); Chiponyola Tomali, Tomali Village, TA Lundu, Chikwawa, 10 June 1996 (SM96/14); Ronex Nyadani, Ndakwera Village, TA Chapananga, Chikwawa, 14 June 1996 (SM96/18). Four and a half kwacha amounted to the same as U.S. 30 cents in 1996.

135. "Farmers Revive Cotton Growing," *Nation,* January 10, 2002, http://www.nation-malawi.com/print.asp?articleID=3054.

136. Mr. F. B. Manani of TA Ngabu (Chikwawa) addressing "The Agricultural Meeting Called and Conveyed [*sic*] by Malawi Congress Party Leaders in Lower Shire on 29th December, 1967," Cotton File (17.16.2R/40370, Ag. 5), MNA.

137. Kalinga, "Master," 378.

138. Forty-four percent of those who sprayed their cotton in 1974–75 got the spraying machines and insecticides from the bigifama (SVADP, "Cotton Survey 1974/75").

139. Some bigifama in the 1990s owned up to four sprayers, including some that they had acquired in the late 1960s and early 1970s. They had purchased some of the machines from other farmers. Many of the older machines were not operational in 1996 because of lack of spare parts: Timoti Davide, Ling'awa Village, TA Kasisi, Chikwawa, 16 May 1996 (SM96/1); Landison July Gawani, Mphamba Village, TA Ngabu, Chikwawa, 20 May 1996 (SM96/5); A. M. Ndapasowa Banda, Mphamba Village, TA Ngabu, Chikwawa, 21 May 1996 (SM96/7); Snake Mthepheya, Kankhomba Village, STA Mbenje, Nsanje, 24 May 1996 (SM96/8); Bonjesi Binzi Namizinga, J. V. Ngalu, Mandere Village, TA Ngabu, Chikwawa, 25 May 1996 (SM96/10); Elizabeth Anthuachino, Selina Kanyezi, Elina Mchawa, Khembo Village, STA Mbenje, Nsanje, 30 May 1996 (SM96/13); Magira Daka, Joseph Edward Muyambitsa Ndakwera, Ndakwera Village, TA Chapananga, Chikwawa, 16 June 1996 (SM96/19).

140. Wikika Mbayenderana, Mbayenderana Village, TA Kasisi, Chikwawa, 16 May 1996 (SM96/2); Mrs. Namaluza Bonongwe, Mbayenderana Village, TA Kasisi, Chikwawa, 17 May 1996 (SM96/3); Magret Jongesi, Mphamba Village, TA Ngabu, Chikwawa, 20 May 1996 (SM96/6); Master Hafulaini, Khembo Village, STA Mbenje, Nsanje, 27 May 1996 (SM96/11); Mrs. Dina Sabe, Mary Sabe, Khembo Village, STA Mbenje, Nsanje, 27 May 1996 (SM96/12); Elizabeth Anthuachino, Selina Kanyezi, Elina Mchawa, Khembo Village, STA Mbenje, Nsanje, 30 May 1996 (SM96/13); Chiponyola Tomali, Tomali Village, TA Lundu, Chikwawa, 10 June 1996 (SM96/14); Keyala Jailosi, James Jimu Kupheka, Baloni Yohane, Tomali Village, TA Lundu, Chikwawa, 10 June 1996 (SM96/15); Msambachulu Muyambitsa Ndakwera, Ndakwera Village, TA Chapananga, Chikwawa, 16 June 1996

(SM96/21); SVADP, "Cotton Survey 1974/75." After the liberalization of the cotton trade in 1995, bigifama came to compete with cotton buyers like the Great Lakes Corporation, who also rented sprayers to their prospective sellers: Bonjesi Binzi Namizinga, J. V. Ngalu, Mandere Village, TA Ngabu, Chikwawa, 25 May 1996 (SM96/10). ADMARC used to give large growers sprayers as bonuses: Snake Mthepheya, Kankhomba Village, STA Mbenje, Nsanje, 24 May 1996 (SM96/8).

141. SVADP, "Cotton Survey 1974/75," 37. I think that the survey exaggerated the generosity of bigifama in its calculation that about a third of the borrowers did not have to pay for pesticides.

142. SVADP, "Cotton Survey 1974/75," 49. *SR* in the text stands for "Spraying Realities."

143. Snake Mthepheya, Kankhomba Village, STA Mbenje, Nsanje, 24 May 1996 (SM96/8); Elizabeth Anthuachino, Selina Kanyezi, Elina Mchawa, Khembo Village, STA Mbenje, Nsanje, 30 May 1996 (SM96/13); Chiponyola Tomali, Tomali Village, TA Lundu, Chikwawa, 10 June 1996 (SM96/14); Elizabeth Jeke, Falena Keyala, Matinesi Laitoni, Victoria Mdzondo, Tomali Village, TA Lundu, Chikwawa, 12 June 1996 (SM96/17); Magira Daka, Joseph Edward Muyambitsa Ndakwera, Ndakwera Village, TA Chapananga, Chikwawa, 16 June 1996 (SM96/19). They did this during the droughts of 1964, 1970, 1980, and 1994: Chikwawa District Monthly Reports (Agriculture), March 1964 (3.5.10R/16559), February 1980 (11.4.9F/40352); Northern Chikwawa District Monthly Reports (Agriculture), March 1970 (14.1.2F/40362), MNA.

144. Northern Chikwawa District Monthly Reports (Agriculture), March 1970 (14.1.2F/40362); Chikwawa District Monthly Reports (Agriculture), January 1980 (11.4.9F/40352), MNA.

145. SVADP, *Monthly Advice* (April 1974): 416–17.

146. Ibid. (February 1975): 3.

147. Ibid. (February 1974): 360. I arrived at this figure on the basis of the information that each season rich and poor peasants sprayed, on the average, 6.2 and 4.1 times respectively. See also ibid. (April 1974): 417.

148. R. W. Kettlewell, *An Outline of Agrarian Problems and Policy in Nyasaland* (Zomba, Malawi: Nyasaland Government Press, 1955): 3.

149. CCDP, "Cotton Survey, 1971/72."

150. SVADP, "Cotton Survey 1974/75," 8. They identified six "Spraying Realities" (or SR), 0, 1, 2, 3, 4, and 5: 0 = those who did not grow cotton; 1 = growers who did not spray; 2 = sprayers with borrowed machines; 3 = sprayers using their own machines; 4 = owners of ULV (ultra-low-volume) sprayers; 5 = owners of both ULV and knapsack sprayers. SR2 and SR3 farmers represented 16.5 and 21.3 percent, respectively, of all the households in the five cotton-growing substrata of Chikwawa. (The 21.3 percent stood for 7,389 households.)

151. NADD, "Garden Survey," chapter 4.

152. Ibid.

153. As was the case in Georgia: Carter, *Hour,* 180.

154. Interview with Timoti Davide, Ling'awa Village, TA Kasisi, Chikwawa, 16 May 1996 (SM96/1).

155. Oral sources place the origins of some businesses that flourished after 1939, particularly fishing and cattle keeping, in the cotton economy of the pre-Bomani era.

156. CCDP, "Agricultural Yield and Social Survey: A Sample Survey of Cotton Spraying Farmers in the Chikwawa Cotton Development Project, Involving Crop Areas and Yields and Incorporating a Socio-Economic Study" (September 1971), appendix B, p. 2, SVADP.

157. Kalinga, "Master."

158. Daison House, Willasi Kacholola, David Nsabwe, Mbayenderana Village, TA Kasisi, Chikwawa, 17 May 1996 (SM96/4); Bonjesi Binzi Namizinga, J.V. Ngalu, Mandere Village, TA Ngabu, Chikwawa, 25 May 1996 (SM96/10); Mrs. Dina Sabe, Mary Sabe, Khembo Village, STA Mbenje, Nsanje, 27 May 1996 (SM96/12); Msambachulu Muyambutsa Ndakwera, Ndakwera Village, TA Chapananga, Chikwawa, 16 June 1996 (SM96/21).

159. Cotton production in the pre-Bomani era was relatively inexpensive and could reproduce itself without capital infusion from other sectors of the economy.

160. Wikika Mbayenderana, Mbayenderana Village, TA Kasisi, Chikwawa, 16 May 1996 (SM96/2); Daison House, Willasi Kacholola, David Nsabwe, Mbayenderana Village, TA Kasisi, Chikwawa, 17 May 1996 (SM96/4); Magret Jongesi, Mphamba Village, TA Ngabu, Chikwawa, 20 May 1996 (SM96/6); A.M. Ndapasowa Banda, Mphamba Village, TA Ngabu, Chikwawa, 21 May 1996 (SM96/7); Mrs. Winalesi Kanyinji, Ndakwera Village, TA Chapananga, Chikwawa, 16 June 1996 (SM96/20).

161. SVADP, "Cotton Survey 1974/75," 17.

162. Ibid., table 2.M. Only 30.6, 18.1, and 30.9 percent of the employees who landed with good government jobs came from SR0, SR1, and SR2 households, respectively. By contrast, 61.5 percent of the members of SR3 households took up such jobs.

163. Ibid., table 2.L. According to the same survey, the corresponding figures for the other four cotton-growing subregions were 17.1, 25, 28.1, and 33.33.

164. See, for example, Berry, "Food Crisis"; idem, *No Condition Is Permanent*.

165. Carter, *Hour,* 199. See also p. 27 for the relationship between economic status and the ability to diversity agricultural practices.

166. Interviews with Magret Jongesi, Mphamba Village, TA Ngabu, Chikwawa, 20 May 1996 (SM96/6); Snake Mthepheya, Kankhomba Village, STA Mbenje, Nsanje, 24 May 1996 (SM96/8).

167. Interviews with Timoti Davide, Ling'awa Village, TA Kasisi, Chikwawa, 16 May 1996 (SM96/1); Mrs. Namaluza Bonongwe, Mbayenderana Village, TA Kasisi, Chikwawa, 17 May 1996 (SM96/3); Landison July Gawani, Mphamba Village, TA Ngabu, Chikwawa, 20 May 1996 (SM96/5); A.M. Ndapasowa Banda, Mphamba Village, TA Ngabu, Chikwawa, 21 May 1996 (SM96/7); Snake Mthepheya, Kankhomba Village, STA Mbenje, Nsanje, 24 May 1996 (SM96/8). Before the introduction of free primary school education in 1995, many children helped their parents in cotton growing to raise money for school fees (Mrs. Dina Sabe, Mary Sabe, Khembo Village, STA Mbenje, Nsanje, 27 May 1996 [SM96/12]), in addition to clothing (Mrs. Namaluza Bonongwe, Mbaenderana Village, TA Kasisi, Chikwawa, 17 May 1996 [SM96/3]).

168. CCDP, "Farm Survey, 1971/72," table H8a.

169. Ibid., Percentage Distribution of Hired Labor Hours by Month: 2, 3, 5, 6, 12, 6, 5, 15, 25, 11, 3, 7 for September, October, November, December, January, February, March, April, May, June, July, and August, respectively.

170. Magira Daka, Joseph Edward Muyambitsa Ndakwera, Ndakwera Village, TA Chapananga, Chikwawa, 16 June 1996 (SM96/19).

171. Keyala Jailosi, James Jimu Kupheka, Baloni Yohane, Tomali Village, TA Lundu, Chikwawa, 10 June 1996 (SM96/15).

172. CCDP, "Farm Survey, 1971/72," table H8a.

173. Ibid.

174. SVADP, "Cotton Survey 1974/75," 44. This survey found that 9, 31, and 60 percent of, respectively, SR1, SR2, and SR3 cotton growers spent money on labor.

175. NADD, "Garden Survey," table 2.13.

176. Strictly speaking, the term *wanchito* denotes any worker. However, in the Tchiri Valley today, it is often used in contradistinction to casual workers or *waganyo* (a term that comes from the Portuguese verb *ganhar*). Some villagers maintain that while wanchito performed all sorts of jobs, you cannot trust waganyo with certain tasks that, like spraying, require special attention and skill: Timoti Davide, Ling'awa Village, TA Kasisi, Chikwawa, 16 May 1996 (SM96/1). For an opposite view, see interviews with Mrs. Namaluza Bonongwe, Mbayenderana Village, TA Kasisi, Chikwawa, 17 May 1996 (SM96/3); Bonjesi Binzi Namizinga, J. V. Ngalu, Mandere Village, TA Ngabu, Chikwawa, 25 May 1996 (SM96/10); Master Hafulaini, Khembo Village, STA Mbenje, Nsanje, 27 May 1996 (SM96/11); Mrs. Dina Sabe, Mary Sabe, Khembo Village, STA Mbenje, Nsanje, 27 May 1996 (SM96/12); Elizabeth Anthuachino, Selina Kanyezi, Elina Mchawa, Khembo Village, STA Mbenje, Nsanje, 30 May 1996 (SM96/13); Keyala Jailosi, James Jimu Kupheka, Baloni Yohane, Tomali Village, TA Lundu, Chikwawa, 10 June 1996 (SM96/15); Elizabeth Jeke, Falena Keyala, Matinesi Laitoni, Victoria Mdzondo, Tomali Village, TA Lundu, Chikwawa, 12 June 1996 (SM96/17).

177. Tiwongolera Bayisi, Njereza Village, TA Kasisi, Chikwawa, 13 April 1995 (SM95/1). It is difficult to allocate farm expenditure by crop operation with regard to regular workers, who did all sorts of farm work: CCDP, "Farm Survey 1972/73" (Evaluation Section, 1974): 30–31, SVADP.

178. CCDP, "Farm Survey, 1971/72," 70.

179. This was the statistical average not only for casual laborers but for all workers (ibid., 69).

180. NADD, "Garden Survey," chapter 5. The survey shows that cotton occupied 12 percent of the smallest gardens but up to 40 percent of the largest fields.

181. Interviews with Daison House, Willasi Kacholola, David Nsabwe, Mbayenderana Village, TA Kasisi, Chikwawa, 17 May 1996 (SM96/4); Bonjesi Binzi Namizinga, J. V. Ngalu, Mandere Village, TA Ngabu, Chikwawa, 25 May 1996 (SM96/10); Mrs. Dina Sabe, Mary Sabe, Khembo Village, STA Mbenje, Nsanje, 27 May 1996 (SM96/12).

182. See Mandala, "Feeding and Fleecing the Native."

183. A notable exception to this is NADD, "Garden Survey."

184. Ibid., chapter 4.

185. Ibid.

186. In four cropping seasons, 1976–77, 1977–78, 1978–79, and 1979–80, the estimated returns to labor for cotton in tambala (100 tambala make a kwacha) per labor day were 39, 46, 43, and 43, respectively. The corresponding figures for maize during the same seasons were 62, 79, 68, and 52. See NADD, "Garden Survey," table 2.4.

187. See, for example, interview with Mrs. Enifa Kwenje, Mrs. Atafinu Petulo, Magret Jimu Mpheka, Tomali Village, TA Lundu, Chikwawa, 12 June 1996 (SM96/16).

CHAPTER 6: THE LOGIC OF THE PEASANT GARDEN

1. N. Helburn, "A Stereotype of Agriculture in Semiarid Turkey," *Geographical Review* 45 (1955): 381, as quoted by H. Gerber, *The Social Origins of the Modern Middle East* (Boulder, CO: Lynne Rienner Publishers, 1987): 110.

2. Port Herald District Monthly Reports (Agriculture), February 1934 (A3/2/201), MNA.

3. Lower River District Annual Reports (Administration), 1948 (NSP3/1/18), MNA.

4. SVADP, 1974 (?). For a similar assessment, see Nsanje District Monthly Reports (Administration), October 1960 (8.7.6F/7310); CCDP, Minutes of Chikwawa Cotton

Project Liaison Committee held at Ngabu Training Centre on 10th December 1970 (14.1.2F/40365), MNA.

5. Berry and Petty, *The Nyasaland Survey Papers*, 223.

6. John Moir to Scott, 28 February 1890, "Moir Family Correspondence, 1878–1940," University of Witwatersrand, Johannesburg.

7. John Moir to Directors of the ALC (Glasgow), 11 (or 10) July 1889, "Moir Family Correspondence, 1878–1940," University of Witwatersrand, Johannesburg. See also John Moir to ALC, 26 July 1888, 22 March 1889; and to Mr. (?), 17 January 1898.

8. The Malawi section of the Dinde is 151 square miles (Minutes of Flood Relief Meeting Held on 6 January 1970 [10.1.9F/53], MNA), and I have assumed the more extensive Dabanyi to be about 200 square miles. The whole valley is 2,644 square miles (747 square miles in Nsanje plus 1,897 in Chikwawa).

9. Young, *Mission to Nyassa*, 36–37, 46.

10. On this, see especially H. Johnston, "Report on the First Three Years' Administration of British Central Africa," 31 March 1894 (FO2/66), PRO; Moir, *After Livingstone*; "Moir Family Correspondence, 1878–1940," University of Witwatersrand, Johannesburg. Also critical are the unpublished diaries (1882–87) of Frederick T. Morrison (University of Edinburgh Library). Morrison was an employee of the ALC.

11. H. Johnston, "Report on the First Three Years' Administration of British Central Africa," 31 March 1894 (FO2/66), PRO.

12. For single women and taxation during and after the Great Depression, see, among others, Lower Shire District Book 4, 1928–32, 2 September 1932, MNA; Great Britain, Colonial Office, Nyasaland Protectorate, *A Report by Eric Smith on the Direct Taxation of Natives in the Nyasaland Protectorate and Other Cognate Matters* (London: Crown Agents for the Colonies, 1937): 10.

13. Colman and Garbett, "Labour Economy."

14. H. Johnston to Secretary of State for Foreign Affairs, 4 February 1894 (FO2/66), PRO.

15. H. Johnston to Sharpe, July–October, 4 July 1894 (FO2/67), PRO.

16. H. Johnston to HM Secretary of State for Foreign Affairs, 22 January 1894 (FO2/66), PRO.

17. Port Herald District Annual Reports (Administration), 1948 (NSP3/1/18), MNA.

18. Ibid., 1943 (NSP2/1/9), MNA.

19. Ibid. (emphasis added).

20. Ibid.

21. Ibid., 1947 (NSP3/1/18), MNA.

22. This happened again in the 1960s and early 1970s: Nsanje District Monthly Reports (Administration), August, September 1965 (10.1.9F/32154), May 1972 (DAM 30722); Chikwawa District Monthly Reports, September 1972 (14.1.2R/40362), MNA.

23. Chief Nyachikadza to DC, 22 March 1970 (10.1.9F/53), MNA. Two years later the closing would kill the fish trade: Nsanje District Monthly Reports (Administration), July 1972 (DAM 30722), MNA.

24. Government Agent (Nsanje) to Secretary to the Prime Minister, 16 March 1966 (10.1.9R/32151, Ag. 9/2/6), MNA.

25. Interview with Mrs. Leni Pereira, Chitsa Village, TA Tengani, Nsanje, 5 November 1991 (EPT91/13).

26. For the regular utilization of the marshes in the early 1970s, see CCDP, "Farm Survey, 1972/73." I think that this survey grossly underestimated the contribution of dimba agriculture.

27. Port Herald District Annual Reports, 1955–56 (8.7.5F/7306), MNA.

28. Lower River Monthly Reports, August 1962 (3.6.10R/16559, Ag. 3), MNA. See also Chikwawa District Monthly Reports (Administration), March 1955 (1DCCK2/2/5), MNA, where it is alleged, "Food ... shortages may occur later due to people planting more cotton than food."

29. Interview with Elizabeth Anthuachino, Selina Kanyezi, Elina Mchawa, Khembo Village, STA Mbenje, Nsanje, 30 May 1996 (SM96/13), MNA. For other sources that make garden preparation a major area of conflict, see Chikwawa District Project Officer's Monthly Reports, October 1982 (11.4.9F/40352), MNA.

30. Chikwawa District Monthly Reports (Administration), May 1958 (no location or reference), MNA. See also South Chikwawa District Monthly Reports (Agriculture), May 65 (3.6.10R/16559, Ag. 3), MNA, which makes reference to the "scarcity in finding labourers."

31. Supervisor (Fabian Anthuacino), South Chikwawa District Monthly Reports (Agriculture), May 1965 (3.6.10R/16559), MNA (emphasis added). The beer drinking was in many cases related to ritual activity (see chapter 2).

32. Not only dimba maize benefited from the neglect of munda cotton farming; rice sometimes absorbed peasant labor from cotton: "This rice production does however tend to cause growers to neglect their cotton gardens" (Chikwawa District Monthly Reports [Agriculture], January 1953 [1DCCK2/2/5], MNA).

33. Chikwawa District Annual Reports (Agriculture), 1952–53 (1DCCK2/2/5), MNA.

34. Chikwawa District Monthly Reports (Agriculture), October 1955 (1DCCK2/2/5), MNA (emphasis added).

35. Ibid., May 1955 (1DCCK2/2/5), MNA.

36. Ibid. See also ibid., June 1955 (1DCCK2/2/5), MNA.

37. Chikwawa District Monthly Reports (Agriculture), 1963–1965 (3.6.10R/16559, Ag. 3), MNA. According to a July 1963 report, almost 28 percent of the total crop was lost because of these and other practices.

38. South Chikwawa District Monthly Reports (Agriculture), May, June 1965 (3.6.10R/16559, Ag. 3), MNA.

39. DA (J.S.J. McCall), Cotton Grown by Natives, 1909: Comparative Statement of Native Grown Seed Cotton Purchased by the African Lakes Company, 1907–1909 (A2/1/3), MNA.

40. Chikwawa District Monthly Reports (Agriculture), March 1955 (1DCCK2/2/5), MNA.

41. Chikwawa District Monthly Reports (General), February 1958 (no location or reference), MNA. See also the section on the munda system in this chapter and Port Herald District Annual Reports (Administration), January 1958 (no reference or location), MNA.

42. Chikwawa District Monthly Reports (Administration), January 1962 (ADM 12/II), MNA.

43. Chikwawa District Annual Reports (Agriculture), 1954–55 (1DCCK2/2/5), MNA.

44. Port Herald District Annual Reports (Administration), 1930 (NSP2/1/3), MNA.

45. See, among others, Chikwawa District Annual Reports (Agriculture), 1954–55 (1DCCK2/2/5); Lower River District Monthly Reports (Agriculture), August 1962 (3.6.10R/16559, Ag. 3), MNA.

46. Chikwawa District Annual Reports (Agriculture), 1954–55 (1DCCK2/2/5), MNA. He ended the report with this comment: "This I consider to be reasonable, however, I think a definite policy should be laid down."

47. Lower River District Monthly Reports (Agriculture), November 1962 (3.6.10R/16559, Ag. 3). See also Chikwawa District Monthly Reports (Administration), November 1962 (ADM 12/II), MNA.

48. Nyasaland Government, *ARDA 1949*, 3. The quote ends, "It was, perhaps, in a way fortunate that their brother African cultivators who had food underlined the advice given so often in the past that the wise man produces economic *and* [*sic*] food crops."

49. For the 1945 and 1966 figures, see J.M. Schoffeleers, *The Lower Shire Valley of Malawi: Its Ecology, Population Distribution, Ethnic Divisions, and Systems of Marriage* (Limbe, Malawi: Montfort Press, 1968): 5.

50. Malawi National Statistical Office, *Population Census, 1977: Preliminary Report* (Zomba, Malawi: Government Press, 1978).

51. Population pressure in the Chididi Hills is a relatively recent development. The region had entered the twentieth century as one of the most sparsely populated areas of the valley. In 1913, for example, the director of agriculture urged his superiors to do "every-thing possible ... to ... encourage settlement in the Port Herald hills" (McCall to Chief Secretary [?], 20 October 1913 [A2/1/9], MNA). But the government did not have to do anything. Starting in the 1940s, villagers who lost their land to permanent inundation in the Dinde headed for the hills and were subsequently joined by other settlers, particularly refugees from Mozambique's liberation and civil wars.

52. Reply to Questionnaire by Dr. Tempany, 1946 (3.17.7F/879); Department of Agriculture (Lilongwe) to DA, Answers to Soil Conservation Questionnaire, 27 February 1946 (3.17.7F/879), MNA.

53. Reply to Questionnaire by Dr. Tempany, 1946 (3.17.7F/879), MNA.

54. Lower RIver District Annual Reports (Administration), 1949 (NSP3/1/18), MNA (emphasis added). This was to happen again in the 1950s: Port Herald District Annual Reports (Agriculture), 1954–55, 1956–57, 1958–59 (8.7.5F/7306), MNA.

55. Chikwawa District Annual Reports (Agriculture), 1961–62 (1 October 1961–30 September 1962) (3.6.10R/16559, Ag. 3), MNA.

56. Department of Agriculture (Blantyre) to DA, Soil Conservation: Lower Shire, 9 August 1947 (2.17.7F/880), MNA.

57. Ibid.

58. Nsanje District Monthly Reports (Administration), March 1965 (10.1.9F/32154), MNA.

59. Ibid., April 1965.

60. Ibid., March 1968 (19.3.3F/14968), MNA.

61. Ibid., May 1965 (10.1.9F/32154), MNA. It was partly because of this disappoint-ment that the leadership chose to provide greater support to "estate" farming; see Minister of Agriculture (Gwanda Chakuamba) to All Field Staff of the Ministry of Agriculture, August 1969 (17.16.2R/40370), MNA; Kydd and Christiansen, "Structural Change in Malawi."

62. On ridge destruction, see, among others, Port Herald District Monthly Reports (Agriculture), October 1960 (8.7.5F/7306); and on the destruction of bunds, see Chikwawa District Annual Reports (Agriculture), 1952–53 (1DCCK2/2/5), MNA.

63. Port Herald District Monthly Reports (Administration), October 1960 (8.7.6F/7310), MNA (emphasis added).

64. Chikwawa District Annual Reports (Agriculture), 1963–64 (1 October 1963–30 September 1964) (3.6.10R/16559, Ag. 3), MNA.

65. Port Herald District Monthly Reports (Administration), March 1968 (19.3.3F/14968), MNA.

66. Ibid., May 1968 (10.1.9F/32154), MNA.

67. Chikwawa District Annual Reports (Agriculture), 1963–64 (1 October 1963–30 September 1964) (3.6.10R/16559, Ag. 3), MNA. See also Nsanje District Monthly Reports (Administration), September 1968 (10.1.9F/32154), MNA.

68. Nsanje District Monthly Reports (Administration), October 1969 (10.1.9F/32154), MNA.

69. Nsanje District Monthly Reports (Administration), January 1967, October 1968, September 1969 (10.1.9F/32154); North Chikwawa District Monthly Reports (Agriculture), August–December 1970 (14.1.2F/40365), MNA.

70. Nsanje District Monthly Reports (Administration), September 1969 (10.1.9F/32154); Chikwawa District Monthly Reports (Administration), September 1969 (14.1.2R/40362), MNA.

71. Chikwawa District Monthly Reports (Administration), November 1969 (14.1.2R/40362), MNA.

72. Indeed, as one unsanitized report put it in 1970–71, one could everywhere see "well ridged gardens among really disappointing cases of shifting cultivation" (North Chikwawa District Annual Reports [Agriculture], 1970–71 [14.1.2F/40365, Ag. 5/2], MNA). The figure for Nsanje South (21%) looks like an overestimate; the resistance to mitumbira was fiercest here.

73. SVADP, "Farm Survey 1973/74 [Part II]: Farm Structure and Cropping Patterns" (Evaluation Section, July 1976): 18, table 6M, SVADP. Only 13 percent of the plots were ridged in Chikwawa in that season.

74. For a similar reaction in colonial Tanzania, see Steven Feierman, *Peasant Intellectuals: Anthropology and History in Tanzania* (Madison: University of Wisconsin Press, 1990).

75. SVADP, "Farm Survey 1973/74 [Part II]," 18.

76. The mounds would prevent Mbona, seen as a snake here, from visiting the land with his blessings of rain.

77. Port Herald District Monthly Reports (Agriculture), July 1933 (A3/2/201), MNA.

78. I have seen only one report referring to finger millet as a dimba crop, but I cannot locate it.

79. Another source of bias against sweet potatoes stems from the fact that the crop has been most popular in Nsanje South, which has not attracted official attention in the post-colonial era because it does not grow cotton. This same region was at the center of official imagination in the pre-Bomani era, when it produced most of the cotton from the country. Officials then covered almost every aspect of the area's economy, including its food crops.

80. NADD, "Garden Survey," 76.

81. In the 1930s, colonial officials identified at least 19 names in the vernacular, although as one report rightly warned, some varieties were known by more than one name. See Port Herald District Monthly Reports (Agriculture), April, July 1930 (A3/3/200); Chikwawa District Annual Report, 1954–55 (1DCCK2/2/5), MNA.

82. Port Herald District Monthly Reports (Agriculture), April 1930 (A3/2/200), MNA. For evidence that millet was ousting sorghum, see, among others, Port Herald District Monthly Reports (Agriculture), May, November 1934 (A3/2/201), MNA.

83. Better known among these were *dembera, kachiliwenda, khasikisakhowa, kotikoti, nkhondo,* and *transvaal.*

84. Port Herald District Monthly Reports (Agriculture), January 1931 (A3/2/200), MNA. See also ibid., March 1932, April 1930, 1933 (A3/2/200); November 1935 (A3/2/201), MNA.

85. According to one estimate, they yielded only between 1,000 and 1,200 pounds per acre on the average: ibid., March 1931 (A3/2/200), MNA.

86. Ibid., December 1930, MNA.

87. On the stem borer (*chilo* sp.), see Port Herald District Monthly Reports (Agriculture), February 1931 (A3/2/200), April 1933 (A3/2/201), MNA. The borer probably lived in a

larval state in the butts of the plants (Port Herald District Monthly Reports, April 1930 [A3/2/200], MNA). Kaswabanda (or Gwengwere) and Ndodzi were subject to these attacks (Port Herald District Monthly Reports [Agriculture], April 1932 [A3/2/200], MNA). Reports that mapira on newly opened gardens were immune from attacks were found to be untrue (ibid.). On witch weed (*Striga asiatica* O. Kuntze), see ibid. April, July 1933 (A3/2/201); and on smut (*Sphacelotheca sorghi*), see ibid., June 1931 (A3/2/200), April, July 1933 (A3/2/201), MNA. Smutted heads of mchewere were sent to the mycologist, who identified them as *Tolyposporium penicillariae* (ibid., June 1931, March 1932 [A3/2/200], MNA). Green ear or downy mildew was supposed to be caused by *Sclerospora graminicola* (ibid.).

88. The belief that the borer lived in a larval state in the butts of the plants led officials to recommend the burning of all stalks (Port Herald District Monthly Reports [Agriculture], April 1930, February 1931 [A3/2/200], MNA)—the same kind of remedy used against the red bollworm.

89. Identified as *Homorocoryphus vicinus* Wlk.

90. Port Herald District Monthly Reports (Agriculture), July 1933 (A3/2/201), MNA. The *mphombo,* which attacked the mchewere crop, was a nocturnal feeder (Port Herald District Monthly Reports [Agriculture], February 1935 [A3/2/201], MNA).

91. Port Herald District Monthly Reports (Agriculture), January 1932 (A3/2/200), MNA.

92. Officials called weaverbirds what Africans refer to as *machocho* or *machete.* The term *waxbill finches* is supposed to refer to what peasants called *dzanjo*. But this may not be the case; officials initially identified dzanjo as a species of Taylor bird (Port Herald District Monthly Reports [Agriculture], July, August 1930 [A3/2/200], MNA).

93. Port Herald District Monthly Reports (Agriculture), July 1930 (A3/2/200), MNA.

94. Ibid., May 1933 (A3/2/201), MNA.

95. Port Herald District Monthly Reports (Agriculture), March 1932 (A3/2/200), MNA. See also ibid., March 1931, MNA, where the British attributed the popularity of the crop to the fact that it "keeps well when stored and is therefore an insurance against famine."

96. Ibid.

97. Port Herald District Monthly Reports (Agriculture), July 1933 (A3/2/201), MNA.

98. I have yet to find an account of the relationship between the general climatic cycle leading to the desiccation of the marshes in 1880–1940 and rainfall patterns in the hills.

99. SVADP, *Atlas of the Lower Shire Valley*, under "Meteorology." In the same period, only 25.61 inches of rain fell around Ndakwera on the valley floor (ibid.).

100. Foskett, *Kirk,* 1:209; Wallis, *Livingstone*, 1:104–5.

101. For what Mr. Frank Barker (agricultural officer) called a "brief and incomplete agricultural description of some of the varieties of rice which are found cultivated on the Lower River," see Port Herald District Annual Reports (Agriculture), December 1934 (A3/2/201), MNA. He listed 13 varieties on the basis of such factors as height, age in days, yield, and so on. The 13 are Nkuta, Ngungunda A, Mpunga Mkhundi, Bungala A, Singano A, Thyolakhosi, Namichila, Rega A, India, Rega B, Ngungunda B, Bangala B, and Singano B.

102. Port Herald District Monthly Reports (Agriculture), April 1931 (A3/2/200), February 1933 (A3/2/201), MNA. It appears that Msafili was also of foreign origin (ibid., February 1933).

103. Port Herald District Monthly Reports (Agriculture), February 1932 (A3/2/200), MNA. The name *machewere* was applied to rice that ripened at the same time as mchewere millet (ibid., March 1932, MNA).

104. Some varieties of the white rice Livingstone saw in the Lower Zambezi originated from North Carolina: Livingstone and Livingstone, *Narrative*, 406.

105. Port Herald District Monthly Reports (Agriculture), February, April, October 1933 (A3/2/201), MNA.

106. Ibid., October 1933. The list included india, khundi, *namichila, rega, ngungunda,* and *nkuta.*

107. Ibid., February 1932 (A3/2/200), November 1933 (A3/2/201), MNA.

108. Ibid., December 1930 (A3/2/200), MNA.

109. Ibid., March, April, June 1931 (A3/2/200), May 1933 (A3/2/201), MNA; interview with: Windo Kampira, Antonio Mwanaleza, Antonio Nyakanyanza, Chanazi Nyakanyanza, Tambo Village, STA Mbenje, Nsanje, 4 July 1995 (TCM95/2).

110. Government attempts to promote rice growing in the valley in the postcolonial era focused on the Taiwanese-sponsored irrigated-rice schemes in the Katunga (Kasinthula), Makhwira, and Mlolo chiefdoms.

111. See, among others, Port Herald District Annual Reports (Agriculture), 1955–56, 1957–58 (8.7.5F/7306); Port Herald District Annual Reports (Administration), 1954 (8.7.5F/7310), MNA.

112. Port Herald District Annual Reports (Agriculture), February 1932 (A3/2/200), MNA. See also ibid., May 1931, MNA. For the persistence of this marketing problem well into the postcolonial era, see, among others, Northern Chikwawa District Monthly Reports (Agriculture), May 1965 (3.6.10R/16559, Ag. 3), MNA. Thus, when pressured for time, villagers often short-circuited the rice cycle. They would, for example, cut the heads while still green, sun-dry them, and turn to other activities like the growing of sweet potatoes: Port Herald District Monthly Reports (Agriculture), April 1932 (A3/2/200), MNA. The MCP apparently fought the cooperative moment before independence. Their subsequent support for the same movement left many local politicians in a bind, as one district commissioner (British) for Chikwawa was only too happy to report: "It is also noted that one of the leading political parties in the country is a strong supporter of the Co-operative movement. This placed Chief Makhwira who has consistently opposed the Lower River Rice Co-operative Society's activities in his area in the awkward position of being on the 'wrong side of the fence'. He therefore had to do a volte face and has assured Government that the scheme is now a good one and will work in his area" (Chikwawa District Monthly Report [Administration], June 1961 [ADM 12/1], MNA).

113. Unlike the Sena, the Mang'anja did not like rice, which they sometimes derisively called *mfunye*—worm. This may be the basis of the following observation by one colonial official: "The Lower River natives do not look upon rice as a staple food. It is only used by bachelors and grass widowers who have no wife to make and cook ufa and have to shift [?] for themselves" (Port Herald District Monthly Reports [Agriculture], February 1932 [A3/2/200], MNA). For more evidence on how the lack of markets adversely affected rice production, see Chikwawa North Monthly Reports (Agriculture), May 1965 (3.6.10R/1655, Ag. 3), MNA.

114. NADD, "Garden Survey," chapter 4, table 4.9. These were followed by Tomali Plain (28%), Makande Plain (21%), Nsanje South (12%), and Nsanje North (11%).

115. Interview with Lendison July Gawani, Mphamba Village, TA Ngabu, Chikwawa, 21 April 1995 (SM95/5)

116. Chikwawa District Monthly Reports (Administration), 16 March–15 April 1952 (19458II), MNA.

117. Ibid., July 1960 (ADM 12/1), MNA.

118. Ibid., April 1961, MNA. See also chapter 4.

119. Chikwawa District Monthly Reports (Agriculture), January 1980 (11.4.9F/40352, Ag. 10/2), MNA.

120. Chikwawa District Monthly Report (Administration), March 1971 (14.1.2R/40362), MNA. That peasants from the area also sell their groundnuts in Mozambique for lack of markets in Malawi, see ibid., April 1969, MNA.

121. In 2003 the Dabanyi was underwater at late as July, which worried growers, eager to open new fields in the marshes: Sister Bertha Khaula, telephone conversation, 18 July 2003 (TCM03/2).

122. Waller papers; Waller diaries, 4:18 (June 20, 1863); see also 4:12 (August 26, 1862); Livingstone and Livingstone, *Narrative,* 102; Foskett, *Kirk,* 1:173; Wallis, *Livingstone,* 1:92.

123. Port Herald District Monthly Reports (Agriculture), March 1932 (A3/2/200), MNA.

124. Ibid., August 1933 (A3/2/201), MNA.

125. Lower Shire District Monthly Reports (Agriculture), March 1931, February 1932 (A3/2/200), MNA.

126. *SAP* 20 (November 1907): 178. See also *SAP* 21 (August 1908): 130; *SAP* 25 (October 1912): 162; *SAP* 26 (January 1913): 11.

127. Peasants in the valley have doggedly resisted cassava or manioc.

128. Most significant among these were *chaina* and *mache.*

129. See especially Lower River District Annual Reports (Administration), 1949 (NSP3/1/18), MNA.

130. See, among others, "Region Could Save $12m in Food Imports," *Financial Gazette* (Harare), http://allafrica.com/stories/printable/200312040171.html.

CHAPTER 7: THE DAILY MEAL

1. African Way of Life Club, "Bantu Wisdom: A Collection of Proverbs" (unpublished MS, Kachebere Major Seminary): item 142.

2. The song was recorded by and reproduced here with the permission of Dr. Enoch Timpunza-Mvula. Oral history does, of course, offer another picture of a mother-in-law, who brews beer to thank her hard-working son-in-law: Chafulumira, *Mbiri ya Amang'anja*, 23–24; interview with Martin Ndauza Leza, Leza Village, TA Makhwira, Chikwawa, 30 January 1980 (TVES1/12).

3. Interview with Mrs. Sigresi Lingstonya Zachepa, Vinancio Zachepa, Njereza Village, TA Kasisi, Chikwawa, 8 July 1995 (TCM95/7).

4. Megan Vaughan is a notable exception. She tried to deal with the problem, although from the perspective of crisis; see her *Story of an African Famine*, 119–47.

5. African Way of Life Club, "Bantu Wisdom," item 145.

6. Although I use the definite article before "alternative vision," I do not believe it is the only theory countering the golden-age theory.

7. Gould, *Time's Arrow Time's Cycle*, 16.

8. Eliade, *The Myth of Eternal Return.*

9. Gould, *Time's Arrow Time's Cycle,* 15–16.

10. Interview with Tiwongolera Bayisi, Njereza Village, TA Kasisi, Chikwawa, 13 April 1995 (SM95/1).

11. Interview with Bernard Inesi Demba, Chapepa Village, TA Ngabu, Nsanje, 10 May 1995 (SM95/9).

12. Two women who draw water from the same well or river would invite one another for a meal, and that would mark the beginning of chidyerano.

13. Henry Genti, Maere Village, TA Mbenje, Nsanje, 8 June 1995 (SM95/17).

14. In this case, colonial anthropology might have exaggerated but did not invent the association between change and moral decay: see Moore and Vaughan, *Cutting Down Trees*.

15. See the poem opening chapter 2, which was recorded by Dr. Samuel Safuli.

16. *Central Africa: A Record of the Work of the Universities Mission* (1895), 13:66–67; Schoffeleers, *River of Blood*, 100; idem, "Mang'anja Religion and History," 49:230.

17. Tiwongolera Bayisi, Njereza Village, TA Kasisi, Chikwawa, 13 April 1995 (SM95/1).

18. Washeni Semba, Khembo Village, STA Mbenje, Nsanje, 8 June 1995 (SM95/19).

19. Laisoni Musaika and Mrs. Musaika, Mtambo Village, TA Makhwira, Chikwawa, 26 May 1995 (SM95/13); Jasten Nasho, Nyangu II Village, TA Makhwira, Chikwawa, 27 May 1995 (SM95/14); Washeni Semba, Khembo Village, STA Mbenje, Nsanje, 8 June 1995 (SM95/19).

20. We will focus on gender, keeping in mind that what is said about women also applies to children.

21. Arnold Kukhala (an employee of Cotton Ginnery Limited), Jambo Village, TA Mbenje, Nsanje, 2 July 1995 (TCM95/1).

22. Berry and Petty, *The Nyasaland Survey Papers*, 222.

23. A.C. Williamson, "Notes on Some Changes in the Malawi Diet over the Last 30 Years," *Society of Malawi Journal* 25, 2 (1972): 52.

24. Moreover, the fact that harvesting coincides with so many other agricultural activities always creates a demand for extra-household labor (see chapter 5).

25. Gregorio Usseni, telephone conversation, 13 May 1998 (TCM98/1).

26. Ibid.; Frederick Lebala and Albert Mvula, Mpangeni Village, TA Kasisi, 18 April 1995 (SM95/3).

27. Gregorio Usseni, telephone conversation, 13 May 1998 (TCM98/1); Henry Genti, Maere Village, TA Mbenje, Nsanje, 8 June 1995 (SM95/17).

28. Helemesi Pepala, Mwalija Village, TA Kasisi, Chikwawa, 18 April 1995 (SM95/4).

29. Gregorio Usseni, telephone conversation, 13 May 1998 (TCM98/1); Frederick Lebala and Albert Mvula, Mpangeni Village, TA Kasisi, 18 April 1995 (SM95/3); Washeni Lazaro, Malemia I Village, TA Ngabu, Chikwawa, 21 April 1995 (SM95/6); Mchelengi Nkhambala, Malemia II Village, TA Ngabu, Chikwawa 21 April 1995 (SM95/7); Mrs. S. Antonio, Magulugulu Village, TA Malemia, Nsanje, 26 April 1995 (SM95/8); Bernard Inesi Demba, Chapepa Village, TA Ngabu, Nsanje, 10 May 1995 (SM95/9); Mrs. Farensa Makaniso, Chazuka I Village, TA Chimombo, Nsanje, 10 May 1995 (SM95/10); Tayipi Alfred, Mafumbi Village, TA Makhwira, Chikwawa, 17 May 1995 (SM95/11).

30. Gregorio Usseni, telephone conversation, 13 May 1998 (TCM98/1).

31. Ibid.; Helemesi Pepala, Mwalija Village, TA Kasisi, Chikwawa, 18 April 1995 (SM95/4); Bernard Inesi Demba, Chapepa Village, TA Ngabu, Nsanje, 10 May 1995 (SM95/9); Mrs. Farensa Makaniso, Chazuka I Village, TA Chimombo, Nsanje, 10 May 1995 (SM95/10).

32. Gregorio Usseni, telephone conversation, 13 May 1998 (TCM98/1). For the container's origin, see interviews with Tiwongolera Bayisi, Njereza Village, TA Kasisi, Chikwawa, 13 April 1995 (SM95/1); Naphiri Chikhambi (headman's wife) and Mrs. Elizabeth Lusiano Mwachumu, Chikhambi Village, TA Kasisi, 13 April 1995 (SM95/2).

33. Gregorio Usseni, telephone conversation, 13 May 1998 (TCM98/1); Helemesi Pepala, Mwalija Village, TA Kasisi, Chikwawa, 18 April 1995 (SM95/4); Mchelengi Nkhambala, Malemia Village (II), TA Ngabu, Chikwawa 21 April 1995 (SM95/7). See the glossary for the botanical term of *chitowe*.

34. For the use of khungulu as an alternative to nkhokwe for storing grains before and after the threshing, see interviews with Mchelengi Nkhambala, Malemia II Village, TA Ngabu, Chikwawa 21 April 1995 (SM95/7); Mrs. S. Antonio, Magulugulu Village, TA Malemia, Nsanje, 26 April 1995 (SM95/8); Laisoni Musaika and Mrs. Musaika, Mtambo Village, TA Makhwira, Chikwawa, 26 May 1995 (SM95/13); Jasten Nasho, Nyangu II Village, TA Makhwira, Chikwawa, 27 May 1995 (SM95/14); Tsamdoka Renso, Mrs. Renso, Dreva Chibonga, one other informant, Chikunkhu Village, TA Tengani, Nsanje, 4 June 1995 (SM95/15); Magireni Theka, Chikunkhu Village, TA Tengani, Nsanje, 6 June 1995 (SM95/16); Elia Mchawa, Erita Switi, Elizabeth Anthuachino, Dina Sabe, and Selina Kanyenzi, Khembo Village, STA Mbenje, Nsanje, 8 June 1995 (SM95/18).

35. Those who had full nkhokwe of food but did not share it with their hungry neighbors were liable to being accused of ntholera, the magic that entices other people's food into one's nkhokwe (see chapters 2 and 4).

36. Lendison July Gawani, Mphamba Village, TA Ngabu, Chikwawa, 21 April 1995 (SM95/5); Mchelengi Nkhambala, Malemia II Village, TA Ngabu, Chikwawa, 21 April 1995 (SM95/7); Mrs. S. Antonio, Magulugulu Village, TA Malemia, Nsanje, 26 April 1995 (SM95/8); Laisoni Musaika and Mrs. Musaika, Mtambo Village, TA Makhwira, Chikwawa, 26 May 1995 (SM95/13); Jasten Nasho, Nyangu II Village, TA Makhwira, Chikwawa, 27 May 1995 (SM95/14); Tsamdoka Renso, Mrs. Renso, Dreva Chibonga, one other informant, Chikunkhu Village, TA Tengani, Nsanje, 4 June 1995 (SM95/15); Magireni Theka, Chikunkhu Village, TA Tengani, Nsanje, 6 June 1995 (SM95/16); Elia Mchawa, Erita Switi, Elizabeth Anthuachino, Dina Sabe, and Selina Kanyenzi, Khembo Village, STA Mbenje, Nsanje, 8 June 1995 (SM95/18).

37. This may be the point to briefly outline some methods of preserving planting seeds. Peasants sometimes select grains for use as seed before threshing, choosing the healthiest millet, sorghum, and maize while on the cob, and hang them in a tree or roof to make sure they were beyond the reach of vermin and weevils (see Mchelengi Nkhambala, Malemia II Village, TA Ngabu, Chikwawa, 21 April 1995 [SM95/7]; Mrs. S.Antonio, Magulugulu Village, TA Malemia, Nsanje, 26 April 1995 [SM95/8]; Jasten Nasho, Nyangu II Village, TA Makhwira, Chikwawa, 27 May 1995 [SM95/14]; Henry Genti, Maere Village, TA Mbenje, Nsanje, 8 June 1995 [SM95/17]). In another method, villagers choose seeds after threshing and store the grains in the same manner as they do for, though separate from, the cereals for consumption.

38. This is largely because, unlike their counterparts in other parts of Malawi, peasants in the valley do not typically turn cassava into ufa flour for nsima.

39. Interview with Mrs. Leni Pereira, Chitsa Village, TA Tengani, Nsanje, 5 November 1991 (EPT91/13).

40. Ibid.

41. There were already mechanical grinding mills in the valley in the 1910s, but these were not for use by villagers; they mostly served the needs of private companies (see chapter 1). See also Williamson, "Notes on Some Changes," which notes that "with a maize diet, the so-called protein gap is not so large as often portrayed" (52).

42. R. T. Ellis, "The Food Properties of Flint and Dent Maize," *East African Agricultural Journal* 24 (April 1959): 251–53.

43. Interview with Mrs. Leni Pereira, Chitsa Village, TA Tengani, Nsanje, 5 November 1991 (EPT91/13). Besides factory-made plates, not much has changed in the way women prepare nsima. Moreover, studies of other Malawian communities in the 1940s suggest that this stability is also spatial. There are striking similarities between what researchers have recorded in the Tchiri Highlands and the Lakeshore areas and my own findings on the Tchiri

Valley (Williamson, *Useful Plants,* 128–29; Berry and Petty, *The Nyasaland Survey Papers,* 239–41). But the beer brewing practices of the valley (see chapter 2) appear to differ quite significantly from those of the highlands (See Williamson, *Useful Plants,* 132–35).

44. Interview with Mrs. Leni Pereira, Chitsa Village, TA Tengani, Nsanje, 5 November 1991 (EPT91/13). Children drink the milky water from the pot.

45. See the glossary for the botanical terms of *chinangwa* and *mbatatesi.*

46. Ms. Chrissie Chawanje, telephone conversation, undated [mid-1990s] (TCMUN/1).

47. J. Barker, "Nyasaland Native Food," *Nyasaland Times*, 1940 (PAM/458/MNA), 4, 21.

48. Ibid., 23.

49. They call the leaves of sesame *umphedza,* while the term *nkhwani* denotes different things among the Mang'anja and Sena. Among the Mang'anja, *nkhwani* refers to pump-kin leaves—see Williamson, *Useful Plants,* 44; D.C. Scott, *A Cyclopaedic Dictionary of the Mang'anja Language Spoken in British Central Africa* (Hants, England: Gregg International Publishers, 1968 [1892])—whereas among the Sena it means the leaves of *khobwe* cowpeas. The Mang'anja call the leaves of khobwe cowpeas *khwanya* (Mrs. Rosta Msaka, personal communication, 21 October 2000 [TCM00/1]).

50. Barker, "Nyasaland Native Food," 8.

51. They sometimes flavor these with tomatoes (ibid., 7–8).

52. Ibid., 11–12.

53. The Sena call catfish *nsomba,* which is otherwise the generic term for all kinds of fish in Chichewa and Chimanga'anja languages.

54. The list includes *dande, makakana, manjole, mphuta, ncheni, nkhonokono, nkupe,* and *usipa.*

55. Barker, "Nyasaland Native Food," 16.

56. Ibid., 8, 14.

57. Ibid., 9–10.

58. This is based on the estimate that there were about 45,200 households in Chikwawa District in the mid-1980s: Chikwawa District Project Officer's Monthly Report, December 1984 (11.4.9F/40352), MNA.

59. People say there is njala if there is no ufa flour for nsima: *SAP* 26 (January 1913): 11.

60. See also J. Barker, "Part Played by Legumes in the Diet of the Nyasaland African with Notes on the Cooking and Palatability of a Number of Different Kinds," *Nyasaland Agricultural Quarterly Journal* 4, 2 (April 1944): 15–26.

61. This is the subject of a recent study: C. Brantley, *Feeding Families: African Realities and British Ideas of Nutrition and Development in Early Colonial Africa* (Portsmouth, NH: Heinemann, 2002).

62. Berry and Petty, *The Nyasaland Survey Papers.* But the evidence remains inconclu-sive on many issues.

63. Malawi Ministry of Health, "Lower Shire Nutrition Survey" (Report of a Nutritional Status and Dietary Survey Carried Out in Ngabu Area, April–May 1970), MNA.

64. Ibid.

65. Interview with Mrs. Sigresi Lingstonya Zachepa, Vinancio Zachepa, Njereza Village, TA Kasisi, Chikwawa, 8 July 1995 (TCM95/7).

66. Liberal translation of a Malawian proverb that runs as follows: "Ali awiri si mantha, kuipa kutha ndiwo m'mbale." I am grateful to Mrs. Rosta Msaka for this proverb.

67. See especially Watts, *Silent Violence.*

68. Interviews with Tiwongolera Bayisi, Njereza Village, TA Kasisi, Chikwawa, 13 April 1995 (SM95/1); Mchelengi Nkhambala, Malemia II Village, TA Ngabu, Chikwawa, 21 April 1995 (SM95/7); Tayipi Alfred, Mafumbi Village, TA Makhwira, Chikwawa, 17

May 1995 (SM95/11); Jasten Nasho, Nyangu II Village, TA Makhwira, Chikwawa, 27 May 1995 (SM95/14); Washeni Semba, Khembo Village, STA Mbenje, Nsanje, 8 June 1995 (SM95/19).

69. That boys used to eat separately in their dormitory, see, among others, Nsayi Bira Mbesa, Tambo Village, STA Mbenje, Nsanje, 5 July 1995 (TCM95/3); Mchelengi Nkhambala, Malemia II Village, TA Ngabu, Chikwawa, 21 April 1995 (SM95/7); Elia Mchawa, Erita Switi, Elizabeth Anthuachino, Dina Sabe, and Selina Kanyenzi, Khembo Village, STA Mbenje, Nsanje, 8 June 1995 (SM95/18). That they joined married men, see, among others, Elena Chagwa, with Asiteva Faifi, Calista Mikaeli, Tsapa Village, TA Kasisi, Chikwawa, 7 July 1995 (TCM95/6); Washeni Semba, Khembo Village, STA Mbenje, Nsanje, 8 June 1995 (SM95/19). Girls do not appear to have left the women's eating group after reaching puberty, although they also slept in an all-girls' dormitory.

70. The Sena words *zjantari* and *siyali* are from the Portuguese *jantar* (lunch) and *ceia* (the noun) or *cear* (the verb) (supper), and no one now seems to know the original Sena nomenclature. This is not, however, the only instance where Portuguese has displaced old and culturally loaded Sena words. Even those Sena who have never been to school greet each other in Portuguese today.

71. The Mang'anja and Sena thus referred to eating as a member of chidyerano as *kudya pa bwalo* and *kudya pa thando,* respectively.

72. It seems that the taboo against eggs is now a thing of the past.

73. Mrs. Leni Pereira, Chitsa Village, TA Tengani, Nsanje, 5 November 1991 (EPT91/13).

74. In the past, chiefs and headpersons used to receive the hind leg of wild and some domesticated animals, but the practice seems to have died out.

75. Mrs. Khembo, Tsapa Village, TA Kasisi, Chikwawa, 30 August 1994 (TCM94/1); Karota Tsaibola, Chikhambi Village, TA Katunga, Chikwawa, 30 August 1994 (TCM94/2); Donaciano Mark and Mrs. Chiwanga, Namila Village, TA Kasisi, Chikwawa, August 1994 (TCM94/3); Mrs. Nkhani, Rabu Village, TA Ngabu, Chikwawa, 1 September, 1994 (TCM94/4); Ester Chibani and Amideresi Abraham, Migano Village, TA Katunga, Chikwawa, August–September 1994 (TCM94/5).

76. Ibid.

77. Ibid.

78. Mrs. Leni Pereira, Chitsa Village, TA Tengani, Nsanje, 5 November 1991 (EPT91/13). Wives who complained about this kind of behavior received unqualified support; the kitchen was a woman's domain. Women also resented and felt betrayed when their husbands monopolized meat and forced them to eat masamba vegetables in a supplementary meal couples took alone inside their houses. Such behavior spoiled the spirit of the snack, which symbolized the couple's intimacy and unity against outsiders, particularly the members of the chidyerano meal. Such behavior on the part of the husband could constitute grounds for divorce: Damison Kulima Tambo, Kolina Chipondeni Tambo, Tambo Village, STA Mbenje, Nsanje, 5 July 1995 (TCM95/4).

79. Rosta Msaka, telephone conversation, 21 October 2000 (TCM00/1).

80. I sometimes got the impression that they wanted me, as an "educated" and therefore more powerful person, to intercede on their behalf with their husbands, just as disgruntled cotton growers always thought I was going to bring their concerns to government officials.

81. Berry and Petty, *The Nyasaland Survey Papers,* 223.

82. People refer to a well-behaved child (or even adult) as *mwana wobvinidwa* and the opposite as *mwana wosabvinidwa* or *mwana wopanda mwambo.* One can be mwana wosabvinidwa or mwana wopanda mwambo even after going through the initiation process.

83. The Sena sometimes call the small second funerary rites *kulilisa* ("to mourn for someone"). According to some sources (Windo Kampira, Antonio Mwanaleza, Antonio

Nyakanyanza, Chanazi Nyakanyanza, Tambo Village, STA Mbenje, Nsanje, 4 July 1995 [TCM95/2]), kulilisa was the only second funeral people held for certain ethnic and social groups, like the Tonga of the Tembo clan and people of mixed African and European descent (*nyakazungu*).

84. For a sampling of the oral sources, see Tiwongolera Bayisi, Njereza Village, TA Kasisi, Chikwawa, 13 April 1995 (SM95/1); Naphiri Chikhambi (headman's wife) and Mrs. Elizabeth Lusiano Mwachumu, Chikhambi Village, TA Kasisi, 13 April 1995 (SM95/2); Helemesi Pepala, Mwalija Village, TA Kasisi, Chikwawa, 18 April 1995 (SM95/4); Washeni Lazaro, Malemia I Village, TA Ngabu, Chikwawa, 21 April 1995 (SM95/6); Mrs. S. Antonio, Magulugulu Village, TA Malemia, Nsanje, 26 April 1995 (SM95/8); Tayipi Alfred, Mafumbi Village, TA Makhwira, Chikwawa, 17 May 1995 (SM95/11).

85. The rituals also served as an occasion for the Magololo and their clients to select new wives and to renew their alliances with members of the powerful nyau village associations; see E. Mandala, "The Kololo Interlude in Southern Malawi: A Study of Political Entrepreneurship in Nineteenth Century Malawi" (M.A. thesis, University of Malawi, 1977): 112–13.

86. J.M. Schoffeleers, "From Socialization to Personal Enterprise: A History of the *Nomi* Labor Societies in Nsanje District of Malawi, c. 1891–1972," *Rural Africana* 20 (Spring 1973): 11–25.

87. J.M. Schoffeleers, "The *Nyau* Societies: Our Present Understanding," *Society of Malawi Journal* 29 (January 1976): 59–68; I. Linden and J.M. Schoffeleers, "The Resistance of the *Nyau* Societies to the Roman Catholic Missions in Colonial Malawi," in *The Historical Study of African Religion,* ed. T.O. Ranger and I. Kimambo (London: Heinemann, 1972) 252–73; I. Linden and J. Linden, *Catholics, Peasants, and Chewa Resistance in Nyasaland, 1889–1939* (London: Heinemann, 1974).

88. Schoffeleers, "From Socialization to Personal Enterprise."

89. *SAP* 38 (September–October 1925): 105; *SAP* 45 (August–September 1932): 108; Chikwawa District Annual Reports (Administration), 1932 (NSC2/1/4), 1936 (S1/66B/37); Port Herald District Annual Reports (Administration), 1932 (S1/43A/33); Lower Shire District Book 4, 1928–32, MNA.

90. For a very vivid and ethnocentric description of mabzyoka, see *SAP* 13, 12 (December 1900): 213; *SAP* 15, 5 (May 1902): 74.

91. Today, peasant women afflicted by the same diseases flock to African Pentecostal Churches.

92. Interview with Windo Kampira, Antonio Mwanaleza, Antonio Nyakanyanza, Chanazi Nyakanyanza, Tambo Village, STA Mbenje, Nsanje, 4 July 1995 (TCM95/2).

93. Washeni Semba, Khembo Village, STA Mbenje, Nsanje, 8 June 1995 (SM95/19).

94. Schoffeleers, *Lower Shire Valley.*

95. Village Headwoman Malita Chimtedza, Chimtedza Village, STA Mbenje, Nsanje, 6 July 1995 (TCM95/5).

96. Ibid.; Elena Chagwa, with Asiteva Faifi, Calista Mikaeli, Tsapa Village, TA Kasisi, Chikwawa, 7 July 1995 (TCM95/6).

97. Linden and Schoffeleers, "The Resistance of the *Nyau* Societies"; Linden and Linden, *Catholics, Peasants, and Chewa Resistance.*

98. Interviews with Nsayi Bira Mbesa, Tambo Village, STA Mbenje, Nsanje, 5 July 1995 (TCM95/3); Damison Kulima Tambo, Kolina Chipondeni Tambo, Tambo Village, STA Mbenje, Nsanje, 5 July 1995 (TCM95/4); Village Headwoman Malita Chimtedza, Chimtedza Village, STA Mbenje, Nsanje, 6 July 1995 (TCM95/5); Elena Chagwa, with Asiteva Faifi, Calista Mikaeli, Tsapa Village, TA Kasisi, Chikwawa, 7 July 1995 (TCM95/6).

99. Village Headwoman Malita Chimtedza, Chimtedza Village, STA Mbenje, Nsanje, 6 July 1995 (TCM95/5).

100. Sen, *Poverty and Famines.*

101. I will let the students of Lévi-Strauss interpret this for themselves.

102. This is the same as *nyama yabaya-baya,* which literally means meat you pick with a fork or something similar.

103. Williamson, *Useful Plants,* 53–54, 87–88, 92–93, 111–12, 127–33.

104. These are baked or roasted pastries for which I have no English equivalents.

105. Bernard Inesi Demba, Chapepa Village, TA Ngabu, Nsanje, 10 May 1995 (SM95/9); see also Washeni Semba, Khembo Village, STA Mbenje, Nsanje, 8 June 1995 (SM95/19).

106. One good example is the Danish beer Carlsberg, which is now brewed in Malawi and competes not only with traditional alcohols but also with imports from South Africa and Zimbabwe.

107. See S. W. Mintz, *Sweetness and Power: The Place of Sugar in Modern History* (New York: Viking Penguin, 1990).

108. According to Williamson (*Useful Plants,* 36–37, 78–80, 137), they also made kachasu from the fermented juice of cashew nuts, cassava, and certain kinds of trees.

109. See also Barker, "Nyasaland Native Food," 18–19.

110. The independent state of Malawi, particularly the more tolerant post-Banda regime, has given up the fight, and villagers brew the liquor in the open.

111. Bernard Inesi Demba, Chapepa Village, TA Ngabu, Nsanje, 10 May 1995 (SM95/9); see also Washeni Semba, Khembo Village, STA Mbenje, Nsanje, 8 June 1995 (SM95/19).

112. Arnold Kukhala (an employee of Cotton Ginnery Limited), Jambo Village, TA Mbenje, Nsanje, 2 July 1995 (TCM95/1); Henry Genti, Maere Village, TA Mbenje, Nsanje, 8 June 1995 (SM95/17).

113. Bernard Inesi Demba, Chapepa Village, TA Ngabu, Nsanje, 10 May 1995 (SM95/9). See also Elia Mchawa, Erita Switi, Elizabeth Anthuachino, Dina Sabe, and Selina Kanyenzi, Khembo Village, STA Mbenje, Nsanje, 8 June 1995 (SM95/18); Arnold Kukhala (an employee of Cotton Ginnery Limited), Jambo Village, TA Mbenje, Nsanje, 2 July 1995 (TCM95/1).

114. See, for example, interviews with Naphiri Chikhambi (headman's wife) and Mrs. Elizabeth Lusiano Mwachumu, Chikhambi Village, TA Kasisi, 13 April 1995 (SM95/2); Mrs. S. Antonio, Magulugulu Village, TA Malemia, Nsanje, 26 April 1995 (SM95/8); Mrs. Farensa Makaniso, Chazuka I Village, TA Chimombo, Nsanje, 10 May 1995 (SM95/10). For the second kind of arrangement, in which women alternated in cooking for the group, see Tiwongolera Bayisi, Njereza Village, TA Kasisi, Chikwawa, 13 April 1995 (SM95/1); Mrs. S. Antonio, Magulugulu Village, TA Malemia, Nsanje, 26 April 1995 (SM95/8); Washeni Semba, Khembo Village, STA Mbenje, Nsanje, 8 June 1995 (SM95/19). But according to Audrey Richards, the Bemba did not like eating several foods, especially ndiwo, at one and the same meal: Richards, *Land, Labour and Diet.*

115. Barker, "Nyasaland Native Food," 2. As she wrote: "Possibly some other wife also will have cooked *so that there are a choice of dishes*" (emphasis added).

116. In the predominantly matrilineal Kasisi chiefdom of Chikwawa, for example, relatives of the wife ate as visitors at 12 of 14 meals.

117. African Way of Life Club, "Bantu Wisdom," item 142.

CONCLUSION: ORDER AND DISORDER COPILOT THE SAME SPACESHIP

1. Gould, *Time's Arrow Time's Cycle,* 8.

BIBLIOGRAPHY

ORAL SOURCES

EPT Series

EPT91/1	Nsayi Mbalanyama Thabwa, Beleu Village, TA Lundu, Chikwawa, 13 October 1991.
EPT91/2	Anthony Bankamu Chipakuza, Chipakuza Village, TA Lundu, Chikwawa, 17 October 1991.
EPT91/3	Kamondo Suliali, location unknown, 19 October 1991.
EPT91/4	Efremu Makwaro, Mphamba Village, TA Ngabu, Chikwawa, 29 October 1991.
EPT91/5	Fernando Caetano Dzinga, Chitengo Village, Nsanje, October 1991.
EPT91/6	Chasasa Nyang'ombe Fole, Odriki Village, TA Chapananga, Chikwawa, October 1991.
EPT91/7	Nadumbo Kanthema, Mangulenje, Chikwawa, October 1991.
EPT91/8	Village Headman Tambo, Tambo Village, STA Mbenje, Nsanje, 3 November 1991.
EPT91/9	Mrs. Kolina Tambo, Tambo Village, STA Mbenje, Nsanje, 3 November 1991.
EPT91/10	Kolina Tambo, Emma Kondwani, Naphiri Mtawa, Everesi Yonasi, Ester Fred, Minima Nelson, Tambo Village, STA Mbenje, Nsanje, 3 November 1991.
EPT91/11	Etinala Fobrika, Nazaret Samuel, Tambo Village (?), STA Mbenje, Nsanje, 3 November 1991.
EPT91/12	Mrs. Patrishu, Mbande Village, TA Lundu, Chikwawa, 5 November 1991.
EPT91/13	Mrs. Leni Pereira, Chitsa Village, TA Tengani, Nsanje, 5 November 1991.
EPT91/14	Dafleni Chimatiro, Mafale Village, TA Lundu, Chikwawa, October–November 1991.
EPT91/15	Mfumu Zimola, Zimola Village, Chikwawa, October–November 1991.
EPT91/16	Unidentified Nsanje Tradition, Bangula (?), Nsanje, October–November 1991.

SM Series

SM95/1	Tiwongolera Bayisi, Njereza Village, TA Kasisi, Chikwawa, 13 April 1995.
SM95/2	Naphiri Chikhambi (headman's wife) and Mrs. Elizabeth Lusiano Mwachumu, Chikhambi Village, TA Kasisi, 13 April 1995.
SM95/3	Frederick Lebala and Albert Mvula, Mpangeni Village, TA Kasisi, 18 April 1995.
SM95/4	Helemesi Pepala, Mwalija Village, TA Kasisi, Chikwawa, 18 April 1995.
SM95/5	Lendison July Gawani, Mphamba Village, TA Ngabu, Chikwawa, 21 April 1995.
SM95/6	Washeni Lazaro, Malemia I Village, TA Ngabu, Chikwawa, 21 April 1995.
SM95/7	Mchelengi Nkhambala, Malemia II Village, TA Ngabu, Chikwawa 21 April 1995.
SM95/8	Mrs. S. Antonio, Magulugulu Village, TA Malemia, Nsanje, 26 April 1995.
SM95/9	Bernard Inesi Demba, Chapepa Village, TA Ngabu, Nsanje, 10 May 1995.
SM95/10	Mrs. Farensa Makaniso, Chazuka I Village, TA Chimombo, Nsanje, 10 May 1995.
SM95/11	Tayipi Alfred, Mafumbi Village, TA Makhwira, Chikwawa, 17 May 1995.
SM95/12	Fuleza Brown, Kasokeza Village, TA Makhwira, Chikwawa, 17 May 1995.
SM95/13	Laisoni Musaika and Mrs. Musaika, Mtambo Village, TA Makhwira, Chikwawa, 26 May 1995.
SM95/14	Jasten Nasho, Nyangu II Village, TA Makhwira, Chikwawa, 27 May 1995.
SM95/15	Tsamdoka Renso, Mrs. Renso, Dreva Chibonga, one other informant, Chikunkhu Village, TA Tengani, Nsanje, 4 June 1995.
SM95/16	Magireni Theka, Chikunkhu Village, TA Tengani, Nsanje, 6 June 1995.
SM95/17	Henry Genti, Maere Village, Mbenje, Nsanje, 8 June 1995.
SM95/18	Elia Mchawa, Erita Switi, Elizabeth Anthuachino, Dina Sabe, and Selina Kanyenzi, Khembo Village, STA Mbenje, Nsanje, 8 June 1995.
SM95/19	Washeni Semba, Khembo Village, STA Mbenje, Nsanje, 8 June 1995.
SM96/1	Timoti Davide, Ling'awa Village, TA Kasisi, Chikwawa, 16 May 1996.
SM96/2	Wikika Mbayenderana, Mbayenderana Village, TA Kasisi, Chikwawa, 16 May 1996.
SM96/3	Mrs. Namaluza Bonongwe, Mbayenderana Village, TA Kasisi, Chikwawa, 17 May 1996.
SM96/4	Daison House, Willasi Kacholola, David Nsabwe, Mbayenderana Village, TA Kasisi, Chikwawa, 17 May 1996.
SM96/5	Landison July Gawani, Mphamba Village, TA Ngabu, Chikwawa, 20 May 1996.
SM96/6	Magret Jongesi, Mphamba Village, TA Ngabu, Chikwawa, 20 May 1996.
SM96/7	A.M. Ndapasowa Banda, Mphamba Village, TA Ngabu, Chikwawa, 21 May 1996.
SM96/8	Snake Mthepheya, Kankhomba Village, STA Mbenje, Nsanje, 24 May 1996.
SM96/9	Mrs. Winesi Khofi, Mrs. Fazita Samuel, Mrs. Esnat Mandere, Mandere Village, TA Ngabu, Chikwawa, 25 May 1996.
SM96/10	Bonjesi Binzi Namizinga, J.V. Ngalu, Mandere Village, TA Ngabu, Chikwawa, 25 May 1996.

SM96/11   Master Hafulaini, Khembo Village, STA Mbenje, Nsanje, 27 May 1996.
SM96/12   Mrs. Dina Sabe, Mary Sabe, Khembo Village, STA Mbenje, Nsanje,
           27 May 1996.
SM96/13   Elizabeth Anthuachino, Selina Kanyezi, Elina Mchawa, Khembo Village,
           STA Mbenje, Nsanje, 30 May 1996.
SM96/14   Chiponyola Tomali, Tomali Village, TA Lundu, Chikwawa,
           10 June 1996.
SM96/15   Keyala Jailosi, James Jimu Kupheka, Baloni Yohane, Tomali Village,
           TA Lundu, Chikwawa, 10 June 1996.
SM96/16   Mrs. Enifa Kwenje, Mrs. Atafinu Petulo, Magret Jimu Mpheka,
           Tomali Village, TA Lundu, Chikwawa, 12 June 1996.
SM96/17   Elizabeth Jeke, Falena Keyala, Matinesi Laitoni, Victoria Mdzondo,
           Tomali Village, TA Lundu, Chikwawa, 12 June 1996.
SM96/18   Ronex Nyadani, Ndakwera Village, TA Chapananga, Chikwawa,
           14 June 1996.
SM96/19   Magira Daka, Joseph Edward Muyambutsa Ndakwera, Ndakwera
           Village, TA Chapananga, Chikwawa, 16 June 1996.
SM96/20   Mrs. Winalesi Kanyinji, Ndakwera Village, TA Chapananga, Chikwawa,
           16 June 1996.
SM96/21   Msambachulu Muyambutsa Ndakwera, Ndakwera Village, TA Chapananga,
           Chikwawa, 16 June 1996.

TCM Series

TCM94/1   Mrs. Khembo, Tsapa Village, TA Kasisi, Chikwawa, 30 August 1994.
TCM94/2   Karota Tsaibola, Chikhambi Village, TA Katunga, Chikwawa,
           30 August 1994.
TCM94/3   Donaciano Mark and Mrs. Chiwanga, Namila Village, TA Kasisi,
           Chikwawa, August 1994.
TCM94/4   Mrs. Nkhani, Rabu Village, TA Ngabu, Chikwawa, 1 September 1994.
TCM94/5   Ester Chibani and Amideresi Abraham, Migano Village, TA Katunga,
           Chikwawa, August–September 1994.
TCM95/1   Arnold Kukhala (an employee of Cotton Ginnery Limited), Jambo
           Village, TA Mbenje, Nsanje, 2 July 1995.
TCM95/2   Windo Kampira, Antonio Mwanaleza, Antonio Nyakanyanza, Chanazi
           Nyakanyanza, Tambo Village, STA Mbenje, Nsanje, 4 July 1995.
TCM95/3   Nsayi Bira Mbesa, Tambo Village, STA Mbenje, Nsanje, 5 July 1995.
TCM95/4   Damison Kulima Tambo, Kolina Chipondeni Tambo, Tambo Village,
           STA Mbenje, Nsanje, 5 July 1995.
TCM95/5   Village Headwoman Malita Chimtedza, Chimtedza Village, STA Mbenje,
           Nsanje, 6 July 1995.
TCM95/6   Elena Chagwa, with Asiteva Faifi, Calista Mikaeli, Tsapa Village, TA
           Kasisi, Chikwawa, 7 July 1995.
TCM95/7   Mrs. Sigresi Lingstonya Zachepa, Vinancio Zachepa, Njereza Village,
           TA Kasisi, Chikwawa, 8 July 1995.
TCM98/1   Gregorio Usseni, telephone conversation, 13 May 1998.
TCM00/1   Rosta Msaka, telephone conversation, 1 October 2000.

TCM01/1   Fabian Anthuacino, telephone conversation, November 2001.
TCM03/1   Peter K. Mandala, telephone conversation, 27 December 2003.
TCM03/2   Sister Bertha Khaula, telephone conversation, 18 July 2003.
TCMUN/1   Ms. Chrissie Chawanje, telephone conversation, undated [mid-1990s].

TVES Series

TVESl/12   Martin Ndauza Leza, Leza Village, TA Makhwira, Chikwawa,
            30 January 1980.
TVES2/3   Mathias Chimtanda Mlilima (former Chief Mlilima), Mlilima Village,
            TA Kasisi, Chikwawa, 26 February 1980.
TVES3/1   Yohane Mzanji, Mtchenyera Village, Sub Traditional Authority Mbenje,
            Nsanje, 1 April 1980.
TVES3/9   Yohane Mzanji, Mtchenyera Village, Sub Traditional Authority Mbenje,
            Nsanje, 3 April 1980.
TVES5/3   Christino Chibanzi, Nsayi Kanting'u, Joakina Sekeni, Nyathando
            Village, TA Ndamera, Nsanje, 8 September 1980.
TVES5/6   Jackson Kwaibvamtowe, Tursida Village, STA Mbenje, Nsanje,
            10 September 1980.
TVES5/8   Kapusi Chimombo, Chimombo Village, TA Chimombo, Nsanje,
            11 September 1980.
TVES5/9   Rampi Masamba, Tizola Village, TA Chimombo, Nsanje,
            11 September 1980.

M/CK Series

M/CK1   Matthias Chimtanda Mlilima (former Chief Mlilima), Mlilima Village,
            TA Kasisi, Chikwawa, 23 January 1976.
M/CK2   Chief Lucias Kasisi, Mr. Piano, Ms. Alindiana, Mr. Lawrence Njereza,
            TA Kasisi, Chikwawa, 25 January 1976.
M/CK4   Chief Joseph Maseya, TA Maseya, Chikwawa, 30 January 1976.

T73 Series

T73/8/2   Moshtishu, Chiphwembwe Village, TA Malemia, Nsanje, 9 and
            14 August 1973.
T73/8/5   David Makoko, Subchief Ostrich Makoko, Makoko Village,
            TA Chimombo, Nsanje, 16 August 1973.
T73/8/6   Chief Ngabu, Mr. Mpachika, Mr. Nyam'dzikwi, Ngabu Village,
            TA Ngabu, Nsanje, 16 August 1973.
T73/8/8   Headman Mphamba, Mphamba Village, TA Malemia, Nsanje,
            19 August 1973.

JMS Series

Schoffeleers, J.M. "Mang'anja Religion and History" (a collection of oral testimonies).

ARCHIVAL AND SPECIAL COLLECTIONS IN MALAWI

Malawi National Archives (MNA), Zomba

Annual, Quarterly, and Monthly Reports: District Administration and Department of Agriculture.

Malawi Ministry of Health, "Lower Shire Nutrition Survey" (Report of a Nutritional Status and Dietary Survey Carried Out in Ngabu Area, April–May 1970).

Shire Valley Agricultural Development Project (SVADP)

Chikwawa Cotton Development Project, "Agricultural Yield and Social Survey: A Sample Survey of Cotton Spraying Farmers in the Chikwawa Cotton Development Project, Involving Crop Areas and Yields and Incorporating a Socio-Economic Study" (September 1971).

Chikwawa Cotton Development Project, "Cattle Census and Sample Survey, 1971–72" (conducted by B.R. Mankhokwe and K.R.A. Oblitas of the Evaluation Section, September 1973).

Chikwawa Cotton Development Project, "Farm Survey, 1971/72: A Report on a Sample Survey Conducted in the 1971/72 Crop Growing Season on Cotton Growing Farming [*sic*] Households in the CCDP Area" (Evaluation Section, March 1973).

Chikwawa Cotton Development Project, "Farm Survey, 1972/73" (Evaluation Section, December 1974).

Ngabu Agricultural Development Division, "Garden Survey Report: Results of Garden Survey Conducted 77/8, 78/9, 79/80" (Evaluation Section, October 1981).

Ngabu Agricultural Development Division, "Initial Stages in the Adaptation of the Train and Visit Extension Approach System" (March 1984).

Ngabu Agricultural Development Division, "A Report on Cotton Production Promotion Campaign Jointly Organized by NADD and David Whitehead and Sons Limited in 1983/84 Season" (November 1987).

Shire Valley Agricultural Development Project, "Cotton Survey 1974/75: A Report of a Sample Survey Conducted in the 1974/75 Crop Growing Season in Households in the SVADP Area" (Evaluation Section, July 1976).

Shire Valley Agricultural Development Project, "Farm Survey 1973/74 [Part I]: Sample Villages" (Evaluation Section, July 1976).

Shire Valley Agricultural Development Project, "Farm Survey 1973/74 [Part II]: Farm Structure and Cropping Patterns" (Evaluation Section, July 1976).

Shire Valley Agricultural Development Project, *Monthly Advice.*

ARCHIVAL AND SPECIAL COLLECTIONS OUTSIDE MALAWI

National Library of Scotland (NLS), Edinburgh

Livingstone Papers.

Public Record Office (PRO), London

Great Britain, Foreign Office, "Africa" (FO2).

Rhodes House, Oxford University

Horace Waller diaries, 11 vols. (1860–64).
Horace Waller papers, MSS Afr s. 16, 10 vols.

University of Edinburgh Library

Frederick T. Morrison diaries (1882–87).

University of Witwatersrand, Johannesburg

John and Fred Moir, "Moir Family Correspondence, 1878–1940."

PERIODICALS AND NEWSPAPERS

Central Africa: A Record of the Work of the Universities Mission (Universities Mission to Central Africa).
Central African Times.
Nyasaland Government Gazette.
Nyasaland Times.
South African Pioneer.

BOOKS, ARTICLES, AND OTHER MATERIALS

African Way of Life Club, "Bantu Wisdom: A Collection of Proverbs" (unpublished MS, Kachebere Major Seminary).

Barker, J., "Nyasaland Native Food," *Nyasaland Times*, 1940 (PAM/458/MNA).

Barker, J., "Part Played by Legumes in the Diet of the Nyasaland African with Notes on the Cooking and Palatability of a Number of Different Kinds," *Nyasaland Agricultural Quarterly Journal* 4, 2 (April 1944): 15–26.

Bates, R., *Markets and States in Tropical Africa* (Berkeley and Los Angeles: University of California Press, 1981).

Beinart, W., "Agricultural Planning and the Late Colonial Technical Imagination: The Lower Shire Valley in Malawi, 1940–1960," in *Malawi: An Alternative Pattern of Development,* ed. K.J. McCracken (Edinburgh: Centre of African Studies, Edinburgh University, 1984): 95–148.

Bennett, N.R., and M. Ylvisaker, eds., *The Central African Journal of Lovell Procter, 1860–64* (Boston: Boston University Press, 1971).

Bernstein, H., "African Peasantries: A Theoretical Framework," *Journal of Peasant Studies* 6, 4 (July 1979): 421–43.

Berry, S., "The Food Crisis and Agrarian Change in Africa: A Review Essay," *African Studies Review* 27, 2 (June 1984): 59–112.

Berry, S., *No Condition Is Permanent: The Social Dynamics of Agrarian Change in Sub-Saharan Africa* (Madison: University of Wisconsin Press, 1993).

Berry, V., and C. Petty, eds., *The Nyasaland Survey Papers, 1938–1943: Agriculture, Food and Health* (London: Academic Books, 1992).

Brantley, C., *Feeding Families: African Realities and British Ideas of Nutrition and Development in Early Colonial Africa* (Portsmouth, NH: Heinemann, 2002).

Bryceson, D. F., "Changes in Peasant Food Production and Food Supply in Relation to the Historical Development of Commodity Production in Pre-Colonial and Colonial Tanganyika," *Journal of Peasant Studies* 7 (April 1980): 281–311.

Bryceson, D. F., *Food Insecurity and the Social Division of Labour in Tanzania, 1919–85* (New York: St. Martin's Press, 1990).

Buchanan, J., *Shire Highlands (East Central Africa): As a Colony and Mission* (London: Blackwell and Sons, 1885).

Bundy, C., "The Emergence and Decline of a South African Peasantry," *African Affairs* 71, 285 (1972): 369–88.

Byerlee, D., and P. Heisey, "Evolution of the African Maize Economy," in *Africa's Emerging Maize Revolution,* ed. D. Byerlee and C. K. Eicher (Boulder, CO: Lynne Rienner, 1997): 9–22.

Carter, J., *An Hour before Daylight: Memories of a Rural Boyhood* (New York: Simon and Schuster, 2001).

Chafulumira, E. W., *Mbiri ya Amang'anja* [A History of the Mang'anja] (Zomba, Malawi: Nyasaland Government, Department of Education, 1948).

Chanoch, M. L., "Development and Change in the History of Malawi," in *The Early History of Malawi,* ed. B. Pachai (London: Longman, 1972): 429–46.

Clark, G., *Onions Are My Husband: Survival and Accumulation by West African Market Women* (Chicago: Chicago University Press, 1994).

Clendennen, G. W., ed., *David Livingstone's Shire Journal, 1861–1864* (Aberdeen, Scotland: Scottish Cultural Press, 1992).

Clendennen, G. W., ed., "The Shire Journal of David Livingstone, 1861–1864" (unpublished MS).

Clendennen, G. W., and I. C. Cunningham, comps., *David Livingstone: A Catalogue of Documents* (Edinburgh: National Library of Scotland, 1979).

Colman, D. R., and G. K. Garbett, "Economic and Sociological Issues in the Development of the Lower Shire Valley" (unpublished paper, Department of Agricultural Economics, University of Manchester, 1974).

Colman, D. R., and G. K. Garbett, "The Labour Economy of a Peasant Community in Malawi" (Second Report of the Socio-Economic Survey of the Lower Shire Valley, unpublished MS, March 1976).

Cotterill, H. B., ed., *Travels and Researches among the Lakes and Mountains of Eastern and Central Africa* (London: Cass, 1968).

Coutinho, J. A., *Memorias de um Velho Marinheiro Soldado de Africa* (Lisbon: Livraria Bertrand, 1941).

Crowder, M., *West Africa under Colonial Rule* (London: Hutchison, 1968).

Cummings, R., "Internal Factors That Generate Famine," in *Drought and Hunger in Africa: Denying Famine a Future,* ed. M. H. Glantz (Cambridge: Cambridge University Press, 1987): 111–26.

De Castro, J., *The Geopolitics of Hunger* (New York: Monthly Review, 1976).

Dias, J. R., "Famine and Disease in the History of Angola, c. 1830–1930," *Journal of African History* 22 (1988): 349–78.

Durkheim, E., *The Elementary Forms of Religious Life*, trans. Karen E. Fields (New York: Free Press, 1995).

Eldredge, E. A., "Drought, Famine and Disease in Nineteenth-Century Lesotho," *African Economic History* 16 (1987): 61–94.

Eliade, M., *The Myth of Eternal Return: Or, Cosmos and History*, trans. Willard R. Trask (Princeton, NJ: Princeton University Press, 1991 [1949]).

Ellis, R. T., "The Food Properties of Flint and Dent Maize," *East African Agricultural Journal* 24 (April 1959): 251–53.

Farrington, F., and R. J. Markx, "Economic Constraints to Cotton Picking and Primary Marketing Relevant to Large-Scale Suppression of Red Bollworm in Malawi" (unpublished MS, Makoka, Malawi, 1976).

Faulkner, H., *Elephant Haunts* (London: Hurst and Blackett, 1868).

Feierman, S., *Peasant Intellectuals: Anthropology and History in Tanzania* (Madison: University of Wisconsin Press, 1990).

Fields, K. E., "Antinomian Conduct at the Millennium: Metaphorical Conceptions of Time in Social Science and Social Life," in *The Political Dimensions of Religion*, ed. Said Amir Arjomand (Albany: State University of New York Press, 1993): 157–68.

Foskett, R., ed., *The Zambesi Journal of Dr. John Kirk, 1858–1863*, 2 vols. (London: Oliver and Boyd, 1965).

Gamitto, A.C.P., *King Kazembe and the Marave, Cheva, Bisa, Bemba, Lunda, and Other Peoples of Southern Africa: Being the Diary of the Portuguese Expedition to That Potante in the Years 1831 and 1832*, 2 vols., trans. I. Cunnison (Lisboa: Junta de Investigações do Ultramar, 1960).

Genovese, E., *Roll, Jordan, Roll: The World the Slaves Made* (New York: Vintage, 1976 [1972]).

Gill, P., *A Year in the Death of Africa: Politics, Bureaucracy and the Famine* (London: Paladin Grafton Books, 1986).

Goody, J., *Production and Reproduction: A Comparative Study of the Domestic Domain* (Cambridge: Cambridge University Press, 1976).

Goody, J., *Technology, Tradition, and the State in West Africa* (Cambridge: Cambridge University Press, 1971).

Gould, S. J., *Time's Arrow Time's Cycle: Myth and Metaphor in the Discovery of Geological Time* (Cambridge: Harvard University Press, 1987).

Great Britain, Colonial Office, Nyasaland Protectorate, *A Report by Eric Smith on the Direct Taxation of Natives in the Nyasaland Protectorate and Other Cognate Matters* (London: Crown Agents for the Colonies, 1937).

Green, D.A.G., "Factors Affecting Cotton Production: Interim Report" (unpublished MS, Rural Development Department, Bunda College of Agriculture, University of Malawi, 1978).

Guyer, J., *An African Niche Economy* (Edinburgh: Edinburgh University Press and the International African Institute, 1997).

Guyer, J., *Family and Farm in Southern Cameroon* (Boston: Boston University African Studies Center, 1984).

Guyer, J., "Food, Cocoa, and the Division of Labor by Sex in Two West African Societies," *Comparative Studies in Society and History* 22, 3 (1980): 355–57.

Guyer, J., "The Food Economy and French Colonial Rule in Central Cameroon," *Journal of African History* 19, 4 (1978): 577–97.

Guyer, J., *Marginal Gains: Monetary Transactions in Atlantic Africa* (Chicago: University of Chicago Press, 2004).

Hay, M. J., and S. Stitcher, eds., *African Women South of the Sahara* (London and New York: Longman, 1984).

Helburn, N., "A Stereotype of Agriculture in Semiarid Turkey," *Geographical Review* 45 (1955): 381, as quoted by H. Gerber, *The Social Origins of the Modern Middle East* (Boulder, CO: Lynne Rienner Publishers, 1987).

Hetherwick, A., *The Romance of Blantyre: How Livingstone's Dream Became True* (London: Clarke, n.d. [1931]).

Holmes, T., ed., *David Livingstone: Letters and Documents, 1841–1872* (Livingstone, Zambia: Livingstone Museum in association with Lusaka: Multimedia Zambia; Bloomington and Indianapolis: Indiana University Press; London: James Currey, 1990).

Hopkins, A.G., "Economic Imperialism in West Africa: Lagos, 1880–92," *Economic History Review* 21 (1968): 580–606.

Horton, R., *Patterns of Thought in Africa and the West: Essays on Magic, Religion and Science* (Cambridge: Cambridge University Press, 1993).

Hyden, G., *Beyond Ujamaa in Tanzania: Underdevelopment and an Uncaptured Peasantry* (Berkeley and Los Angeles: University of California Press, 1980).

Iliffe, J., *The African Poor: A History* (Cambridge: Cambridge University Press, 1987).

Iliffe, J., *Africans: The History of a Continent* (New York: Cambridge University Press, 1995).

Iliffe, J., *Famine in Zimbabwe, 1890–1960* (Gweru, Zimbabwe: Mambo Press, 1990).

Isaacman, A., *Cotton is the Mother of Poverty: Peasants, Work, and Rural Struggle in Colonial Mozambique* (Portsmouth, NH: Heinemann, 1996).

Johnston, H.H., *British Central Africa: An Attempt to Give Some Account of a Portion of the Territories under British Influence North of the Zambesi* (London: Methuen, 1897).

Jones, E.L., *The European Miracle: Environments, Economics and Geopolitics in the History of Europe and Asia* (Cambridge: Cambridge University Press, 1981, 1987): 154–56.

Kalinga, O.J.M., "The Master Farmers' Scheme in Nyasaland, 1950–1962: A Study of a Failed Attempt to Create a 'Yeoman' Class," *African Affairs* 92 (1993): 367–87.

Kavinya, F., "An Appraisal of Crop Production Constraints in the Shire Valley Agricultural Development Project" (M.A. thesis, University College of Wales, Aberystwth, 1979).

Kerr, W.M., *The Far Interior: A Narrative of Travel and Adventure from the Cape of Good Hope across the Zambezi to the Lake Regions of Central Africa,* 2 vols. (London: Sampson Low, Marston, Searle and Rivington, 1887).

Kettlewell, R.W., *An Outline of Agrarian Problems and Policy in Nyasaland* (Zomba, Malawi: Nyasaland Government Press, 1955).

Kjekshus, H., *Ecology Control and Economic Development in East African History: The Case of Tanganyika, 1850–1950* (London: Heinemann, 1977).

Kotre, J.N., *White Gloves, How We Create Ourselves through Memory* (New York: Norton, 1995).

Kydd, J., and R. Christiansen, "Structural Change in Malawi since Independence: Consequences of a Development Strategy Based on Large-Scale Agriculture," *World Development* 10, 5 (1982): 355–75.

Kydd, J.G., and N.J. Spooner, *The World Bank's Analysis of Malawian Agriculture: Changing Perspectives, 1966 to 1985* (Washington, D.C.: World Bank, 1987).

Lele, U., N. van de Walle, and M. Gbetibouo, *Cotton in Africa: An Analysis of Differences in Performance,* MADIA Discussion Paper 7 (Washington, D.C.: World Bank, 1989).

Liebenow, G.J., "Food Self-Sufficiency in Malawi: Are Successes Transferable?" in *Drought and Hunger in Africa: Denying Famine a Future,* ed. M.H. Glantz (Cambridge: Cambridge University Press, 1987): 369–92.

Likaka, O., *Rural Society and Cotton in Colonial Zaire* (Madison: University of Wisconsin Press, 1997).

Linden, I., and J. Linden, *Catholics, Peasants, and Chewa Resistance in Nyasaland, 1889–1939* (London: Heinemann, 1974).

Linden, I., and J.M. Schoffeleers, "The Resistance of the *Nyau* Societies to the Roman Catholic Missions in Colonial Malawi," in *The Historical Study of African Religion*, ed. T.O. Ranger and I. Kimambo (London: Heinemann, 1972): 252–73.

Livingstone, D., and C. Livingstone, *Narrative of an Expedition to the Zambesi and Its Tributaries and of the Discoveries of the Lakes Shirwa and Nyassa* (London: Murray, 1865; New York: Harper and Brothers, 1866).

Livingstone, W.P., *Laws of Livingstonia: A Narrative of Missionary Adventure and Achievement* (London: Hodder and Stoughton, n.d.).

Lofchie, M., "The Decline of African Agriculture: An Internalist Perspective," in *Drought and Hunger in Africa: Denying Famine a Future*, ed. M.H. Glantz (Cambridge: Cambridge University Press, 1987): 85–109.

Macdonald, D., *Africana: The Heart of Heathen Africa* (London: Dawson of Paul Mall, 1969).

Malawi Congress Party, "Nsanje Calendar of Events" (unpublished, 1966).

Malawi National Statistical Office, *Population Census, 1977: Preliminary Report* (Zomba, Malawi: Government Press, 1978).

Mandala, E., *Black Englishmen: The Magololo Chiefs of Malawi and the Europeans, 1855–1913* (forthcoming).

Mandala, E., "Feeding and Fleecing the Native: How the Nyasaland Transport System Distorted a New Food Market, 1890s–1920s," *Journal of Southern African Studies* (forthcoming).

Mandala, E., "Gold-Seekers, *Prazo*-Holders and Capitalists in Mozambique: A Review," *Canadian Journal of African Studies* 18 (1983): 545–47.

Mandala, E., "The Kololo Interlude in Southern Malawi: A Study of Political Entrepreneurship in Nineteenth Century Malawi" (M.A. thesis, University of Malawi, 1977).

Mandala, E., "The Nature and Substance of Mang'anja and Kololo Oral Traditions: A Preliminary Survey" *Society of Malawi Journal* 31 (January 1978): 1–14.

Mandala, E., "The Tengani Chieftaincy and Its Relations with Other Chieftaincies in Nsanje District" (Final Year Students Seminar Papers, Chancellor College, University of Malawi, 1973–74).

Mandala, E., *Work and Control in a Peasant Economy: A History of the Lower Tchiri Valley in Malawi, 1859–1960* (Madison: University of Wisconsin Press, 1990).

Mbiti, J.S., *African Religions and Philosophy* (New York: Anchor Books, 1970 [1969]).

McCracken, J., *American Historical Review* 97, 6 (February 1992): 261–62.

Miller, J., "The Significance of Drought, Disease and Famine in the Agriculturally Marginal Zones of West-Central Africa," *Journal of African History* 23 (1982): 17–61.

Mintz, S.W., *Sweetness and Power: The Place of Sugar in Modern History* (New York: Viking Penguin, 1990).

Moir, F.L.M., *After Livingstone: An African Trade Romance* (London: Hodder and Stoughton, n.d.).

Moore, H.L., and M. Vaughan, *Cutting Down Trees: Gender, Nutrition, and Agricultural Change in the Northern Province of Zambia, 1890–1990* (Portsmouth, NH: Heinemann, 1994).

Newitt, M.D.D., "Drought in Mozambique, 1823–1831," *Journal of Southern African Studies* 15, 1 (1988): 15–35.

Newman, L.F., ed., *Hunger in History: Food Shortage, Poverty, and Deprivation* (Cambridge, MA: Basil Blackwell, 1990).

Ng'ong'ola, C.H.S., "Statutory Law and Agrarian Change in Malawi" (Ph.D. dissertation, London University, 1983).

Nurse, G.T., "Seasonal Hunger among the Ngoni and Ntumba of Central Malawi," *Africa* 45, 1 (1975): 1–11.

Nyasaland Protectorate, *Annual Report of the Department of Agriculture* (Zomba, Malawi: Government Press).

O'Keefe, P., and B. Wisner, "African Drought: The State of the Game," in *The African Environment,* ed. P. Richards (London: International African Institute, 1975): 31–39.

Ogbu, J.U., "Seasonal Hunger in Tropical Africa as a Cultural Phenomenon," *Africa* 13, 4 (1973): 317–32.

Pachai, B., *Malawi: The History of the Nation* (London: Longman, 1973).

Palmer, R., "The Agricultural History of Rhodesia," in *The Roots of Rural Poverty in Central and Southern Africa,* ed. R. Palmer and N. Parsons (Berkeley and Los Angeles: University of California Press, 1977): 221–54.

Pelissier, R., *Revue francaise d'histoire d'outre-mer* 81, 302 (1994): 117–18.

Ranger, T., "Connections between 'Primary Resistance' Movements and Modern Mass Nationalism in East and Central Africa," *Journal of African History* 9, 3 (1968): 437–53; 4 (1968): 631–41.

Rankin, D.J., *The Zambesi Basin and Nyasaland* (London: Blackwell and Sons, 1893).

Rau, B., *From Feast to Famine: Official Cures and Grassroots Remedies to Africa's Food Crisis* (Atlantic Highlands, NJ, and London: Zed Press, 1991).

Richards, A.I., *Hunger and Work in a Savage Tribe* (London: Oxford University Press, 1932).

Richards, A.I., *Land, Labour and Diet in Northern Rhodesia: An Economic Study of the Bemba Tribe* (London: Oxford University Press, 1952, 1961 [1939]).

Rowley, H., *The Story of the Universities Mission to Central Africa* (New York: Negro Universities Press, 1969 [1867]).

Ruthenberg, H., *Farming Systems in the Tropics,* 3rd ed. (London: OUP, 1980).

Schoffeleers, J.M., "The Chisumphi and Mbona Cults in Malawi: A Comparative History," in *Guardians of the Land: Essays on Central African Territorial Cults,* ed. J.M. Schoffeleers (Gwelo, Zimbabwe: Mambo, 1978): 147–85.

Schoffeleers, J.M., "Crisis, Criticism, and Critique: An Interpretative Model of Territorial Mediumship among the Chewa," *Journal of Social Science* 3 (1974): 74–80.

Schoffeleers, J.M., "From Socialization to Personal Enterprise: A History of the *Nomi* Labor Societies in Nsanje District of Malawi, c. 1891–1972," *Rural Africana* 20 (Spring 1973): 11–25.

Schoffeleers, J.M., ed., *Guardians of the Land: Essays on Central African Territorial Cults* (Gwelo, Zimbabwe: Mambo, 1978).

Schoffeleers, J.M., *The Lower Shire Valley of Malawi: Its Ecology, Population Distribution, Ethnic Divisions, and Systems of Marriage* (Limbe, Malawi: Montfort Press, 1968).

Schoffeleers, J.M., "The *Nyau* Societies: Our Present Understanding," *Society of Malawi Journal* 29 (January 1976): 59–68.

Schoffeleers, J.M., "The Political Role of the Mbona Cult of the Mang'anja," in *The Historical Study of African Religion,* ed. T.O. Ranger and I. Kimambo (London: Heinemann, 1972): 73–94.

Schoffeleers, J.M., *River of Blood: The Genesis of a Martyr Cult in Southern Malawi, c. A.D. 1600* (Madison: University of Wisconsin Press, 1992).

Schoffeleers, J.M., "Social and Symbolic Aspects of Spirit Worship Among the Mang'anja" (Ph.D. thesis, Oxford University, 1968).

Scott, D.C., *A Cyclopaedic Dictionary of the Mang'anja Language Spoken in British Central Africa* (Hants, England: Gregg International Publishers, 1968 [1892]).

Sen, A., *Poverty and Famines: An Essay on Entitlement and Deprivation* (Oxford: Clarendon Press, 1981).

Shaw, T., "Towards the Political Economy of the African Crisis: Diplomacy, Debates, and Dialectics," in *Drought and Hunger in Africa: Denying Famine a Future,* ed. M.H. Glantz (Cambridge: Cambridge University Press, 1987): 126–47.

Shire Valley Agricultural Development Project, *An Atlas of the Lower Shire Valley, Malawi* (Blantyre, Malawi: Department of Surveys, 1975).

Spear, T., *Mountain Farmers: Moral Economies of Land and Agricultural Development in Arusha and Meru* (Berkeley and Los Angeles: University of California Press, 1997).

Suret-Canale, J., "The Economic Balance Sheet of French Colonialism in West Africa," in *African Social Studies: A Radical Reader,* ed. P. Gutkind and P. Waterman (New York: Monthly Review, 1977): 125–34.

Tabler, E.C., ed., *The Zambezi Papers of Richard Thornton: Geologist to Livingstone's Zambezi Expedition,* 2 vols. (London: Chatto and Windus, 1963).

Thomas, M., and G. Whittington, eds., *Environment and Land Use in Africa* (London: Methuen, 1969).

Vail, L., "Ecology and History: The Example of Eastern Zambia," *Journal of Southern African Studies* 3, 2 (1976): 129–55.

Vail, L., "Railway Development and Colonial Underdevelopment: The Nyasaland Case," in *The Roots of Rural Poverty in Central and Southern Africa,* ed. R. Palmer and N. Parsons (Berkeley and Los Angeles: University of California Press, 1977): 365–95.

Vansina, J., *Living with Africa* (Madison: University of Wisconsin Press, 1994).

Vansina, J., *The Tio Kingdom of the Middle Congo, 1880–1892* (London: IAI, 1973).

Vaughan, M., *The Story of an African Famine: Gender and Famine in Twentieth-Century Malawi* (Cambridge: Cambridge University Press, 1987).

Wallis, J.P.R., ed., *The Zambesi Expedition of David Livingstone, 1858–63,* 2 vols. (London: Chatto and Windus, 1956).

Wallis, J.P.R., ed., *The Zambesi Journal of James Stewart, 1862–1863* (London: Chatto and Windus, 1952).

Watts, M., "Drought, Environment and Food Security: Some Reflections on Peasants, Pastoralists and Commoditization in Dryland West Africa," in *Drought and Hunger in Africa: Denying Famine a Future,* ed. M.H. Glantz (Cambridge: Cambridge University Press, 1987): 171–211.

Watts, M., *Silent Violence: Food, Famine and Peasantry in Northern Nigeria* (Berkeley and Los Angeles: University of California Press, 1983).

Webster, J.B., "Drought and Migration: The Lake Malawi Littoral as a Region of Refuge," in *Proceedings of the Symposium on Drought in Botswana, National Museum, Gaborone, Botswana, June 5th to 8th, 1978,* ed. M.T. Hinchey (Gaborone, Botswana: Botswana Society in collaboration with Clark University Press; Hanover, NH: distributed by University Press of New England, 1979): 148–57.

Webster, J.B., "Noi! Noi! Famines as an Aid to Interlacustrine Chronology," in *Chronology, Migration and Drought in Interlacustrine Africa,* ed. J.B. Webster (New York: Africana Publishing Company, Dalhousie University Press, 1979): 1–37.

Weiss, B., *The Making and Unmaking of the Haya Lived World: Consumption, Commoditization, and Everyday Practice* (Durham, NC: Duke University Press, 1996).

Werner, A., *The Natives of British Central Africa* (New York: Negro University Press, 1969).

White, L., "Working Lives in the Lower Shire," *Journal of African History* 34, 1 (1993): 158–59.

Williamson, A.C., "Notes on Some Changes in the Malawi Diet over the Last 30 Years," *Society of Malawi Journal* 25, 2 (1972): 49–53.

Williamson, J., *Useful Plants of Malawi* (Zomba, Malawi: Government Press, 1972 [1956]).

World Bank, *Accelerated Development in Sub-Saharan Africa* (Washington, D.C.: World Bank, 1981).

Young, E.D., *Mission to Nyassa* (London: John Murray, 1877).

Young, E.D., *The Search after Livingstone: A Diary Kept during the Investigation of His Reported Murder* (London: Letts, 1868).

Zeleza, P.T., *Manufacturing African Studies and Crises* (Dakar: Senegal: CODESRIA, 1997).

INDEX

About the Author

ELIAS C. MANDALA was born in Malawi and received his Bachelors and Masters from the University of Malawi. In 1977, he came to the United States as a Fulbright Scholar, where he did further graduate work at the Universities of Minnesota and Wisconsin (Madison). After obtaining his Ph.D. from Minnesota, he started teaching at the University of Rochester, where he is now a full professor in the Department of History. He has authored many articles on the agrarian history of Southern Malawi and his *Work and Control in a Peasant Economy: A History of the Lower Tchiri Valley in Malawi, 1859-1960* (University of Wisconsin Press) was a finalist for the 1990 Herskovits award.